SUNSET BOOKS
VICE PRESIDENT, GENERAL MANAGER
Richard A. Smeby
VICE PRESIDENT, EDITORIAL DIRECTOR
Bob Doyle
PRODUCTION DIRECTOR
Lory Day
OPERATIONS DIRECTOR
Rosann Sutherland
MARKETING MANAGER
Linda Barker
ART DIRECTOR
Vasken Guiragossian
SPECIAL SALES
Brad Moses

PRODUCTION SPECIALIST
Linda M. Bouchard
PREPRESS COORDINATOR
Eligio Hernandez
ASSOCIATE EDITOR
Carrie Dodson Davis

10 9 8 7 6 5 4 3 2 1
First Printing January 2006

Library of Congress Control Number 2005933861.

ISBN-13: 978-0-376-01198-5
ISBN-10: 0-376-01198-X
Printed in the United States of America.

For additional copies of *Best-selling One-story Home Plans* or any other Sunset book, call 1-800-526-5111 or visit us at www.sunset.com.

COVER
Plan #011D-0013 (page 195) by Alan Mascord Design Associates. Photograph by Bob Greenspan.

table of contents

Plan #584-022D-0026. For more information please see page 173.

Plan #584-007D-0010. For more information please see page 89.

Plan #584-065D-0041. For more information please see page 188.

about this book

Choosing a home plan can be a daunting task. With our collection of best-selling one-story plans we've made it simpler. By categorizing this book into sections, it will be easier to locate specific styles based on your lifestyle needs.

For those just starting out, sections ***Under 1,799 Square Feet*** and ***Over 1,800 Square Feet*** may be most useful. Since square footage is usually based on budget, these two sections offer an array of styles all within specific square footage parameters.

An ***Atrium Ranch*** may be ideal for those with teenagers. This style usually features living areas for recreation and relaxation on the lower level and bedrooms on the main level for more privacy. While the family with toddlers will need bedrooms near each other for convenience and an enclosed staircase for safety reasons.

The ***Retirement*** plans generally include two bedrooms with the option to convert a third bedroom into an office or den.

Some people may be looking for a more relaxed, cozier feel to their home. The ***Cottage*** plans offer this style.

Vacation homes usually include many windows for sweeping rear views of seaside, lakeside, mountains or wooded backdrops.

For those of you with lot restrictions, we offer ***Narrow Lot*** plans with a maximum width of 50 feet.

Throughout this book you will find plans featuring many different styles for many different budgets from some of the nation's leading designers and architects. Browse through our plan pages to discover the home of your dreams.

Plan #584-016D-0047. For more information please see page 214 .

what is the right plan for you?

Many of the homes you see may appear to be just what you're looking for. But are they? One way to find out is to carefully analyze what you want in a home. This is an important first step we'll show you how to take.

For most people, budget is the most critical element in narrowing the choices. Generally, the size of the home, or, specifically, the square footage of living area is the most important criteria in establishing the cost of a new home.

Your next task is to consider the style of home you want. Should it be traditional, contemporary, one-story or two-story? If yours is an infill lot in an existing neighborhood, is the design you like compatible with the existing residential architecture? If not, will the subdivision permit you to build the design of your choice?

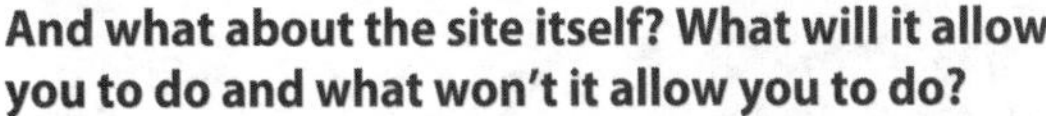

And what about the site itself? What will it allow you to do and what won't it allow you to do?

Site topography is the first consideration in floor plan development. Slopes, both gentle and steep, will affect the home design you select. If you want a multi-level home with a walk-out basement that appears to be a single-story residence from the street, you need a lot that slopes from front to back. And what about the garage? Do you prefer access at street level or a lower level?

Next, there is the issue of orientation, that is, the direction in which you want the house to face. Considering the north-south or east-west orientation of the site itself, will the plan you choose allow you to enjoy sweeping views from the living room? Does the design have a lot of glass on the south side that will permit you to take advantage of the sun's warmth in winter?

Now for the tough part; figuring out what you want inside the house to satisfy your needs and lifestyle. To a large extent, that may depend on where you are in life – just starting out, whether you have toddlers or teenagers, whether you're an "empty-nester," or retired.

Next, think about the components of the home. Do you want, or need, both a living room and family room or would just one large great room suffice? Do you want, or need, both a breakfast room and a formal dining room? How many bedrooms, full baths and half baths do you need? How much storage? And what about space for working from home, hobbies or a workshop?

When you've completed your wish list, think about how you want your home to function. In architectural terms, think about spatial relationships and circulation, or in other words, the relationship of each of the components to one another.

For example, to deliver groceries conveniently, the kitchen should be directly accessible from the garage. To serve meals efficiently, the dining area should be adjacent to the kitchen. The same principle applies to other areas and components of the home. Consider the flow from entry foyer to living, sleeping, and food preparation areas.

Experts in the field suggest that the best way to determine your needs is to begin by listing everything you like or dislike about your current home.

As you study your favorite home plan, ask yourself if it's possible to close off certain spaces to eliminate noise from encroaching upon others. For instance, if you enjoy listening to music, you don't want it drowned out by a droning dishwasher or blaring TV being watched by another member of the family nearby. Similarly, sleeping areas and bathrooms should be remote from living areas. After you've come to terms with the types and relationship of rooms you want in your dream home, you can then concentrate on the size and features you want for each of those spaces.

If cooking is a hobby and you entertain frequently, you might want a large gourmet kitchen or even the ever-so-popular outdoor kitchen. If you like openness and a laid-back environment, you might want a large family room with picture windows, a fireplace, vaulted ceiling, and exposed wood beams. A central living area directly accessible to an outdoor deck or patio is the ultimate in casual, relaxed style.

Deciding what you want in your dream home, where you want it, and how you want it to look is thought provoking and time consuming, but careful planning and thought will have a great return on investment when it comes to you and your family's happiness.

quick & easy customizing

make changes to your home plan in 4 steps

Here's an affordable and efficient way to make changes to your plan.

1. Select the house plan that most closely meets your needs. Purchase of a reproducible master is necessary in order to make changes to a plan.

2. Call 1-800-367-7667 to place your order. Tell the sales representative you're interested in customizing a plan. A $50 nonrefundable consultation fee will be charged. You will then be instructed to complete a customization checklist indicating all the changes you wish to make to your plan. You may attach sketches if necessary. If you proceed with the custom changes the $50 will be credited to the total amount charged.

3. FAX the completed customization checklist to our design consultant at 1-866-477-5173 or e-mail at customize@hdainc.com. Within 24-48* business hours you will be provided with a written cost estimate to modify your plan. Our design consultant will contact you by phone if you wish to discuss any of your changes in greater detail.

4. Once you approve the estimate, a 75% retainer fee is collected and customization work gets underway. Preliminary drawings can usually be completed within 5-10* business days. Following approval of the preliminary drawings your design changes are completed within 5-10* business days. Your remaining 25% balance due is collected prior to shipment of your completed drawings. You will be shipped five sets of revised blueprints or a reproducible master, plus a customized materials list if required.

Sample Modification Pricing Guide

The average prices specified below are provided as examples only. They refer to the most commonly requested changes, and are subject to change without notice. Prices for changes will vary or differ, from the prices below, depending on the number of modifications requested, the plan size, style, quality of original plan, format provided to us (originally drawn by hand or computer), and method of design used by the original designer. To obtain a detailed cost estimate or to get more information, please contact us.

Categories	Average Cost*
Adding or removing living space	Quote required
Adding or removing a garage	Starting at $400
Garage: Front entry to side load or vice versa	Starting at $300
Adding a screened porch	Starting at $280
Adding a bonus room in the attic	Starting at $450
Changing full basement to crawl space or vice versa	Starting at $495
Changing full basement to slab or vice versa	Starting at $495
Changing exterior building material	Starting at $200
Changing roof lines	Starting at $360
Adjusting ceiling height	Starting at $280
Adding, moving or removing an exterior opening	$65 per opening
Adding or removing a fireplace	Starting at $90
Modifying a non-bearing wall or room	$65 per room
Changing exterior walls from 2"x4" to 2"x6"	Starting at $200
Redesigning a bathroom or a kitchen	Starting at $120
Reverse plan right reading	Quote required
Adapting plans for local building code requirements	Quote required
Engineering and Architectural stamping and services	Quote required
Adjust plan for handicapped accessibility	Quote required
Interactive Illustrations (choices of exterior materials)	Quote required
Metric conversion of home plan	Starting at $400

*Prices and Terms are subject to change without notice.

plan #584-001D-0013

price code D

plan information	
total living area:	1,882
bedrooms:	3
baths:	2
garage:	2-car
foundation type:	
basement	

special features

- wide, handsome entrance opens to the vaulted great room with fireplace
- living and dining areas are conveniently joined but still allow privacy
- private covered porch extends breakfast area
- practical passageway runs through the laundry and mud room from the garage to the kitchen
- vaulted ceiling in master bedroom

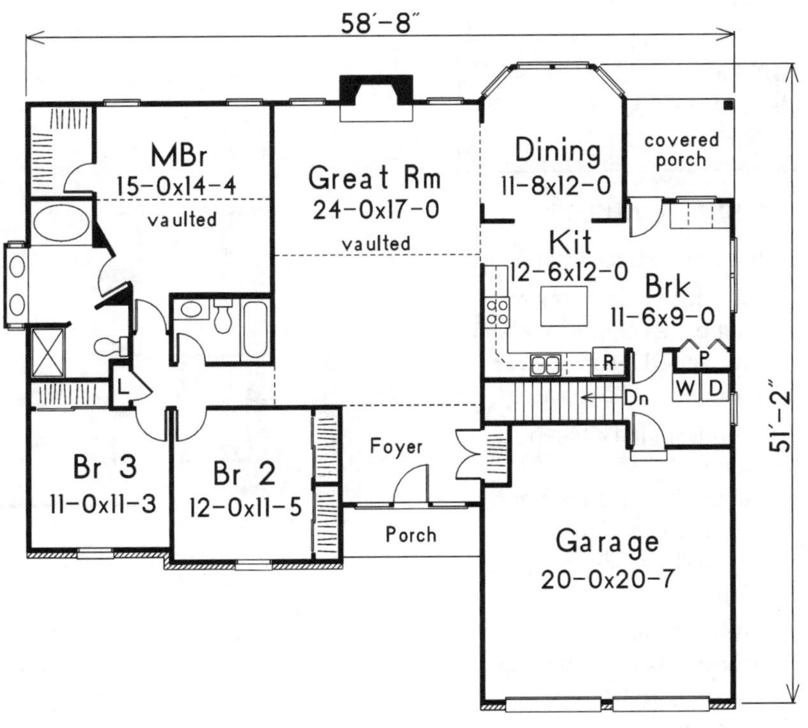

plan #584-007D-0017 price code C

plan information

total living area:	1,882
bedrooms:	4
baths:	2
garage:	2-car side entry
foundation type:	basement

special features

- handsome brick facade
- spacious great room and dining area combination is brightened by unique corner windows and patio access
- well-designed kitchen incorporates a breakfast bar peninsula, sweeping casement window above sink and a walk-in pantry island
- master bedroom features a large walk-in closet and private bath with bay window

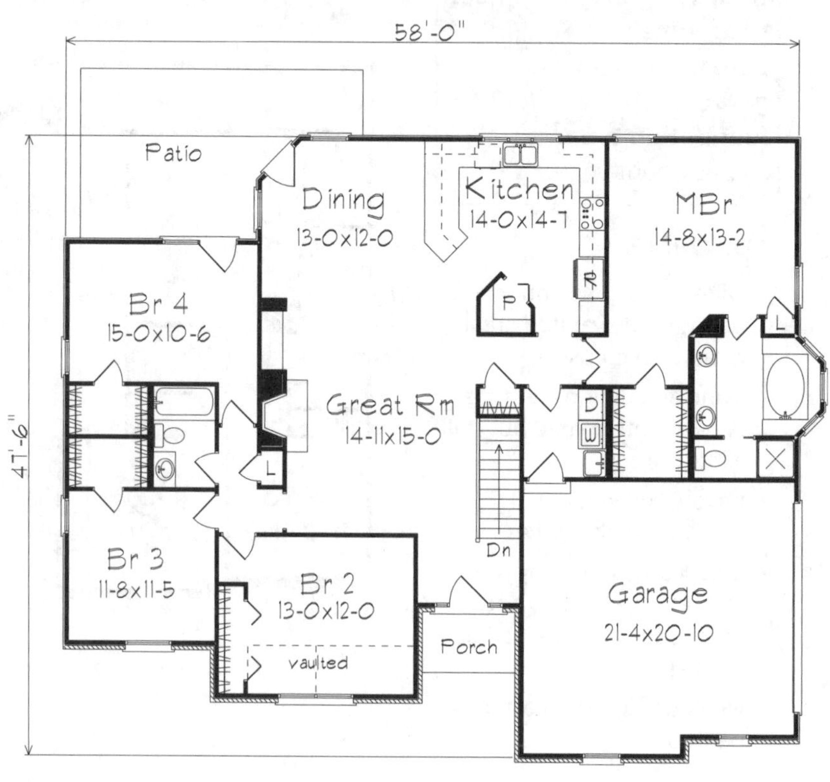

plan information	
total living area:	1,195
bedrooms:	3
baths:	2
garage:	2-car
foundation type:	
basement	

special features

- dining room opens onto the patio
- master bedroom features a vaulted ceiling, private bath and walk-in closet
- coat closets are located by both the entrances
- convenient secondary entrance is located at the back of the garage

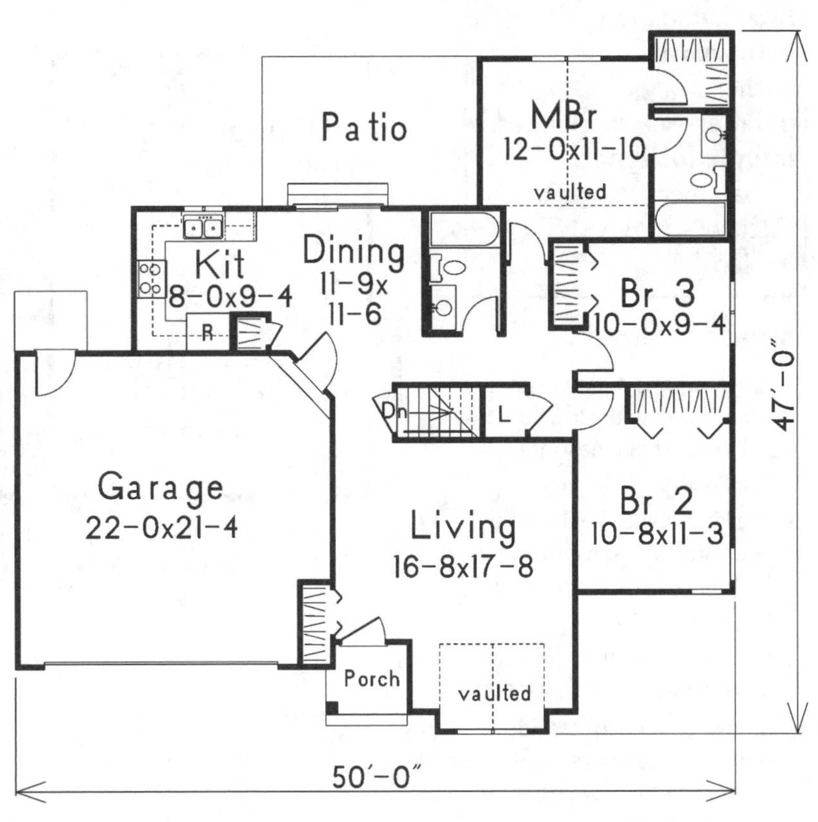

plan #584-008D-0010

price code A

plan information

total living area:	1,440
bedrooms:	3
baths:	2
garage:	2-car side entry
foundation types:	
basement standard	
crawl space	
slab	

special features

- foyer adjoins massive-sized great room with sloping ceiling and tall masonry fireplace
- the kitchen connects to the spacious dining room and features a pass-through to the breakfast bar
- master bedroom enjoys a private bath and two closets
- an oversized two-car side entry garage offers plenty of storage for bicycles, lawn equipment, etc.

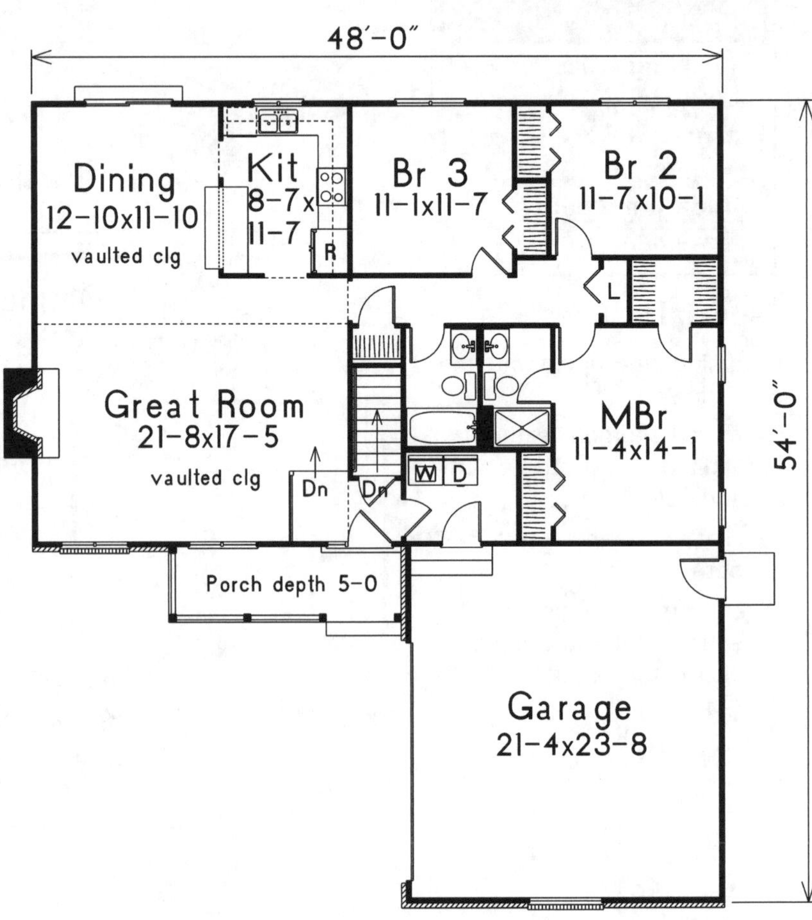

plan #584-001D-0031

price code B

plan information	
total living area:	1,501
bedrooms:	3
baths:	2
garage:	2-car side entry
foundation types:	
basement standard	
crawl space	
slab	

special features

- spacious kitchen with dining area is open to the outdoors
- convenient utility room is adjacent to garage
- master bedroom features a private bath, dressing area and access to the large covered porch
- large family room creates openness

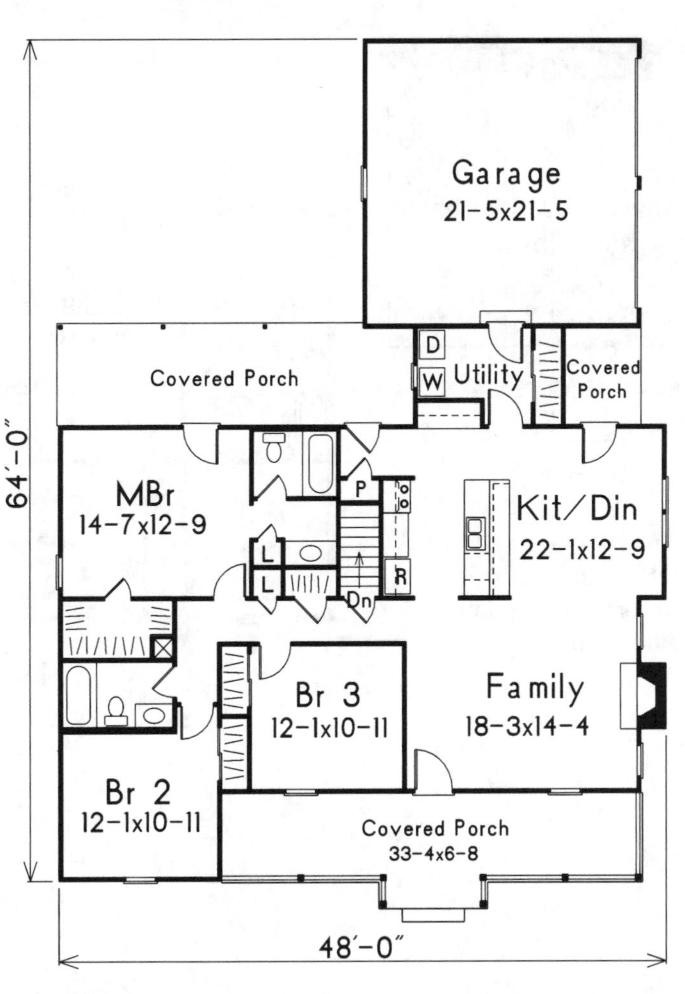

plan #584-020D-0005

price code B

plan information

total living area:	1,770
bedrooms:	3
baths:	2
garage:	2-car side entry
foundation types:	
slab standard	
crawl space	

special features

- open floor plan makes this home feel spacious
- 12' ceilings in kitchen, living, breakfast and dining areas
- kitchen is the center of activity with views into all gathering places

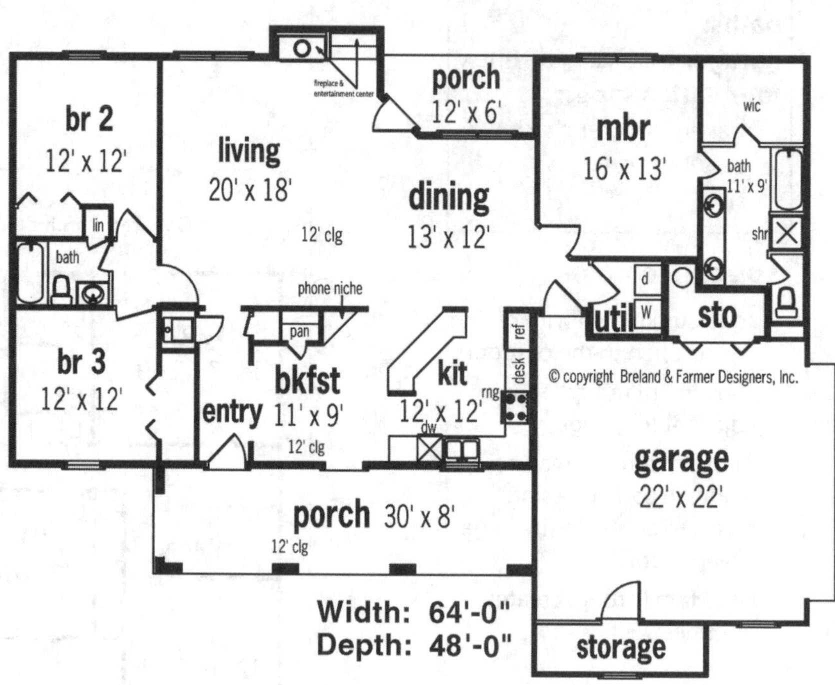

plan #584-003D-0002

price code B

plan information

total living area:	1,676
bedrooms:	3
baths:	2
garage:	2-car
foundation types:	
basement standard	
crawl space	
slab	

special features

- the living area skylights and large breakfast room with bay window provide plenty of sunlight
- the master bedroom has a walk-in closet and both the secondary bedrooms have large closets
- vaulted ceilings, plant shelving and a fireplace provide a quality living area

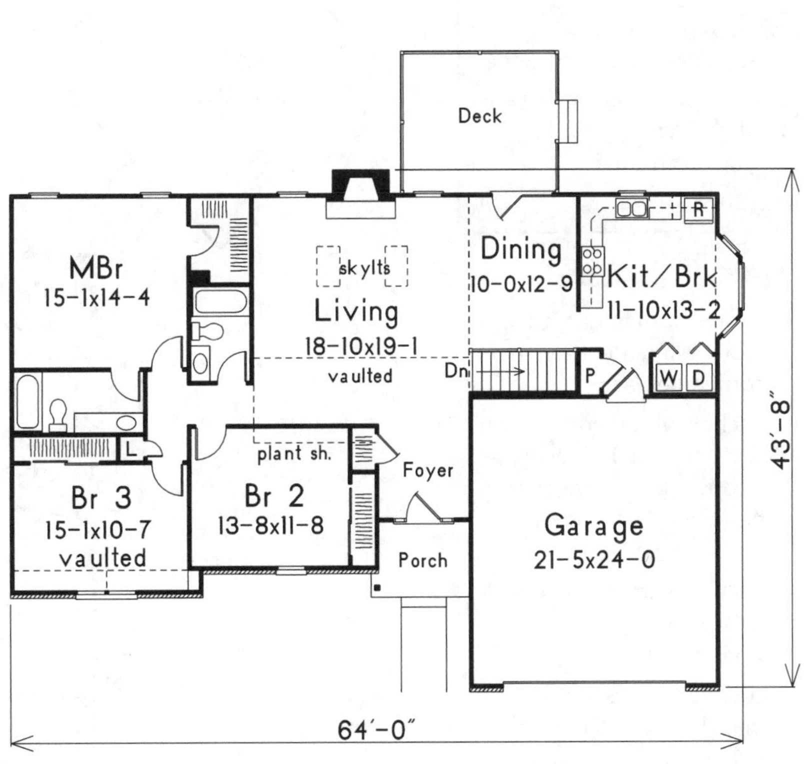

plan #584-040D-0003

price code B

plan information

total living area:	1,475
bedrooms:	3
baths:	2
garage:	2-car detached side entry
foundation types:	
slab standard	
crawl space	

special features

- family room features a high ceiling and prominent corner fireplace
- kitchen with island counter and garden window makes a convenient connection between the family and dining rooms
- hallway leads to three bedrooms all with large walk-in closets
- covered breezeway joins the main house and garage
- full-width covered porch entry lends a country touch

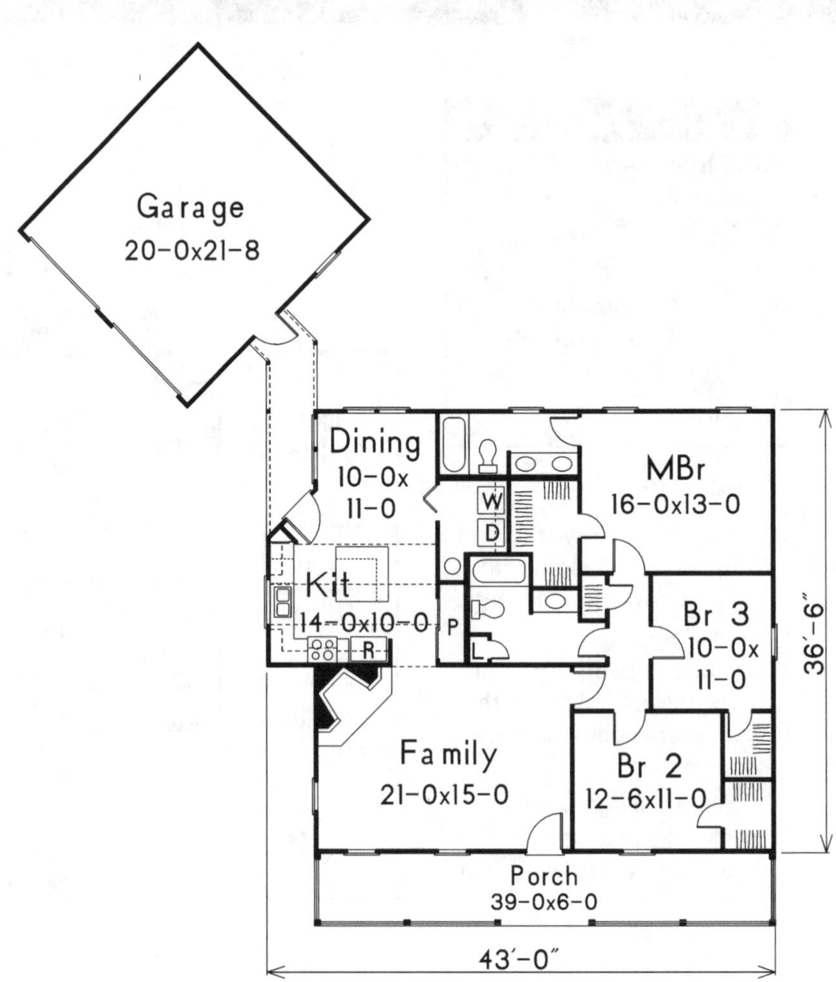

plan #584-001D-0045

price code AA

plan information

total living area:	1,197
bedrooms:	3
baths:	1
foundation types:	
crawl space standard	
basement	
slab	

special features

- the U-shaped kitchen includes ample workspace, breakfast bar, laundry area and direct access to the outdoors
- large living room has a convenient coat closet
- bedroom #1 features a large walk-in closet

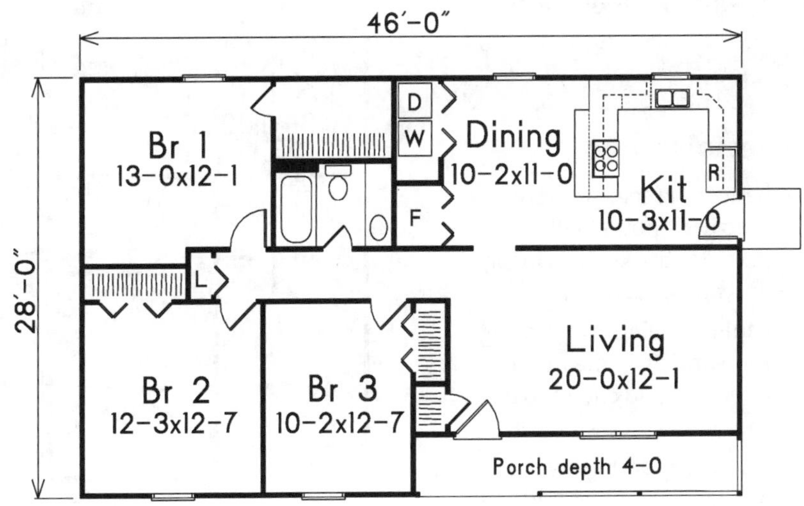

plan #584-053D-0037

price code A

plan information

total living area:	1,388
bedrooms:	3
baths:	2
garage:	2-car
foundation types:	
crawl space standard	
slab	

special features

- handsome see-through fireplace offers a gathering point for the kitchen, family and breakfast rooms
- vaulted ceiling and large bay window in the master bedroom add charm to this room
- a dramatic angular wall and large windows add brightness to the kitchen and breakfast room
- kitchen, breakfast and family rooms have vaulted ceilings, adding to this central living area

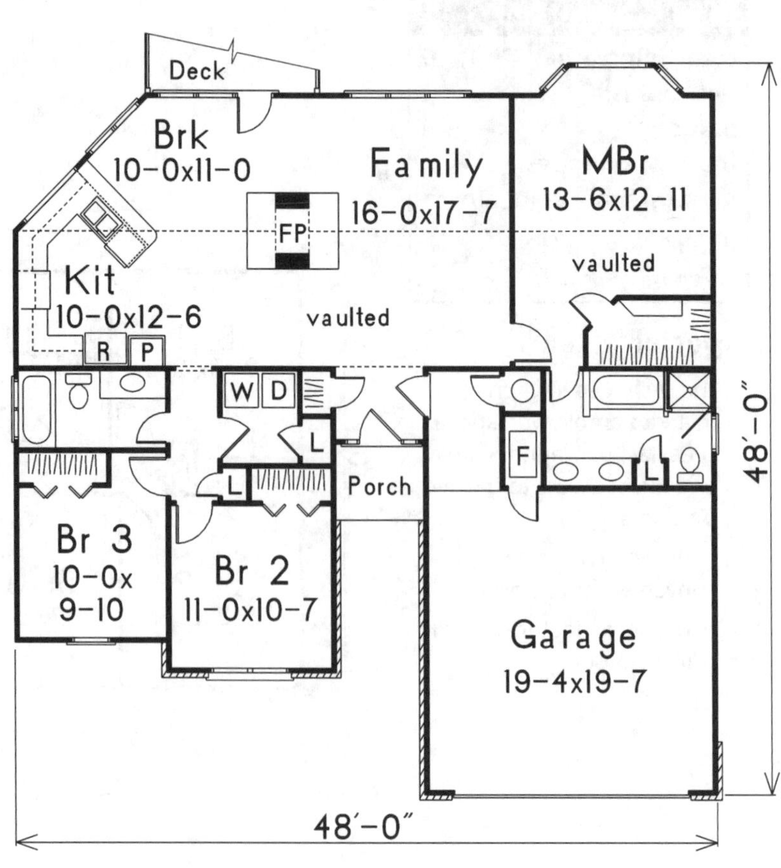

plan #584-011D-0004

price code D

plan information	
total living area:	1,997
bedrooms:	4
baths:	2 1/2
garage:	3-car
foundation type:	
crawl space	

special features

- corner fireplace warms the vaulted family room located near the kitchen
- a spa tub and shower enhance the master bath
- plenty of closet space throughout

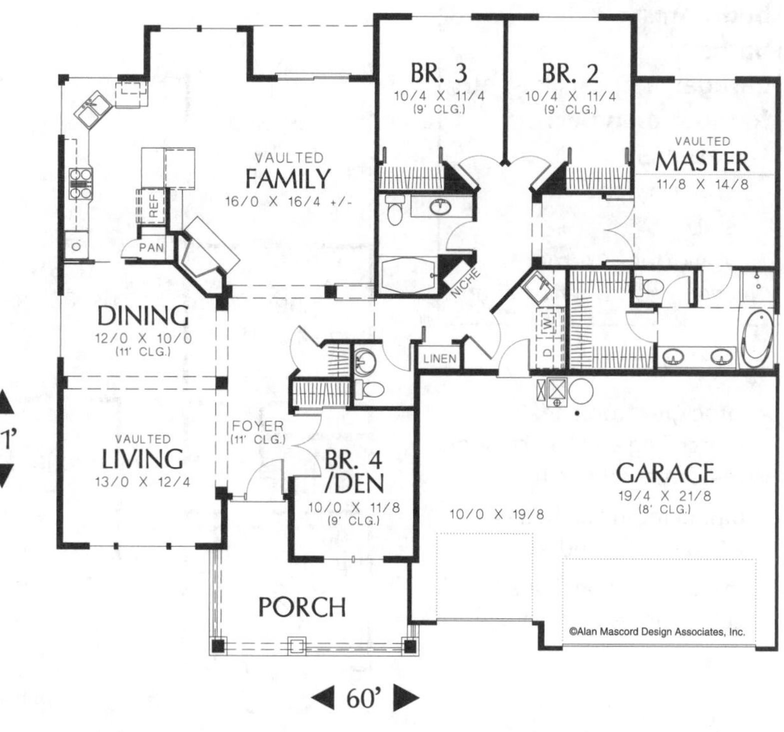

plan #584-016D-0040

price code C

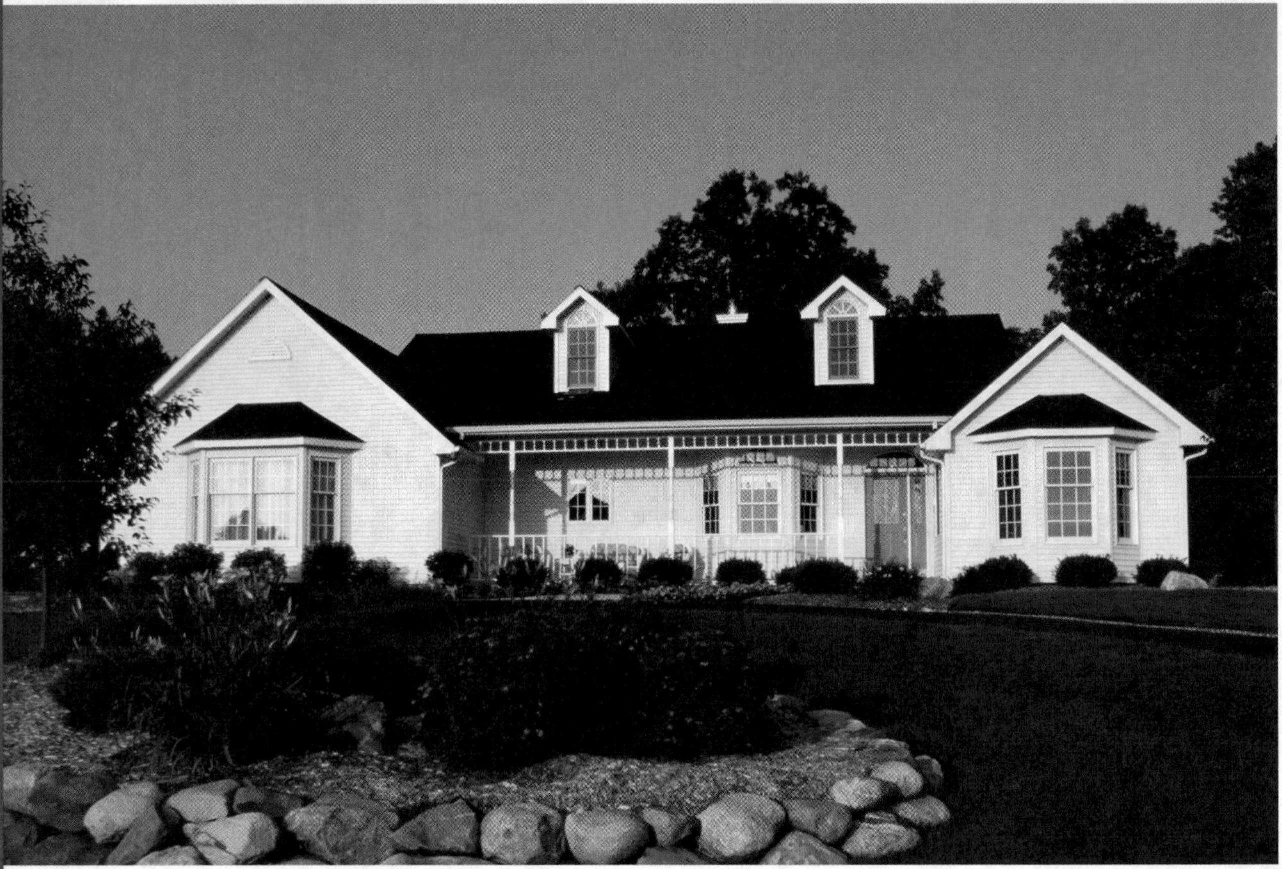

plan information

total living area:	1,595
bedrooms:	3
baths:	2
garage:	2-car side entry
foundation types:	
basement	
crawl space	
slab	
walk-out basement	
please specify when ordering	

special features

- large great room features a tray ceiling and French doors to a screened porch
- dining room and bedroom #2 have bay windows
- master bedroom has a tray ceiling and a bay window

Width 59'-0"
Depth 47'-0"

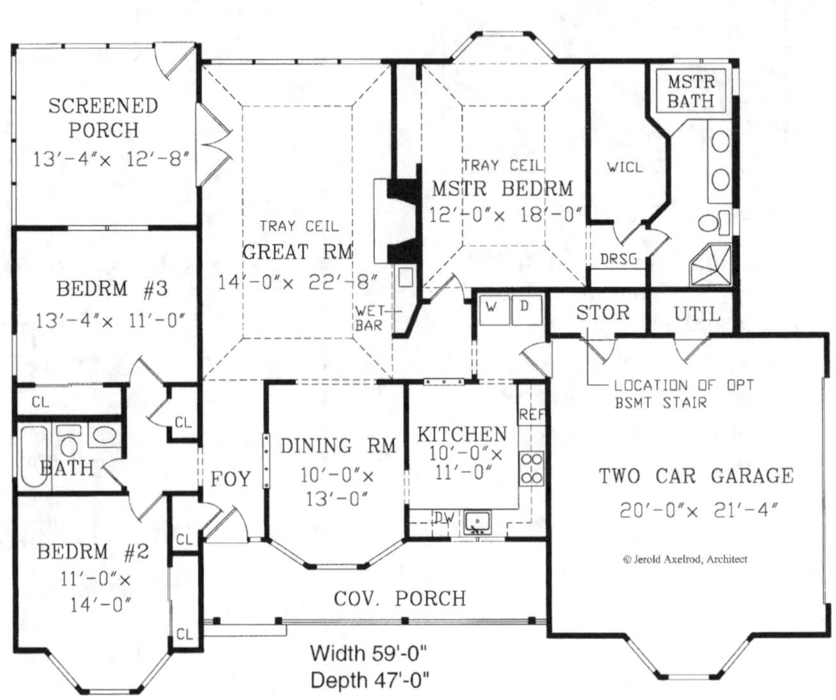

plan #584-047D-0022

price code B

J.N. HANSEN P.T.L.

plan information	
total living area:	1,768
bedrooms:	3
baths:	2
garage:	2-car
foundation type:	
slab	

special features

- uniquely designed vaulted living and dining rooms combine making great use of space
- informal family room has a vaulted ceiling, plant shelf accents and kitchen overlook
- sunny breakfast area conveniently accesses kitchen

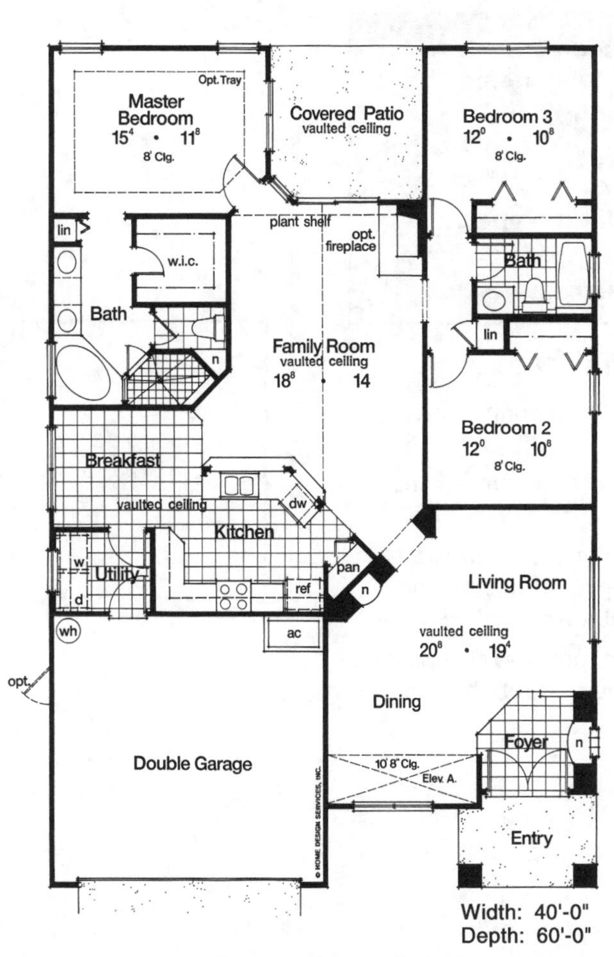

Width: 40'-0"
Depth: 60'-0"

plan #584-001D-0021

price code A

plan information

total living area:	1,416
bedrooms:	3
baths:	2
garage:	2-car
foundation types:	
crawl space standard	
basement	

special features

- excellent floor plan eases traffic
- master bedroom features private bath
- foyer opens to both a formal living room and informal great room
- great room has access to the outdoors through sliding doors

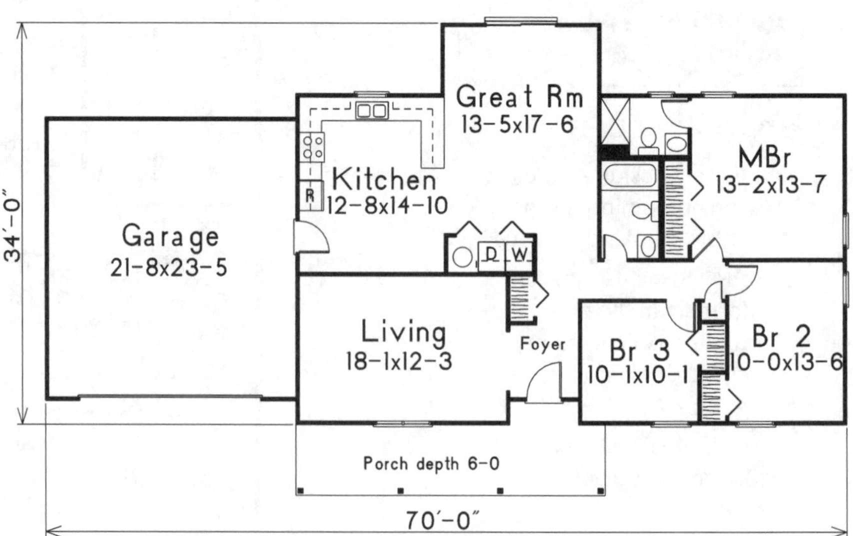

plan #584-016D-0027

price code A

plan information

total living area: 1,480
bedrooms: 3
baths: 2
garage: 2-car side entry
foundation types:
basement
crawl space
slab
please specify when ordering

special features

- split bedroom floor plan has private master bedroom with large bath and walk-in closet
- fabulous great room features 11' high stepped ceiling, fireplace and media center
- floor plan designed to be fully accessible for the handicapped

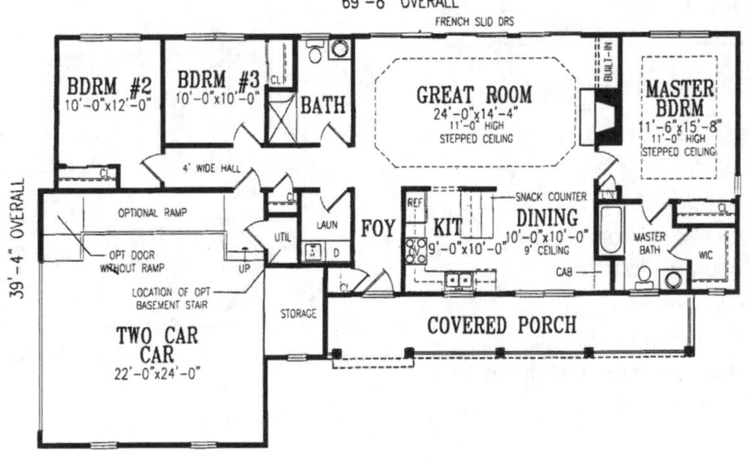

plan #584-058D-0024

price code B

plan information

total living area:	1,598
bedrooms:	3
baths:	2
garage:	2-car
foundation type: basement	

special features

- additional storage area in garage
- double-door entry into master bedroom with luxurious master bath
- entry opens into large family room with vaulted ceiling and open stairway to basement

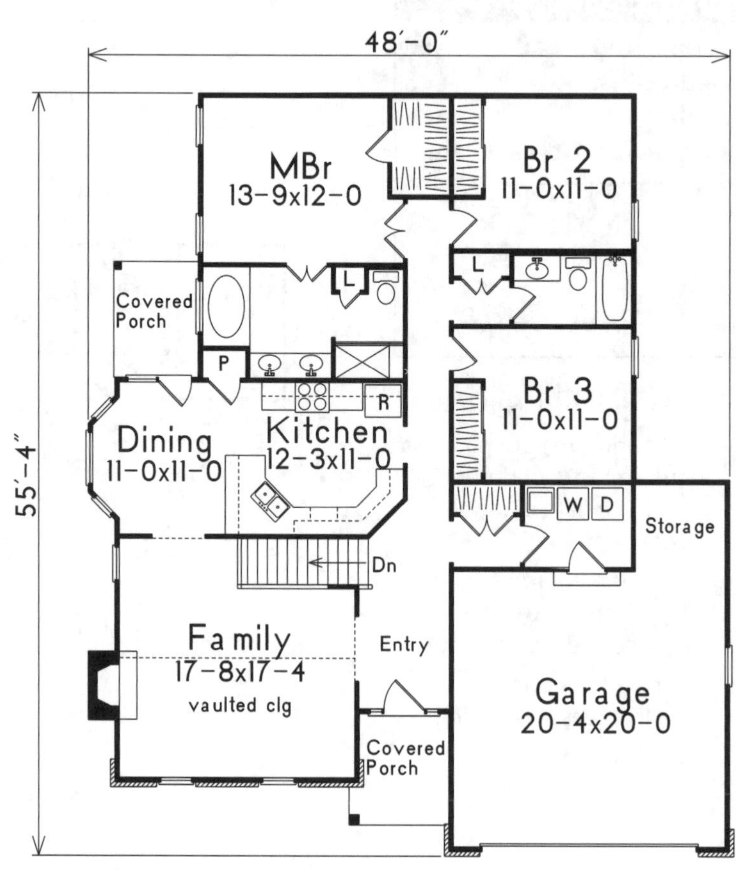

plan #584-014D-0005

price code A

plan information	
total living area:	1,314
bedrooms:	3
baths:	2
garage:	2-car
foundation type: basement	

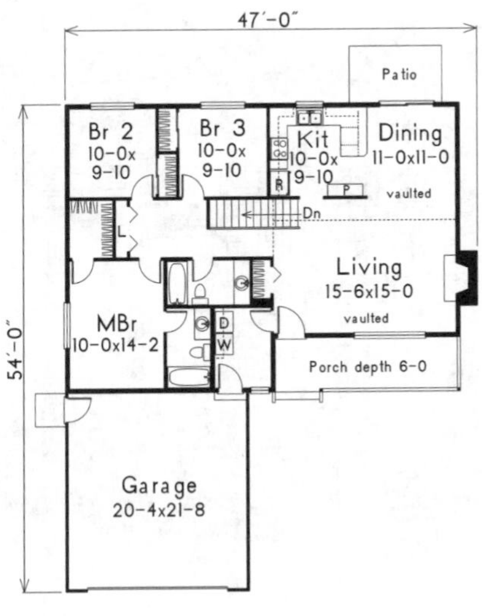

special features

- energy efficient home with 2" x 6" exterior walls
- covered porch adds immediate appeal and welcoming charm
- open floor plan combined with a vaulted ceiling offers spacious living
- functional kitchen is complete with a pantry and eating bar
- cozy fireplace in the living room
- private master bedroom features a large walk-in closet and bath

---

plan #584-008D-0110

price code B

plan information	
total living area:	1,500
bedrooms:	3
baths:	2
garage:	2-car
foundation type: basement	

special features

- living room features a cathedral ceiling and opens to the breakfast room
- breakfast room has a spectacular bay window and adjoins a well-appointed kitchen with generous storage
- laundry room is convenient to the kitchen and includes a large closet
- large walk-in closet gives the master bedroom abundant storage

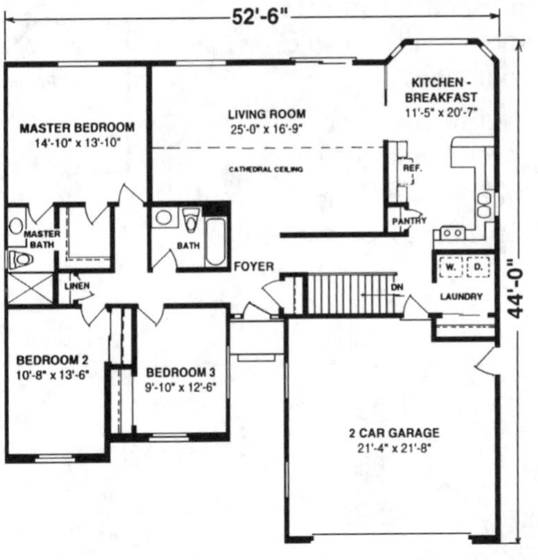

plan #584-067D-0001

price code A

plan information	
total living area:	1,200
bedrooms:	3
baths:	2
garage:	2-car
foundation types:	
basement	
crawl space	
slab	
please specify when ordering	

special features

- large great room extends the entire depth of the home and also accesses the outdoors
- a U-shaped kitchen keeps everything within reach
- convenient laundry room is located just off the kitchen

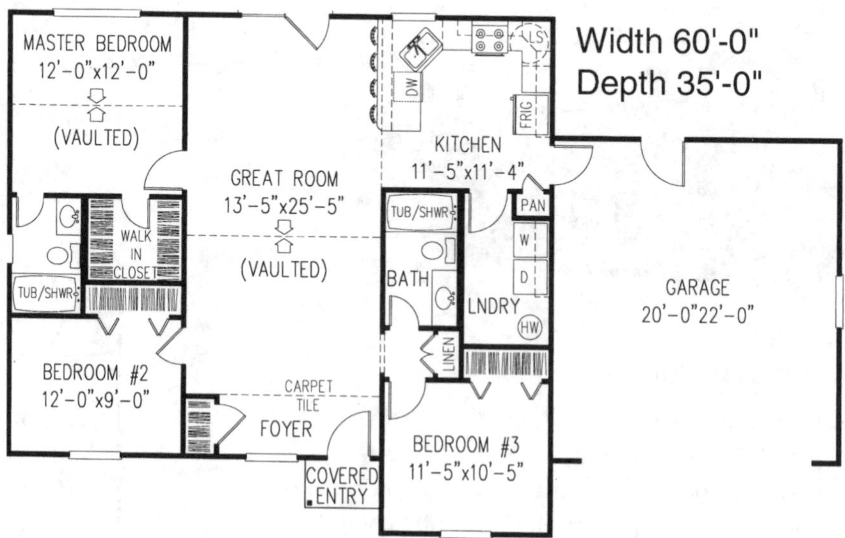

plan #584-061D-0001

price code B

plan information

total living area:	1,747
bedrooms:	4
baths:	2
garage:	2-car
foundation type:	
slab	

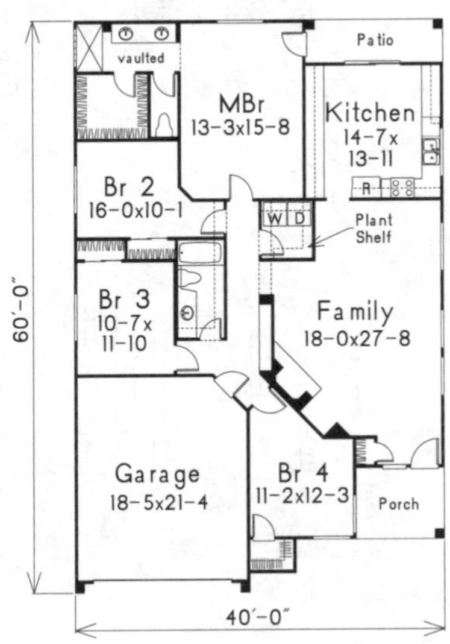

special features

- entry opens into large family room with coat closet, angled fireplace and attractive plant shelf
- kitchen and master bedroom access covered patio
- functional kitchen includes ample workspace

---

plan #584-014D-0004

price code B

plan information

total living area:	1,689
bedrooms:	3
baths:	2
garage:	2-car
foundation types:	
basement standard	
crawl space	
slab	

special features

- distinct covered entrance
- open living and dining areas include vaulted ceilings, a corner fireplace and access to the rear deck
- stylish angled kitchen offers large counter workspace and nook
- master bedroom boasts a spacious bath with step-up tub, separate shower and large walk-in closet

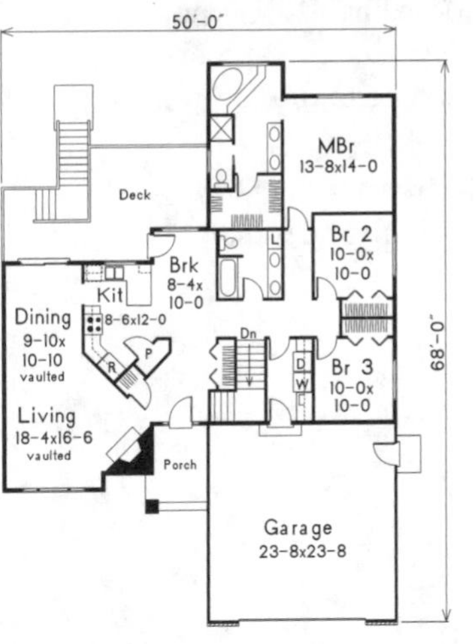

plan #584-020D-0003

price code A

plan information	
total living area:	1,420
bedrooms:	3
baths:	2
garage:	2-car
foundation types:	
slab standard	
crawl space	

special features

- energy efficient home with 2" x 6" exterior walls
- living room has a 12' ceiling, corner fireplace and atrium doors leading to the covered porch
- secluded master suite has a garden bath and walk-in closet

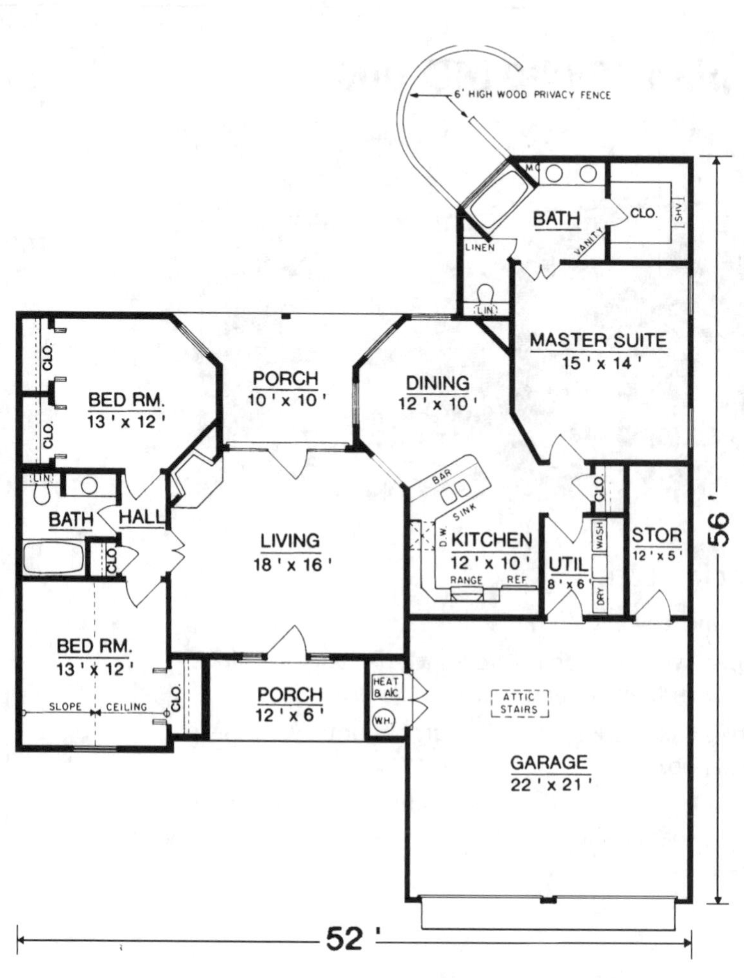

plan #584-039D-0002

price code A

plan information

total living area:	1,333
bedrooms:	3
baths:	2
garage:	2-car carport
foundation types:	
crawl space	
slab	
please specify when ordering	

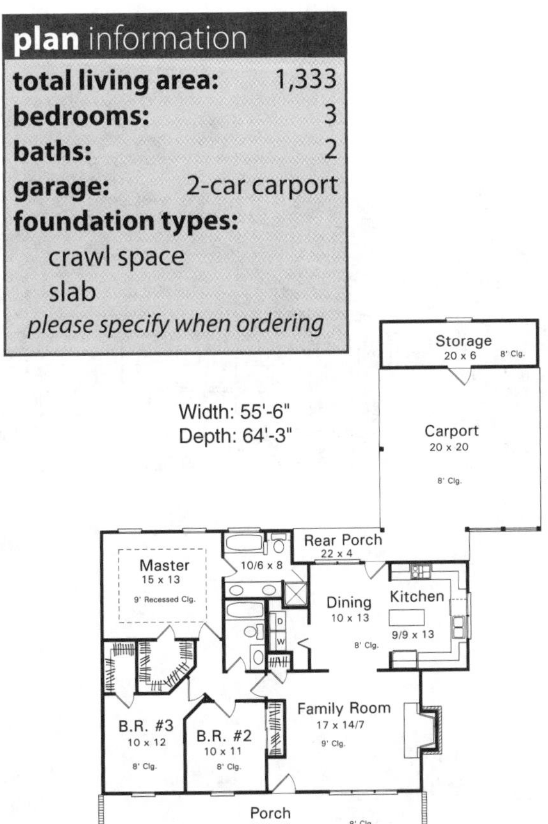

special features

- country charm with a covered front porch
- dining area looks into the family room with fireplace
- master suite has a walk-in closet and private bath

---

plan #584-014D-0007

price code A

plan information

total living area:	1,453
bedrooms:	3
baths:	2
garage:	2-car
foundation types:	
basement standard	
crawl space	

special features

- decorative vents, window trim, shutters and brick blend to create dramatic curb appeal
- energy efficient home with 2" x 6" exterior walls
- kitchen opens to the living area and includes a salad sink in the island as well as a pantry and handy laundry room
- exquisite master bedroom is highlighted by a vaulted ceiling, dressing area with walk-in closet, private bath and spa tub/shower

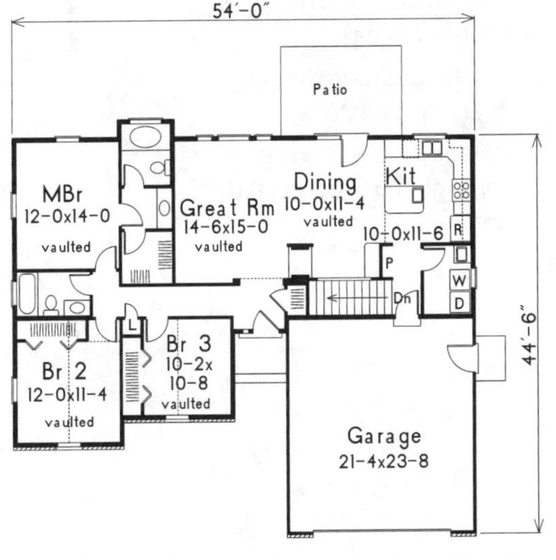

plan #584-008D-0054

price code B

plan information

total living area:	1,574
bedrooms:	3
baths:	2
garage:	2-car
foundation types:	
basement standard	
crawl space	

special features

- foyer enters into an open great room with corner fireplace and rear dining room with adjoining kitchen
- two secondary bedrooms share a full bath
- master bedroom has a spacious private bath
- garage accesses home through mud room/utility area

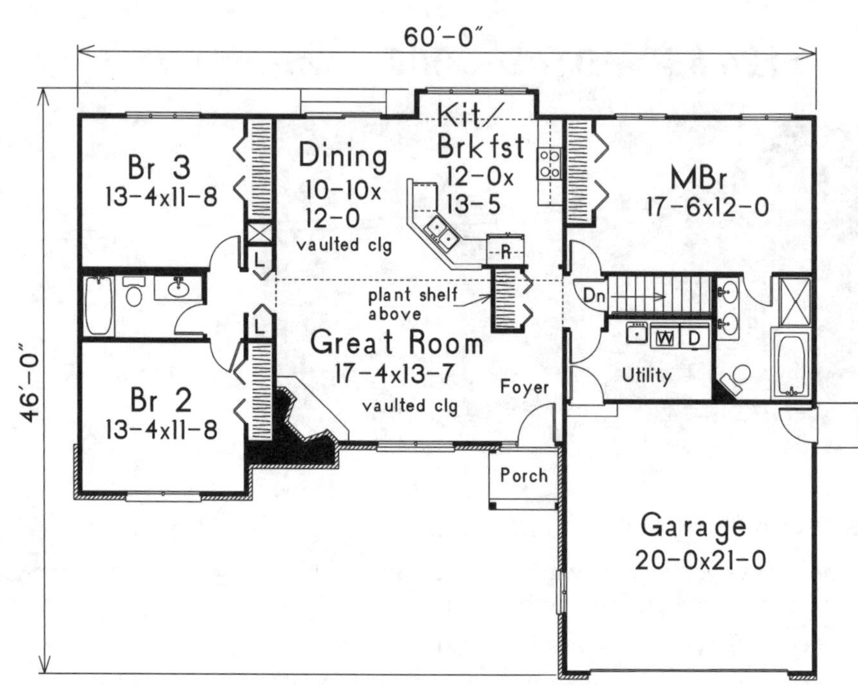

plan #584-018D-0008

price code C

plan information

total living area:	2,109
bedrooms:	3
baths:	2
garage:	2-car side entry
foundation types:	
slab standard	
crawl space	

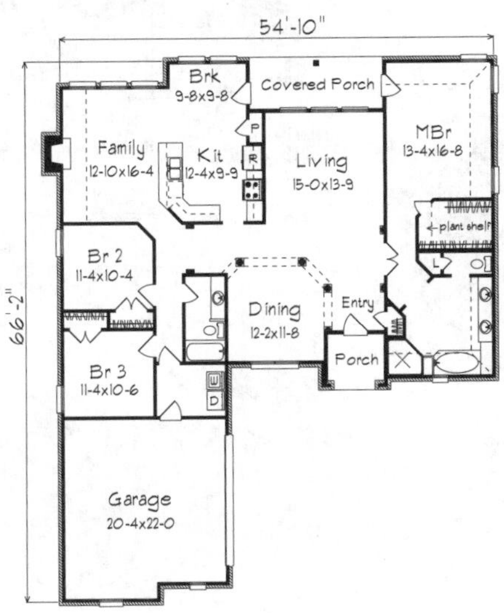

special features

- 12' ceilings in the living and dining rooms
- the kitchen is designed as an integral part of the family and breakfast rooms
- the secluded and generously sized master bedroom includes a plant shelf, walk-in closet and private bath with separate tub and shower
- stately columns and circle-top window frame the dining room

plan #584-053D-0035

price code B

plan information

total living area:	1,527
bedrooms:	3
baths:	2
garage:	2-car side entry
foundation types:	
basement standard	
crawl space	
slab	

special features

- convenient laundry room is located off the garage
- vaulted ceiling in living room slopes to foyer and dining area creating a spacious entrance
- galley kitchen provides an easy passage to both the breakfast and dining areas
- master bedroom is complete with a large master bath, platform tub and shower, plus roomy walk-in closets

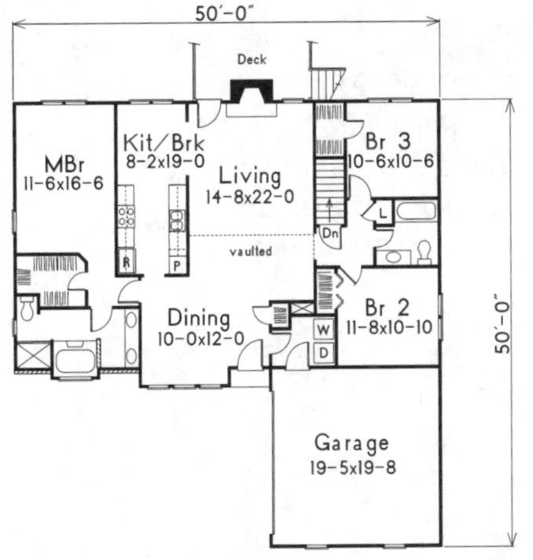

plan #584-037D-0010

price code B

plan information

total living area:	1,770
bedrooms:	3
baths:	2
garage:	2-car
foundation type:	slab

special features

- distinctive covered entrance leads into spacious foyer
- master bedroom, living and dining rooms feature large windows for plenty of light
- oversized living room has a high ceiling and large windows that flank the fireplace
- kitchen includes a pantry and large planning center
- master bedroom has a high vaulted ceiling, deluxe bath, and private access outdoors

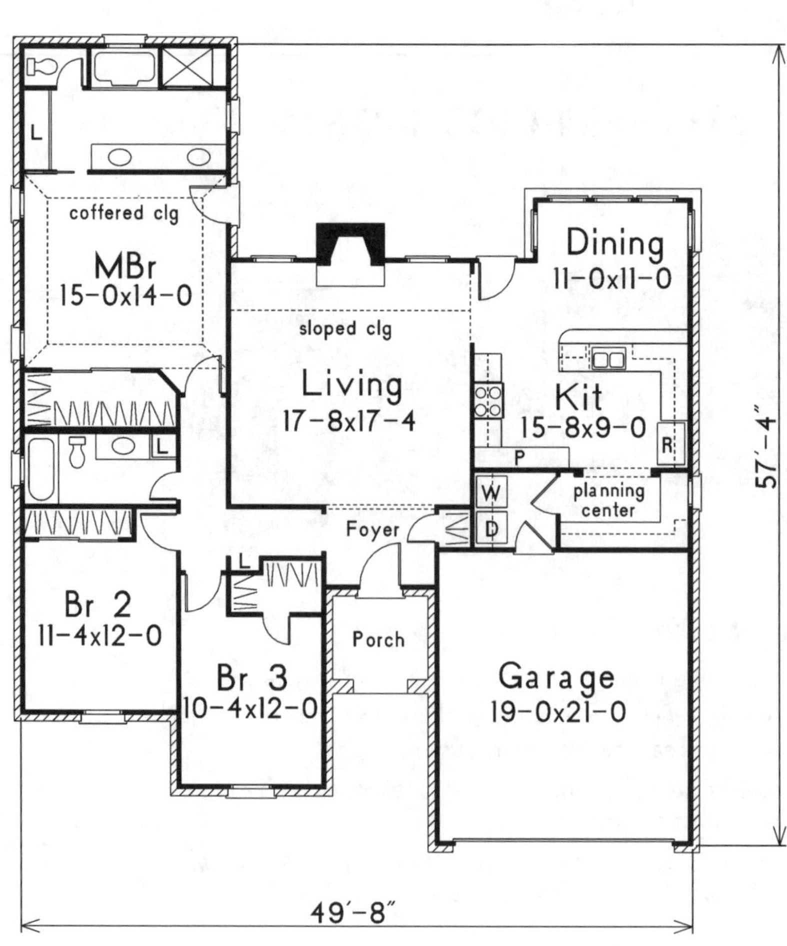

plan #584-022D-0011

price code B

plan information

total living area:	1,630
bedrooms:	3
baths:	2
garage:	2-car
foundation type:	
basement	

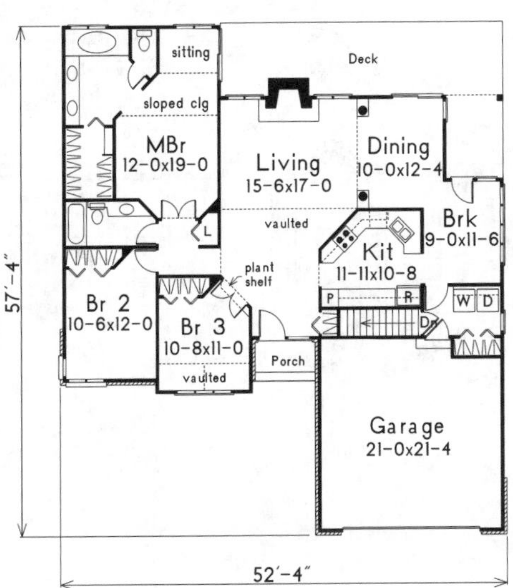

special features

- crisp facade and full windows front and back offer open viewing
- wrap-around rear deck is accessible from breakfast room, dining room and master bedroom
- vaulted ceilings in the living room and master bedroom
- sitting area and large walk-in closet complement the master bedroom

---

plan #584-001D-0034

price code B

plan information

total living area:	1,642
bedrooms:	3
baths:	2
garage:	2-car
foundation types:	
basement standard	
crawl space	
slab	

special features

- walk-through kitchen boasts a vaulted ceiling and corner sink overlooking the family room
- vaulted family room features a cozy fireplace and access to the rear patio
- master bedroom includes a sloped ceiling, walk-in closet and private bath

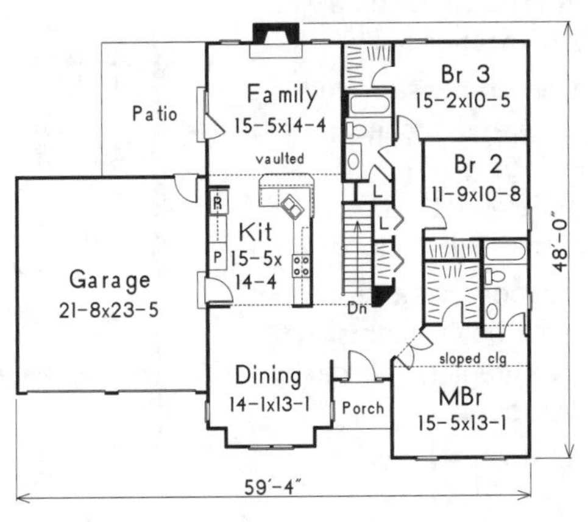

plan #584-021D-0007

price code D

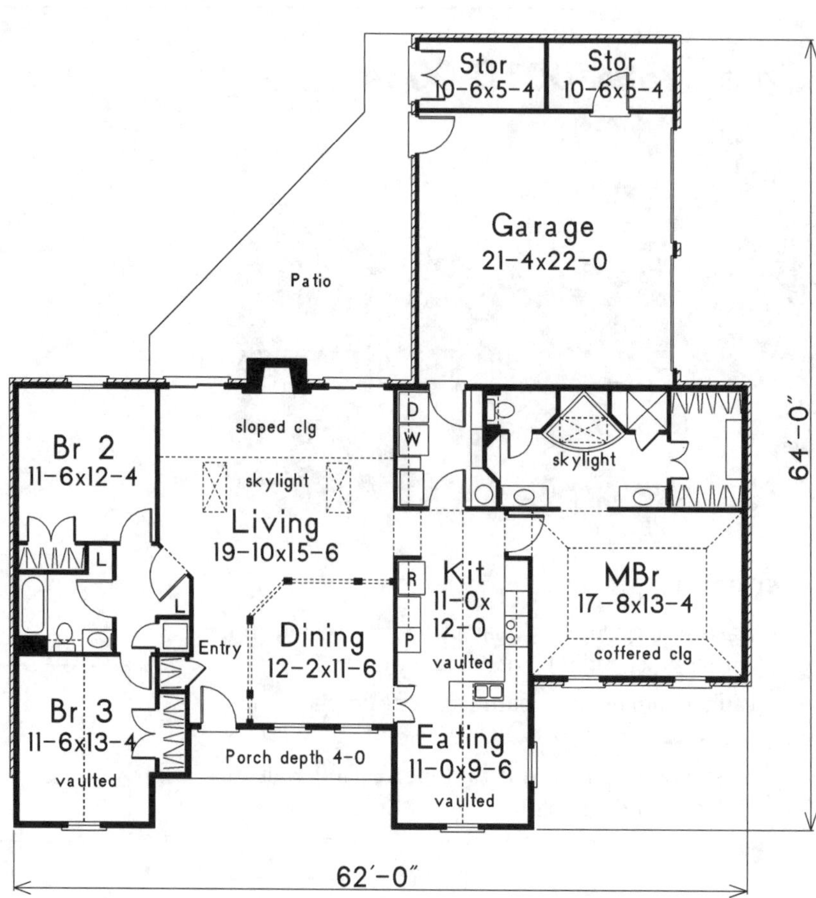

plan information

total living area:	1,868
bedrooms:	3
baths:	2
garage:	2-car side entry
foundation types:	
slab standard	
crawl space	

special features

- luxurious master bath is impressive with an angled quarter-circle tub, separate vanities and large walk-in closet
- energy efficient home with 2" x 6" exterior walls
- dining room is surrounded by a series of arched openings which complement the open feeling of this design
- living room has a 12' ceiling accented by skylights and a large fireplace flanked by sliding doors
- large storage areas

plan #584-001D-0001

price code B

plan information	
total living area:	1,605
bedrooms:	3
baths:	2
garage:	2-car
foundation types:	
basement standard	
slab	
crawl space	

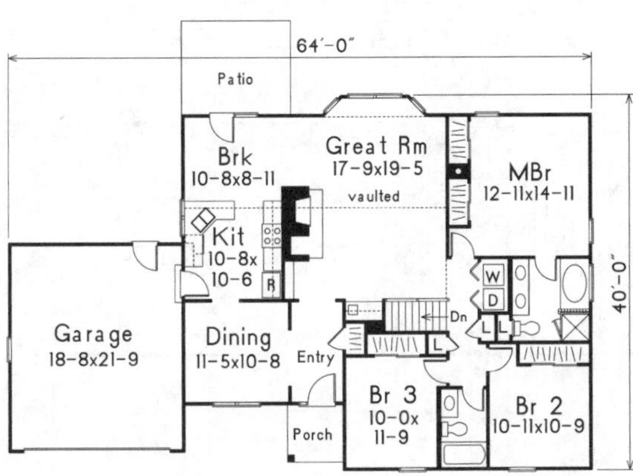

special features

- vaulted ceilings in great room, kitchen and breakfast area
- spacious great room features a large bay window, fireplace, built-in bookshelves and a convenient wet bar
- the formal dining room and breakfast area are perfect for entertaining or everyday living
- master bedroom has a spacious bath with oval tub and separate shower

---

plan #584-022D-0027

price code C

plan information	
total living area:	1,847
bedrooms:	3
baths:	2
garage:	2-car
foundation type:	
slab	

special features

- kitchen includes an island cooktop and sunny breakfast area
- master bedroom features a vaulted ceiling and a skylighted bath with large tub, separate shower and walk-in closet
- service bar eases entertaining in the vaulted dining and living rooms
- family room, complete with corner fireplace, accesses outdoor patio

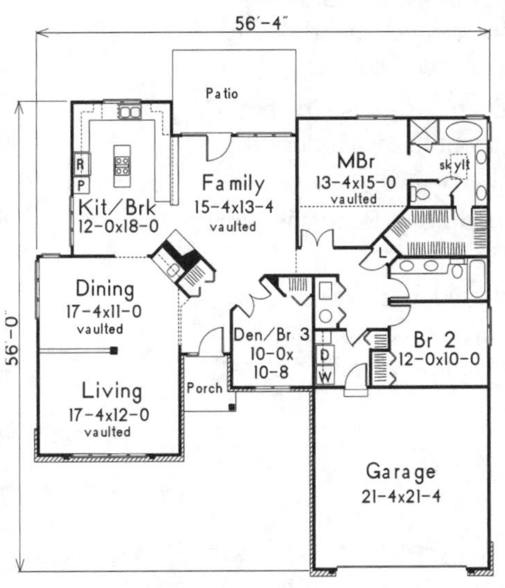

plan #584-037D-0031

price code C

rear view

plan information	
total living area:	1,923
bedrooms:	3
baths:	2
garage:	2-car
foundation type: slab	

special features

- the foyer opens into a spacious living room with fireplace and splendid view of the covered porch
- kitchen has a walk-in pantry adjacent to the laundry area and breakfast room
- all bedrooms feature walk-in closets
- secluded master bedroom includes unique angled bath with spacious walk-in closet

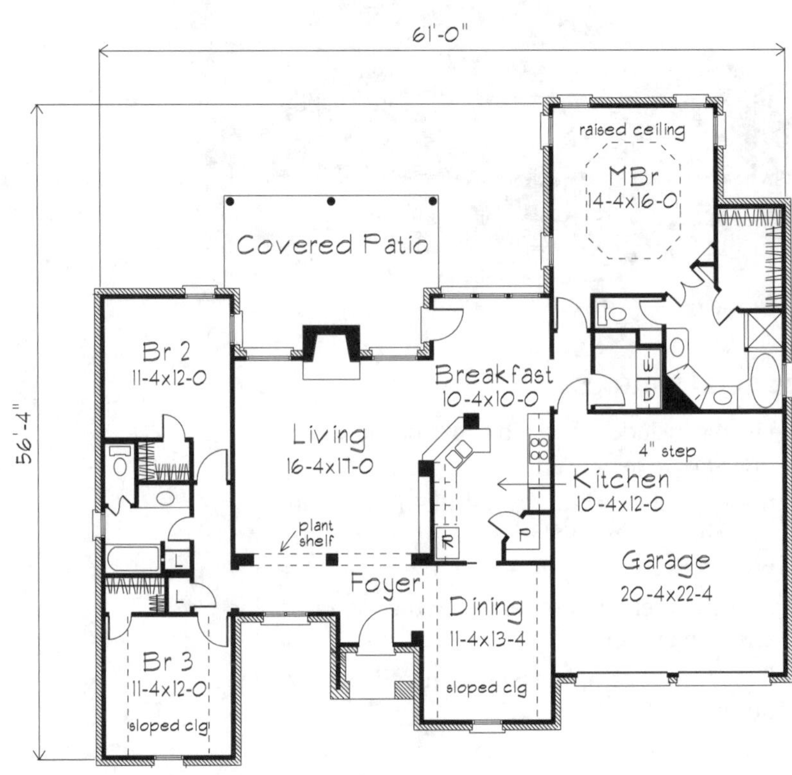

plan #584-007D-0042

price code AA

plan information

total living area:	914
bedrooms:	2
baths:	1
garage:	2-car drive under
foundation type: basement	

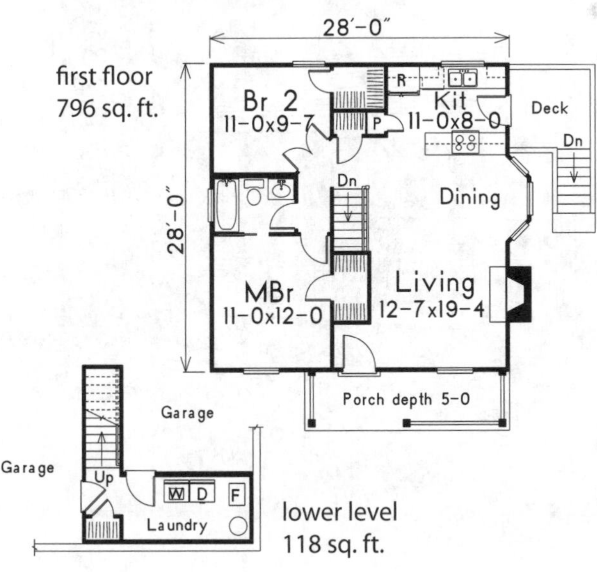

special features

- large porch for leisure evenings
- dining area with bay window, open stair and pass-through kitchen create openness
- basement includes generous garage space, storage area, finished laundry and mechanical room

---

plan #584-008D-0148

price code AAA

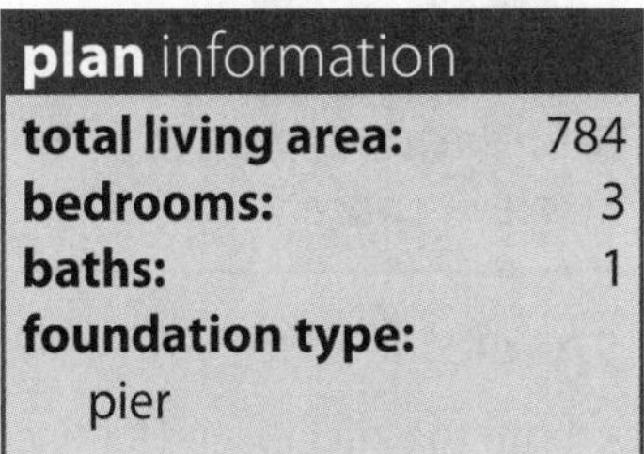

plan information

total living area:	784
bedrooms:	3
baths:	1
foundation type: pier	

special features

- outdoor relaxation will be enjoyed with this home's huge wrap-around wood deck
- upon entering the spacious living area, a cozy free-standing fireplace, sloped ceiling and corner window wall catch the eye
- charming kitchen features a pass-through peninsula to the dining area

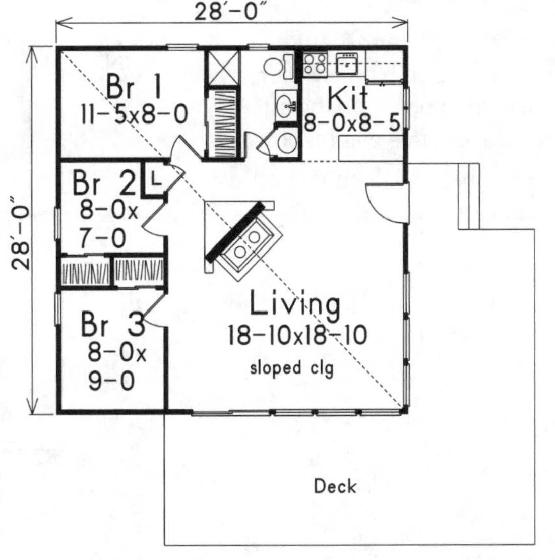

plan #584-058D-0004

price code AA

plan information	
total living area:	962
bedrooms:	2
baths:	1
foundation type:	
crawl space	

special features

- both the kitchen and family room share warmth from the fireplace
- charming facade features a covered porch on one side, screened porch on the other and attractive planter boxes
- an L-shaped kitchen boasts a convenient pantry

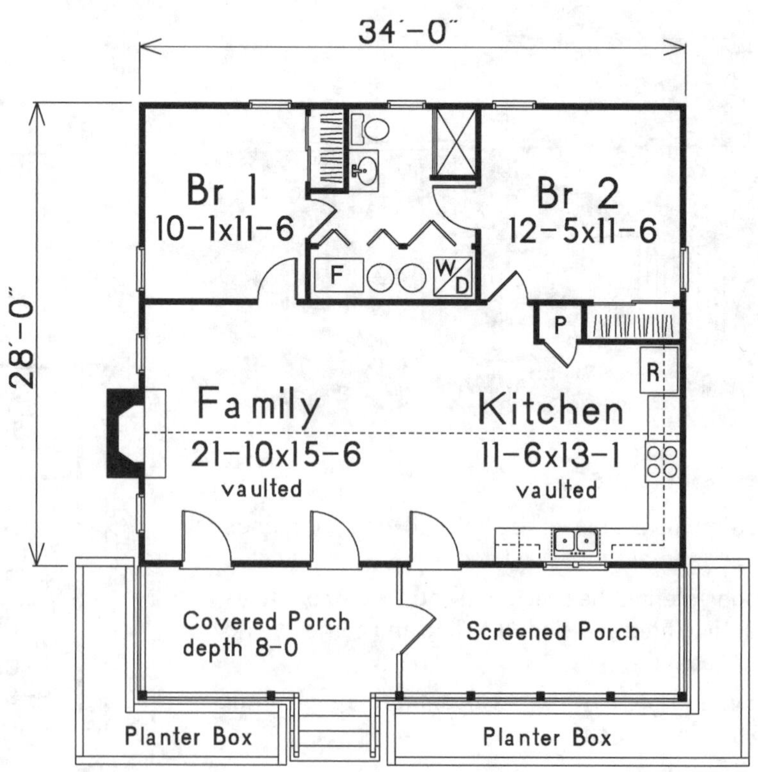

plan #584-008D-0133

price code AAA

plan information	
total living area:	624
bedrooms:	2
baths:	1
foundation type:	
pier	

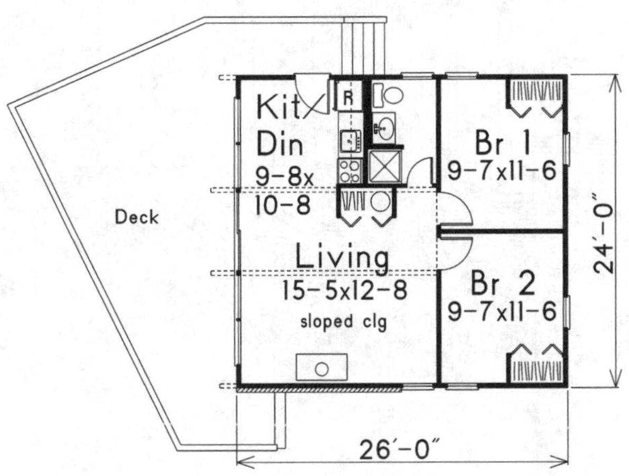

special features

- the combination of stone, vertical siding, lots of glass and a low roof line creates a cozy retreat
- vaulted living area features a free-standing fireplace that heats the adjacent stone wall
- efficient kitchen includes a dining area and view onto an angular deck
- two bedrooms share a hall bath with shower

---

plan #584-078D-0025

price code D

plan information	
total living area:	1,015
bedrooms:	2
baths:	1
foundation types:	
basement	
crawl space	
please specify when ordering	

special features

- a massive fieldstone fireplace separates the living and dining spaces, both of which feature beamed and vaulted ceilings
- one bedroom enjoys a walk-in closet, private entry to bath and French doors accessing the porch making it an ideal master suite
- the cozy kitchen is fully equipped and conveniently adjacent to a well-planned utility room

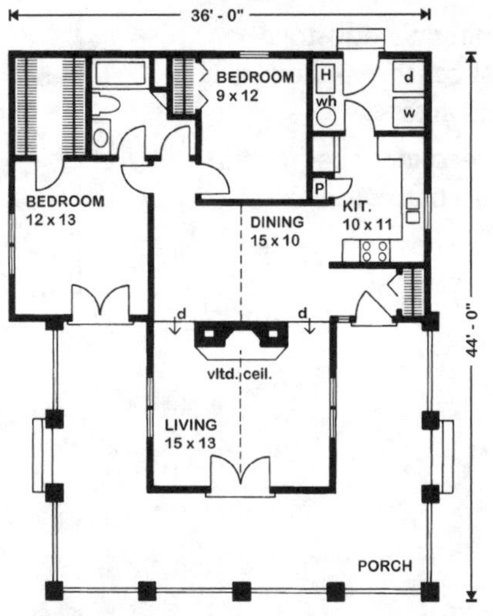

plan #584-062D-0049

price code A

plan information	
total living area:	1,292
bedrooms:	3
baths:	2
foundation type:	
crawl space	

special features

- master bedroom features a walk-in closet, private bath and access to the outdoors onto an expansive deck
- prominent woodstove enhances the vaulted living/dining area
- two secondary bedrooms share a bath
- kitchen has a convenient snack counter

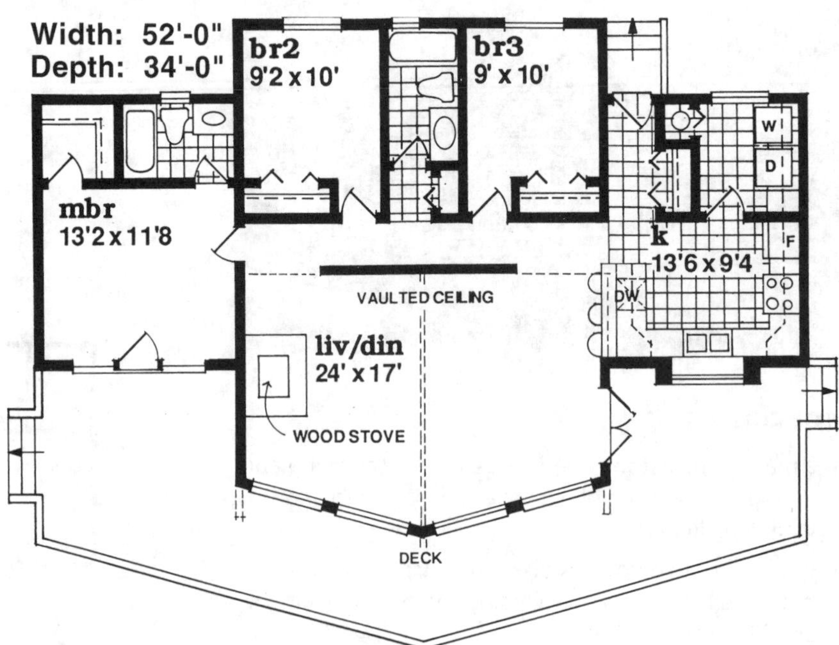

plan #584-001D-0085

price code AAA

plan information

total living area:	720
bedrooms:	2
baths:	1
foundation types:	
crawl space standard	
slab	

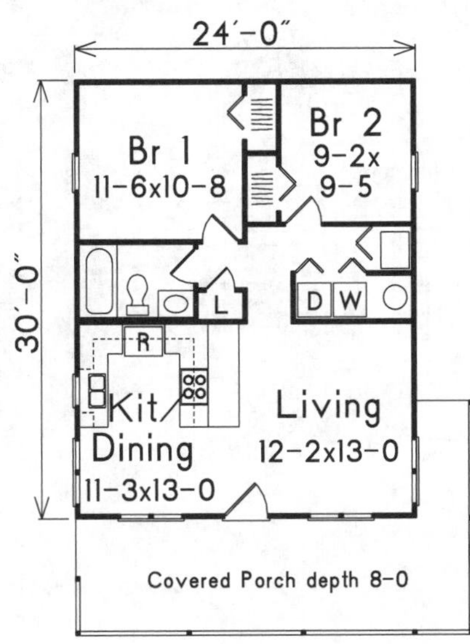

special features

- abundant windows in living and dining rooms provide generous sunlight
- secluded laundry area with handy storage closet
- a U-shaped kitchen with large breakfast bar opens into living area
- large covered deck offers plenty of outdoor living space

---

plan #584-058D-0030

price code AA

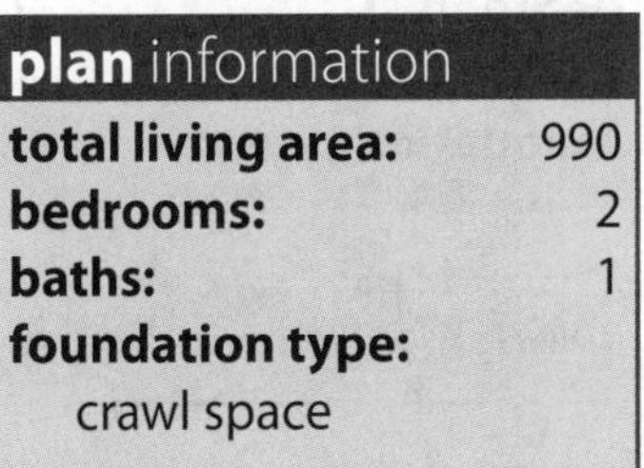

plan information

total living area:	990
bedrooms:	2
baths:	1
foundation type:	
crawl space	

special features

- the wrap-around porch creates a relaxing retreat
- combined family and dining rooms boast a vaulted ceiling
- space for an efficiency washer and dryer unit offers convenience

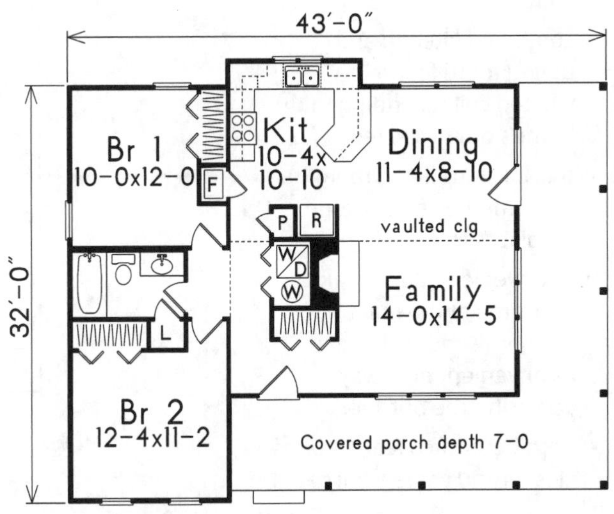

plan #584-078D-0032

price code D

plan information

total living area:	895
bedrooms:	2
baths:	1
foundation types:	
basement	
crawl space	
please specify when ordering	

special features

- compact yet efficient floor plan
- combined kitchen and dining room features a vaulted ceiling adding to the home's open, airy feel
- the spacious living room is warmed by a fieldstone fireplace
- a convenient laundry alcove is located at the rear of the home and includes a convenient doorway accessing the outdoors
- both bedrooms feature large closets and share a full bath

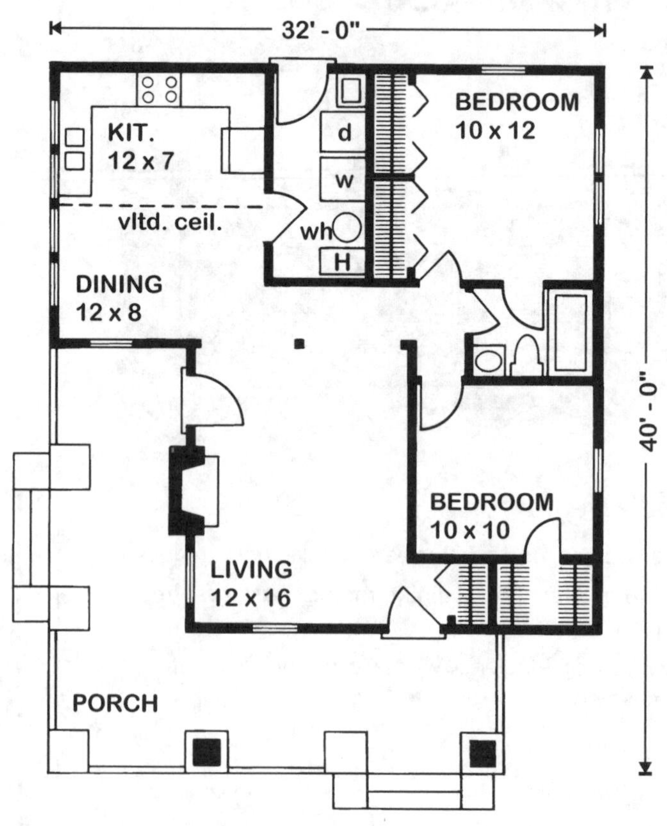

plan #584-008D-0153

price code AAA

plan information	
total living area:	792
bedrooms:	2
baths:	1
foundation types:	
crawl space standard	
slab	

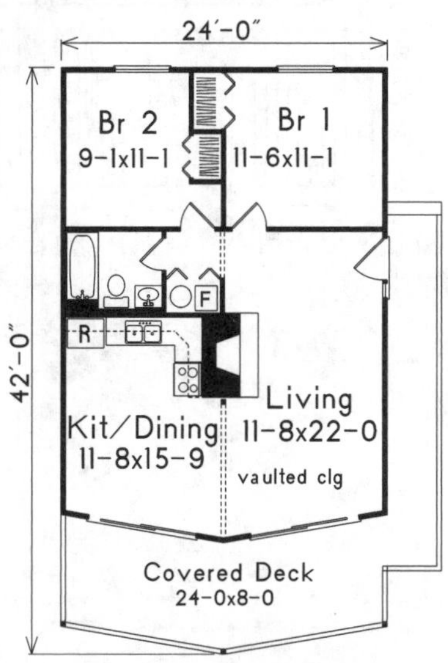

special features

- attractive exterior features wood posts and beams, wrap-around deck with railing and glass sliding doors with transoms
- kitchen, living and dining areas enjoy sloped ceilings, a cozy fireplace and views over the deck
- two bedrooms share a bath just off the hall

---

plan #584-078D-0023

price code D

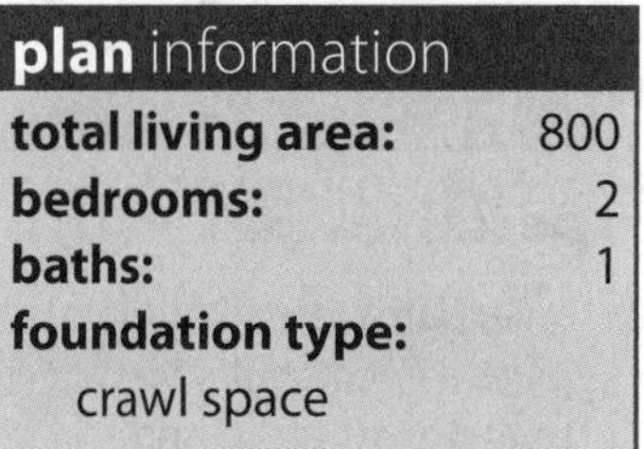

plan information	
total living area:	800
bedrooms:	2
baths:	1
foundation type:	
crawl space	

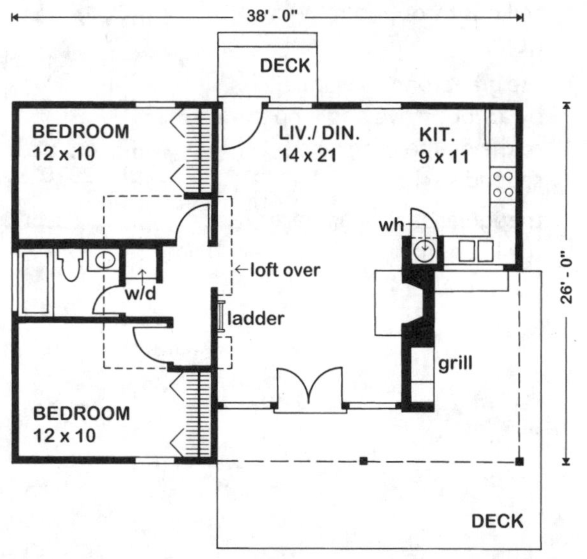

special features

- the open floor plan gives this home a casual feeling perfect for a vacation hideaway or compact home
- the vaulted ceiling and floor-to-ceiling windows enhance the living room
- the large covered deck is ideal for entertaining with a barbecue pit built into the stone fireplace
- a ship's ladder accesses the unique sleeping or storage loft located above the bedrooms

plan #584-062D-0053 price code A

plan information

total living area:	1,405
bedrooms:	3
baths:	2
foundation types:	
basement	
crawl space	
please specify when ordering	

special features

- an expansive wall of glass gives a spectacular view to the great room and accentuates the high vaulted ceilings throughout the design
- the great room is warmed by a woodstove and is open to the dining room and L-shaped kitchen
- triangular snack bar graces the kitchen

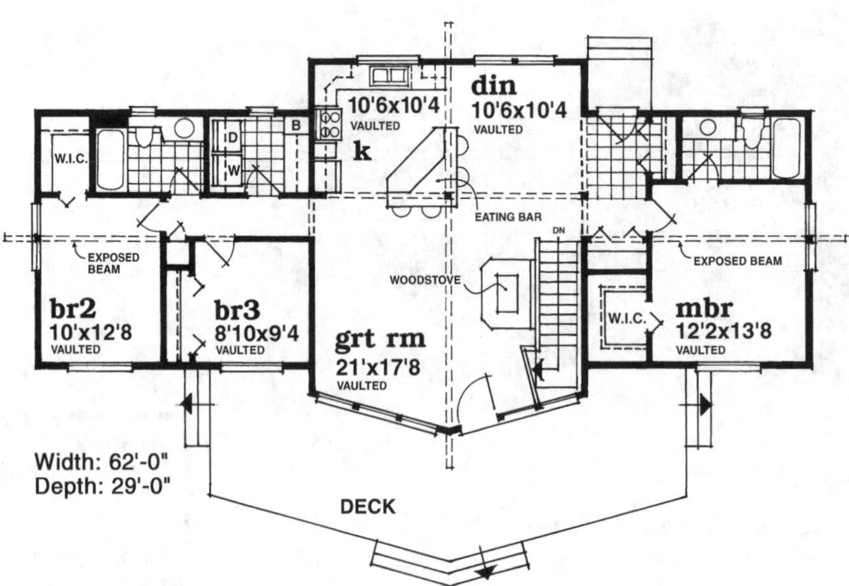

plan information	
total living area:	1,321
bedrooms:	3
baths:	2
garage:	1-car rear entry
foundation type:	basement

special features

- rear entry garage and elongated brick wall add to the appealing facade
- dramatic vaulted living room includes corner fireplace and towering feature windows
- breakfast room is immersed in light from two large windows and glass sliding doors

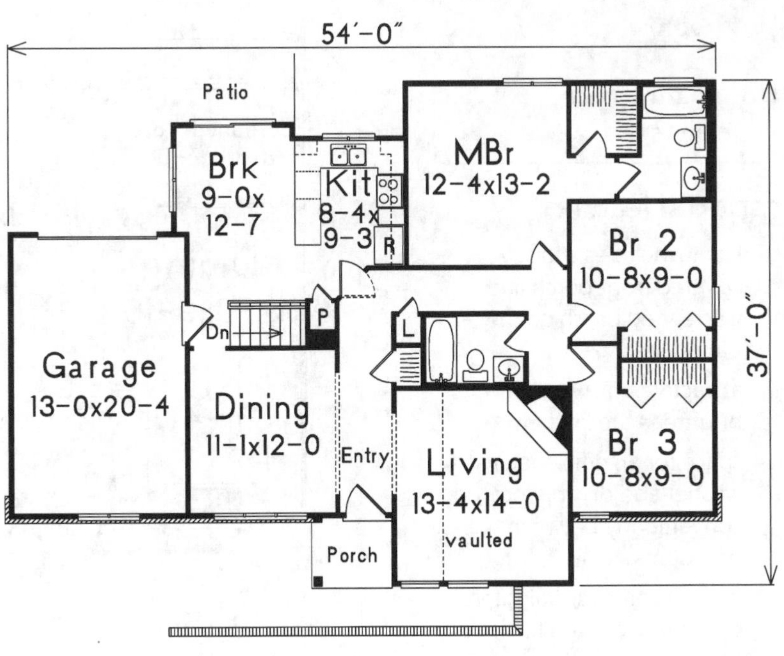

plan #584-058D-0013

price code AA

plan information	
total living area:	1,073
bedrooms:	2
baths:	1
foundation type: crawl space	

special features

- home includes a lovely covered front porch and a screened porch off the dining area
- attractive box window brightens the kitchen
- space for an efficiency washer and dryer is located conveniently between the bedrooms
- family room is spotlighted by a fireplace with flanking bookshelves and spacious vaulted ceiling

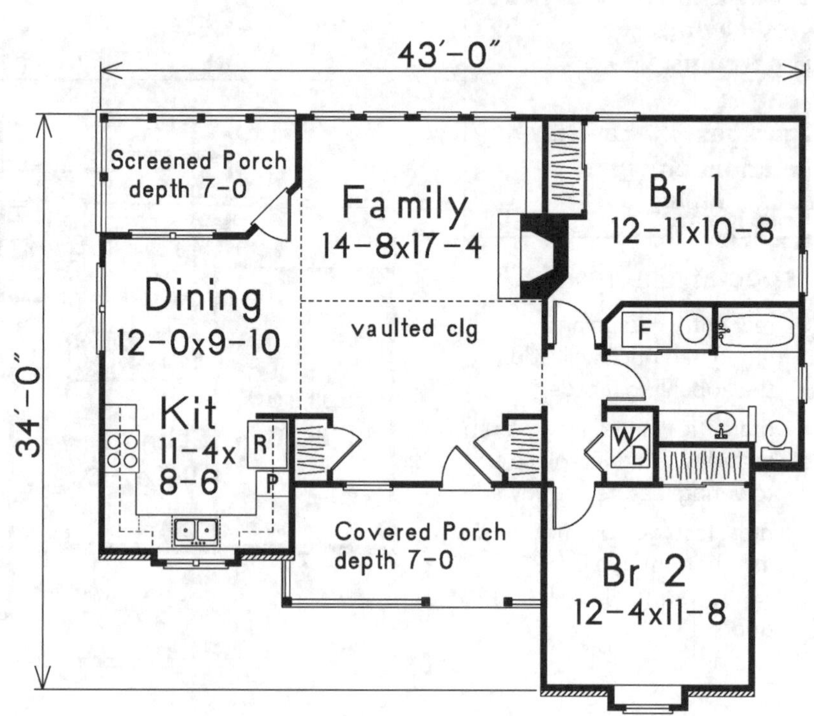

plan #584-008D-0158

price code B

plan information	
total living area:	1,584
bedrooms:	3
baths:	2
foundation types:	
basement standard	
crawl space	
slab	

special features

- vaulted living and dining rooms feature a stone fireplace, ascending spiral staircase and a separate vestibule with guest closet
- space-saving kitchen has an eat-in area and access to the deck
- bedroom #1 has private access to a full bath

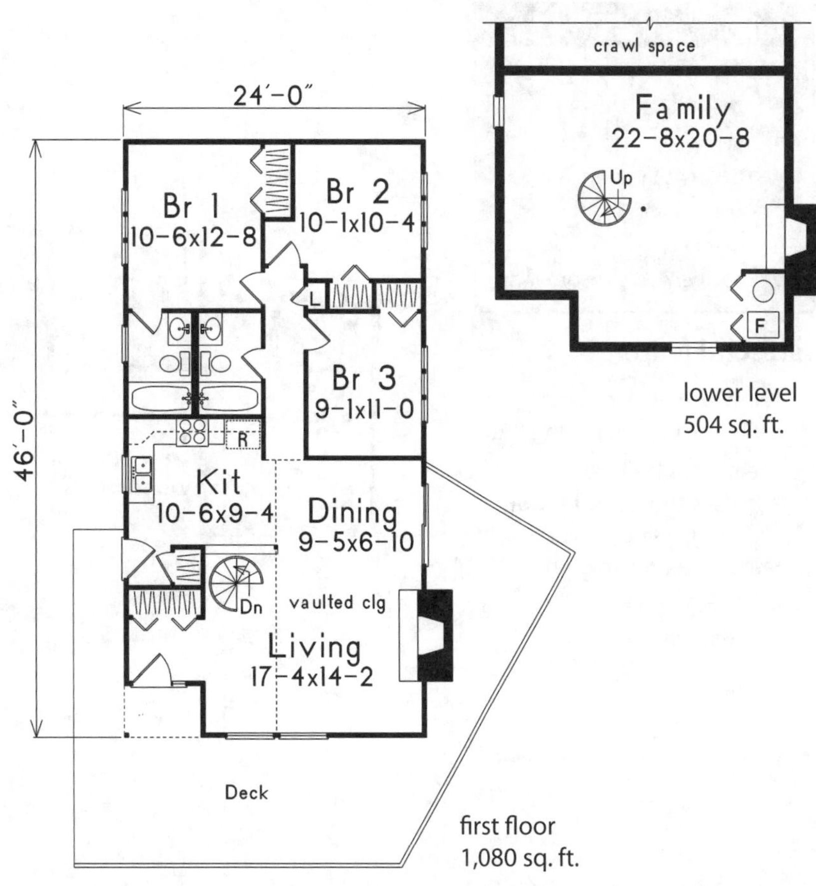

lower level
504 sq. ft.

first floor
1,080 sq. ft.

plan #584-062D-0047

price code A

plan information	
total living area:	1,230
bedrooms:	3
baths:	2
foundation types:	
crawl space	
basement	
please specify when ordering	

special features

- full-width deck creates plenty of outdoor living area
- the master bedroom accesses the deck through sliding glass doors and features a private bath
- vaulted living room has a woodstove

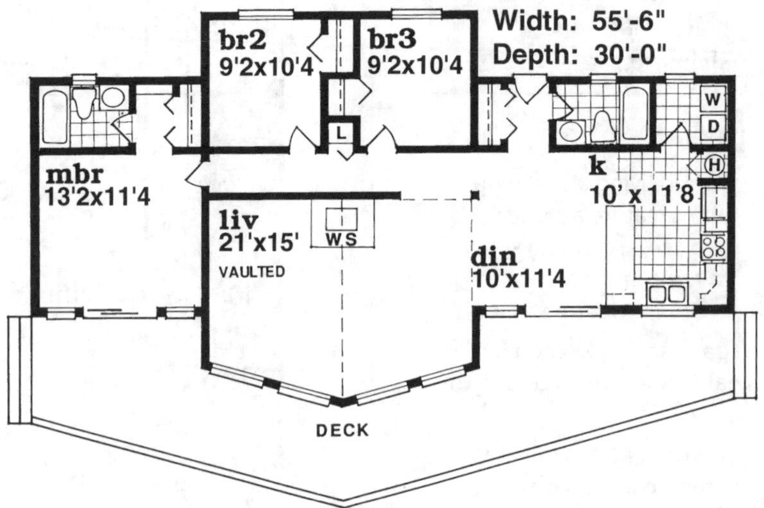

plan information

total living area:	1,176
bedrooms:	4
baths:	2
foundation types:	
crawl space standard	
slab	

special features

- efficient kitchen offers plenty of storage, a dining area and a stylish eating bar
- a gathering space is created by the large central living room
- closet and storage space throughout help keep sporting equipment organized and easily accessible
- each end of home is comprised of two bedrooms and a full bath

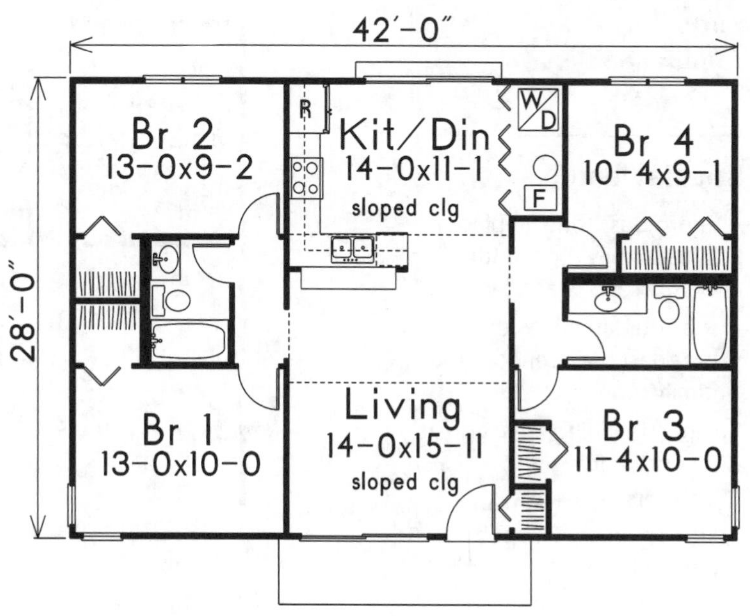

plan #584-058D-0012

price code AA

plan information

total living area:	1,143
bedrooms:	2
baths:	1
foundation type:	
crawl space	

special features

- enormous stone fireplace in the family room adds warmth and character
- spacious kitchen with breakfast bar overlooks the family room
- separate dining area is great for entertaining
- vaulted family room and kitchen create an open atmosphere

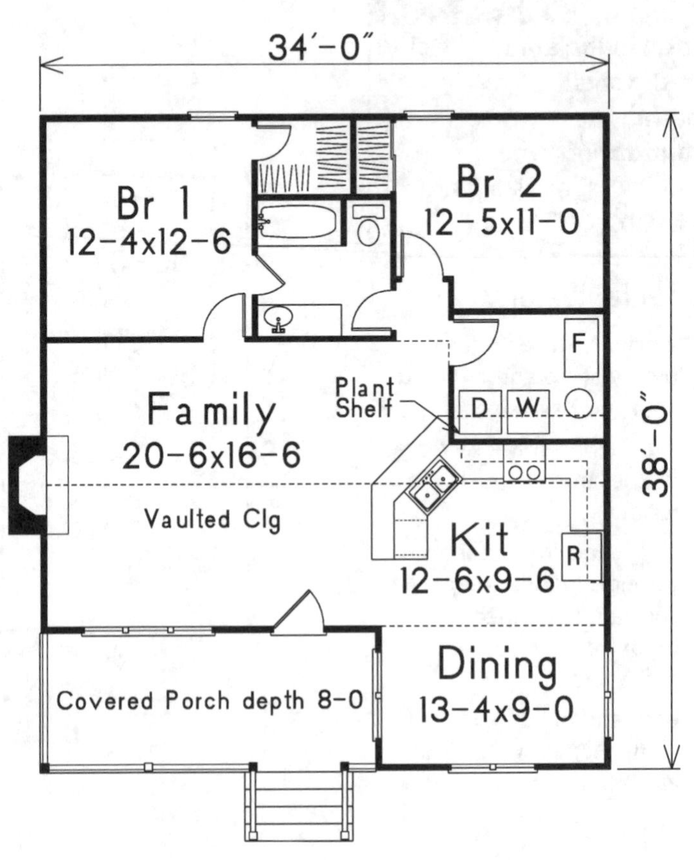

plan #584-007D-0037

price code A

plan information

total living area: 1,403
bedrooms: 3
baths: 2
garage: 2-car drive under
foundation type: basement

special features

- impressive living areas for a modest-sized home
- special master/hall bath has linen storage, step-up tub and lots of window light
- spacious closets everywhere you look

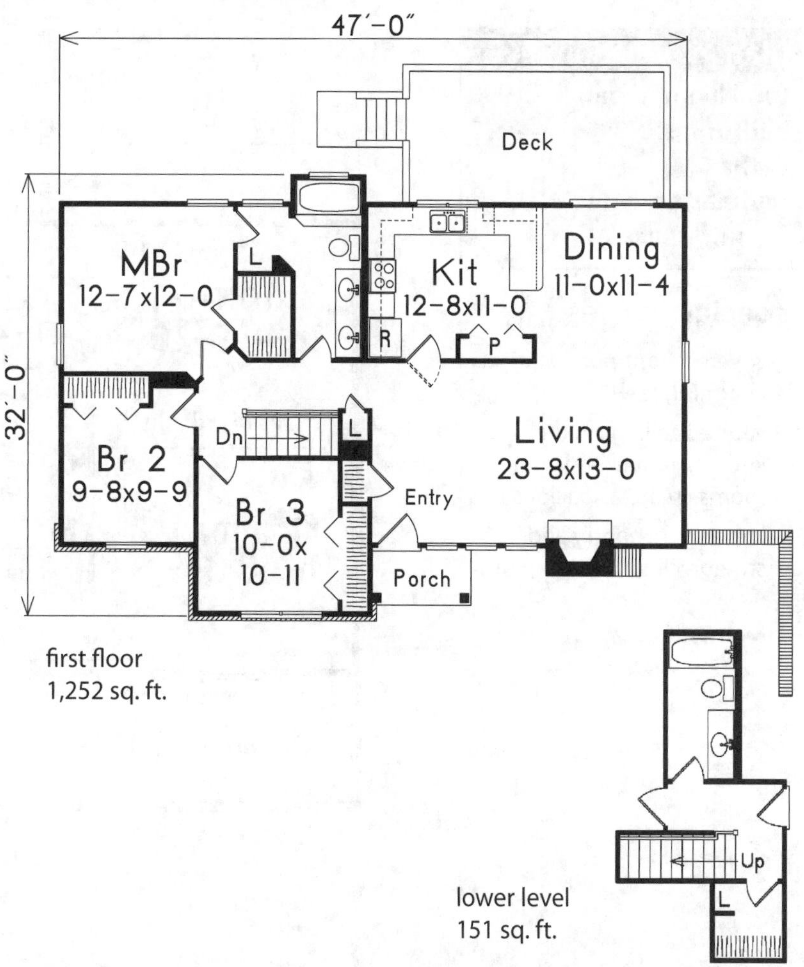

first floor
1,252 sq. ft.

lower level
151 sq. ft.

plan #584-058D-0031

price code AA

plan information	
total living area:	990
bedrooms:	2
baths:	1
foundation type: crawl space	

special features

- covered front porch adds a charming feel
- vaulted ceilings in the kitchen, family and dining rooms create a spacious feel
- large linen, pantry and storage closets throughout

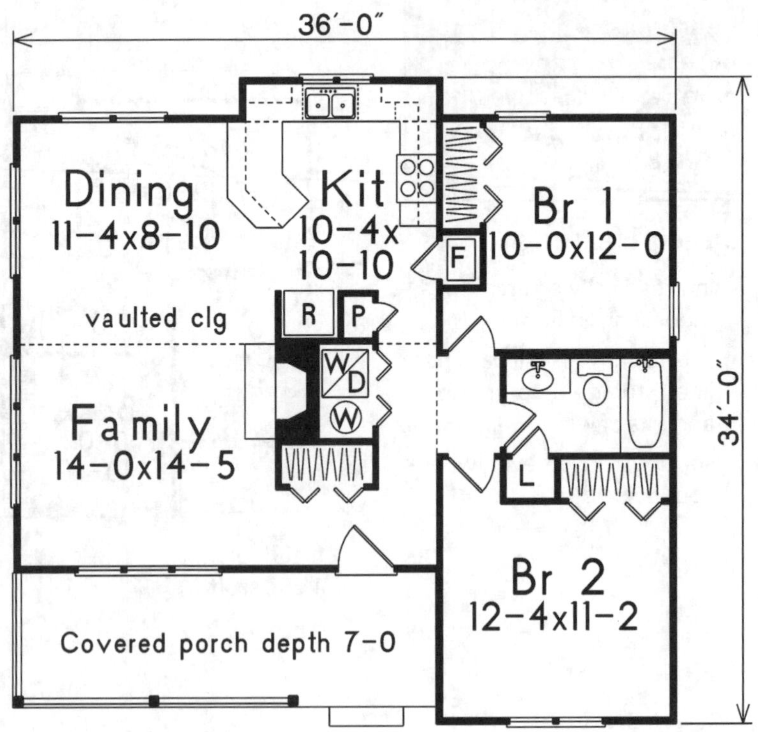

plan #584-008D-0131

price code AA

plan information	
total living area:	960
bedrooms:	2
baths:	1
foundation type:	
crawl space	

special features

- interesting roof and wood beams overhang a generous-sized deck
- family room is vaulted and opens to the dining area and kitchen
- pullman-style kitchen has been skillfully designed
- two bedrooms and hall bath are located at the rear of home

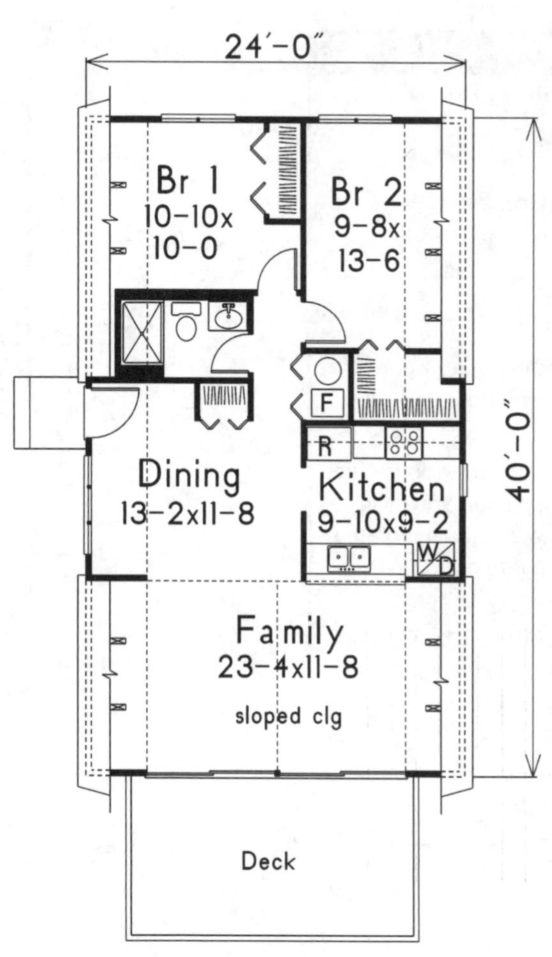

plan #584-007D-0105

price code AA

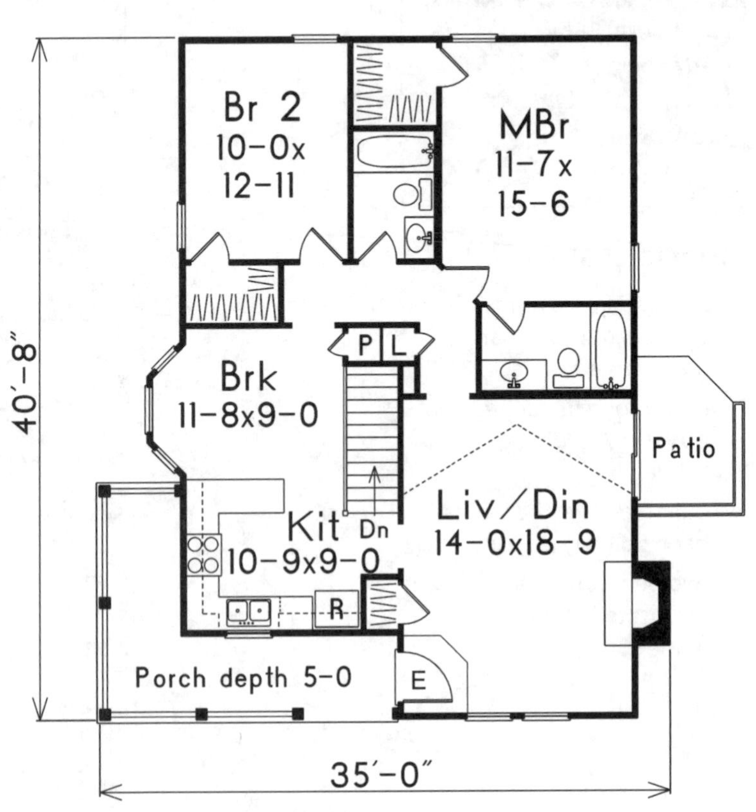

plan information	
total living area:	1,084
bedrooms:	2
baths:	2
foundation type:	
basement	

special features

- delightful country porch for quiet evenings
- the living room offers a front feature window which invites the sun and includes a fireplace and dining area with private patio
- the U-shaped kitchen features lots of cabinets and bayed breakfast room with built-in pantry
- both bedrooms have walk-in closets and access to their own bath

plan information

total living area:	950
bedrooms:	2
baths:	1
garage:	1-car
foundation type: basement	

special features

- deck is attached to the kitchen, perfect for outdoor dining
- vaulted ceiling, open stairway and fireplace complement the great room
- bedroom #2 with a sloped ceiling and box-bay window can convert to a den
- master bedroom has a walk-in closet, plant shelf, separate dressing area and private access to bath
- kitchen has garage access and opens to the great room

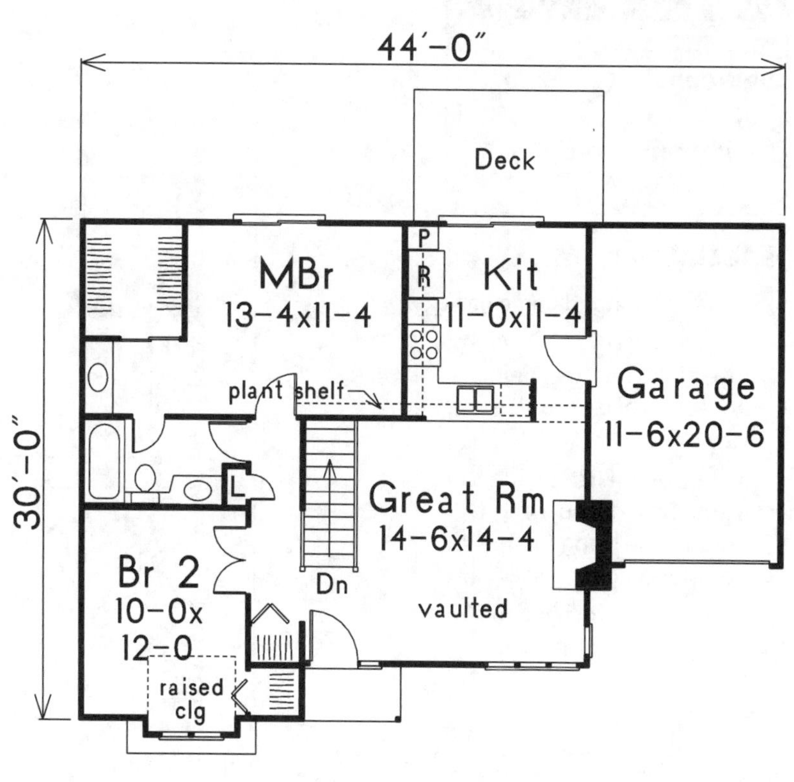

plan #584-008D-0154

price code AAA

plan information

total living area:	527
bedrooms:	1
baths:	1
foundation type:	
crawl space	

special features

- cleverly arranged home has it all
- foyer spills into the dining nook with access to side views
- an excellent kitchen offers a long breakfast bar and borders the living room with free-standing fireplace
- a cozy bedroom has a full bath just across the hall

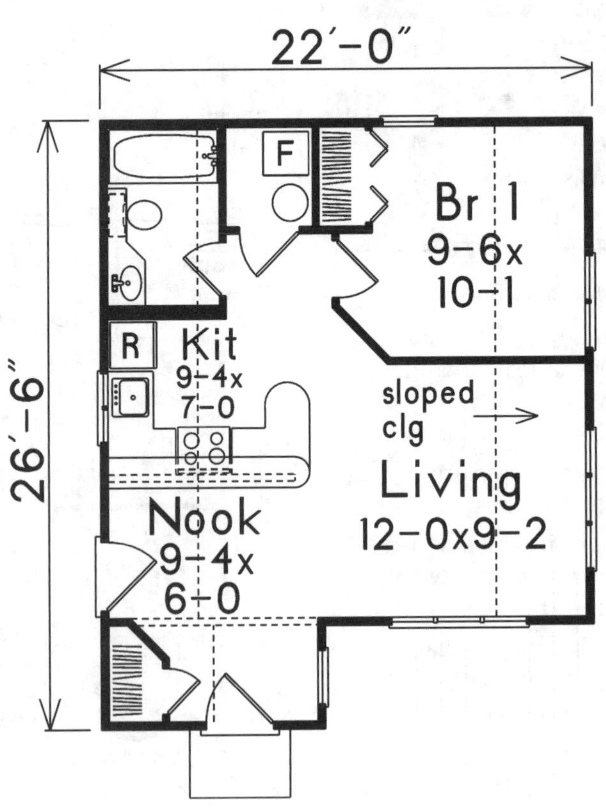

plan #584-008D-0151

price code C

plan information

total living area:	1,806
bedrooms:	3
baths:	2
foundation type:	
basement	

special features

- wrap-around deck, great for entertaining, enhances appearance
- side entry foyer accesses two rear bedrooms, hall bath and living and dining area
- an L-shaped kitchen is open to the dining area
- lots of living area is provided on the lower level, including a spacious family room with a fireplace and sliding doors to the patio under the deck

lower level
742 sq. ft.

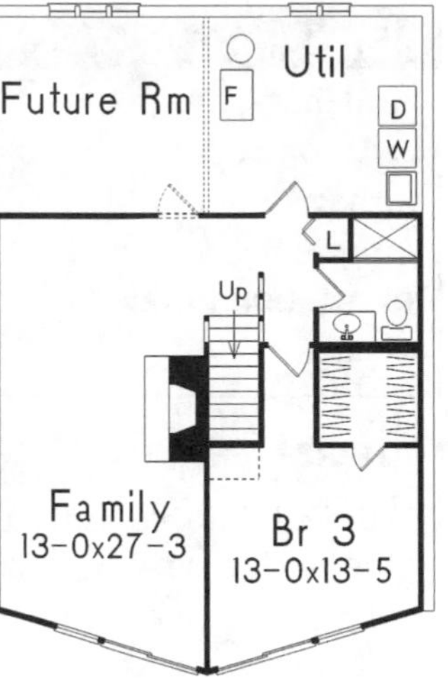

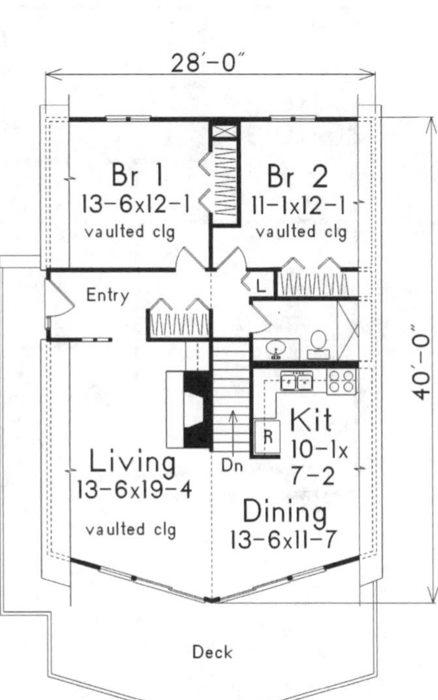

first floor
1,064 sq. ft.

plan #584-040D-0013

price code A

plan information	
total living area:	1,304
bedrooms:	3
baths:	2
garage:	2-car
foundation type:	
slab	

special features

- covered entrance leads into the family room with a cozy fireplace
- 10' ceilings in kitchen, dining and family rooms
- master bedroom features a coffered ceiling, walk-in closet and private bath
- efficient kitchen includes large window over the sink

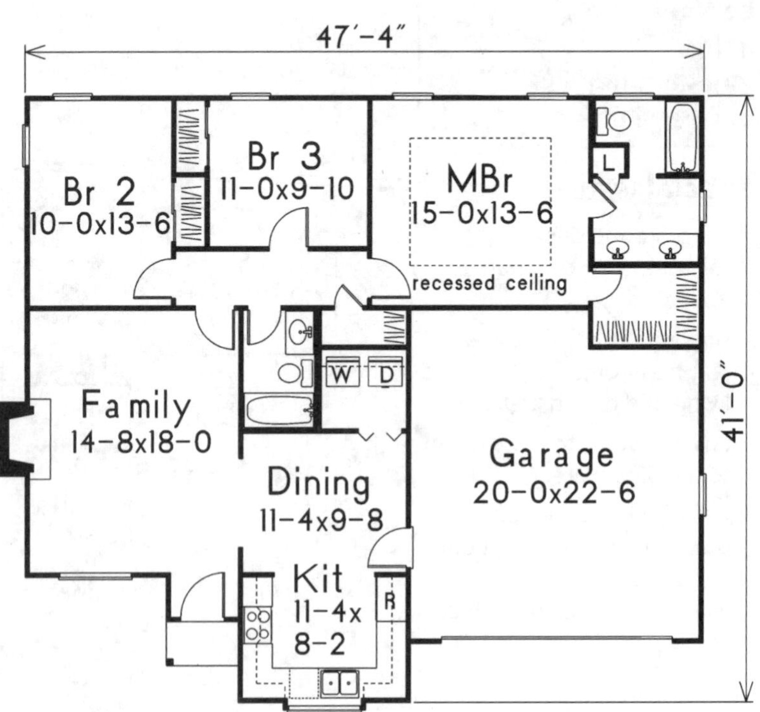

plan information

total living area:	864
bedrooms:	2
baths:	1
foundation types:	
crawl space standard	
basement	
slab	

special features

- kitchen is L-shaped and features a convenient pantry
- easy access to laundry area, linen closet and storage closet
- both bedrooms include ample closet space

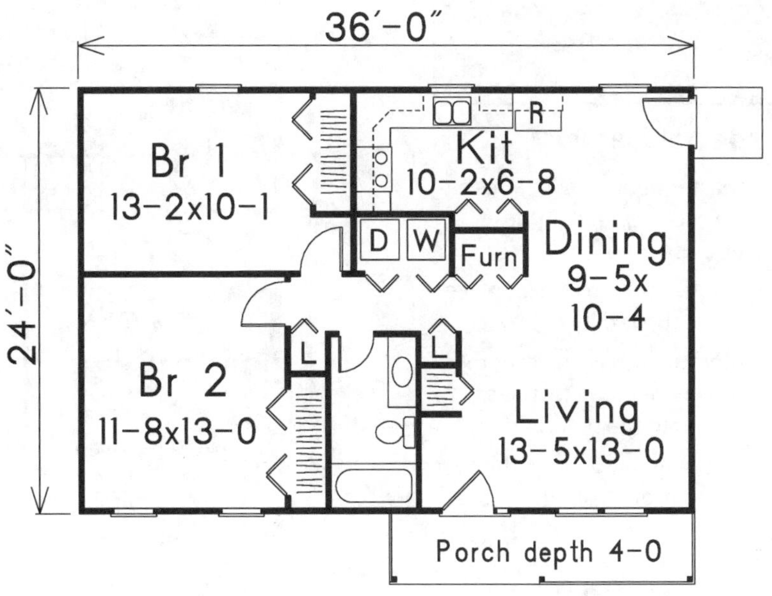

plan #584-040D-0010

price code A

plan information

total living area:	1,496
bedrooms:	3
baths:	2
garage:	2-car drive under
foundation type:	basement

special features

- master bedroom features a tray ceiling, walk-in closet and spacious bath
- vaulted ceiling and fireplace grace the family room
- dining room is adjacent to the kitchen and features access to the rear porch
- convenient access to the utility room from the kitchen

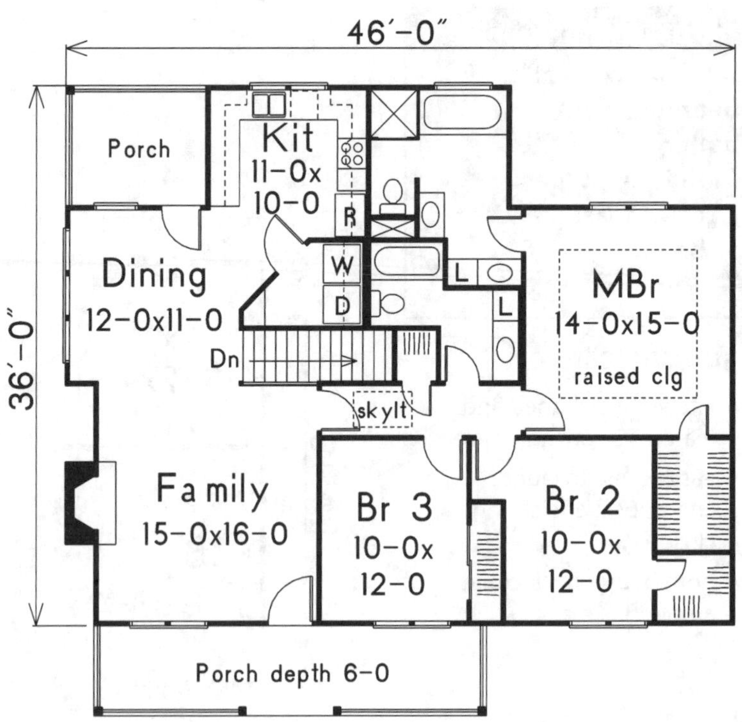

plan #584-001D-0093

price code AA

plan information	
total living area:	1,120
bedrooms:	3
baths:	1 1/2
foundation types:	
crawl space standard	
basement	
slab	

special features

- master bedroom includes a half bath with laundry area, linen closet and kitchen access
- kitchen has charming double-door entry, breakfast bar and a convenient walk-in pantry
- welcoming front porch opens to a large living room with coat closet

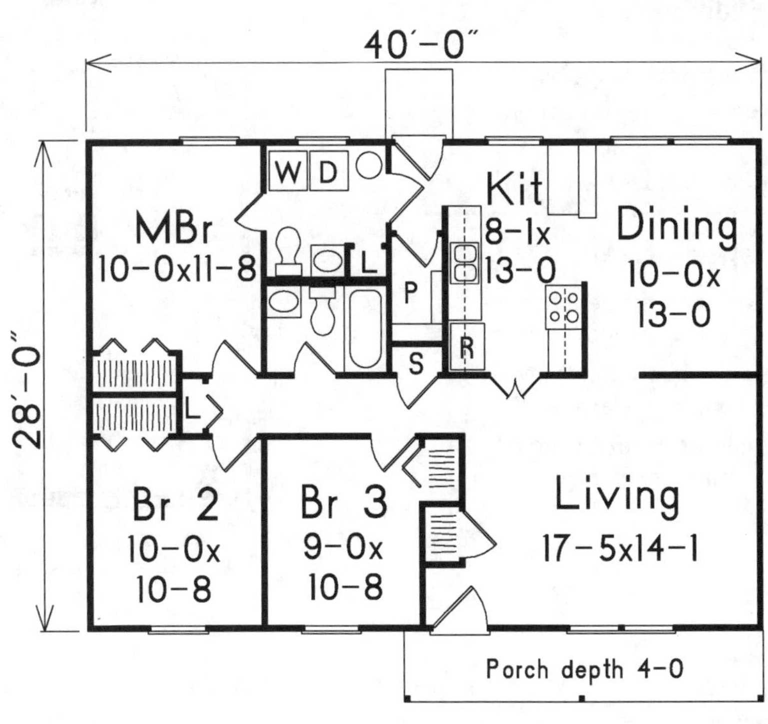

plan #584-062D-0035

price code A

plan information	
total living area:	1,358
bedrooms:	3
baths:	2
foundation types:	
walk-out basement	
crawl space	
please specify when ordering	

special features

- energy efficient home with 2" x 6" exterior walls
- covered veranda invites outdoor relaxation
- living room is warmed by a masonry fireplace

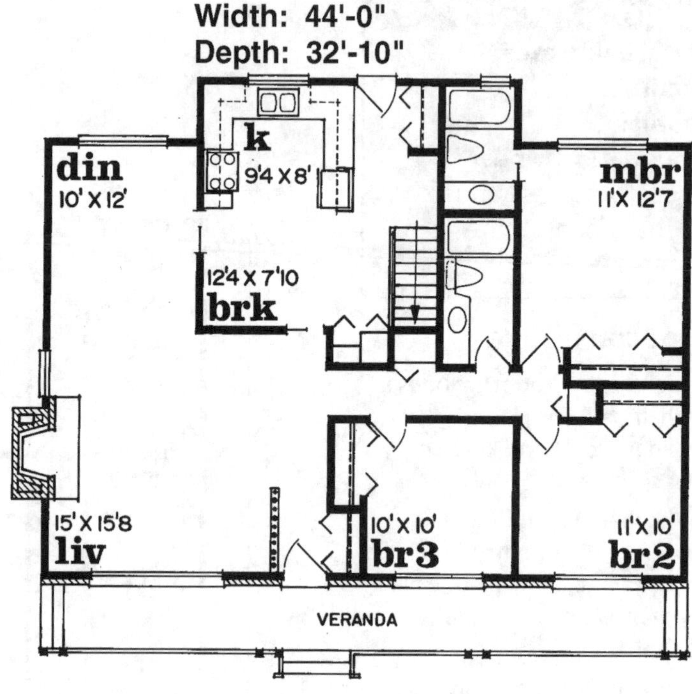

plan #584-007D-0104 price code AA

plan information	
total living area:	969
bedrooms:	2
baths:	1
garage:	1-car rear entry
foundation type:	walk-out basement

special features

- eye-pleasing facade enjoys stone accents with country porch for quiet evenings
- a bayed dining area, cozy fireplace and atrium with sunny two-story windows are the many features of the living room
- step-saver kitchen includes a pass-through snack bar
- 325 square feet of optional living area on the lower level

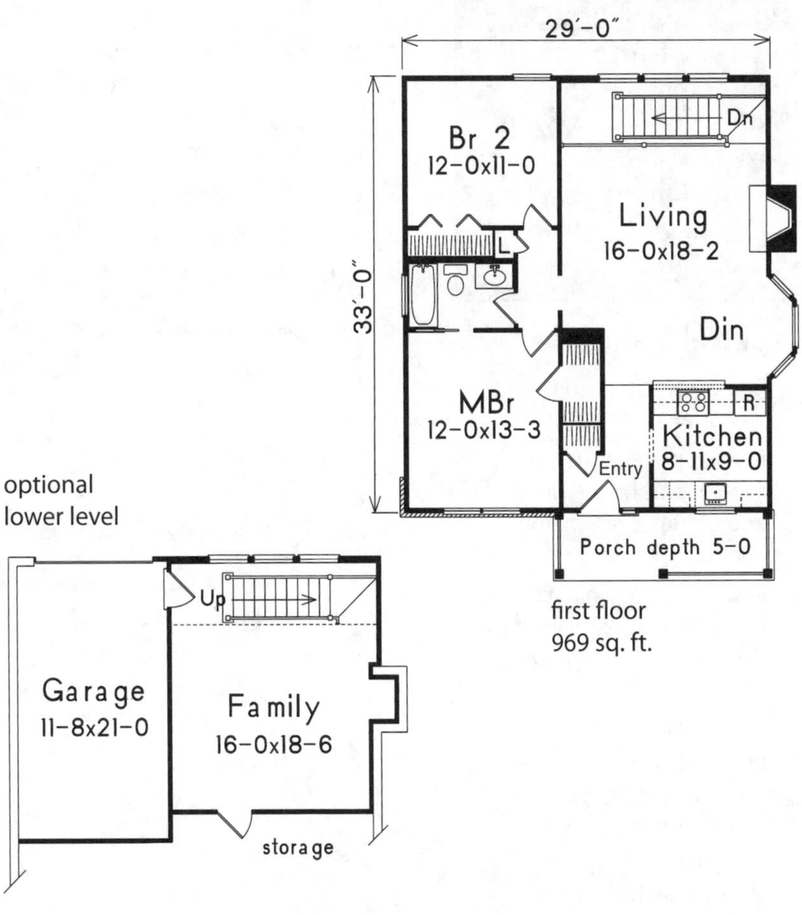

optional lower level

first floor 969 sq. ft.

plan #584-017D-0008

price code B

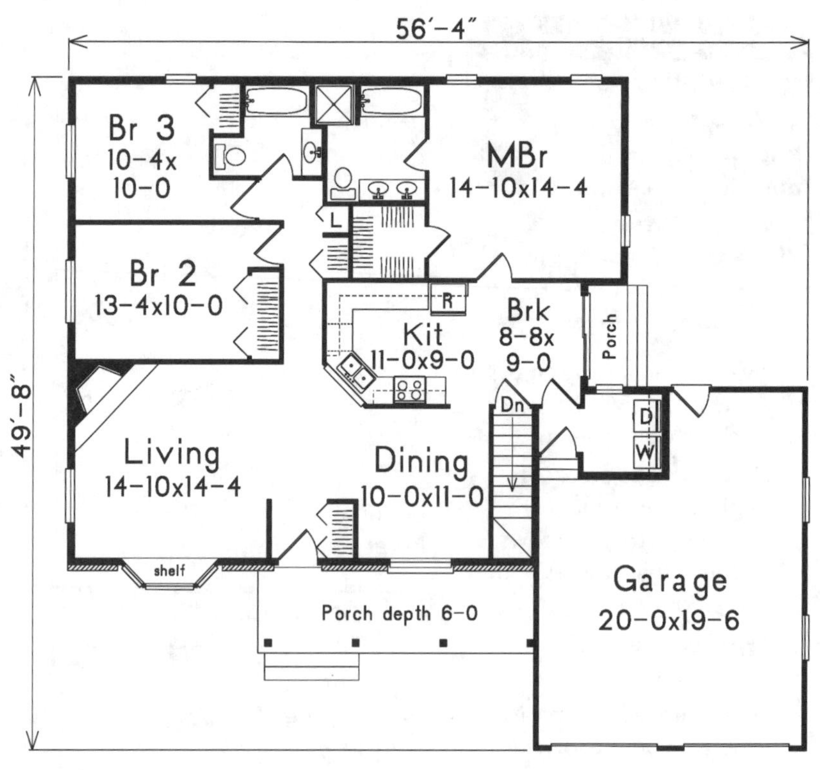

plan information

total living area:	1,466
bedrooms:	3
baths:	2
garage:	2-car
foundation types:	
basement standard	
slab	

special features

- energy efficient home with 2" x 6" exterior walls
- foyer separates the living room from the dining room and contains a generous coat closet
- large living room features a corner fireplace, bay window and pass-through to the kitchen
- informal breakfast area opens to a large terrace through sliding glass doors which brighten area
- master bedroom has a large walk-in closet and private bath

plan #584-058D-0009

price code AAA

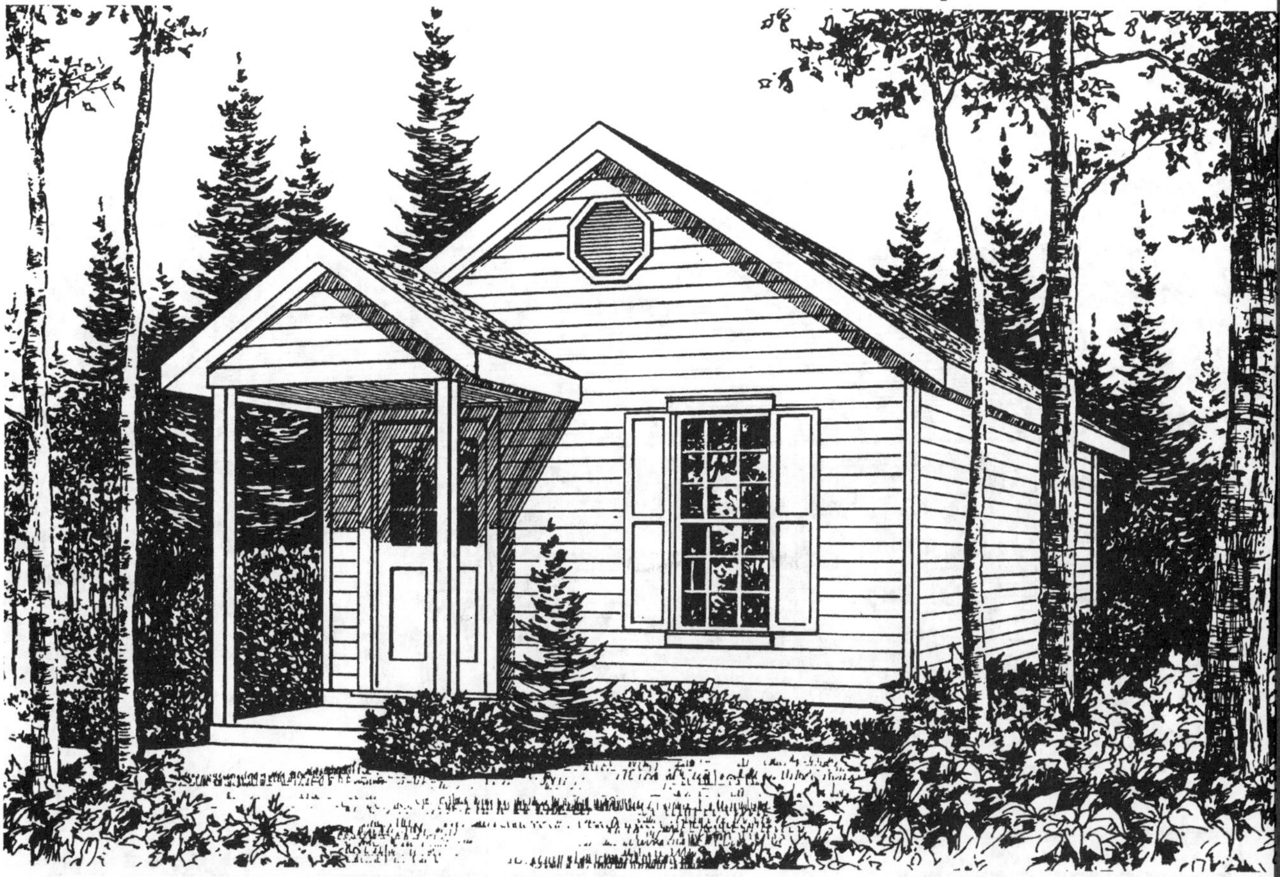

plan information	
total living area:	448
bedrooms:	1
baths:	1
foundation type: slab	

special features

- bedroom features a large walk-in closet ideal for storage
- combined dining/sitting area is ideal for relaxing
- galley-style kitchen is compact and efficient
- covered porch adds to front facade

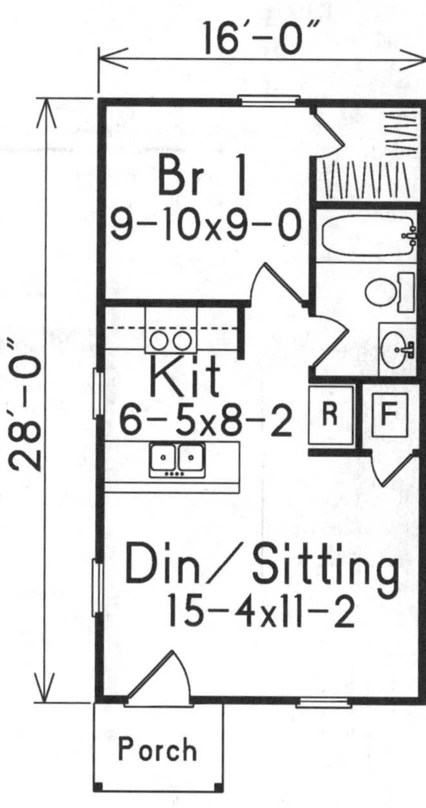

plan #584-020D-0015

price code AA

plan information

total living area: 1,191
bedrooms: 3
baths: 2
garage: 2-car side entry
foundation types:
slab standard
crawl space

special features

- energy efficient home with 2" x 6" exterior walls
- master bedroom is located near living areas for maximum convenience
- living room has a cathedral ceiling and stone fireplace

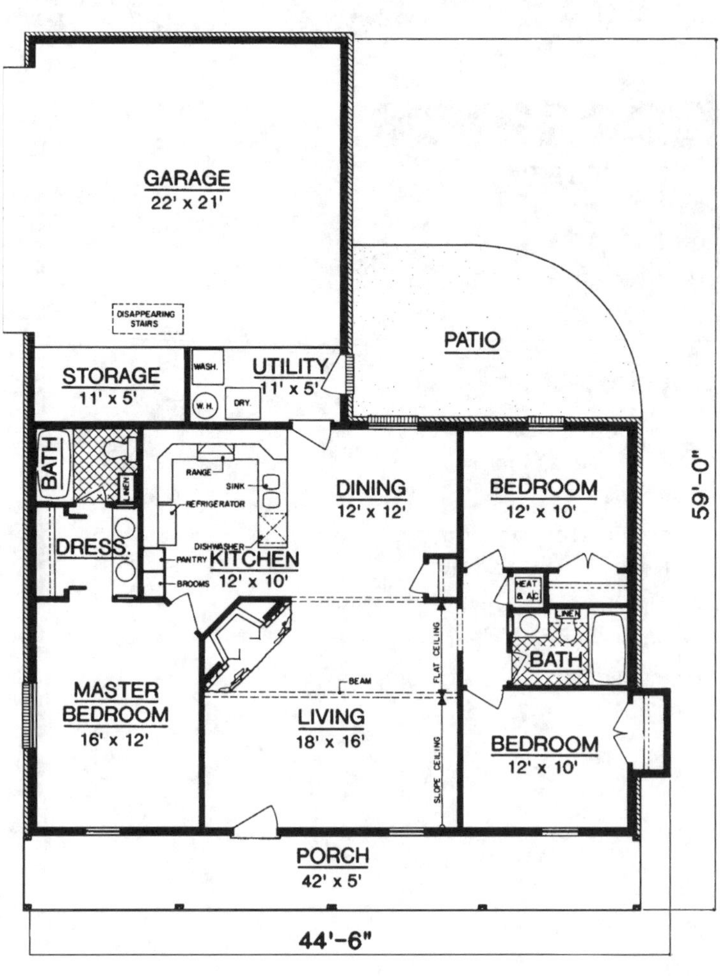

plan #584-037D-0025

price code D

plan information	
total living area:	2,481
bedrooms:	3
baths:	2
garage:	3-car side entry
foundation type:	
slab	

special features

- varied ceiling heights throughout this home
- master bedroom features a built-in desk and pocket-door entrance into the large master bath
- master bath includes a corner vanity and garden tub
- breakfast area accesses the courtyard

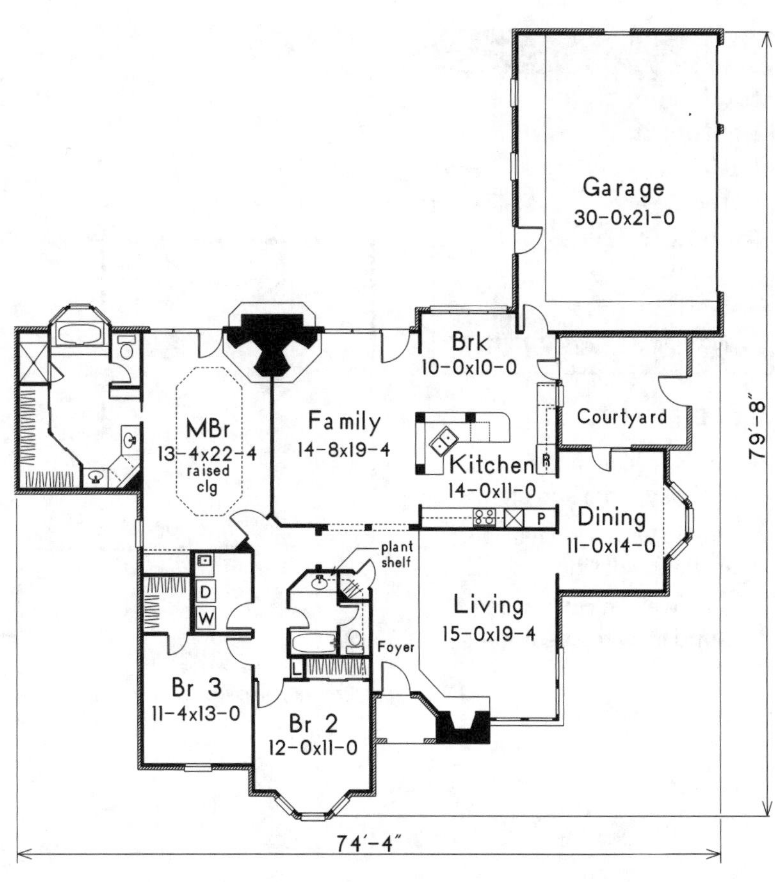

plan #584-039D-0001

price code A

plan information	
total living area:	1,253
bedrooms:	3
baths:	2
garage:	2-car
foundation types:	
crawl space	
slab	
please specify when ordering	

special features

- sloped ceiling and fireplace in family room add drama
- The U-shaped kitchen is efficiently designed
- large walk-in closets are found in all the bedrooms

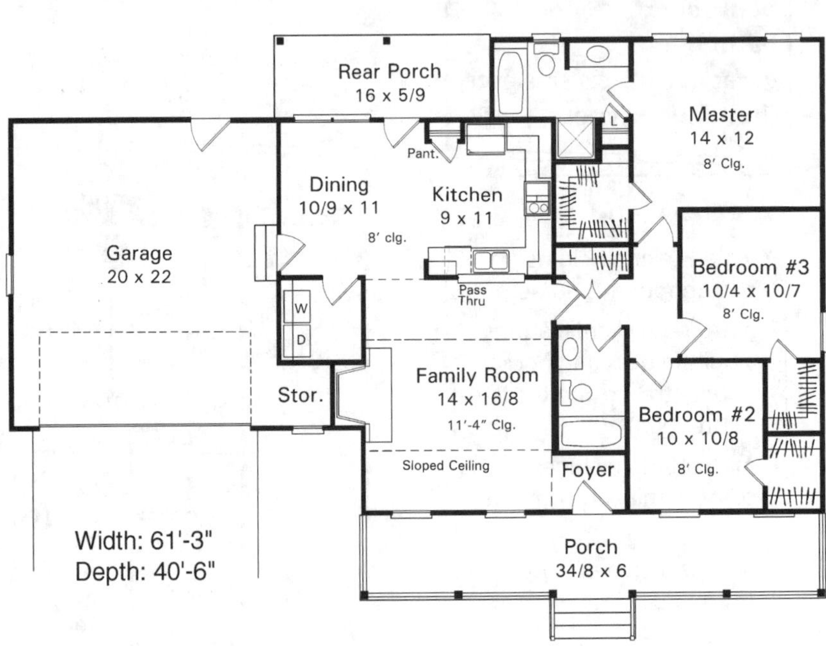

plan #584-058D-0010

plan information

total living area:	676
bedrooms:	1
baths:	1
foundation type:	
crawl space	

special features

- see-through fireplace between bedroom and living area adds character
- combined dining and living areas create an open feeling
- full-length front covered porch is perfect for enjoying the outdoors
- additional storage available in utility room

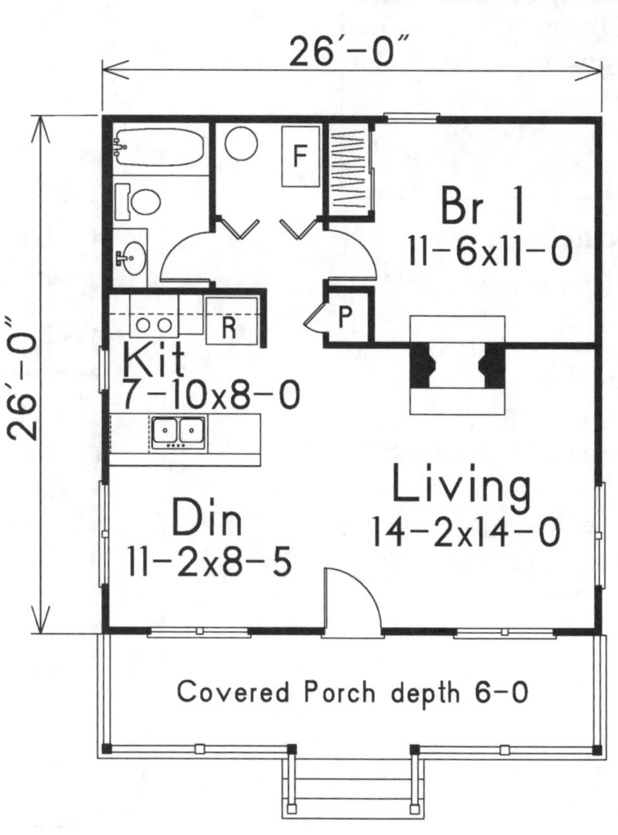

plan #584-007D-0029 price code AAA

plan information	
total living area:	576
bedrooms:	1
baths:	1
foundation type:	
crawl space	

special features

- perfect country retreat features vaulted living room and entry with skylights and plant shelf above
- a double-door entry leads to the vaulted bedroom with bath access
- kitchen offers generous storage and pass-through breakfast bar

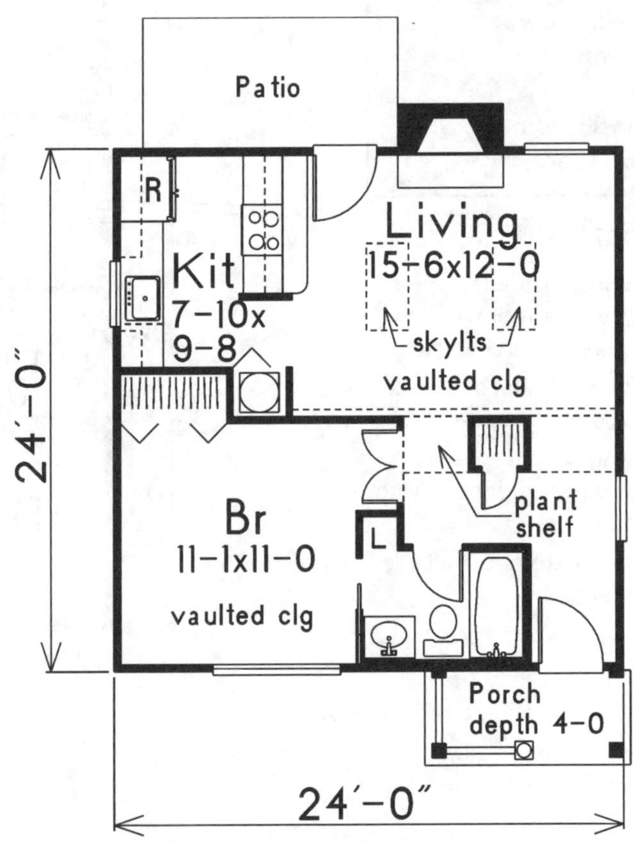

plan #584-058D-0014 price code AAA

plan information	
total living area:	416
bedrooms:	1
baths:	1
foundation type: slab	

special features

- open floor plan creates a spacious feeling
- covered porch has rustic appeal
- plenty of cabinetry and workspace in the kitchen
- large linen closet is centrally located and close to the bath

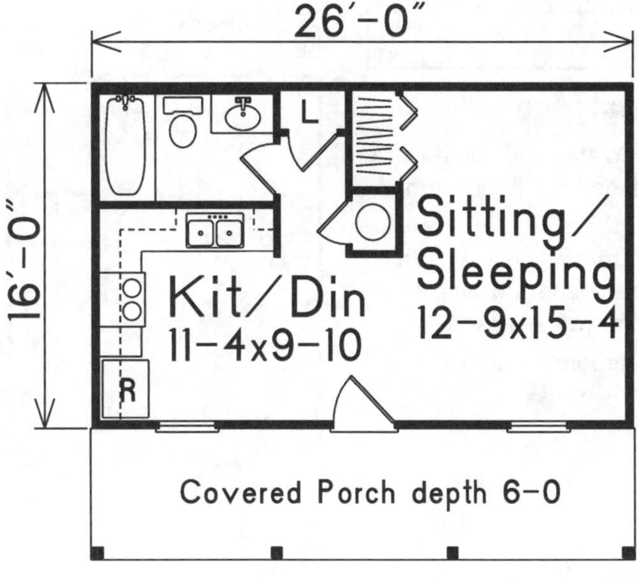

plan #584-062D-0041 price code B

plan information

total living area:	1,541
bedrooms:	3
baths:	2
garage:	2-car
foundation types:	
basement	
crawl space	
please specify when ordering	

special features

- dining area offers access to a screened porch for outdoor dining and entertaining
- country kitchen features a center island and a breakfast bay for casual meals
- great room is warmed by a woodstove

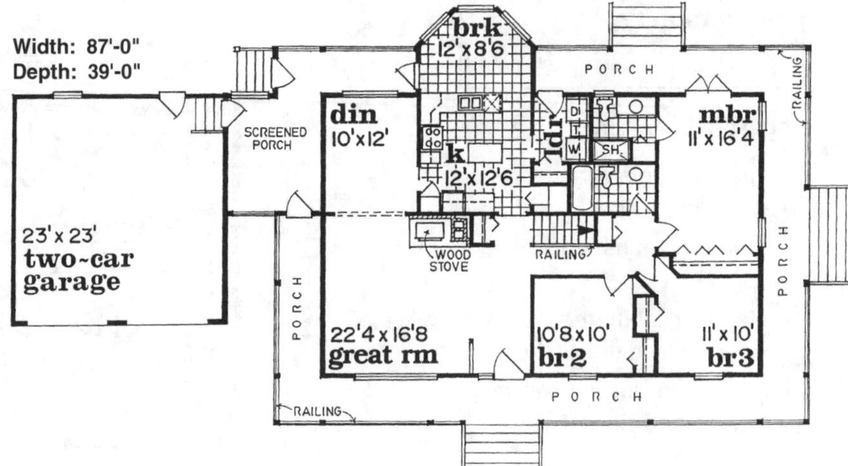

plan information

total living area:	1,280
bedrooms:	2
bath:	1
foundation types:	
basement	
crawl space	
please specify when ordering	

special features

- the combined kitchen, living and dining rooms are enhanced by vaulted ceilings, French doors and a cozy fireplace
- two bedrooms comprise the left side of the home and include French doors leading to the porch
- a large loft overlooks the living areas below and provides an additional 340 square feet of living space

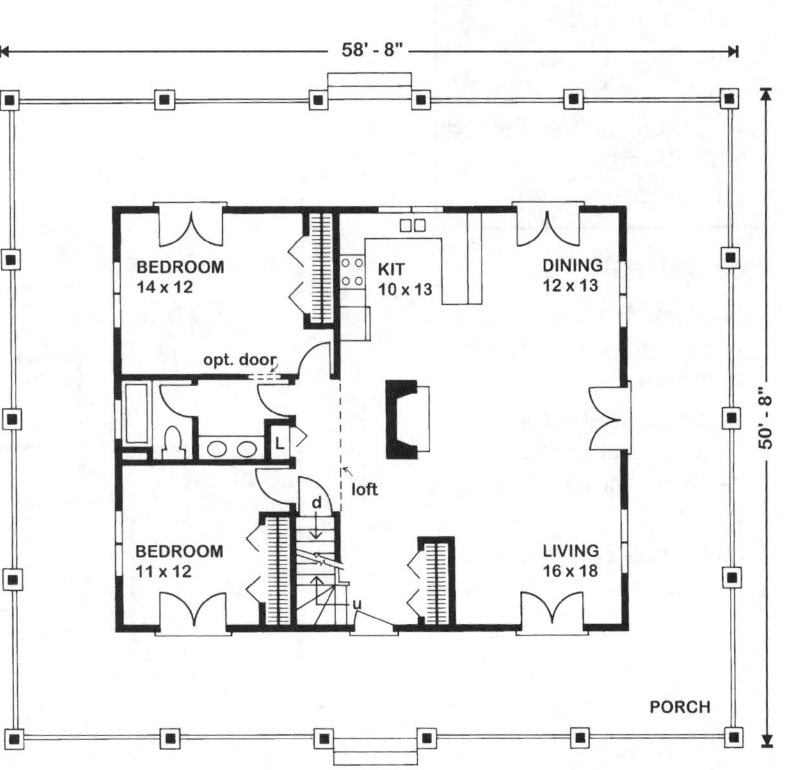

plan #584-007D-0030 price code AA

plan information

total living area:	1,140
bedrooms:	3
baths:	2
garage:	2-car drive under
foundation type:	basement

special features

- open and spacious living and dining areas for family gatherings
- well-organized kitchen features an abundance of cabinetry and a built-in pantry
- roomy master bath features a double-bowl vanity

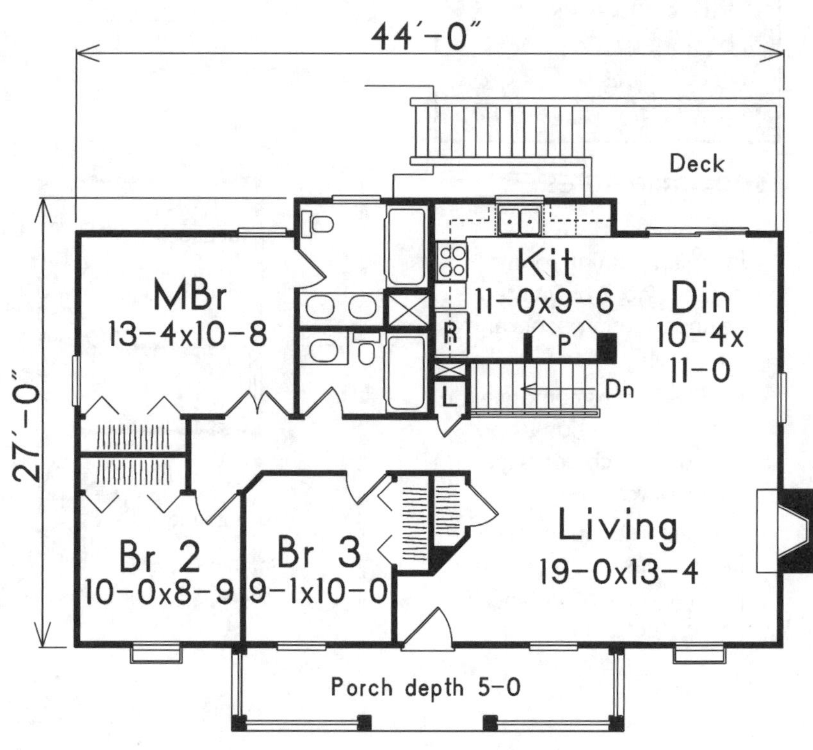

plan #584-056D-0001

price code E

Christine Canova 9/02

plan information	
total living area:	1,624
bedrooms:	3
baths:	2
foundation types:	
crawl space	
slab	
please specify when ordering	

special features

- large covered deck leads to two uncovered decks accessible by the master bedroom and bedroom #3
- well-organized kitchen overlooks into the breakfast area and family room
- laundry closet is located near the secondary bedrooms

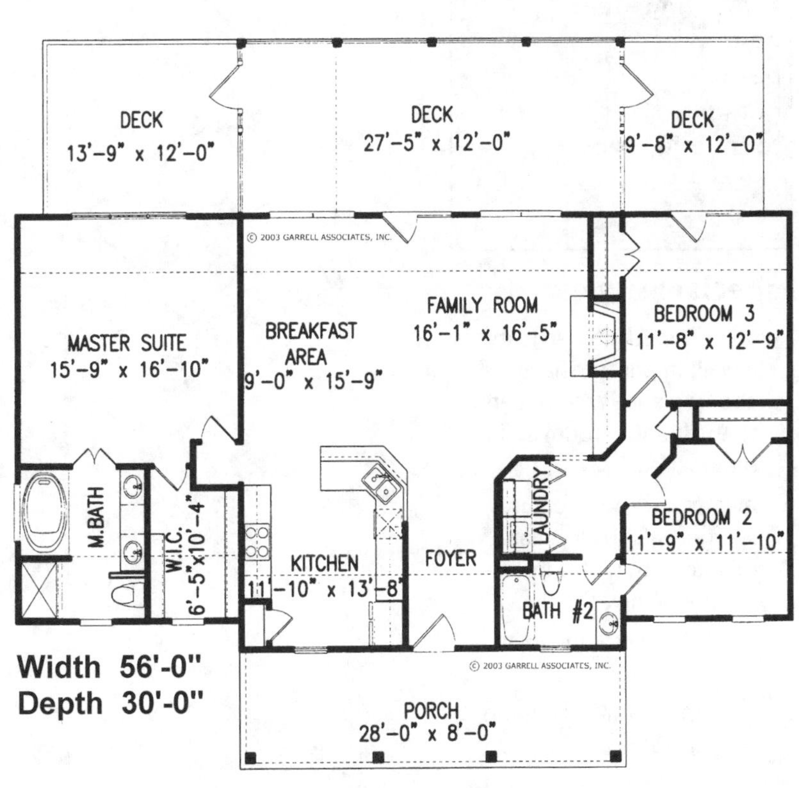

plan #584-040D-0026

price code B

plan information

total living area:	1,393
bedrooms:	3
baths:	2
garage:	2-car detached
foundation types:	
crawl space standard	
slab	

special features

- an L-shaped kitchen features a walk-in pantry, island cooktop and is convenient to the laundry room and dining area
- master bedroom features a large walk-in closet and private bath with separate tub and shower
- convenient storage/coat closet in hall
- view to the patio from the dining area

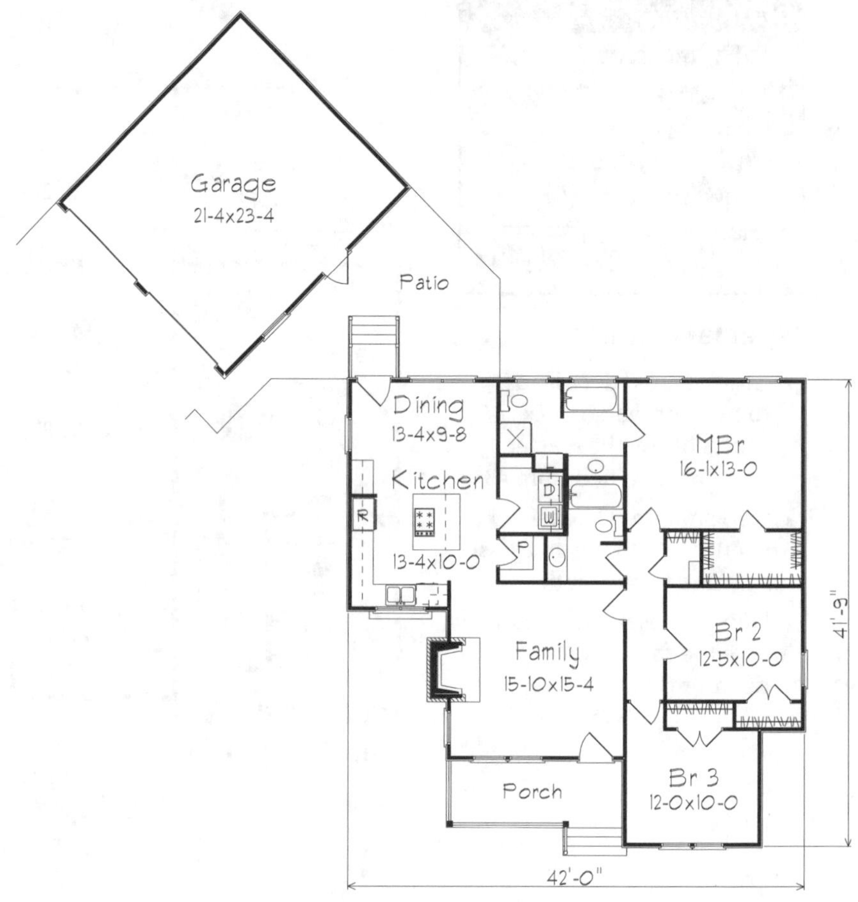

plan #584-007D-0103

price code A

plan information	
total living area:	1,231
bedrooms:	2
baths:	2
garage:	1-car drive under
foundation type:	walk-out basement

special features

- stone accents and Dutch gables provide an enchanting appearance
- the spacious living room offers a masonry fireplace, atrium with window wall and is open to a dining area with bay window
- kitchen has a breakfast counter, lots of cabinet space and glass sliding doors to a balcony

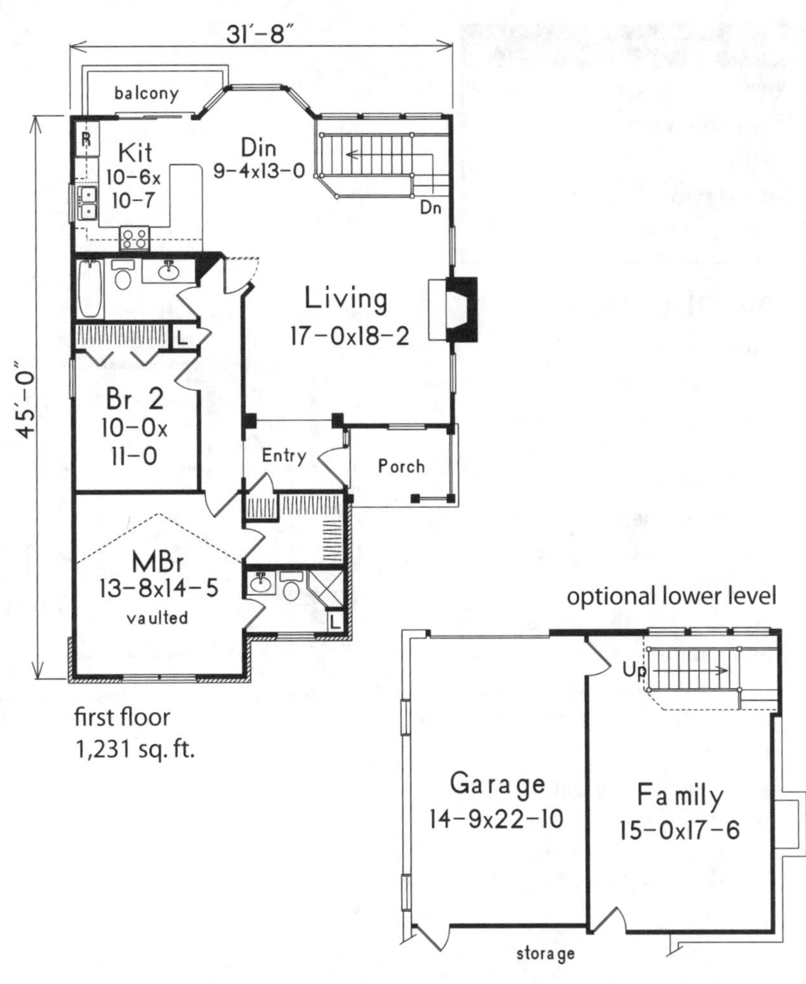

first floor
1,231 sq. ft.

optional lower level

plan #584-007D-0043 price code AAA

plan information

total living area:	647
bedrooms:	1
baths:	1
foundation type: crawl space	

special features

- large vaulted room for living/sleeping has plant shelves on each end, stone fireplace and wide glass doors for views
- roomy kitchen is vaulted and has a bayed dining area and fireplace
- step down into a sunken and vaulted bath featuring a 6'-0" whirlpool tub-in-a-bay with shelves at each end for storage
- a large palladian window adorns each end of the cottage giving a cheery atmosphere throughout

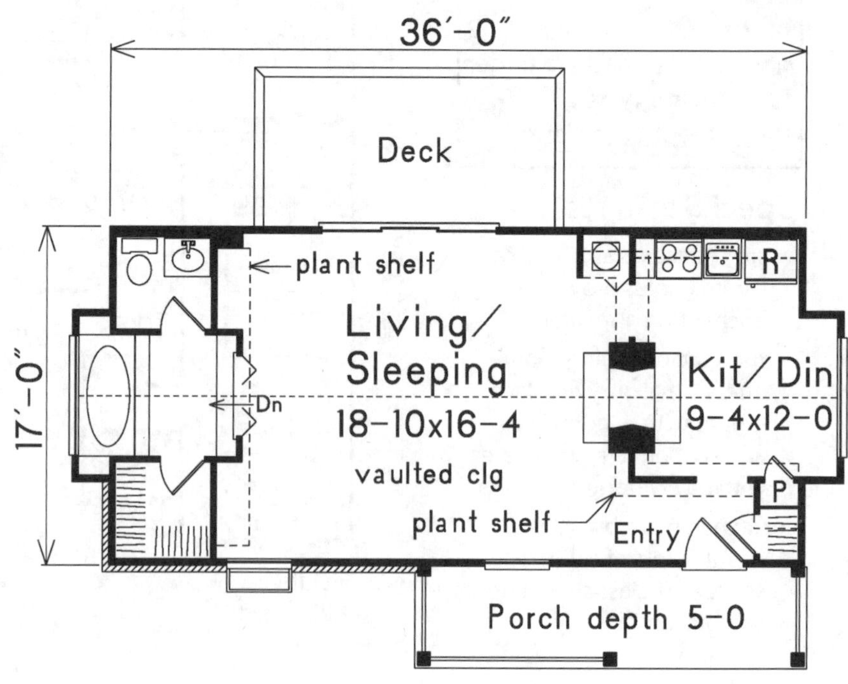

plan #584-052D-0002

price code A

plan information

total living area:	1,208
bedrooms:	3
baths:	2
garage:	2-car drive under
foundation type:	basement

special features

- master bath is graced with an oversized tub, plant shelf and double vanity
- a U-shaped kitchen promotes organization while easily accessing the dining area
- hall bath includes a laundry closet for convenience

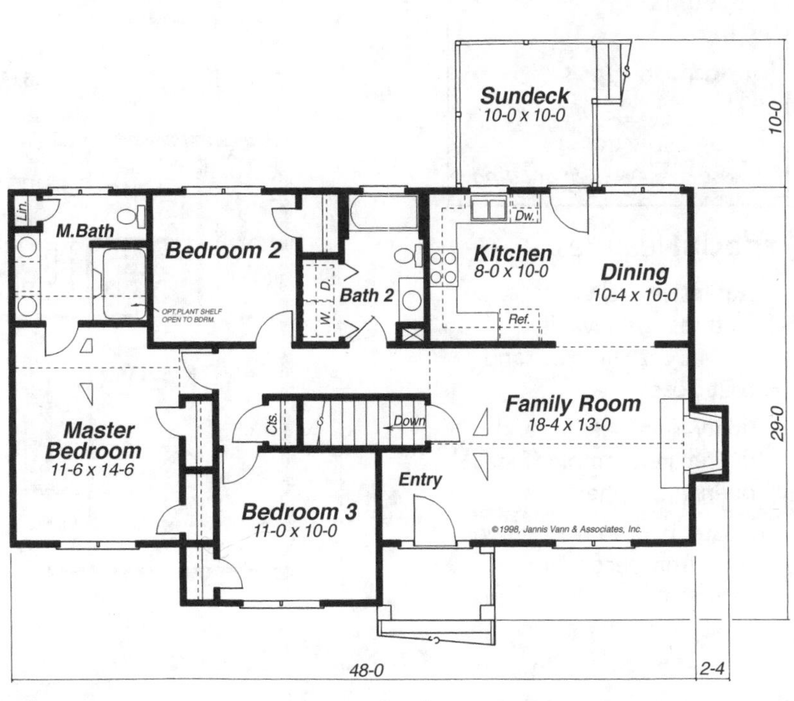

plan #584-069D-0006

price code A

plan information	
total living area:	1,277
bedrooms:	3
baths:	2
foundation types:	
slab	
crawl space	
please specify when ordering	

special features

- expansive great room features an 11' vaulted ceiling, cozy fireplace and coat closet
- utility room, kitchen and dining area combine for an open atmosphere
- master bedroom is located away from secondary bedrooms for privacy

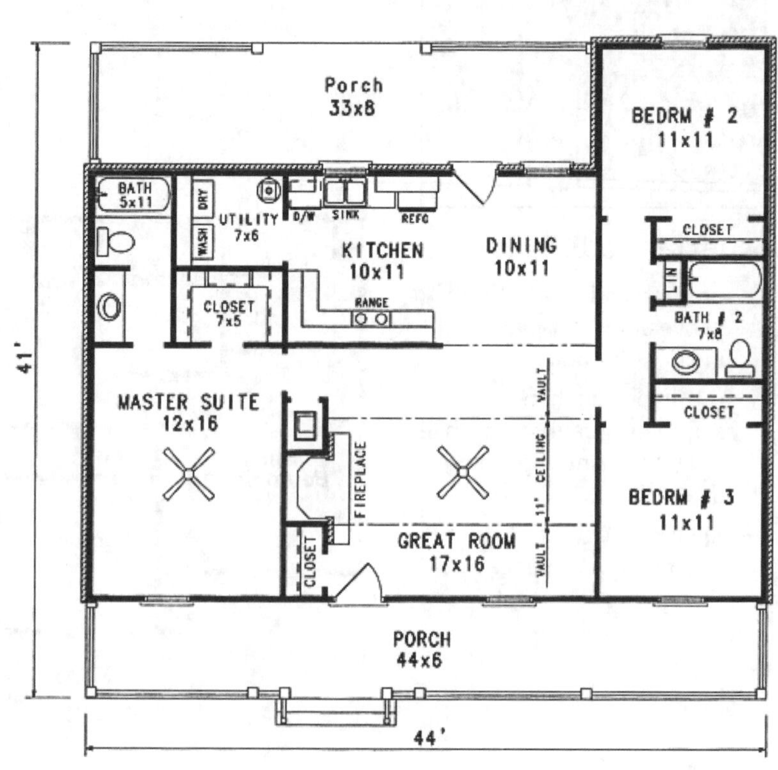

plan #584-078D-0033

price code D

plan information	
total living area:	995
bedrooms:	2
baths:	1
foundation type: crawl space	

special features

- decorative facade enhances the old-world ambiance of the home
- the cozy living room features a rustic beamed ceiling and traditional hearth fireplace
- kitchen adjoins dining room and includes a corner pantry
- two bedrooms comprise the left side of the home and enjoy ample closet space and bright windows

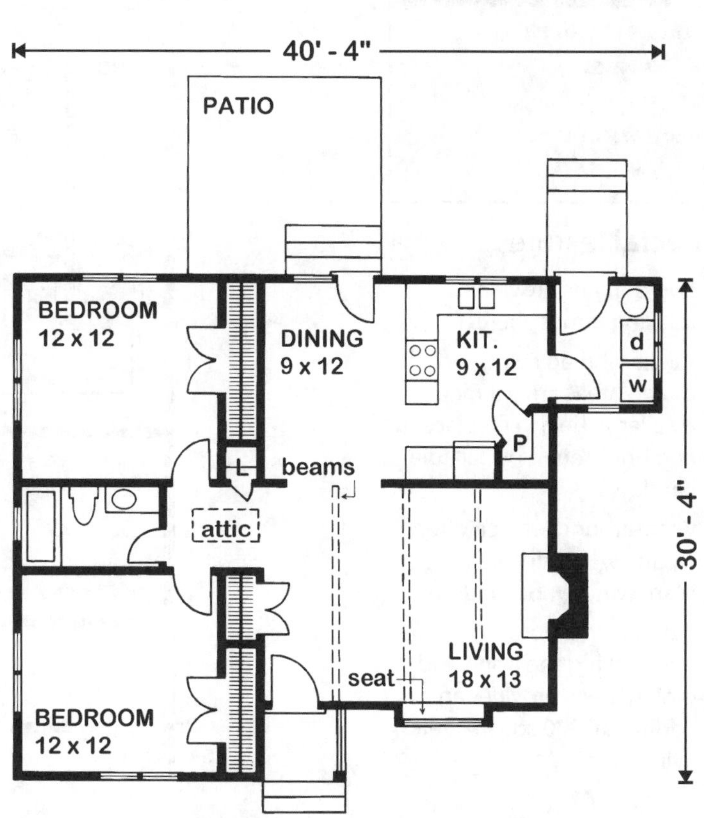

plan #584-078D-0011 price code D

plan information	
total living area:	950
bedrooms:	2
baths:	1
foundation type: crawl space	

special features

- two porches provide relaxing atmospheres
- the combined living and dining areas are warmed by a large hearth fireplace and brightened by palladian windows
- wrap-around kitchen offers a pantry, laundry area and plant window beyond sink
- a spectacular loft overlooking the living and dining areas provides an additional 270 square feet of living area

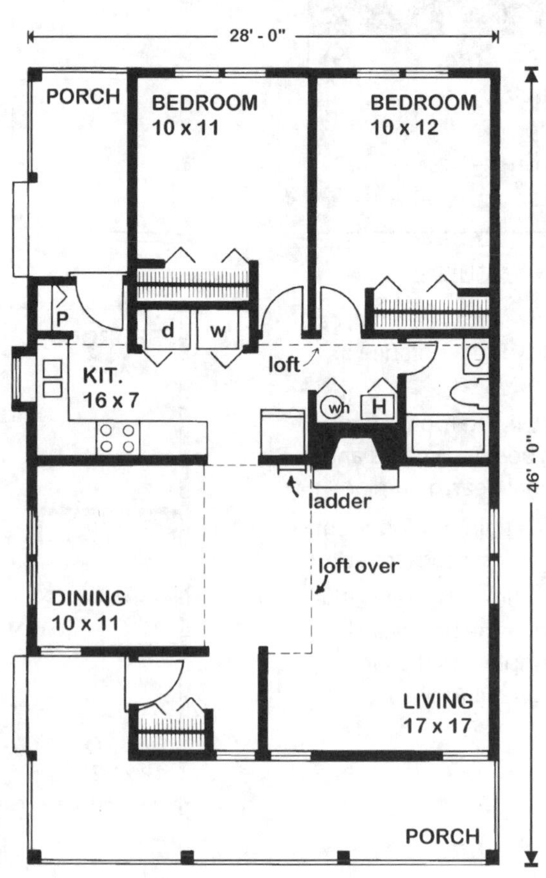

plan #584-058D-0033 price code A

plan information	
total living area:	1,440
bedrooms:	2
baths:	2
garage:	2-car side entry
foundation type:	basement

special features

- open floor plan with access to covered porches in front and back
- lots of linen, pantry and closet space throughout
- laundry/mud room between the kitchen and garage is a convenient feature

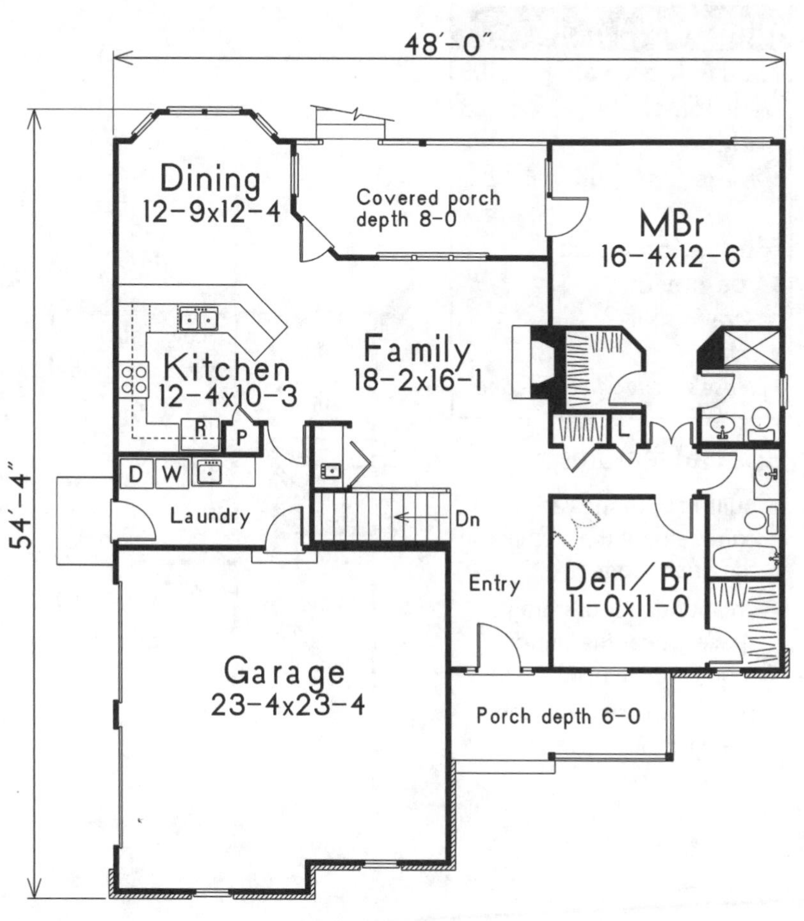

plan #584-016D-0062 price code A

plan information

total living area:	1,380
bedrooms:	3
baths:	2
garage:	optional 2-car side entry

foundation types:
basement
crawl space
slab
please specify when ordering

special features

- built-in bookshelves complement the fireplace in the great room
- an abundance of storage space is near the laundry room and kitchen
- covered porch has a view of the backyard

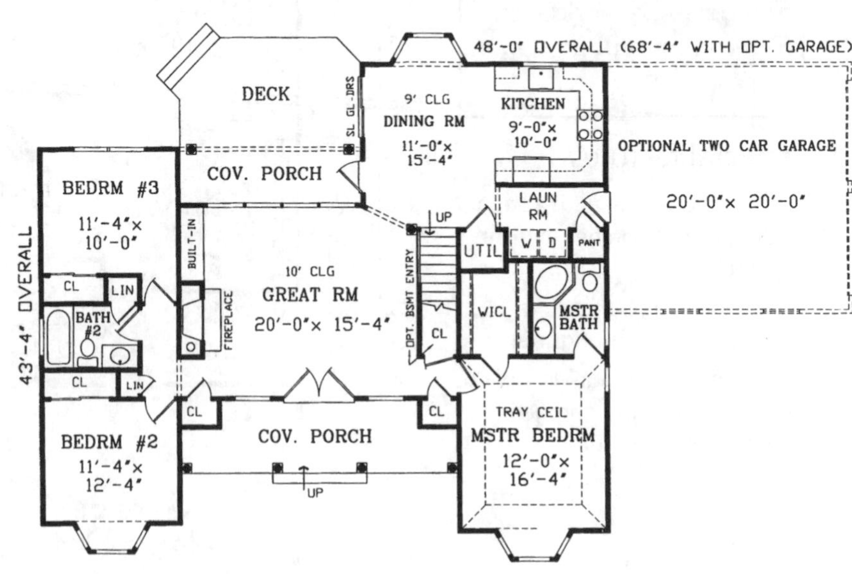

plan #584-008D-0159

price code AAA

plan information

total living area:	733
bedrooms:	2
baths:	1
foundation type:	
pier	

special features

- bedrooms are separate from the kitchen and living area for privacy
- lots of closet space throughout this home
- centrally located bath is easily accessible
- kitchen features a door accessing the outdoors and a door separating it from the rest of the home

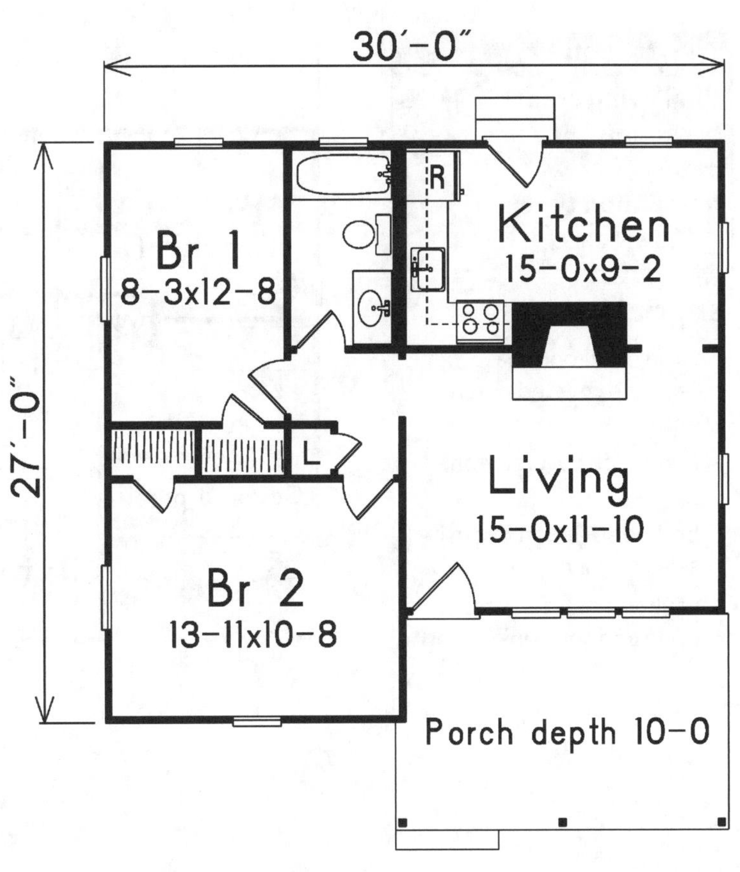

plan #584-058D-0029

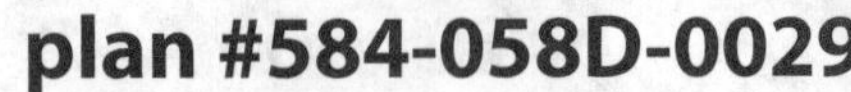

price code AA

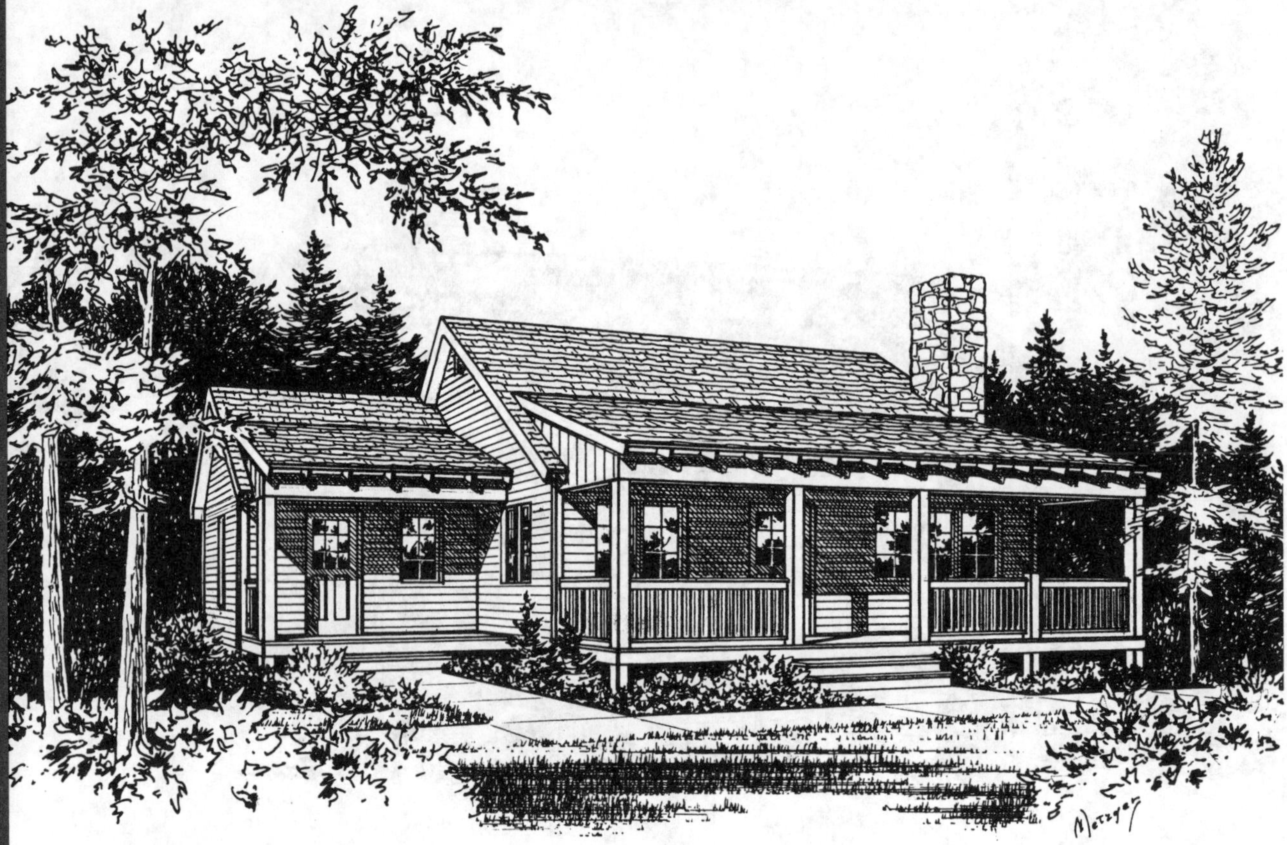

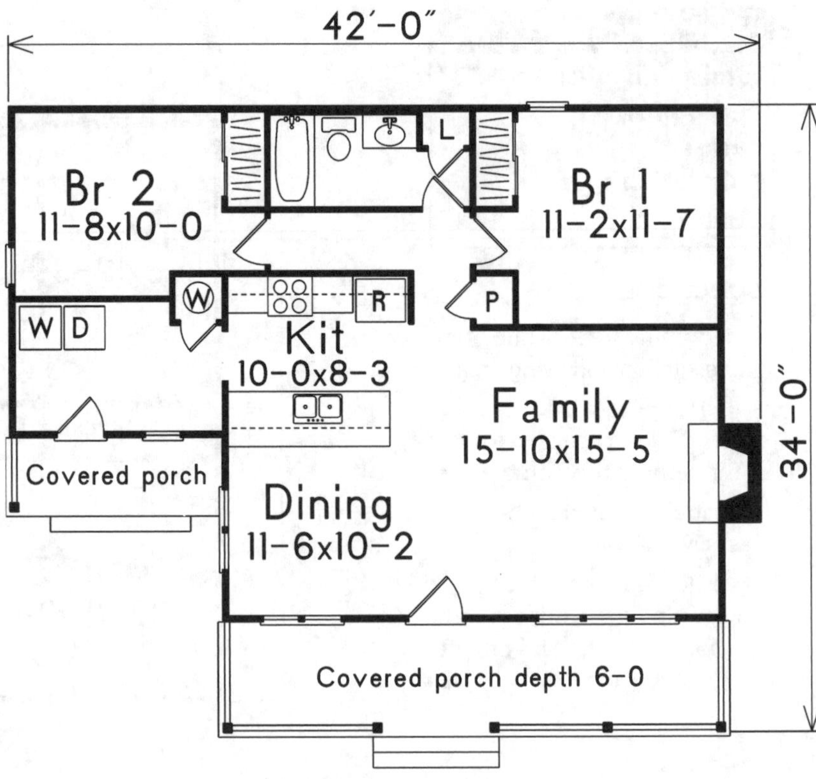

plan information

total living area:	1,000
bedrooms:	2
baths:	1
foundation type: crawl space	

special features

- large mud room has a separate covered porch entrance
- full-length covered front porch
- bedrooms are on opposite sides of the home for privacy
- vaulted ceiling creates an open and spacious feeling

rear view

plan information

total living area:	1,684
bedrooms:	3
baths:	2
garage:	2-car drive under
foundation type:	walk-out basement

special features

- delightful wrap-around porch is anchored by a full masonry fireplace
- the vaulted great room includes a large bay window, fireplace, dining balcony and atrium window wall
- double walk-in closets, large luxury bath and sliding doors to exterior balcony are a few fantastic features of the master bedroom
- atrium opens to 611 square feet of optional living area on the lower level

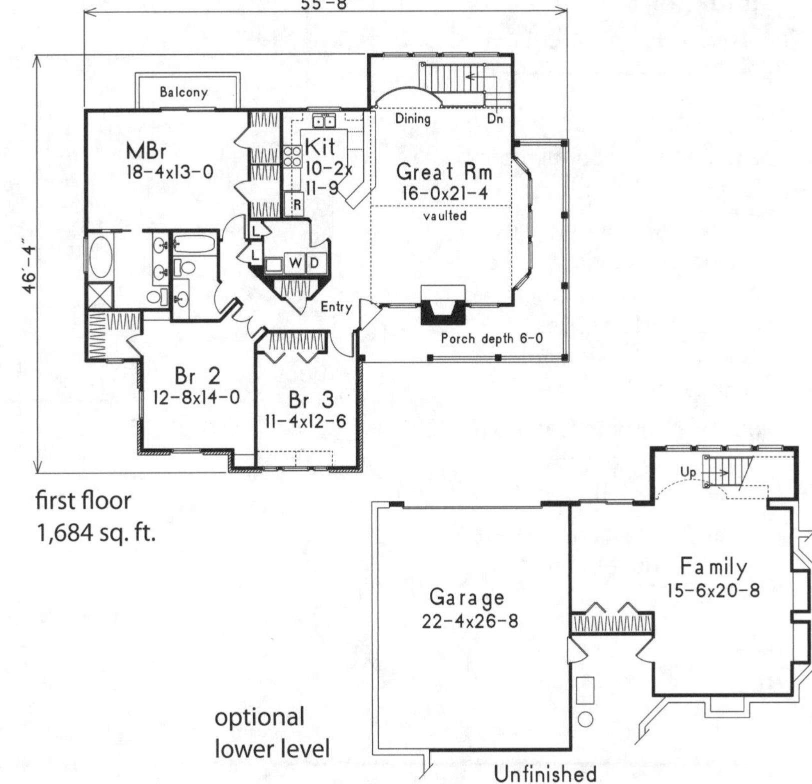

first floor
1,684 sq. ft.

optional
lower level

plan #584-007D-0068

price code B

rear view

plan information

total living area:	1,384
bedrooms:	2
baths:	2
garage:	1-car side entry
foundation type:	walk-out basement

special features

- wrap-around country porch for peaceful evenings
- vaulted great room enjoys a large bay window, stone fireplace, pass-through kitchen and awesome rear views through atrium window wall
- master bedroom features a double-door entry, walk-in closet and a fabulous bath
- atrium opens to 611 square feet of optional living area below

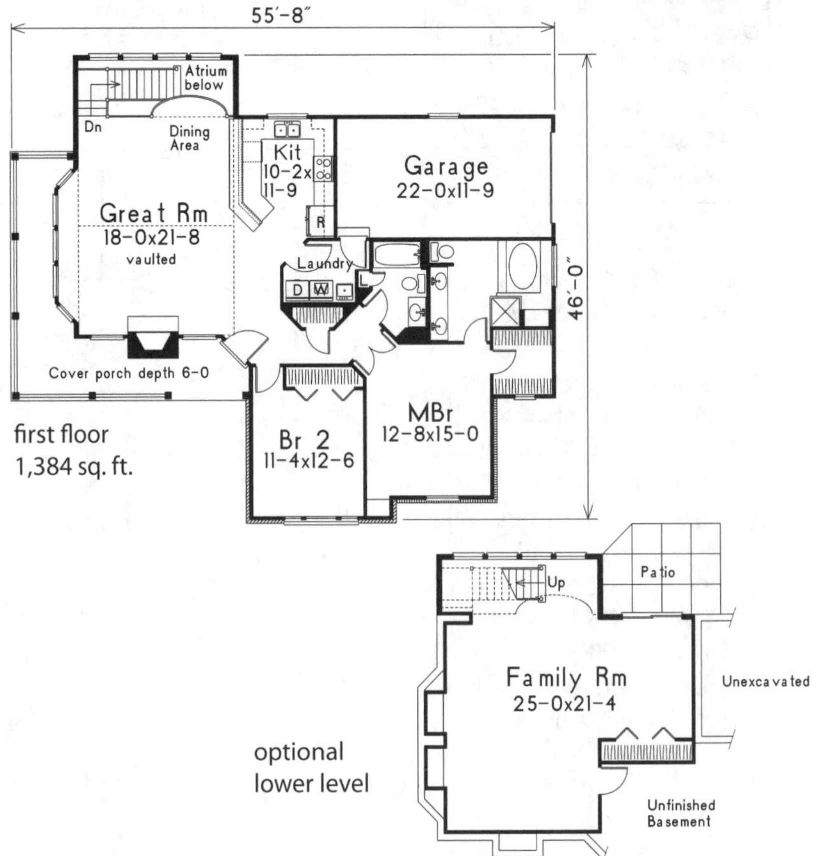

first floor
1,384 sq. ft.

optional
lower level

plan #584-007D-0066

price code D

plan information

total living area:	2,408
bedrooms:	4
baths:	3
garage:	3-car side entry
foundation type:	walk-out basement

special features

- large vaulted great room overlooks atrium and window wall, adjoins dining room, spacious breakfast room with bay and pass-through kitchen
- a special private bedroom with bath, separate from other bedrooms, is perfect for mother-in-law suite or children home from college
- atrium opens to 1,100 square feet of optional living area below

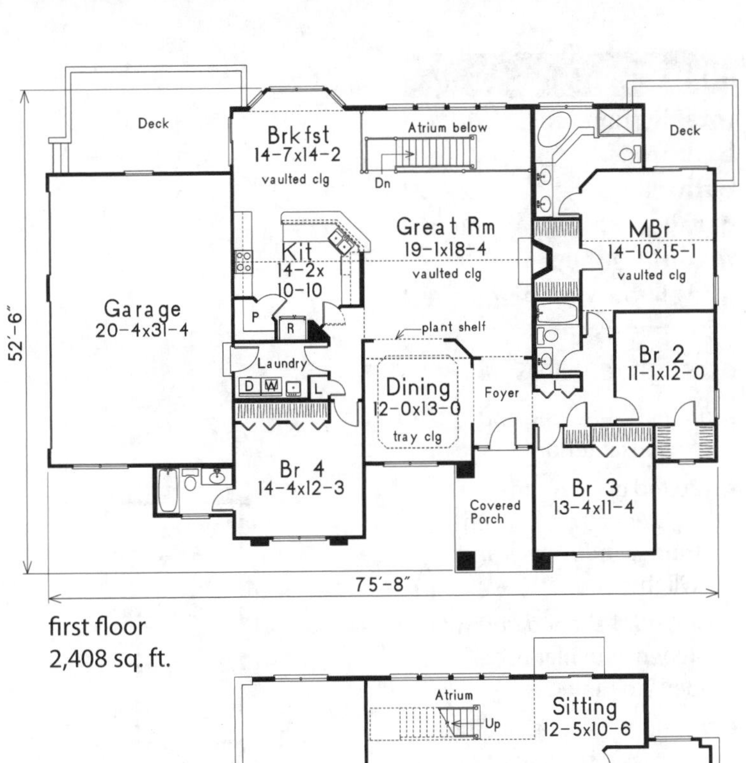

first floor
2,408 sq. ft.

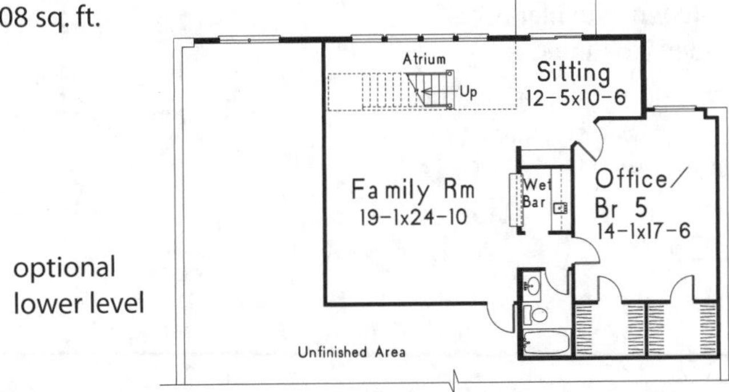

optional
lower level

plan #584-007D-0018

price code C

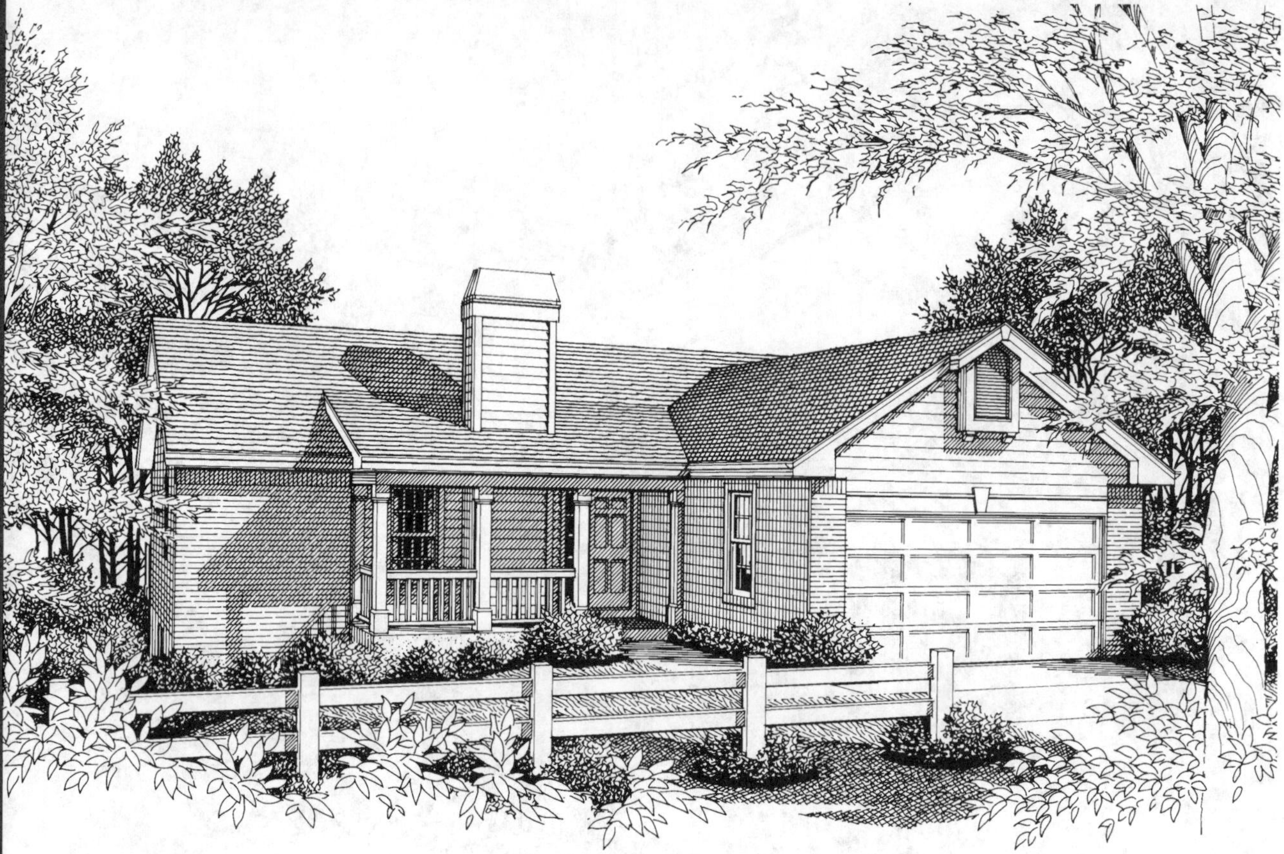

plan information

total living area:	1,941
bedrooms:	4
baths:	2 1/2
garage:	2-car
foundation type:	
walk-out basement	

special features

- dramatic, exciting and spacious interior
- vaulted great room is brightened by a sunken atrium window wall and skylights
- vaulted U-shaped gourmet kitchen with plant shelf opens to dining room
- first floor half bath features space for a stackable washer and dryer

lower level
945 sq. ft.

first floor
996 sq. ft.

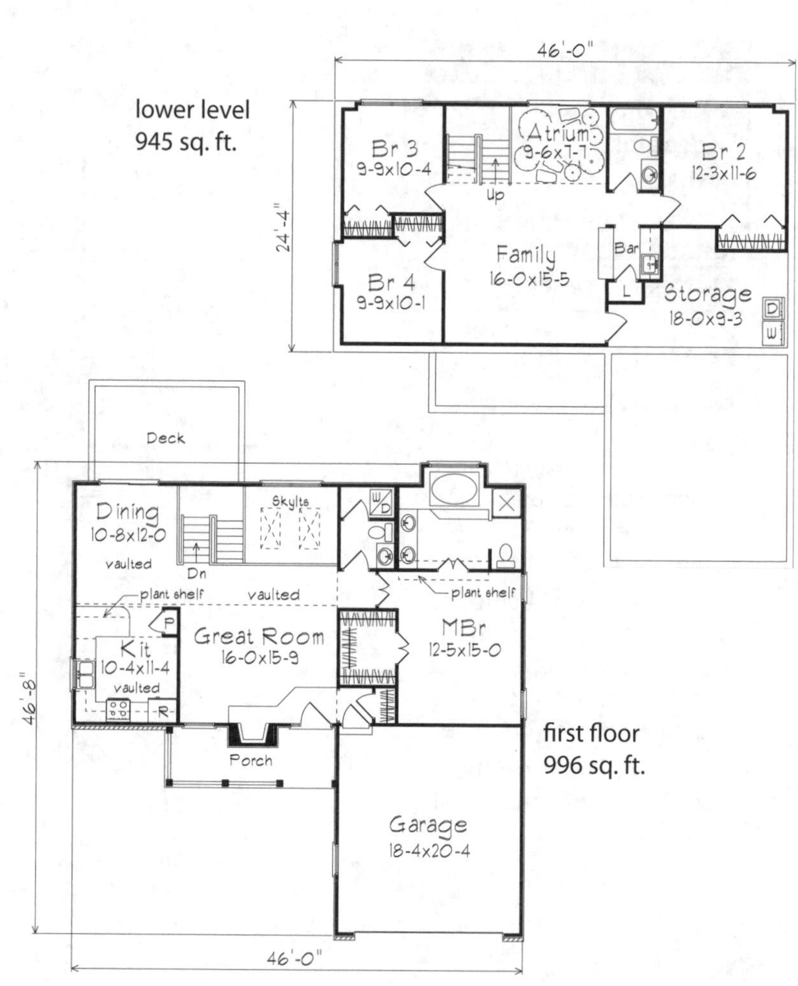

plan #584-007D-0056

price code E

rear view

plan information

total living area:	3,199
bedrooms:	3
baths:	2 1/2
garage:	3-car side entry
foundation type:	walk-out basement

special features

- grand-scale kitchen features bay-shaped cabinetry built over an atrium that overlooks a two-story window wall
- a second atrium dominates the master bedroom that boasts a sitting area with bay window as well as a luxurious bath that has a whirlpool tub open to the garden atrium and lower level study

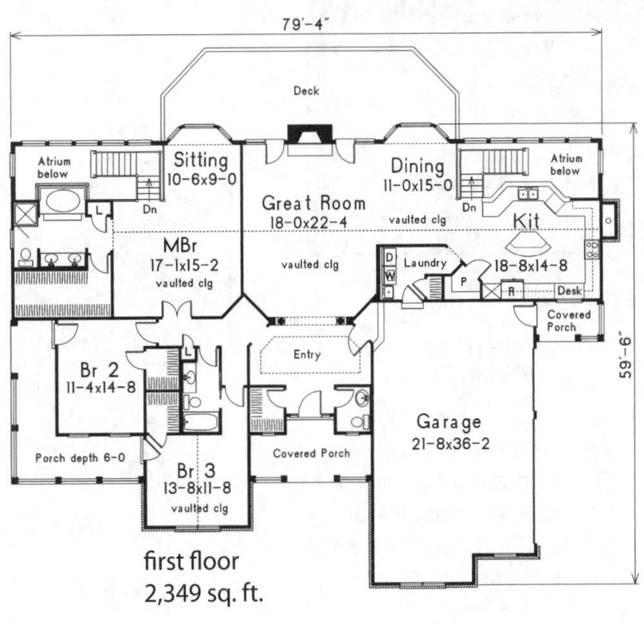

first floor
2,349 sq. ft.

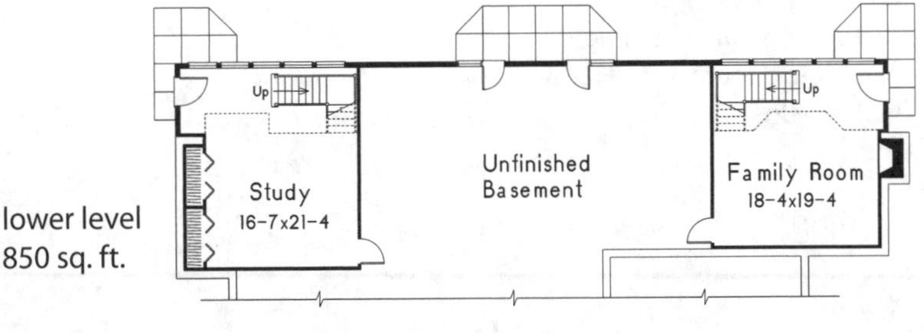

lower level
850 sq. ft.

plan #584-007D-0053

price code D

rear view

plan information	
total living area:	2,334
bedrooms:	3
baths:	2
garage:	2-car
foundation type:	
walk-out basement	

special features

- roomy front porch gives home a country flavor
- vaulted great room boasts a fireplace, TV alcove, pass-through snack bar to kitchen and atrium featuring bayed window wall and an ascending stair to family room
- oversized master bedroom features a vaulted ceiling, double-door entry and large walk-in closet

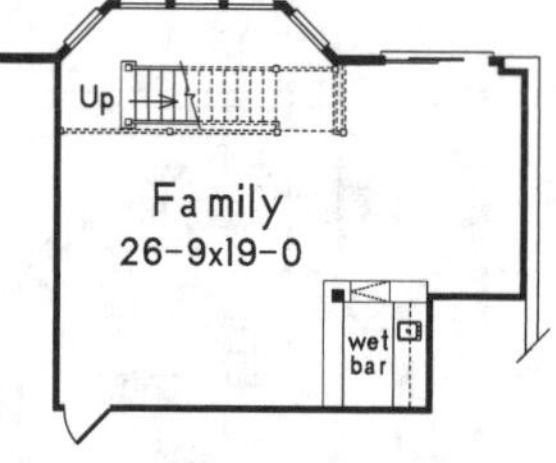

lower level
557 sq. ft.

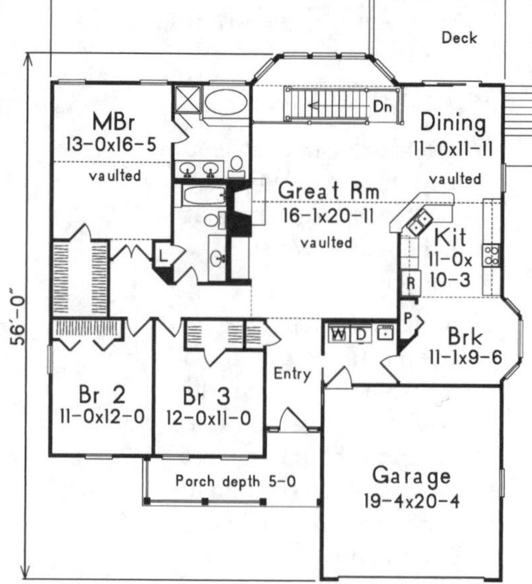

first floor
1,777 sq. ft.

plan #584-007D-0010

price code C

rear view

plan information

total living area:	1,721
bedrooms:	3
baths:	2
garage:	3-car
foundation types:	
walk-out basement - standard	
crawl space	
slab	

special features

- roof dormers add great curb appeal
- vaulted dining and great rooms are immersed in light from the atrium window wall
- breakfast room opens onto the covered porch
- functionally designed kitchen
- 1,604 square feet on the first floor and 117 square feet on the lower level

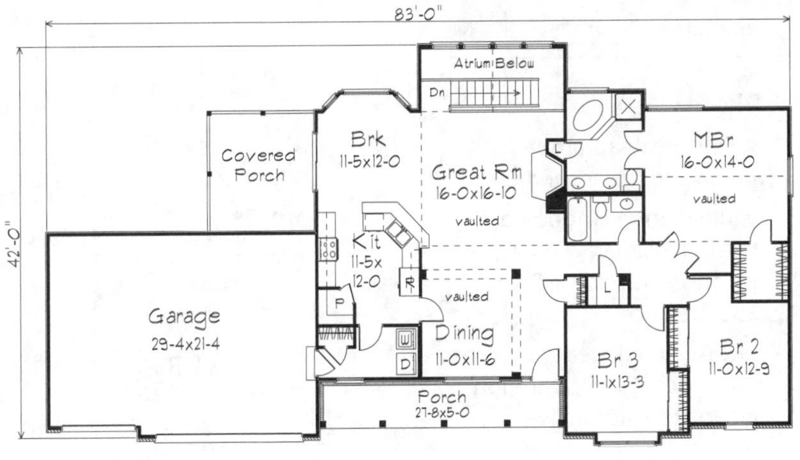

plan #584-007D-0039

price code B

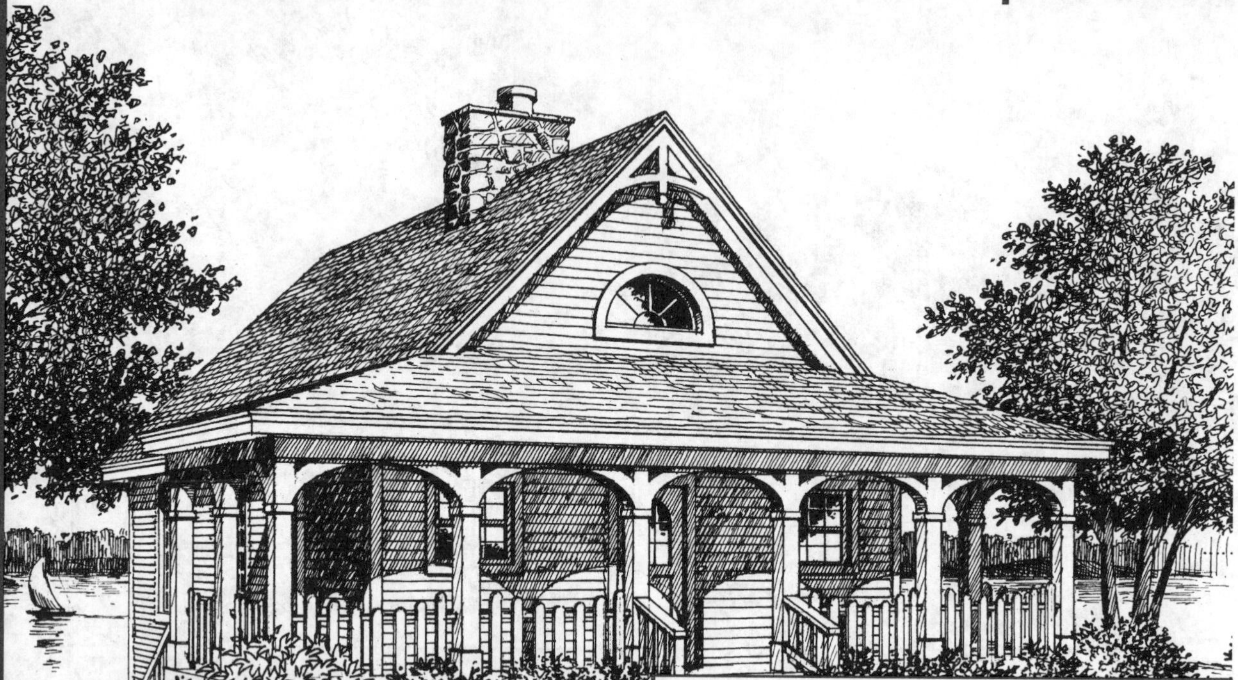

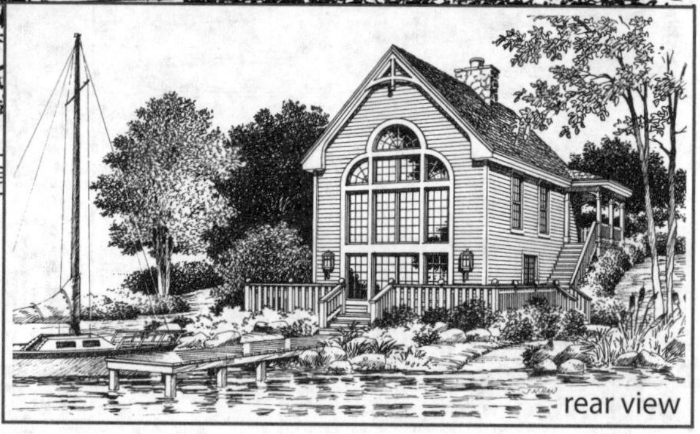

rear view

plan information	
total living area:	1,563
bedrooms:	2
baths:	1 1/2
foundation type:	
basement	

special features

- enjoyable wrap-around porch and lower sundeck
- vaulted entry is adorned with a palladian window, plant shelves, stone floor and fireplace
- huge vaulted great room has magnificent views through a two-story atrium window wall

lower level
858 sq. ft.

first floor
705 sq. ft.

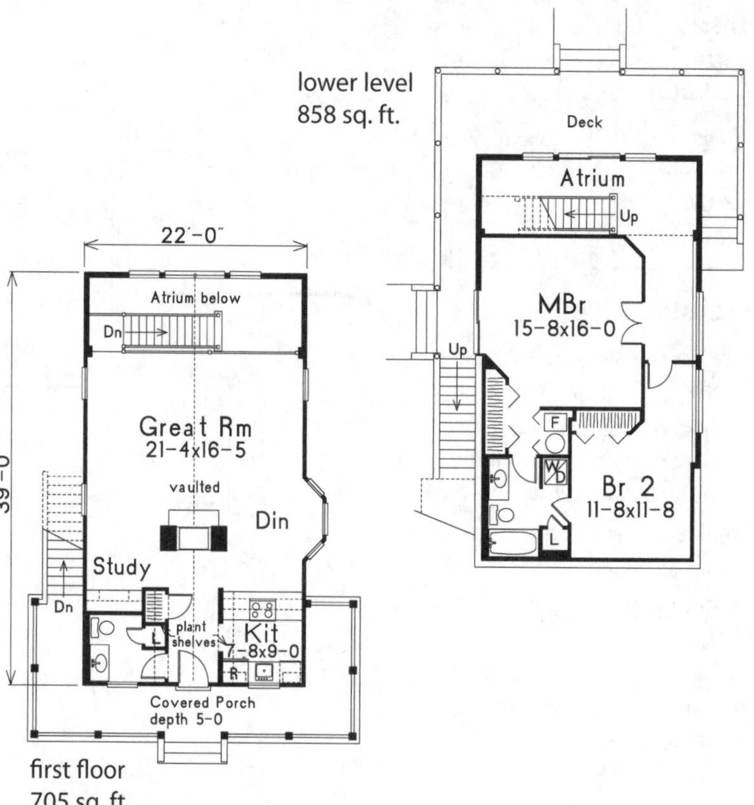

plan #584-007D-0004

price code D

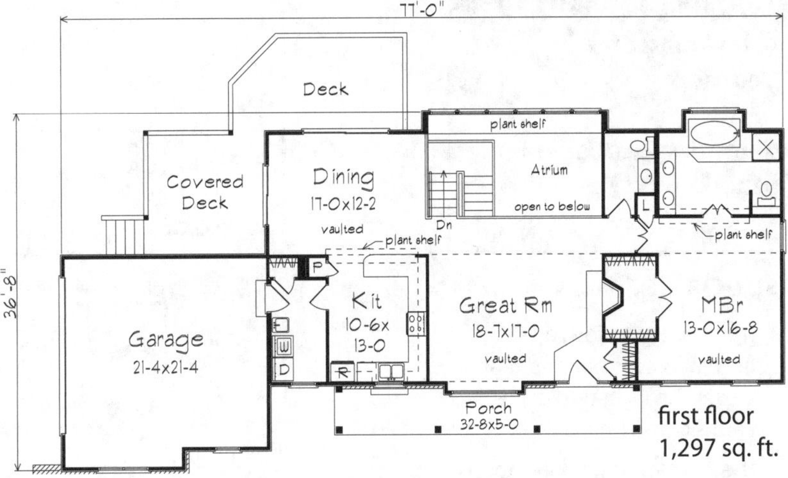

first floor
1,297 sq. ft.

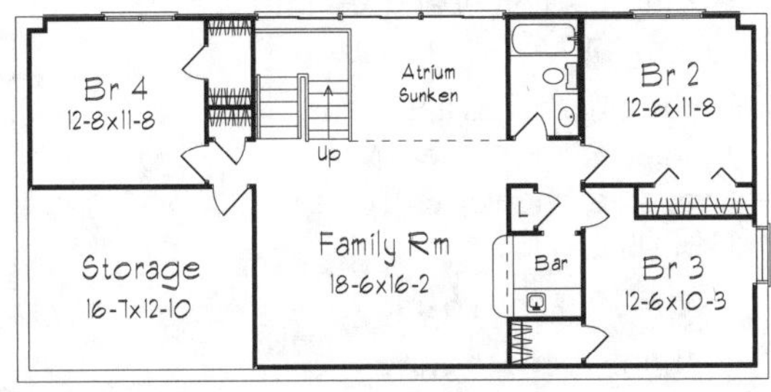

lower level
1,234 sq. ft.

plan information	
total living area:	2,531
bedrooms:	4
baths:	2 1/2
garage:	2-car side entry
foundation type:	walk-out basement

special features

- charming porch with dormers leads into vaulted great room with atrium
- well-designed kitchen and breakfast bar adjoin an extra-large laundry/mud room
- double sinks, tub with window above and plant shelf complete the vaulted master bath

plan #584-#007D-0069

price code C

rear view

plan information

total living area:	2,070
bedrooms:	3
baths:	2
garage:	2-car drive under
foundation type:	walk-out basement

special features

- great room enjoys a fireplace, wet bar and rear views through two-story vaulted atrium
- the U-shaped kitchen opens to the breakfast area and features a walk-in pantry, computer center and atrium overlook
- master bath has a Roman whirlpool tub, TV alcove, separate shower/toilet area and linen closet
- extra storage in garage
- atrium opens to 1,062 square feet of optional living area below

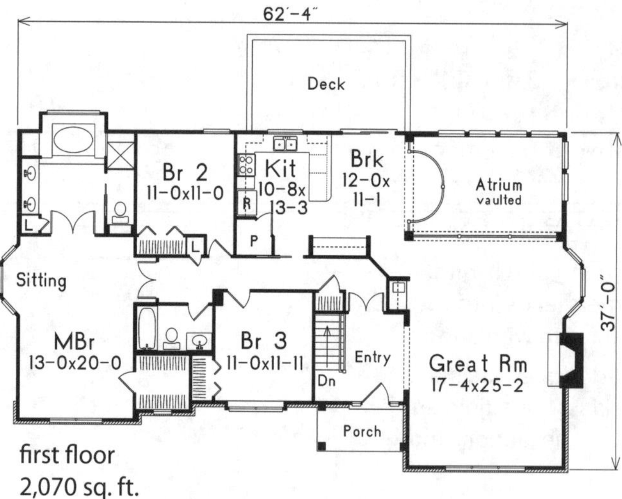

first floor
2,070 sq. ft.

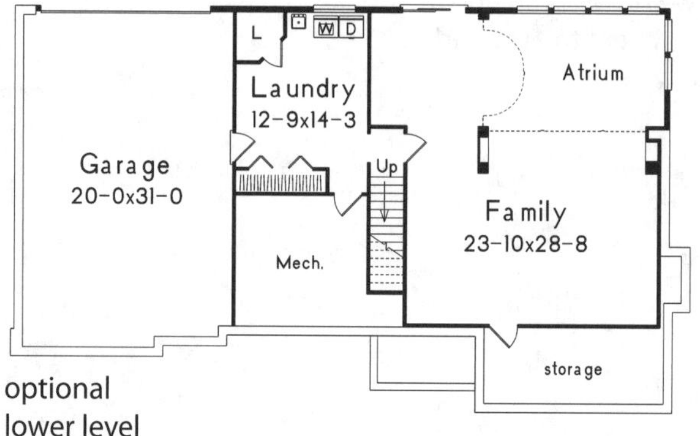

optional
lower level

plan #584-058D-0025

price code C

plan information

total living area:	2,164
bedrooms:	3
baths:	2 1/2
garage:	2-car side entry
foundation type:	basement

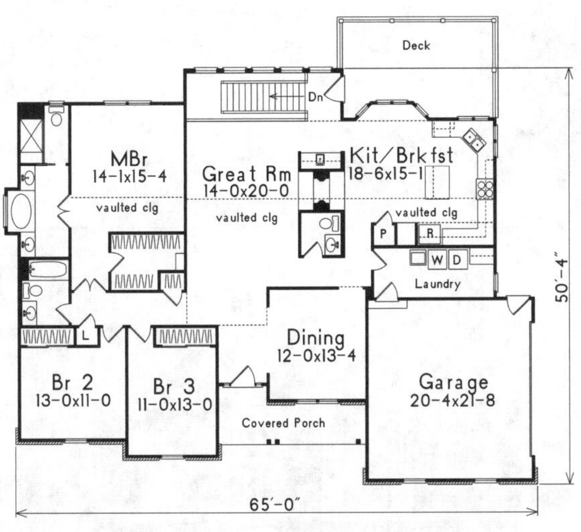

special features

- great design for entertaining with a wet bar and see-through fireplace in the great room
- plenty of closet space
- vaulted ceilings enlarge the master bedroom, great room and kitchen/breakfast area
- great room features an excellent view to the rear of the home

---

plan #584-058D-0017

price code D

plan information

total living area:	2,412
bedrooms:	4
baths:	2
garage:	3-car side entry
foundation type:	walk-out basement

special features

- coffered ceiling in dining room adds character and spaciousness
- great room is enhanced by a vaulted ceiling and atrium window wall
- spacious and well-planned kitchen includes counterspace dining and overlooks breakfast room and beyond to the deck
- luxurious master bedroom features an enormous walk-in closet, private bath and easy access to the laundry area

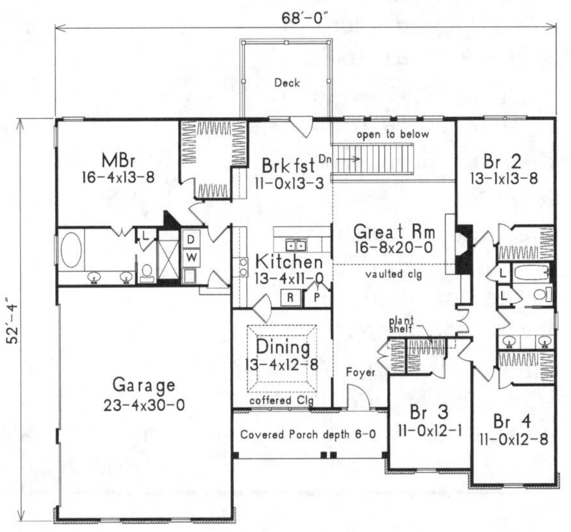

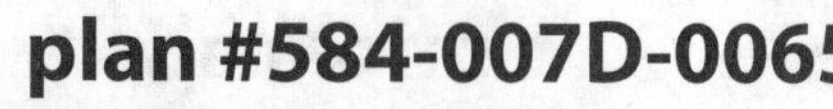

plan #584-007D-0065

price code D

rear view

plan information	
total living area:	2,218
bedrooms:	4
baths:	2
garage:	2-car
foundation type:	
walk-out basement	

special features

- vaulted great room has an arched colonnade entry, bay windowed atrium with staircase and a fireplace
- vaulted kitchen enjoys bay doors to deck, pass-through breakfast bar and walk-in pantry
- breakfast room offers bay window and snack bar open to kitchen with the large laundry room nearby
- atrium opens to 1,217 square feet of optional living area below

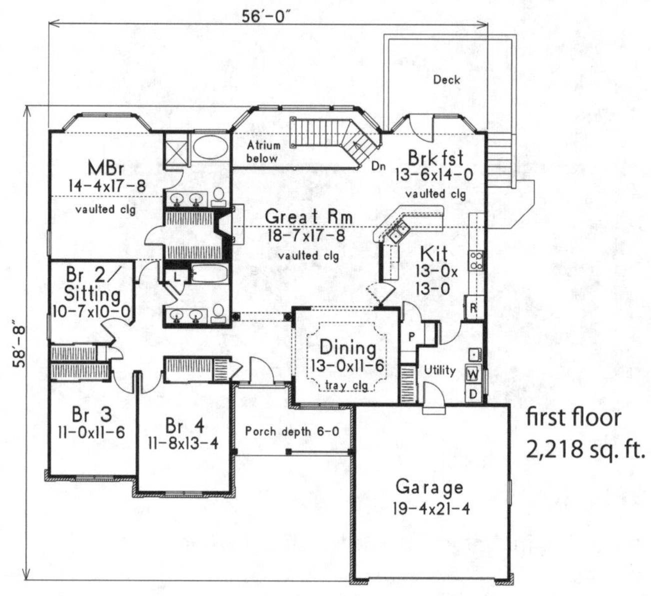

first floor
2,218 sq. ft.

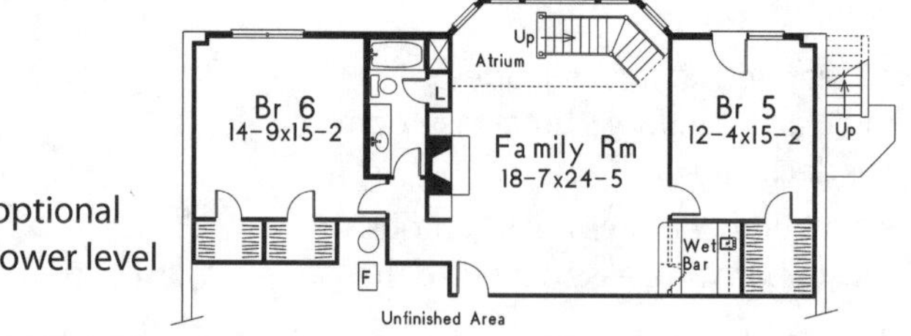

optional
lower level

plan #584-001D-0036

price code A

plan information	
total living area:	1,320
bedrooms:	3
baths:	2
foundation type: crawl space	

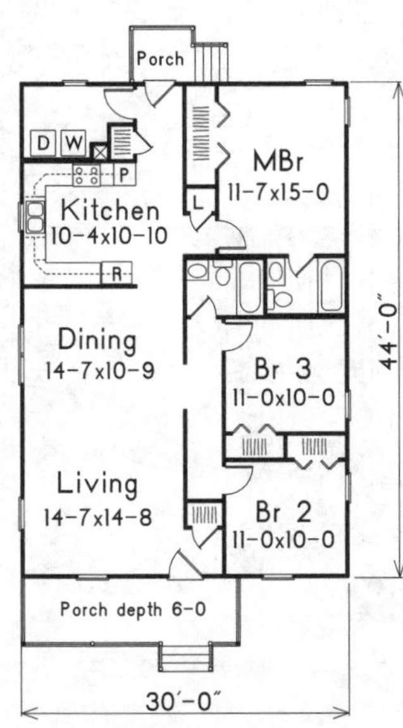

special features

- functional U-shaped kitchen features pantry
- large living and dining areas join to create an open atmosphere
- secluded master bedroom includes private full bath
- covered front porch opens into large living area with convenient coat closet
- utility/laundry room is located near the kitchen

plan #584-001D-0033

price code B

special features

- master bedroom has a private entry from the outdoors
- garage is adjacent to the utility room with convenient storage closet
- large family and dining areas feature a fireplace and porch access
- pass-through kitchen opens directly to cozy breakfast area

plan information	
total living area:	1,624
bedrooms:	3
baths:	2
garage:	2-car side entry
foundation types: basement standard, crawl space, slab	

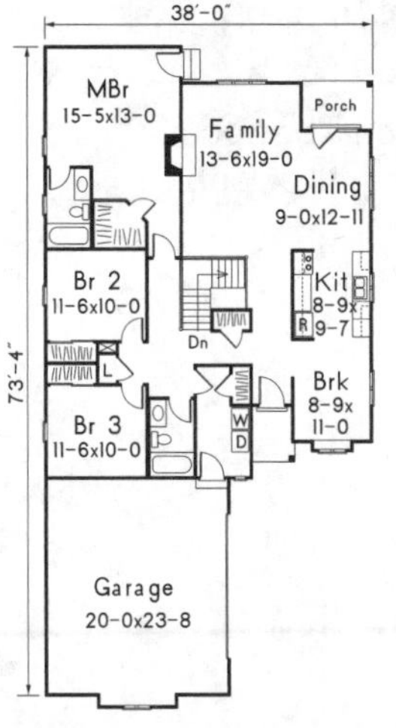

plan #584-007D-0102 price code A

plan information	
total living area:	1,452
bedrooms:	4
baths:	2
foundation type:	
basement	

special features

- large living room features a cozy corner fireplace, bayed dining area and access from entry with guest closet
- forward master bedroom enjoys having its own bath and linen closet
- three additional bedrooms share a bath with a double-bowl vanity

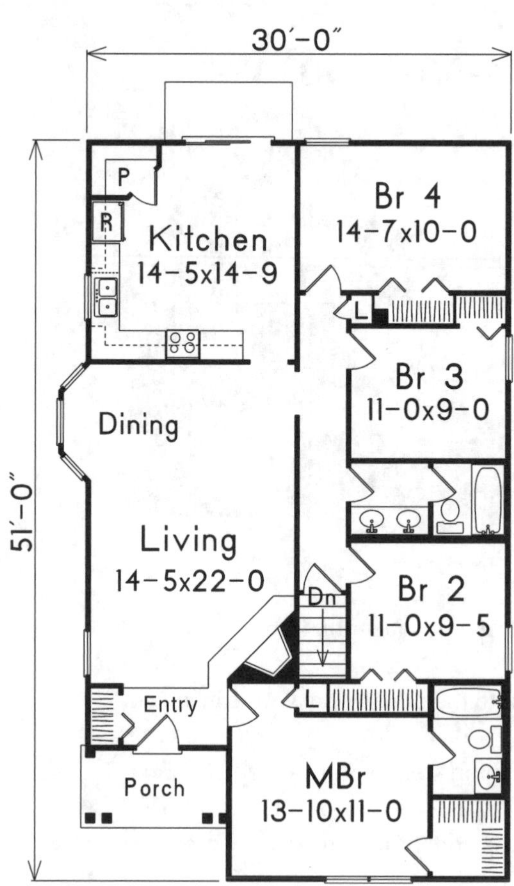

plan #584-007D-0031

price code AA

plan information

total living area:	1,092
bedrooms:	3
baths:	1 1/2
garage:	1-car
foundation type:	
basement	

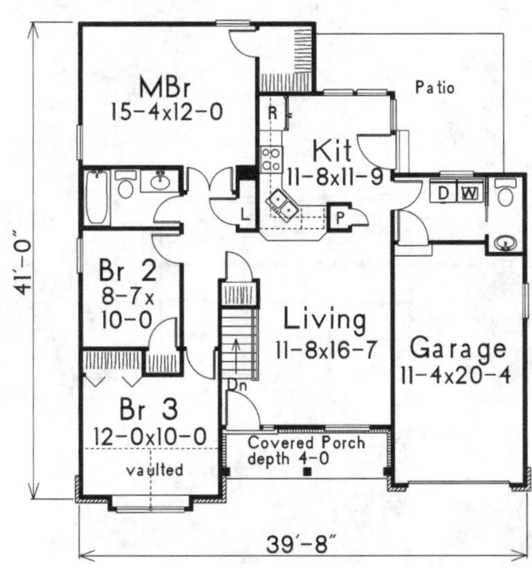

special features

- box window and inviting porch with dormers create a charming facade
- eat-in kitchen offers a pass-through breakfast bar, corner window wall to patio, pantry and convenient laundry with half bath
- master bedroom features a double-door entry and walk-in closet

---

plan #584-022D-0020

price code AA

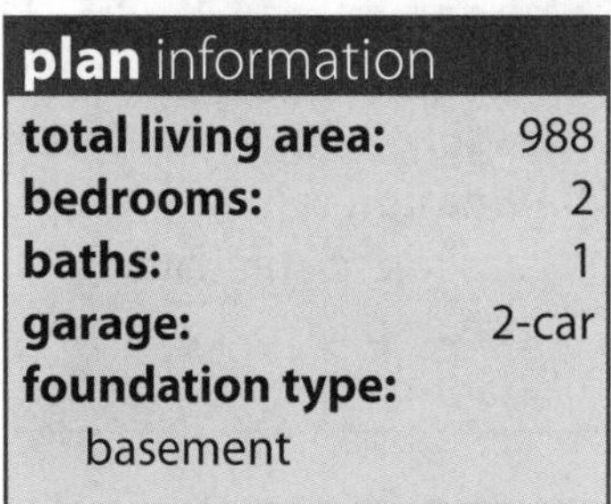

plan information

total living area:	988
bedrooms:	2
baths:	1
garage:	2-car
foundation type:	
basement	

special features

- great room features corner fireplace
- vaulted ceiling and corner windows add space and light in great room
- eat-in kitchen with vaulted ceiling accesses deck for outdoor living
- master bedroom features separate vanities and private access to the bath

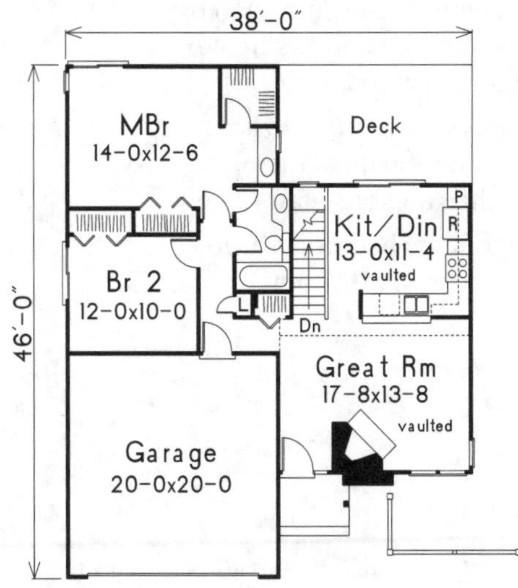

plan #584-007D-0060

price code B

plan information	
total living area:	1,268
bedrooms:	3
baths:	2
garage:	2-car
foundation types:	
basement standard	
crawl space	
slab	

special features

- multiple gables, large porch and arched windows create a classy exterior
- innovative design provides openness in great room, kitchen and breakfast room
- secondary bedrooms have private hall with bath

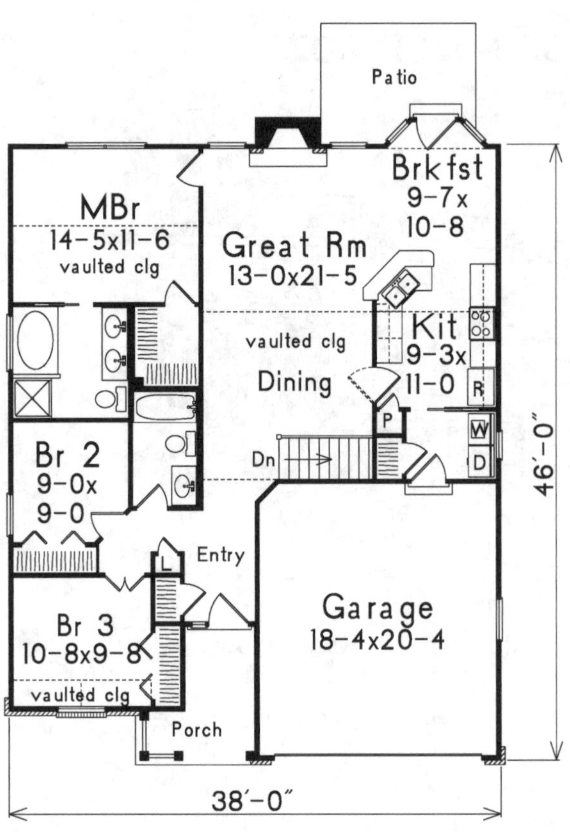

plan #584-058D-0003

price code AA

plan information	
total living area:	1,020
bedrooms:	2
baths:	1
foundation type: slab	

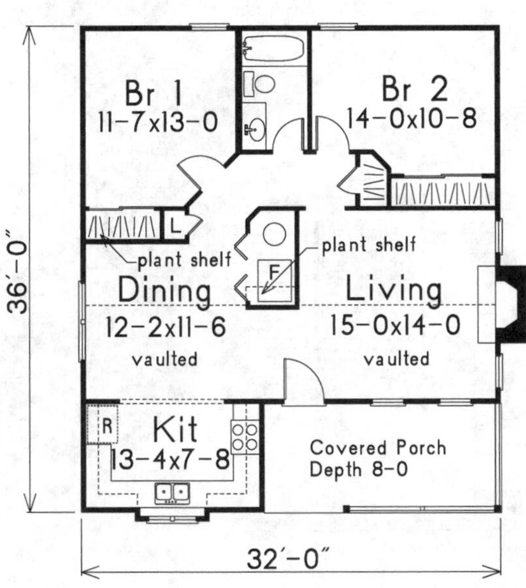

special features

- living room is warmed by a fireplace
- dining and living rooms are enhanced by vaulted ceilings and plant shelves
- a U-shaped kitchen features a large window over the sink

plan #584-045D-0014

price code AA

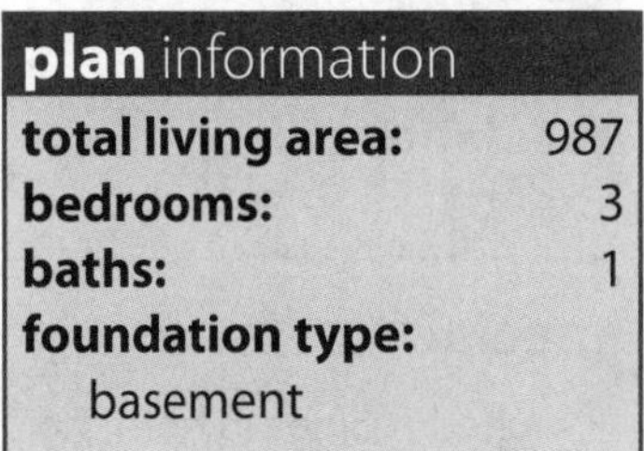

plan information	
total living area:	987
bedrooms:	3
baths:	1
foundation type: basement	

special features

- galley kitchen opens into the cozy breakfast room
- convenient coat closets are located by both entrances
- dining/living room offers an expansive open area
- breakfast room has access to the outdoors
- front porch is great for enjoying outdoor living

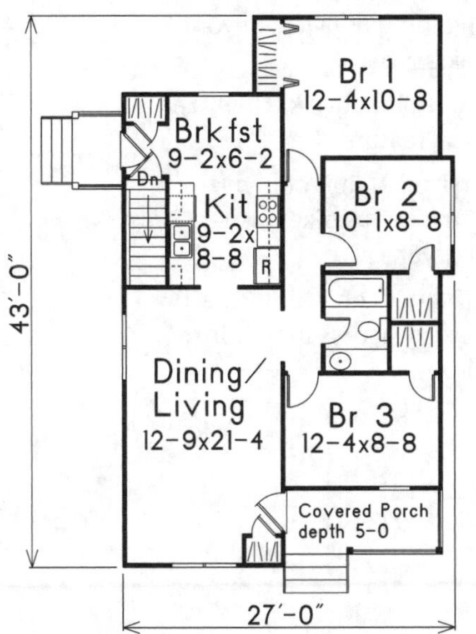

plan #584-058D-0007

price code AA

plan information	
total living area:	1,103
bedrooms:	2
baths:	1
foundation type: slab	

special features

- vaulted ceilings in both the family room and kitchen with dining area just beyond breakfast bar
- plant shelf above kitchen is a special feature
- oversized utility room has space for a full-size washer and dryer
- hall bath is centrally located with easy access from both bedrooms

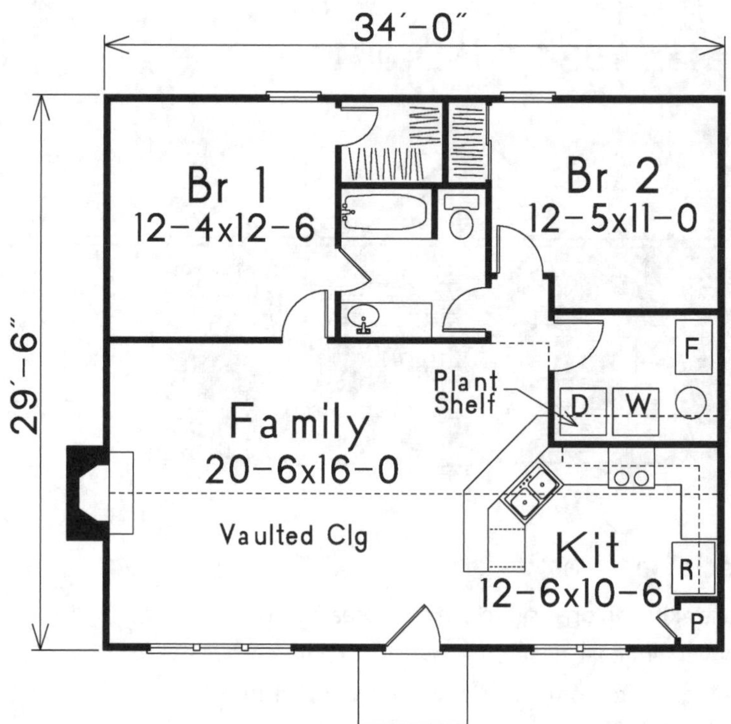

plan #584-007D-0061

price code A

plan information	
total living area:	1,340
bedrooms:	3
baths:	2
garage:	2-car drive under
foundation type: basement	

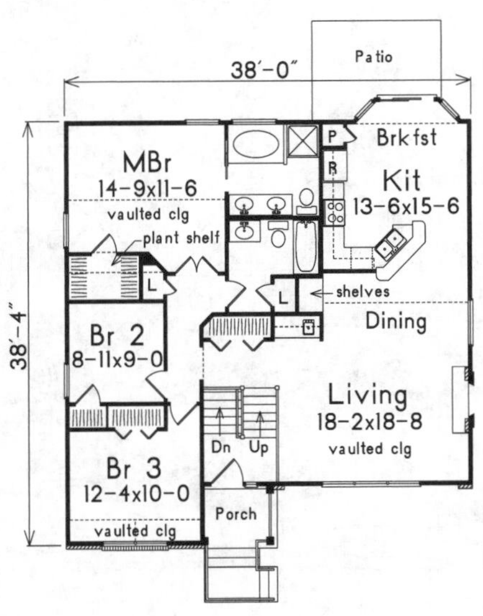

special features

- grand-sized vaulted living and dining rooms offer fireplace, wet bar and breakfast counter open to a spacious kitchen
- vaulted master bedroom features a double-door entry, walk-in closet and an elegant bath
- basement includes a huge two-car garage and space for a bedroom/bath expansion
- extra storage in garage

---

plan #584-056D-0023

price code E

plan information	
total living area:	1,277
bedrooms:	3
baths:	2
garage:	2-car
foundation type: slab	

special features

- both the family room and master bedroom have direct access to an outdoor deck
- the kitchen is compact, yet efficient
- columns add distinction between the dining and family rooms

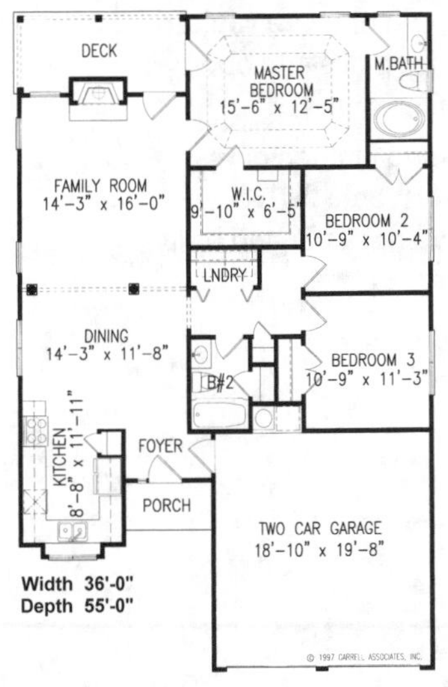

plan #584-007D-0107

price code AA

plan information

total living area:	1,161
bedrooms:	3
baths:	2
foundation type:	
basement	

special features

- brickwork and feature window add elegance to this home for a narrow lot
- living room enjoys a vaulted ceiling, fireplace and opens to kitchen
- a U-shaped kitchen offers a breakfast area with bay window, snack bar and built-in pantry

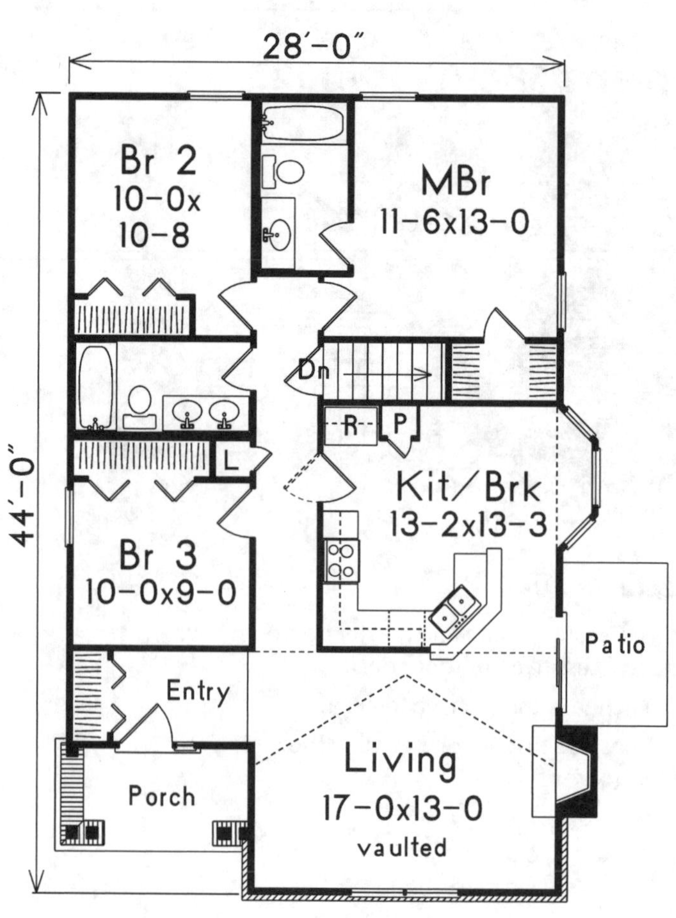

plan #584-022D-0024

price code AA

plan information

total living area:	1,127
bedrooms:	2
baths:	2
garage:	2-car
foundation type:	
basement	

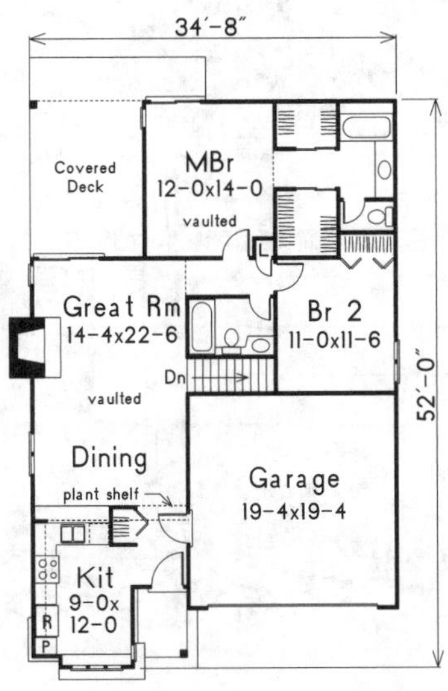

special features

- plant shelf joins kitchen and dining room
- vaulted master bedroom has double walk-in closets, deck access and private bath
- great room features vaulted ceiling, fireplace and sliding doors to covered deck
- ideal home for a narrow lot

plan #584-020D-0016

price code C

plan information

total living area:	1,380
bedrooms:	3
baths:	2
garage:	2-car side entry
foundation types:	
slab standard	
crawl space	

special features

- living room has a sloped ceiling and corner fireplace
- kitchen features a breakfast bar overlooking the dining room
- master suite is separate from other bedrooms for privacy
- large utility/storage area

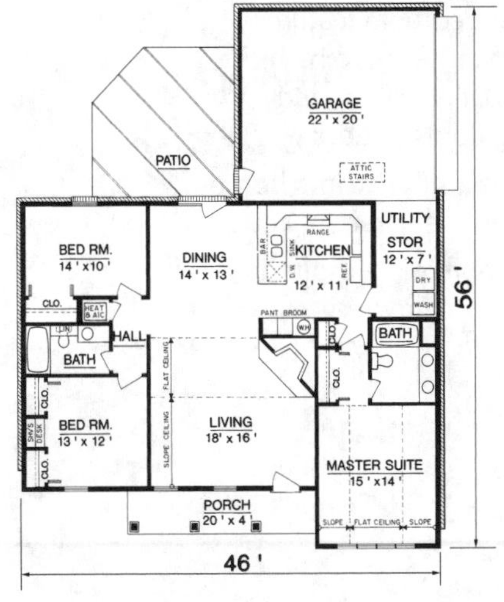

plan #584-022D-0021

price code AA

plan information	
total living area:	1,020
bedrooms:	2
baths:	1
garage:	2-car
foundation type:	
basement	

special features

- kitchen features open stairs, pass-through to great room, pantry and deck access
- master bedroom features private entrance to bath, large walk-in closet and sliding doors to deck
- informal entrance into home through the garage
- great room has a vaulted ceiling and fireplace

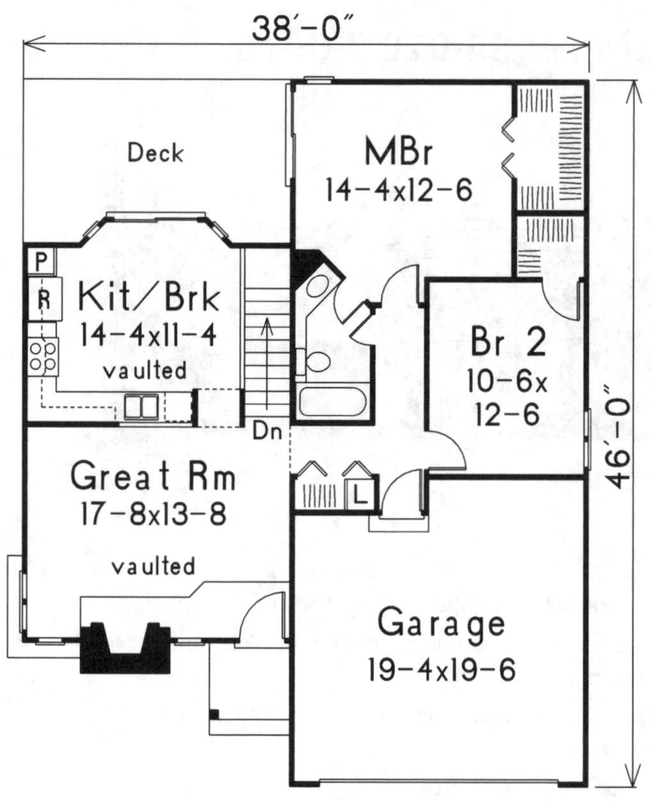

plan #584-001D-0035

price code A

plan information

total living area:	1,396
bedrooms:	3
baths:	2
garage:	1-car carport
foundation types:	
basement standard	
crawl space	

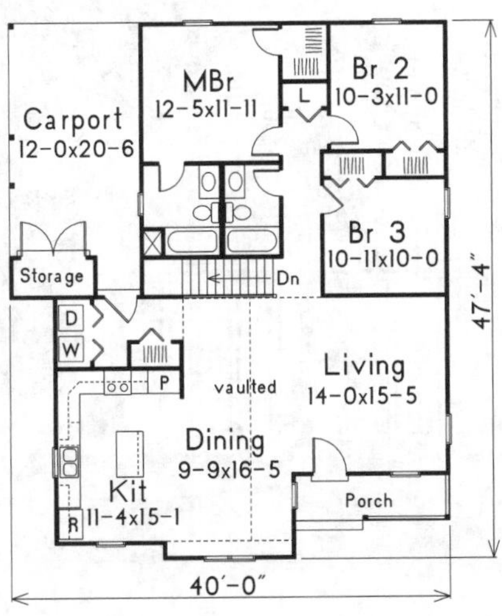

special features

- gabled front adds interest to facade
- living and dining rooms share a vaulted ceiling
- master bedroom features a walk-in closet and private bath
- functional kitchen boasts a center work island and convenient pantry

---

plan #584-022D-0022

price code A

plan information

total living area:	1,270
bedrooms:	3
baths:	2
garage:	2-car
foundation type:	
basement	

special features

- spacious living area features angled stairs, vaulted ceiling, exciting fireplace and deck access
- master bedroom includes a walk-in closet and private bath
- dining and living rooms join to create an open atmosphere
- eat-in kitchen has a convenient pass-through to dining room

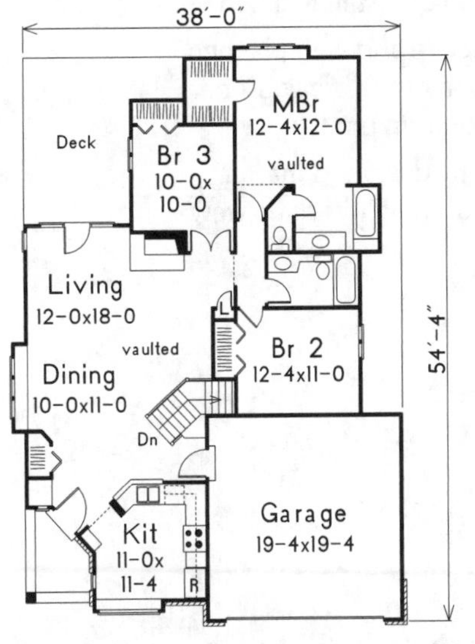

plan #584-007D-0044

price code B

plan information	
total living area:	1,516
bedrooms:	3
baths:	2
garage:	2-car
foundation type:	basement

special features

- spacious great room is open to dining area with a bay and unique stair location
- attractive and well-planned kitchen offers breakfast bar and built-in pantry
- smartly designed master bedroom enjoys patio view

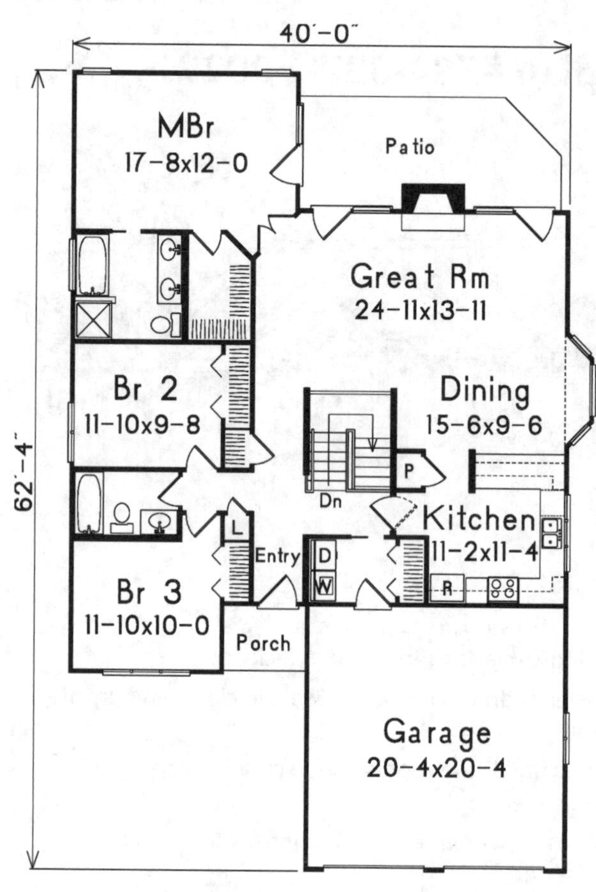

plan #584-014D-0006

price code B

plan information

total living area:	1,588
bedrooms:	3
baths:	2
garage:	2-car
foundation types:	
basement standard	
crawl space	
slab	

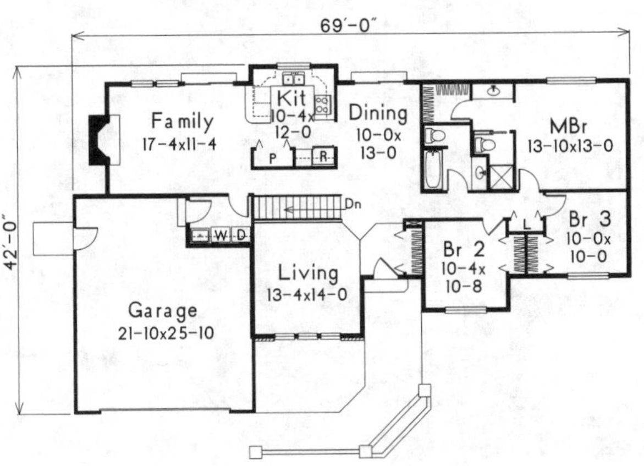

special features

- family and dining rooms access the rear patio
- angled walkway leads guests by an attractive landscape area
- master bedroom enjoys a separate dressing area, walk-in closet and private bath
- sunken living room features an attractive railing on two sides
- the U-shaped kitchen is complete with a large pantry and eating bar

---

plan #584-001D-0091

price code A

plan information

total living area:	1,344
bedrooms:	3
baths:	2
foundation types:	
crawl space standard	
basement	
slab	

special features

- kitchen has side entry, laundry area, pantry and joins family/dining area
- master bedroom includes a private bath
- linen and storage closets in hall
- covered porch opens to the spacious living room with a handy coat closet

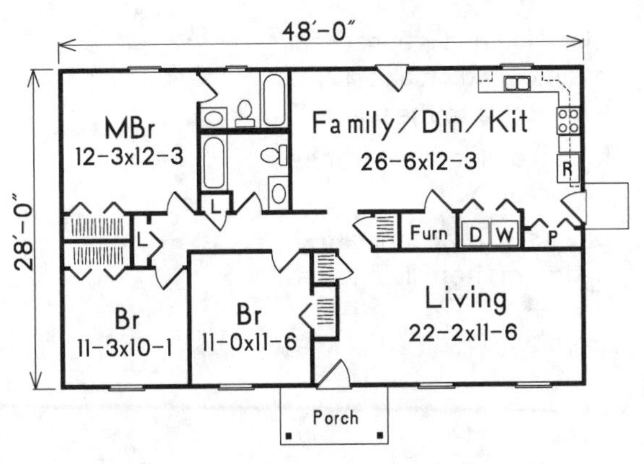

plan #584-040D-0011

price code B

plan information

total living area:	1,739
bedrooms:	3
baths:	2
garage:	2-car side entry
foundation type:	slab

special features

- utility room has convenient laundry sink
- vaulted ceiling lends drama to the family room with fireplace and double French doors
- island kitchen is enhanced by adjoining breakfast area with access to the patio
- formal dining room features a 10' ceiling
- private hallway separates bedrooms from living area

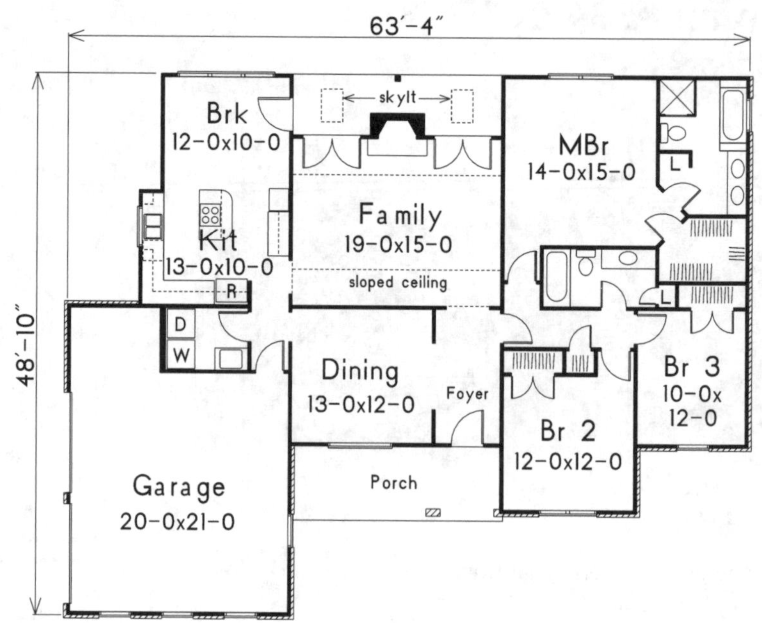

plan #584-001D-0030

price code A

plan information	
total living area:	1,416
bedrooms:	3
baths:	2
garage:	2-car
foundation types:	
basement standard	
crawl space	
slab	

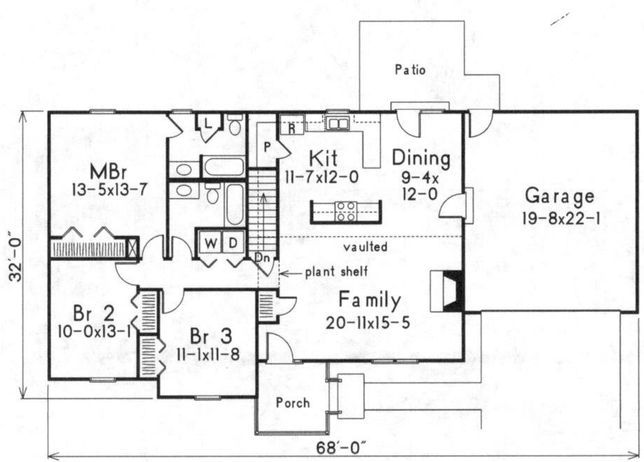

special features

- family room includes fireplace, elevated plant shelf and vaulted ceiling
- patio is accessible from dining area and garage
- centrally located laundry area
- oversized walk-in pantry

---

plan #584-013D-0002

price code B

plan information	
total living area:	1,197
bedrooms:	3
baths:	2
garage:	2-car
foundation types:	
crawl space	
slab	
please specify when ordering	

special features

- dining area is adjacent to living room ideal for gathering
- private master bath has a vaulted ceiling, double vanity, separate tub and shower
- plant shelf in family room adds charm

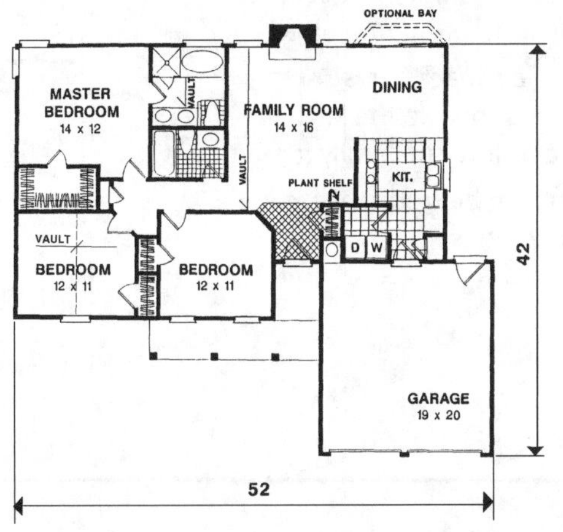

plan #584-039D-0007

price code B

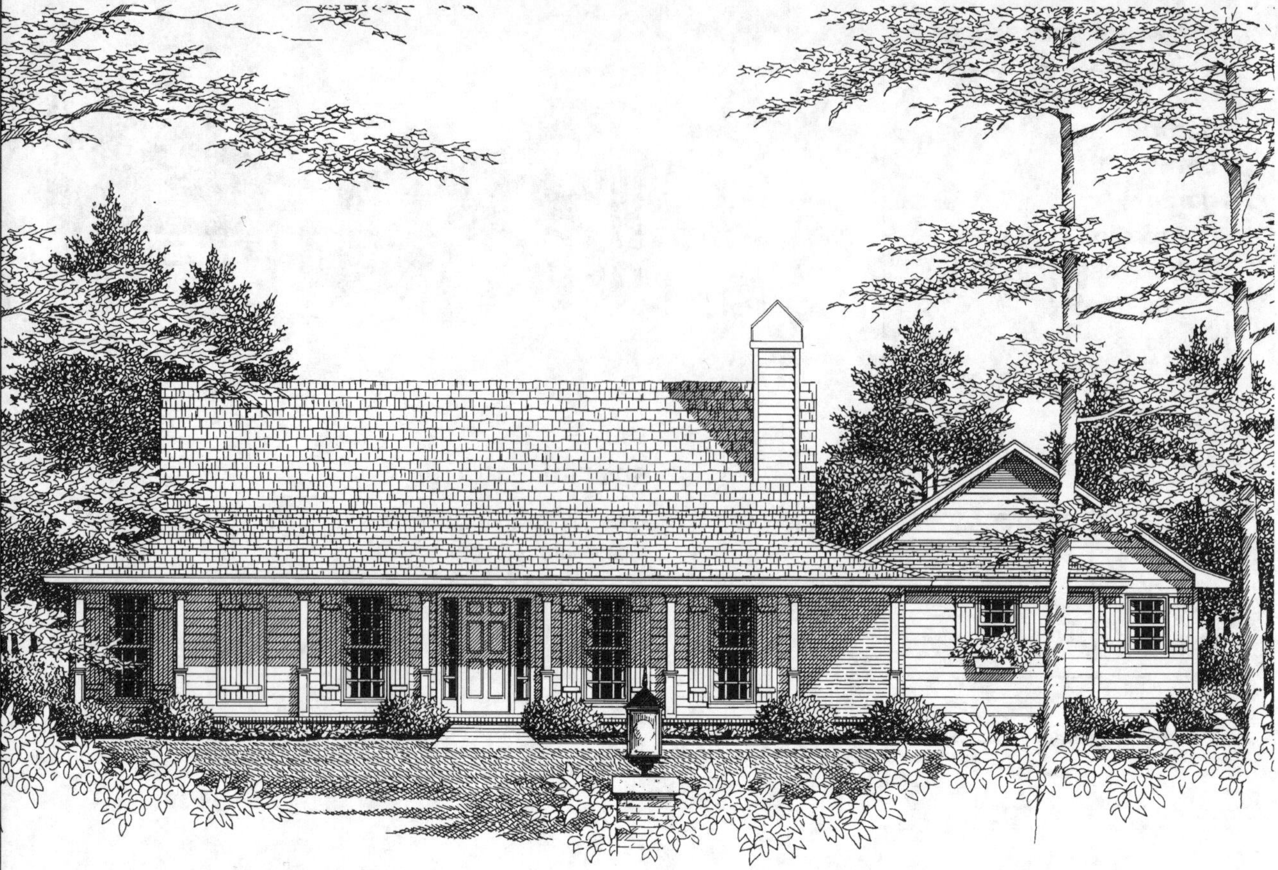

plan information

total living area:	1,550
bedrooms:	3
baths:	2
garage:	2-car detached side entry

foundation types:
slab
crawl space
please specify when ordering

special features

- wrap-around front porch is an ideal gathering place
- handy snack bar is positioned so the kitchen flows into the family room
- master bedroom has many amenities

With Garage
Width: 68'-3"
Depth: 73'-8"

Without Garage
Width: 50'-9"
Depth: 42'-1"

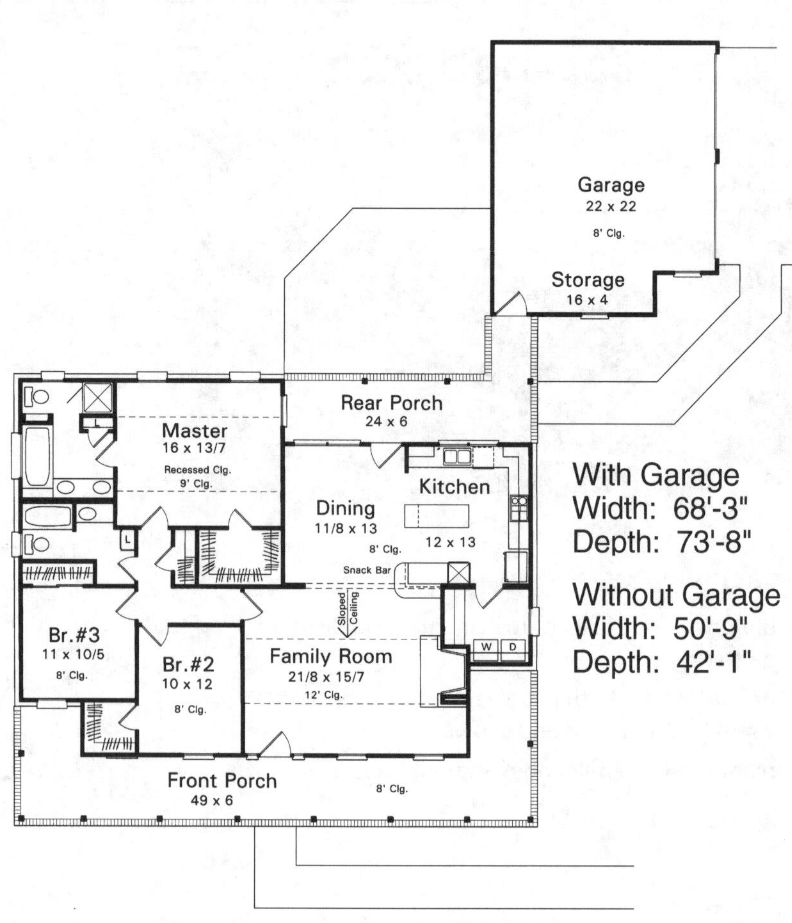

plan #584-008D-0013

price code A

plan information

total living area:	1,345
bedrooms:	3
baths:	2
garage:	2-car side entry
foundation types:	
basement standard	
crawl space	
slab	

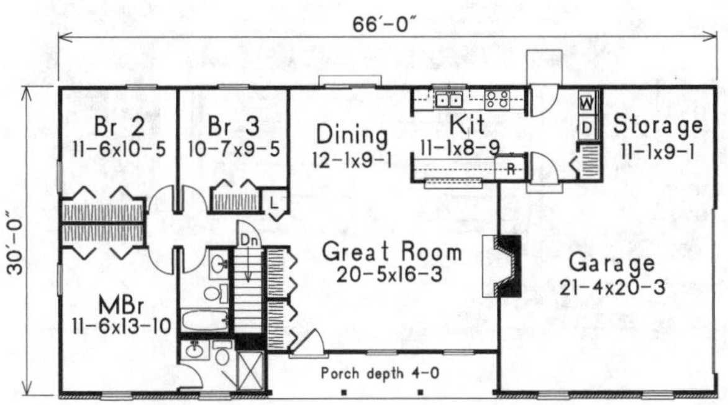

special features

- brick front details add a touch of elegance
- master bedroom has a private full bath
- great room combines with the dining area creating a sense of spaciousness
- garage includes a handy storage area which could easily convert to a workshop space

---

plan #584-014D-0008

price code AA

plan information

total living area:	1,135
bedrooms:	3
baths:	2
garage:	2-car
foundation types:	
basement standard	
crawl space	

special features

- living and dining rooms feature vaulted ceilings and a corner fireplace
- energy efficient home with 2" x 6" exterior walls
- master bedroom offers a vaulted ceiling, private bath and generous closet space
- compact but functional kitchen is complete with a pantry and adjacent utility room

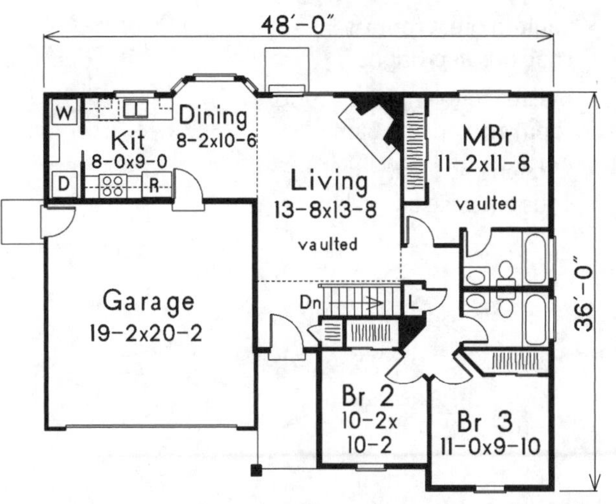

plan #584-035D-0001

price code B

plan information

total living area:	1,715
bedrooms:	3
baths:	2
garage:	2-car
foundation types:	
walk-out basement	
crawl space	
slab	
please specify when ordering	

special features

- vaulted great room is spacious and bright
- master suite enjoys a sitting room and private bath
- kitchen has plenty of counterspace and cabinetry

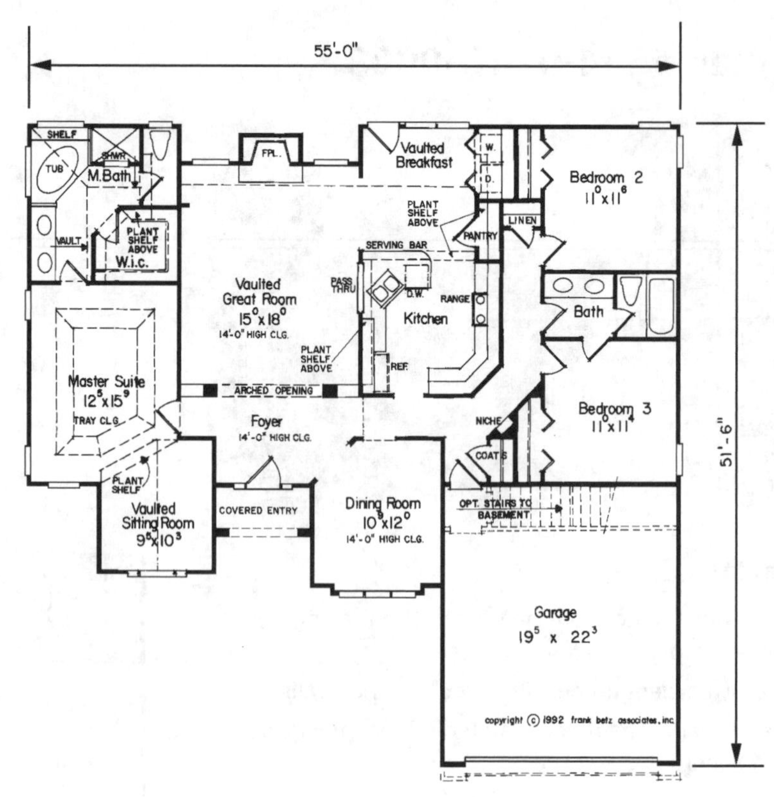

plan #584-045D-0010

price code B

plan information	
total living area:	1,558
bedrooms:	2
baths:	2
garage:	2-car rear entry
foundation type:	basement

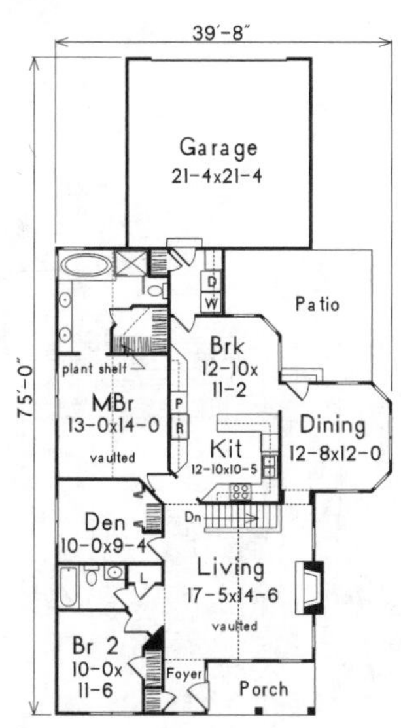

special features

- illuminated spaces are created by visual access to the outdoor living areas
- vaulted master bedroom features a private bath with whirlpool tub, separate shower and large walk-in closet
- convenient laundry area has garage access
- practical den or third bedroom
- a U-shaped kitchen is adjacent to the sunny breakfast area

---

plan #584-051D-0053

price code A

plan information	
total living area:	1,461
bedrooms:	3
baths:	2
garage:	2-car
foundation type:	basement

special features

- casual dining room
- cathedral ceilings in the great room and dining area give the home a spacious feel
- relaxing master bedroom boasts an expansive bath and large walk-in closet

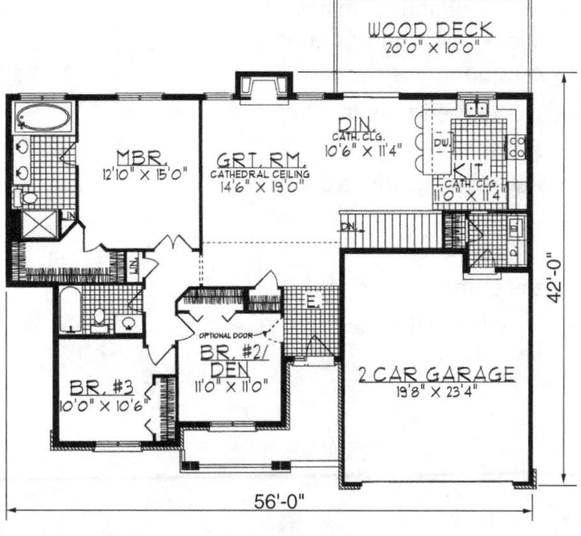

plan #584-001D-0053

price code A

plan information

total living area:	1,344
bedrooms:	3
baths:	2
garage:	2-car
foundation types:	
crawl space standard	
basement	
slab	

special features

- family/dining room has sliding glass doors to the outdoors
- master bedroom features a private bath
- hall bath includes a double-bowl vanity for added convenience
- the U-shaped kitchen features a large pantry and laundry area

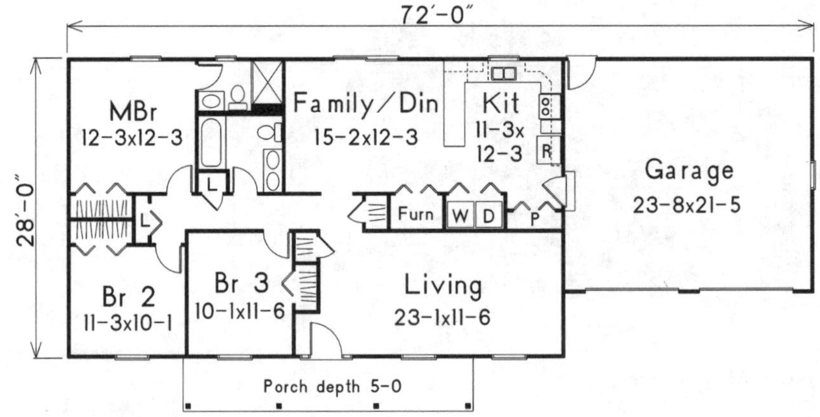

plan #584-065D-0038

price code B

plan information	
total living area:	1,663
bedrooms:	3
baths:	2
garage:	2-car side entry
foundation type:	basement

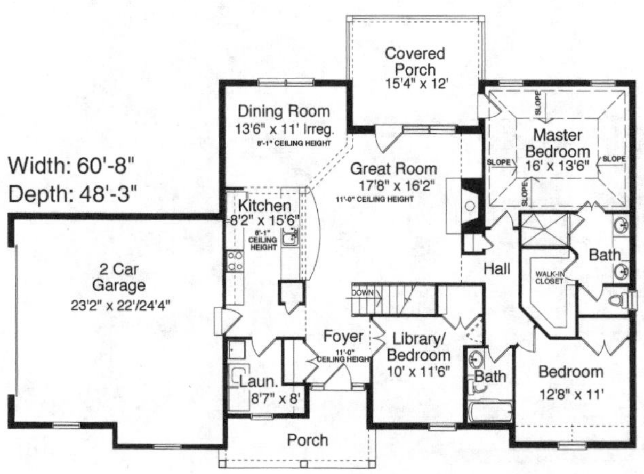

special features

- the open great room, dining area and kitchen combine to form the main living area
- an 11' ceiling tops the great room and foyer for added openness
- the rear covered porch provides a cozy and relaxing atmosphere
- the master bedroom enjoys a sloped ceiling and a private entrance to the covered porch

---

plan #584-052D-0035

price code B

plan information	
total living area:	1,770
bedrooms:	3
baths:	2
garage:	2-car drive under
foundation type:	basement

special features

- compartmentalized hall bath is convenient and functional
- walk-in pantry in kitchen maintains organization
- superb master bath is spacious and well equipped

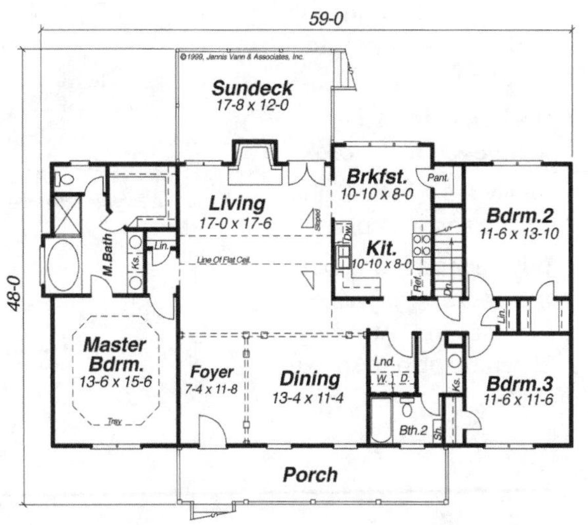

plan #584-040D-0014

price code B

plan information	
total living area:	1,595
bedrooms:	3
baths:	2
garage:	2-car side entry
foundation types:	
slab standard	
crawl space	

special features

- dining room has a convenient built-in desk and provides access to the outdoors
- the L-shaped kitchen features an island cooktop
- family room has a high ceiling and a fireplace
- private master bedroom includes a large walk-in closet and bath with separate tub and shower units

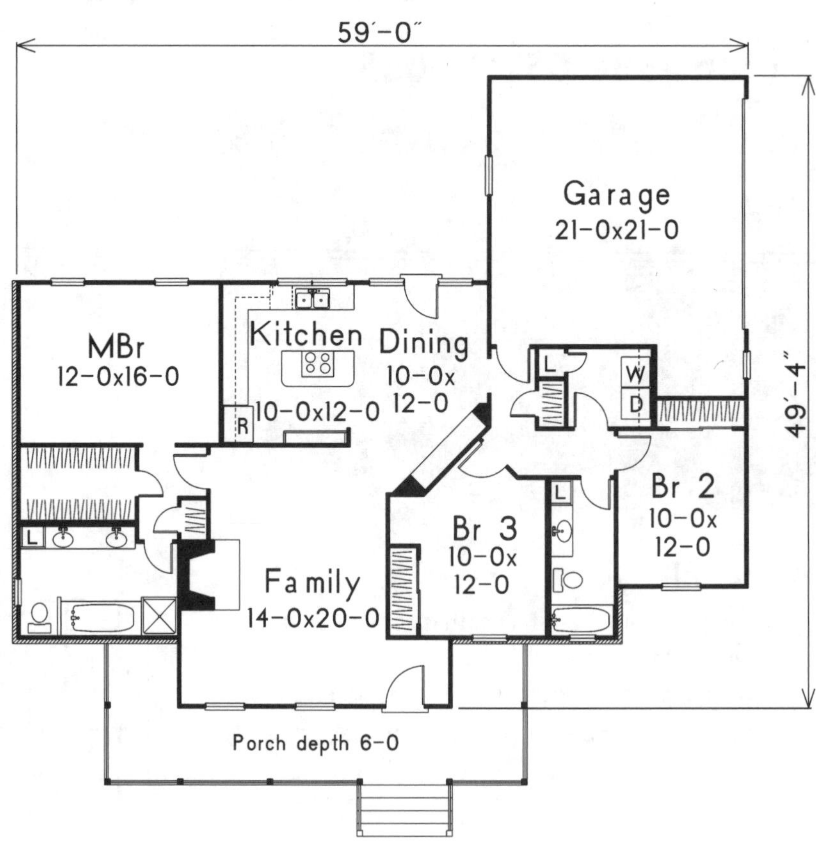

plan #584-053D-0002

price code C

plan information

total living area:	1,668
bedrooms:	3
baths:	2
garage:	2-car drive under
foundation type:	basement

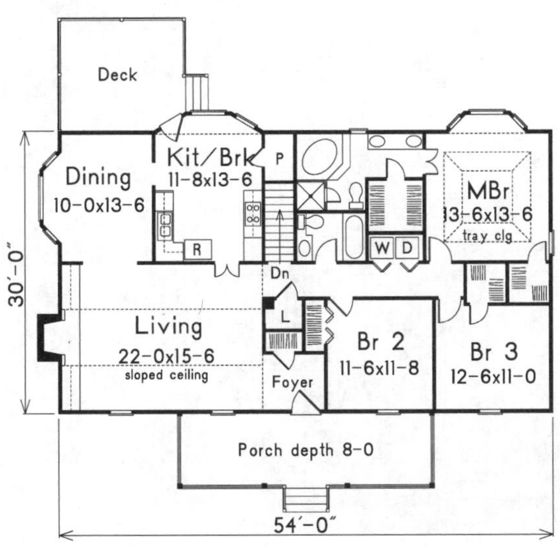

special features

- large bay windows grace the breakfast area, master bedroom and dining room
- extensive walk-in closets and storage spaces are located throughout the home
- handy covered entry porch
- large living room has a fireplace, built-in bookshelves and sloped ceiling

---

plan #584-053D-0036

price code B

plan information

total living area:	1,567
bedrooms:	3
baths:	2
garage:	2-car drive under
foundation type:	basement

special features

- front gables and extended porch add charm to facade
- large bay windows add brightness to breakfast and dining rooms
- the master bath boasts an oversized tub, separate shower, double sinks and a large walk-in closet
- living room features a vaulted ceiling and a prominent fireplace

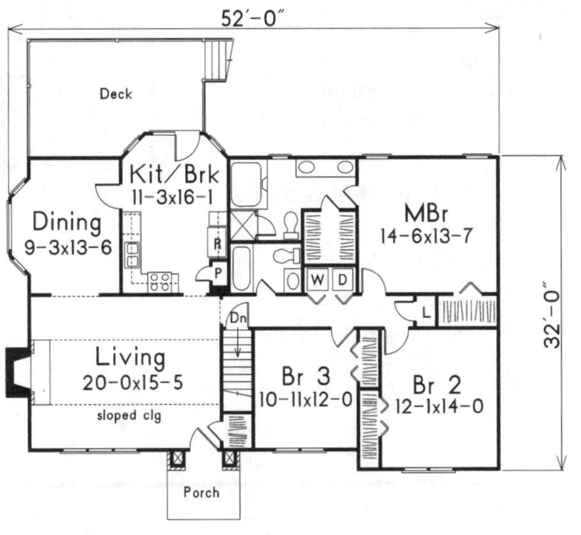

plan #584-077D-0001

price code C

plan information

total living area:	1,638
bedrooms:	3
baths:	2
garage:	2-car side entry

foundation types:

basement
crawl space
slab

please specify when ordering

special features

- great room features a fireplace with flanking doors that access the covered porch
- the centrally located kitchen serves the breakfast and dining areas with ease
- plenty of storage area is located in the garage

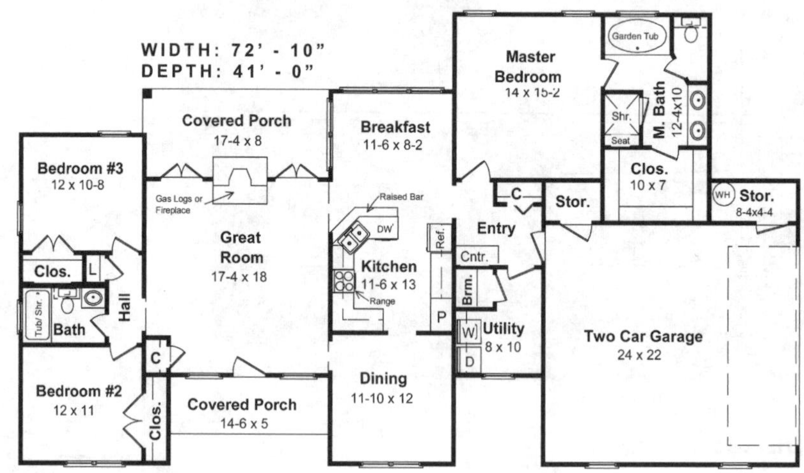

plan #584-069D-0014

price code B

plan information

total living area:	1,680
bedrooms:	3
baths:	2
garage:	2-car
foundation types:	
slab	
crawl space	
please specify when ordering	

special features

- master suite has two walk-in closets and a private bath
- kitchen has snack bar that overlooks into an angled dining area
- a covered porch extends the living area to the outdoors
- extra storage in garage

plan #584-053D-0040

price code A

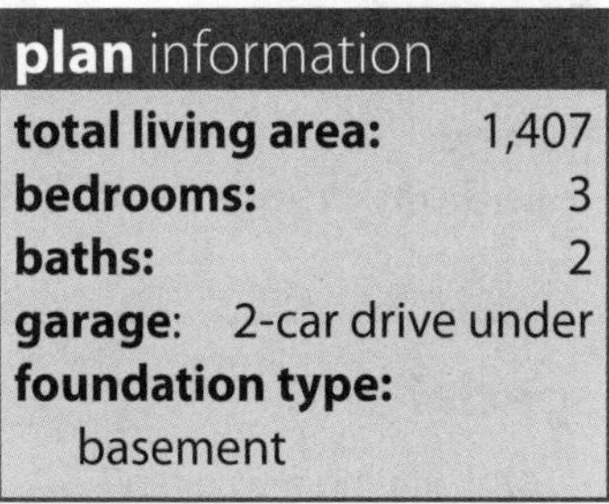

plan information

total living area:	1,407
bedrooms:	3
baths:	2
garage:	2-car drive under
foundation type:	
basement	

special features

- large living room has a fireplace and access to the rear deck
- kitchen and dining area combine to create an open gathering area
- convenient laundry room and broom closet
- master bedroom includes a private bath with large vanity and separate tub and shower

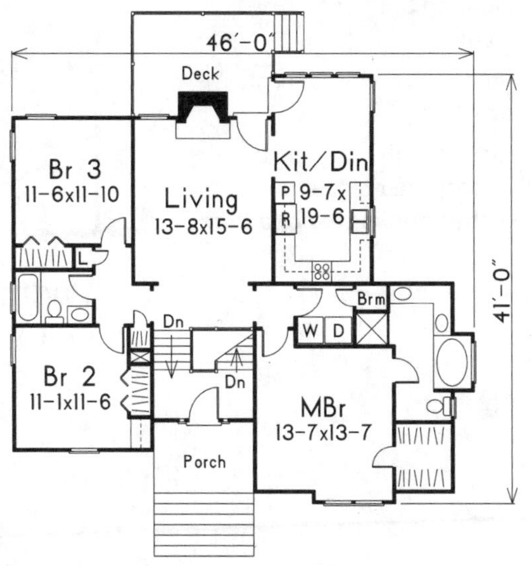

plan #584-047D-0020

price code B

plan information

total living area:	1,783
bedrooms:	3
baths:	2
garage:	2-car
foundation type:	
slab	

special features

- formal living and dining rooms in the front of the home
- kitchen overlooks breakfast area
- conveniently located laundry area is near the kitchen and master bedroom

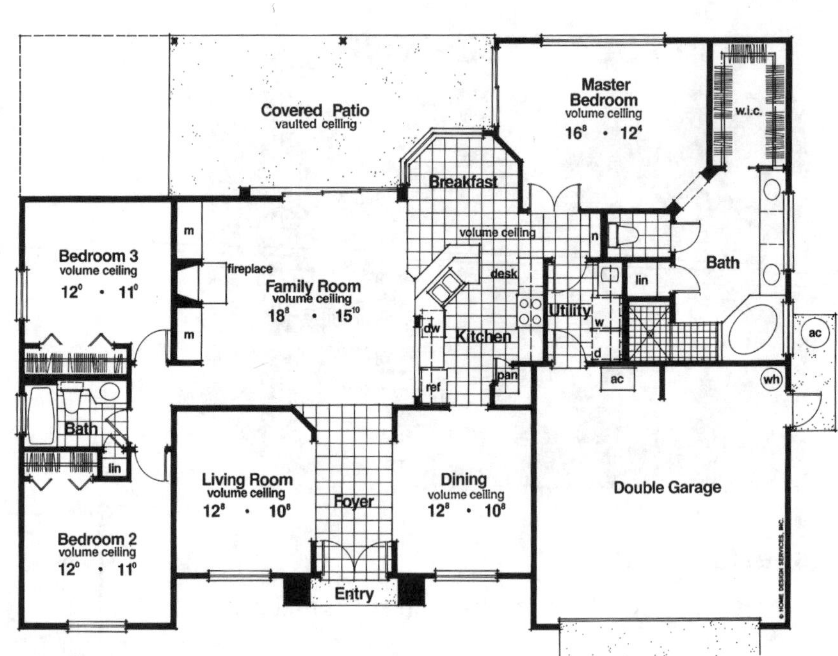

Width: 60'-0"
Depth: 45'-0"

plan #584-067D-0002

price code B

plan information	
total living area:	1,627
bedrooms:	3
baths:	2
garage:	2-car
foundation types:	
crawl space	
slab	
please specify when ordering	

special features

- cathedral ceiling in living room adds drama to this space
- cozy corner dining area just off the kitchen is convenient
- large master bedroom is cheerful with many windows and includes its own bath and walk-in closet

---

plan #584-053D-0045

price code B

plan information	
total living area:	1,698
bedrooms:	3
baths:	2
garage:	2-car drive under
foundation type:	
basement	

special features

- kitchen includes a walk-in pantry and corner sink that faces the living area
- breakfast room is highlighted by an expanse of windows and access to deck
- recessed foyer opens into the vaulted living room with fireplace
- master bedroom features a private bath with large walk-in closet

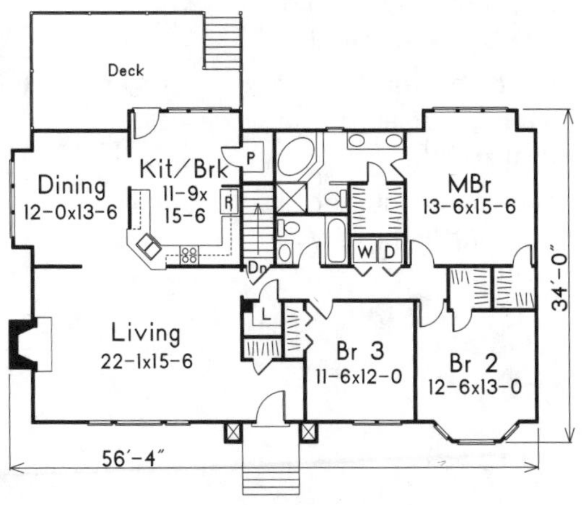

plan #584-053D-0053

price code B

plan information	
total living area:	1,609
bedrooms:	4
baths:	2
garage:	2-car
foundation type:	
basement	

special features

- efficient kitchen includes a corner pantry and adjacent laundry room
- breakfast room boasts plenty of windows and opens onto rear deck
- master bedroom features a tray ceiling and private deluxe bath
- entry opens into large living area with fireplace

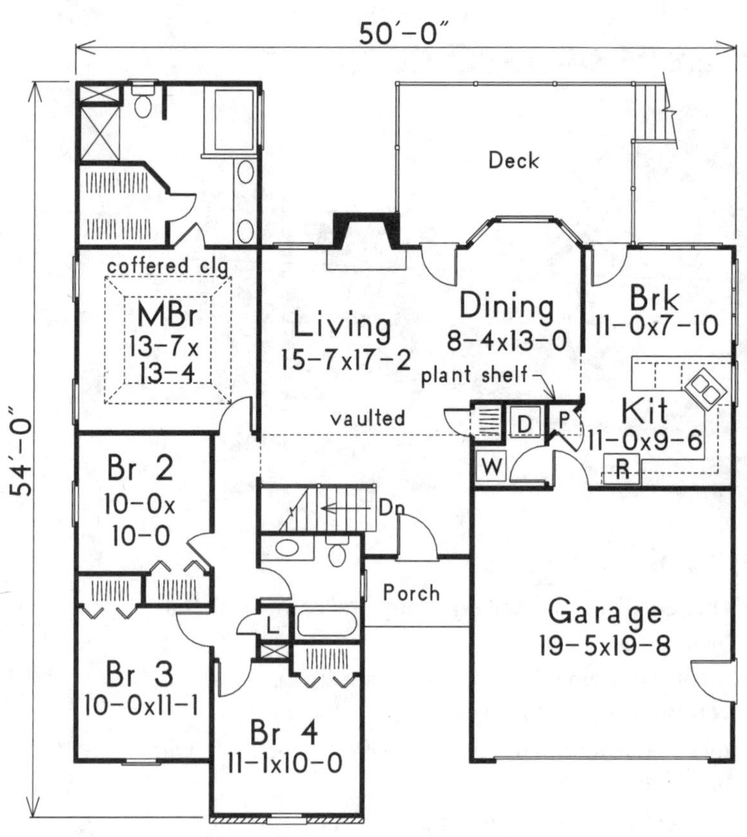

plan #584-053D-0048

price code B

plan information

total living area: 1,697
bedrooms: 3
baths: 2
garage: 2-car drive under
foundation type:
basement

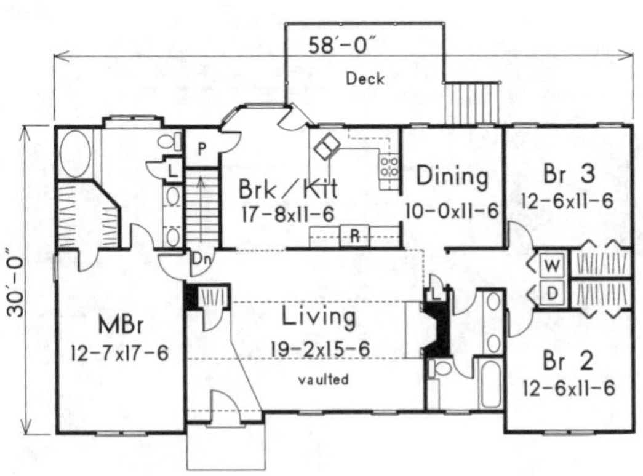

special features

- secondary bedrooms share a bath with private dressing area
- large living room enjoys a fireplace and vaulted ceiling
- secluded master bedroom boasts a private deluxe bath
- open kitchen and breakfast area include a pantry and rear access to sun deck

---

plan #584-053D-0047

price code A

plan information

total living area: 1,438
bedrooms: 3
baths: 2
garage: 2-car side entry
foundation types:
crawl space standard
slab

special features

- vaulted living and dining rooms unite to provide an open space for entertaining
- secondary bedrooms share a full bath
- compact kitchen maintains organization
- vaulted master bedroom includes a private bath, large walk-in closet and access to the patio

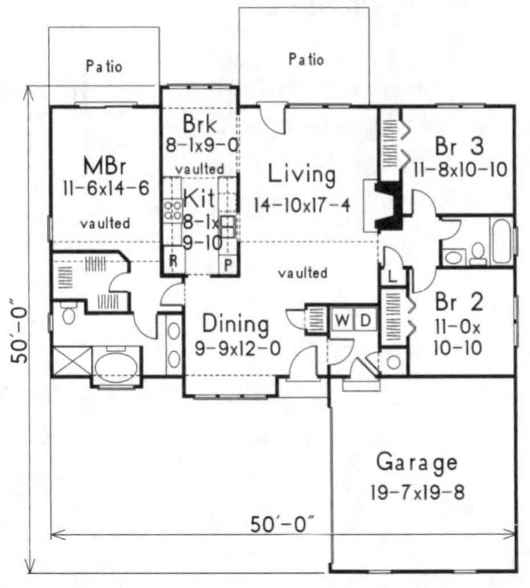

plan #584-047D-0019

price code B

plan information	
total living area:	1,783
bedrooms:	3
baths:	2
garage:	2-car
foundation type:	
slab	

special features

- grand foyer leads to family room
- walk-in pantry in kitchen
- master bath has a step-down doorless shower, huge vanity and a large walk-in closet

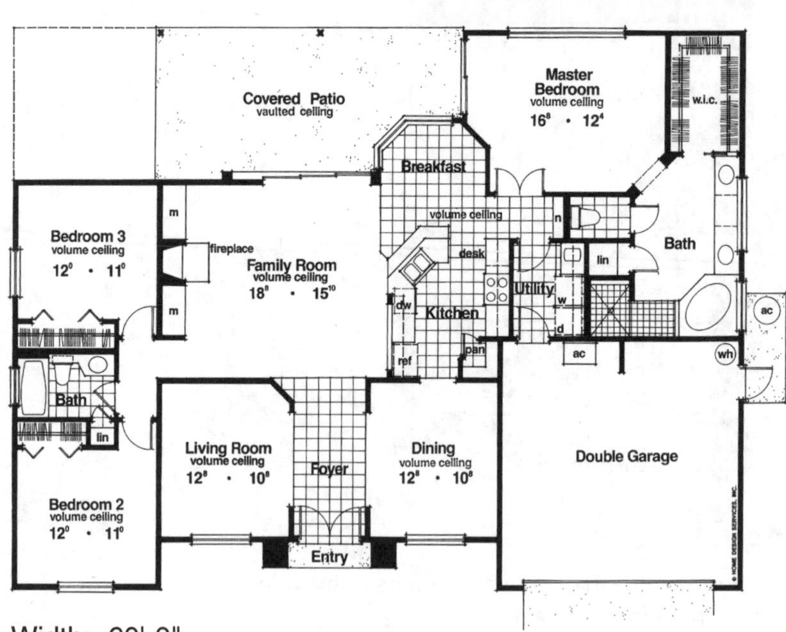

Width: 60'-0"
Depth: 45'-0"

plan #584-065D-0039

price code B

plan information

total living area: 1,794
bedrooms: 3
baths: 2
garage: 2-car side entry
foundation type: walk-out basement

special features

- the great room with sloped ceiling and a fireplace connects with the kitchen and dining area for an open atmosphere
- seating at the snack bar, angled walls and French doors to a covered porch from the dining area create spectacular surroundings
- optional lower level has an additional 1,130 square feet of living area

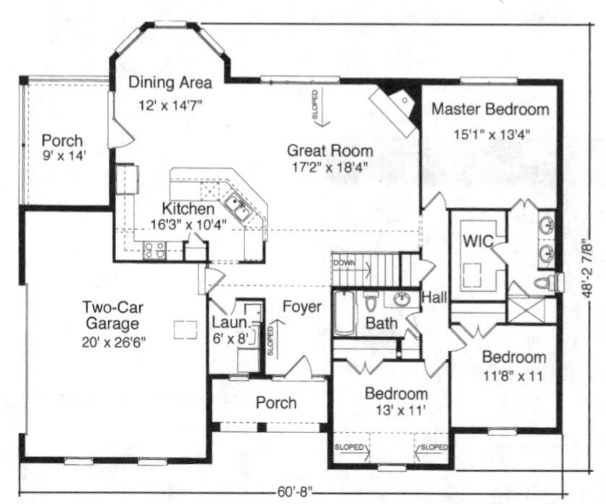

first floor
1,794 sq. ft.

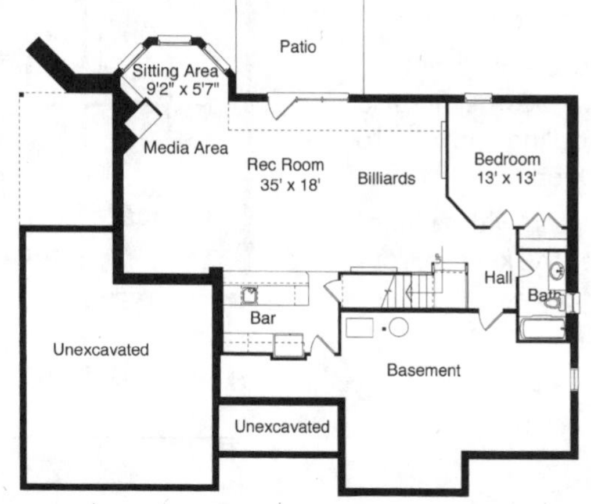

optional
lower level

plan #584-065D-0022

price code B

plan information	
total living area:	1,593
bedrooms:	3
baths:	2
garage:	2-car
foundation type:	basement

special features

- the rear porch is a pleasant surprise and perfect for enjoying the outdoors
- great room is filled with extras like a corner fireplace, sloping ceiling and view to the outdoors
- a large island with seating separates the kitchen from the dining area

plan #584-067D-0004

price code B

plan information

total living area:	1,698
bedrooms:	3
baths:	2 1/2
garage:	2-car side entry

foundation types:

basement
crawl space
slab

please specify when ordering

special features

- vaulted master bedroom has a private bath and a walk-in closet
- decorative columns flank the entrance to the dining room
- open great room is perfect for gathering family together
- extra storage in garage

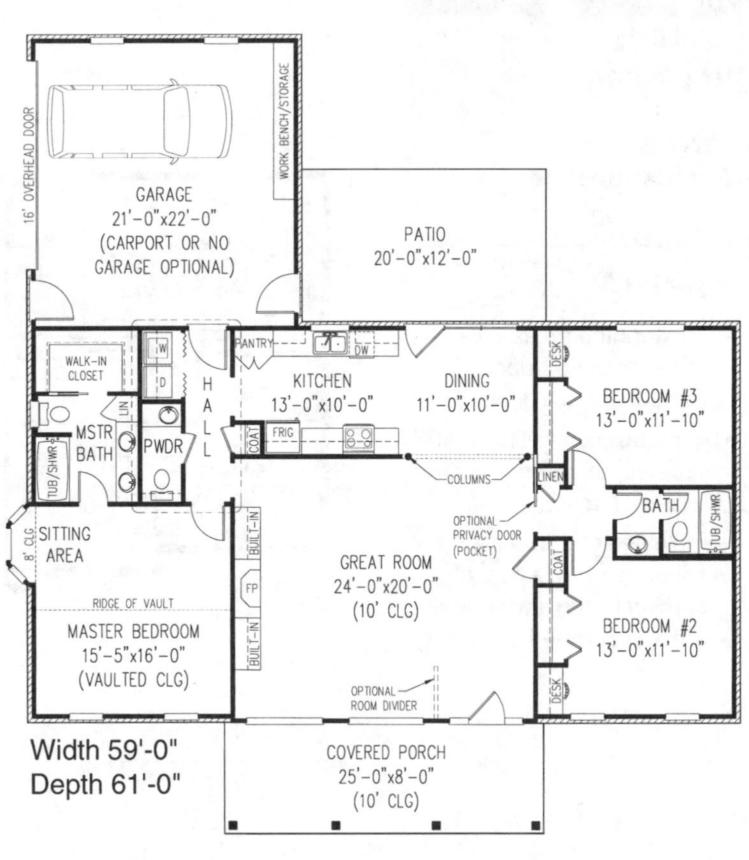

Width 59'-0"
Depth 61'-0"

plan #584-065D-0005

price code B

plan information

total living area:	1,782
bedrooms:	3
baths:	2
garage:	2-car
foundation type:	
basement	

special features

- outstanding breakfast area accesses the outdoors through French doors
- generous counterspace and cabinets combine to create an ideal kitchen
- the master bedroom is enhanced with a beautiful bath featuring a whirlpool tub and double-bowl vanity

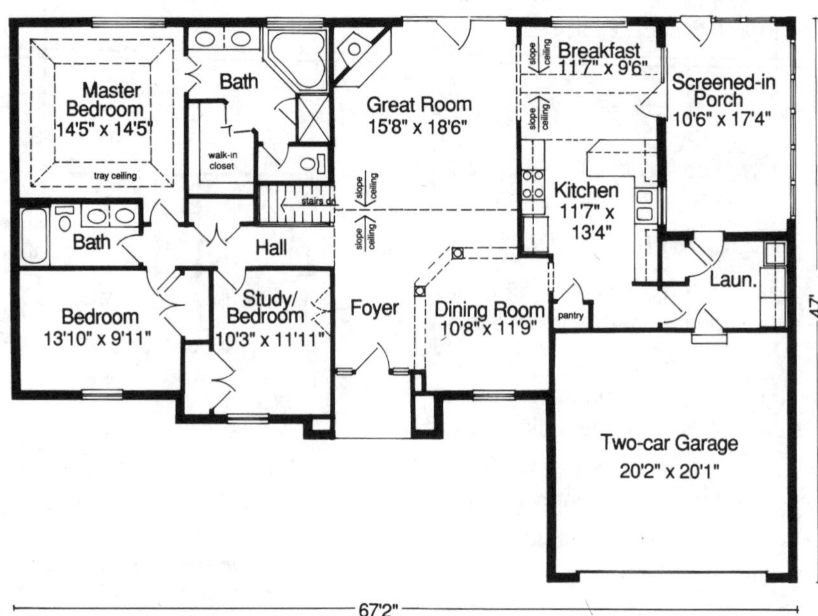

plan #584-069D-0009

price code A

plan information

total living area:	1,409
bedrooms:	3
baths:	2
garage:	2-car
foundation types:	
slab	
crawl space	
please specify when ordering	

special features

- striking fireplace in the living room
- eating bar off kitchen provides extra seating for dining
- large master suite has its own bath

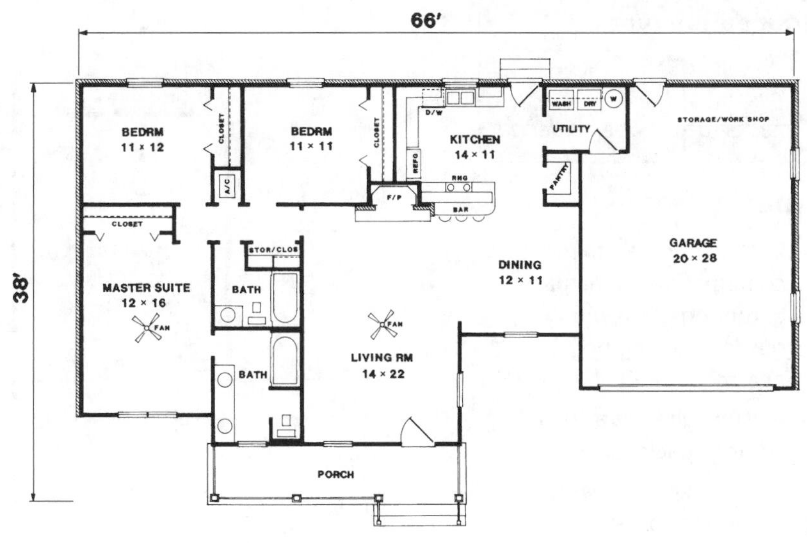

plan #584-055D-0039

price code A

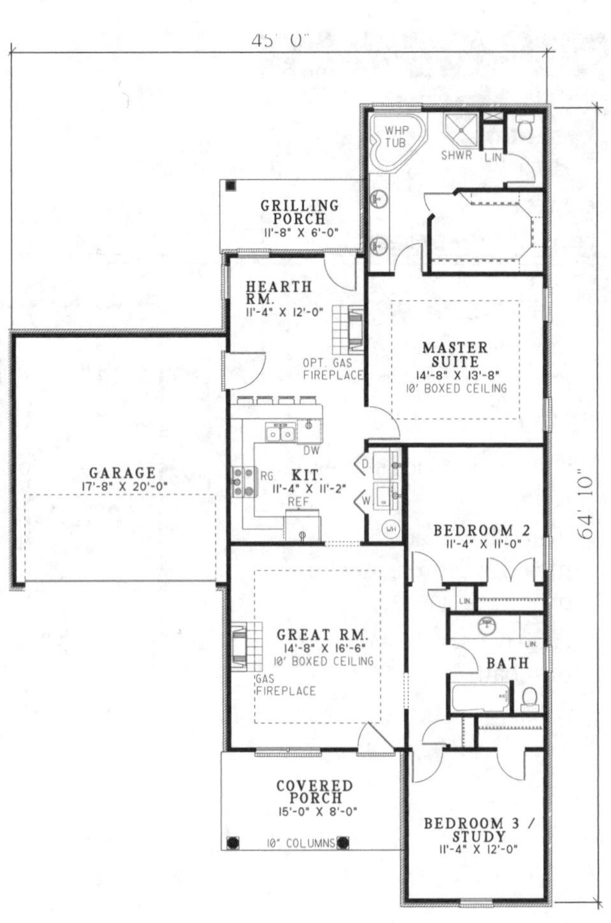

plan information

total living area:	1,425
bedrooms:	3
baths:	2
garage:	2-car
foundation types:	
crawl space	
slab	
please specify when ordering	

special features

- kitchen and hearth room combination is a natural gathering place with outdoor grilling porch nearby
- master suite has a 10' ceiling adding spaciousness
- bedroom #3 can easily be converted to a study

plan #584-035D-0045

price code B

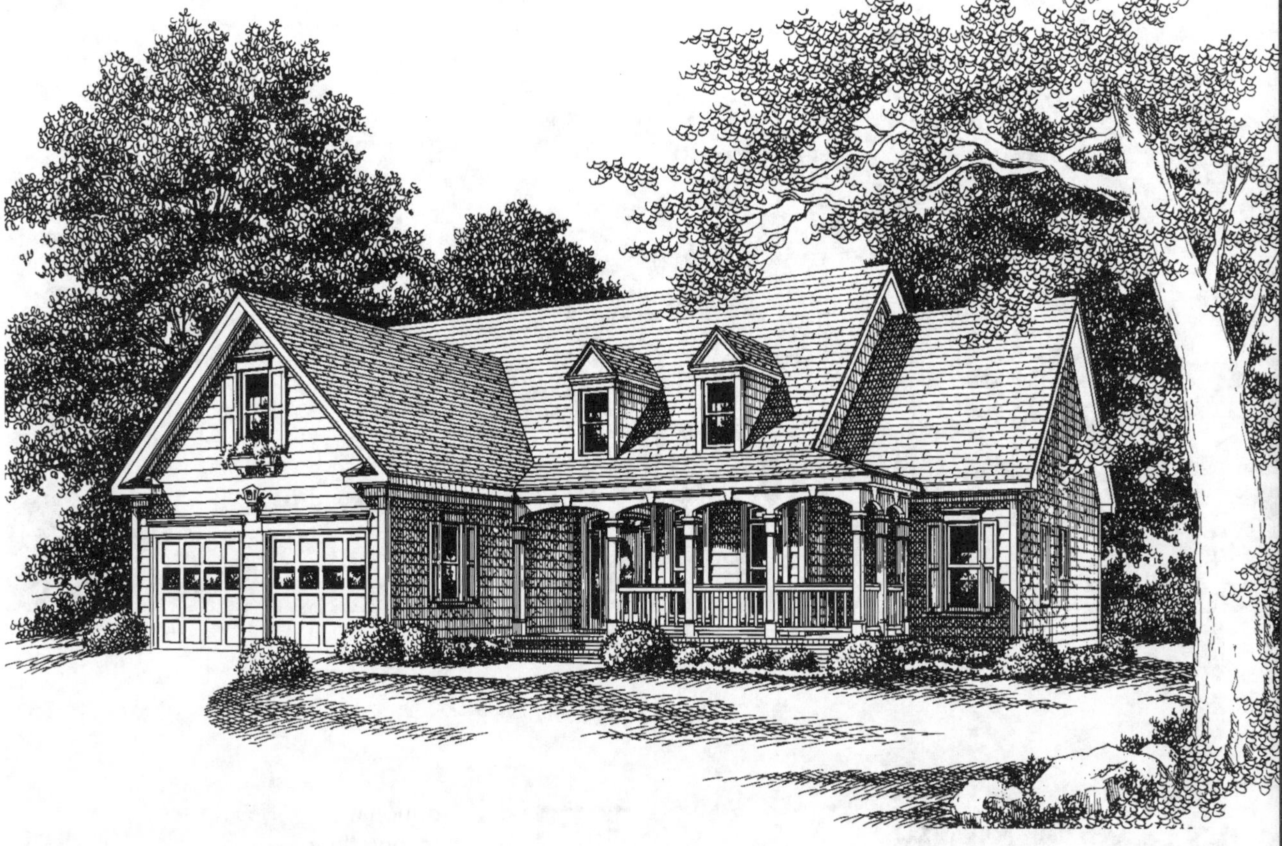

plan information

total living area:	1,749
bedrooms:	3
baths:	2
garage:	2-car
foundation types:	
walk-out basement	
slab	
crawl space	
please specify when ordering	

special features

- tray ceiling in master suite
- a breakfast bar overlooks the vaulted great room
- additional bedrooms are located away from master suite for privacy
- optional bonus room above the garage has an additional 308 square feet of living area

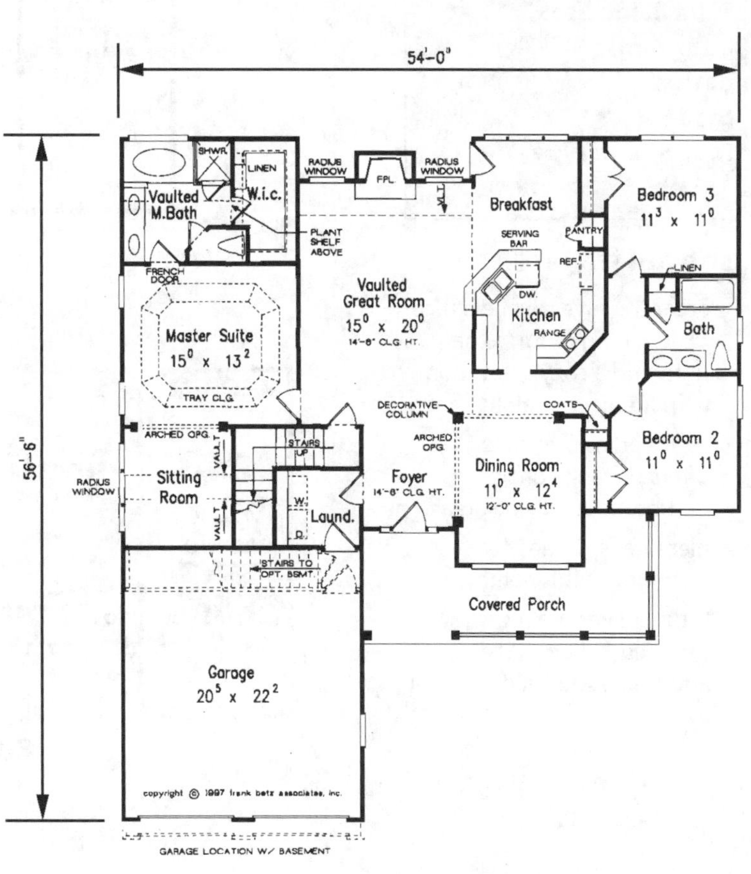

plan #584-025D-0012

price code B

plan information

total living area:	1,634
bedrooms:	3
baths:	2
garage:	2-car
foundation type: slab	

special features

- enter the foyer to find a nice-sized dining room to the right and a cozy great room with fireplace straight ahead
- secluded master suite offers privacy from other bedrooms and living areas
- plenty of storage throughout this home
- future playroom on the second floor has an additional 256 square feet of living area

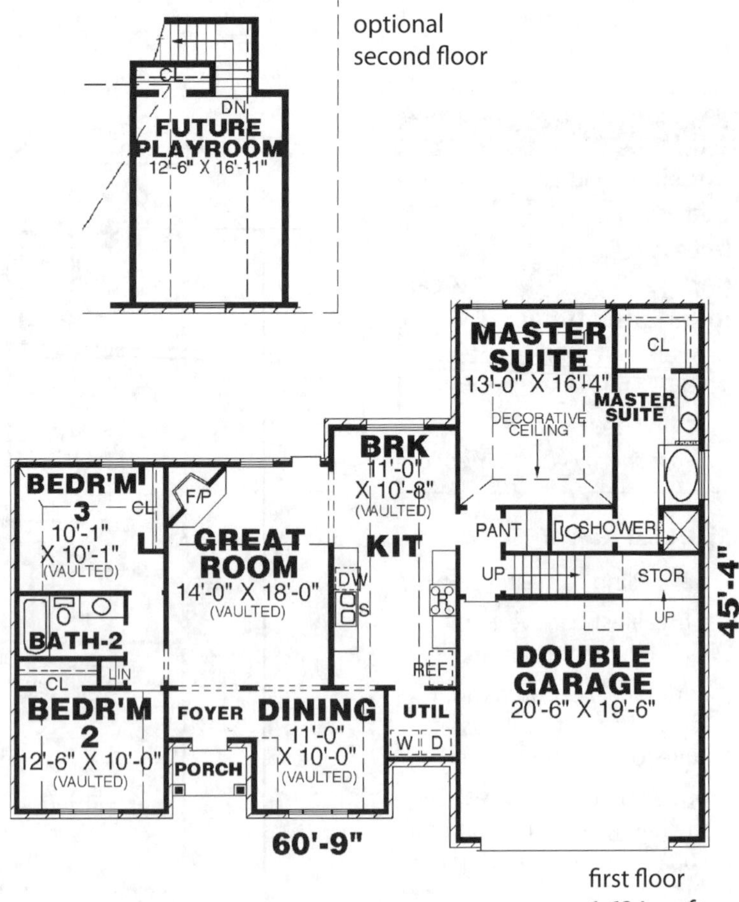

optional second floor

first floor 1,634 sq. ft.

plan information

total living area:	1,097
bedrooms:	3
baths:	2
garage:	optional 2-car side entry

foundation types:
basement
crawl space
slab
please specify when ordering

special features

- a U-shaped kitchen wraps around center island
- master bedroom includes its own private bath and walk-in closet
- living room provides expansive view to the rear

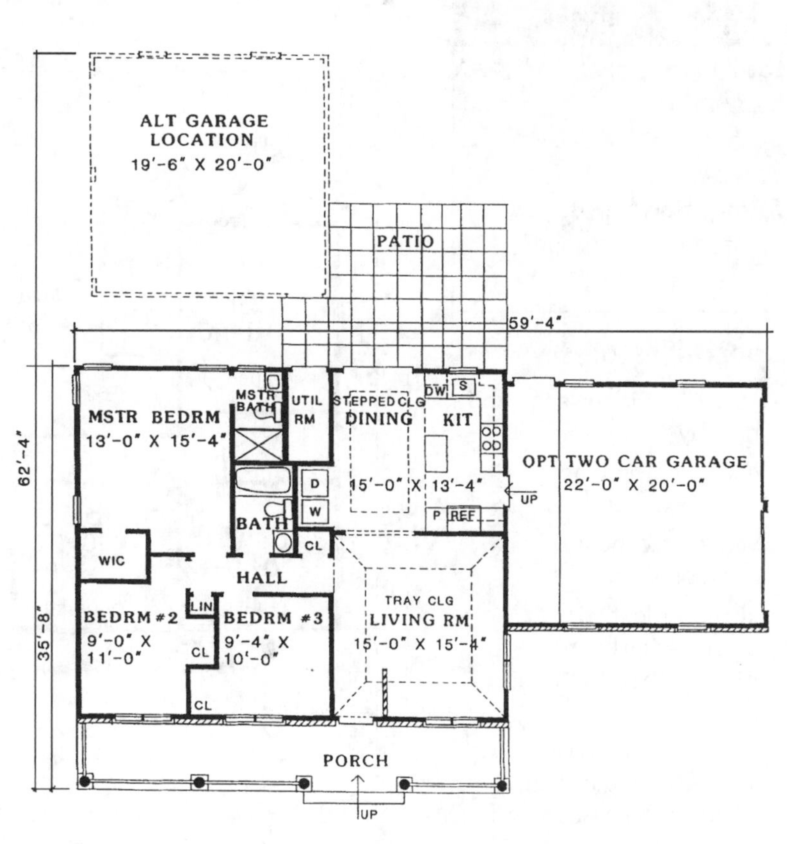

plan #584-014D-0009

price code A

plan information

total living area:	1,428
bedrooms:	3
baths:	2
garage:	2-car
foundation types:	
basement standard	
crawl space	

special features

- 10' ceilings in the entry and hallway
- energy efficient home with 2" x 6" exterior walls
- vaulted secondary bedrooms
- kitchen is loaded with amenities including an island with salad sink and pantry
- master bedroom with vaulted ceiling includes a large walk-in closet and private bath

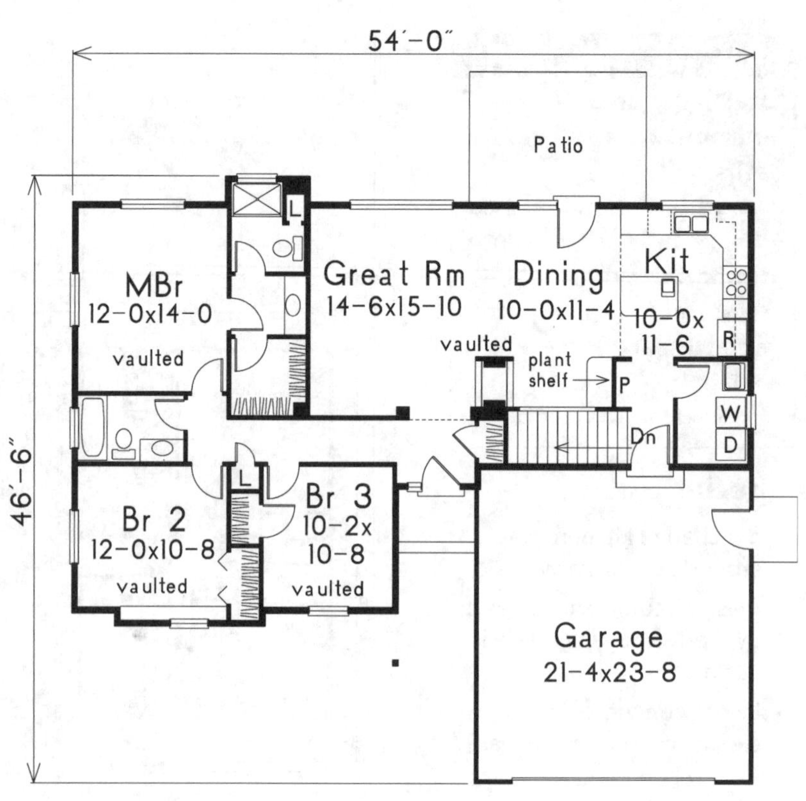

plan #584-008D-0122

price code A

plan information

total living area:	1,364
bedrooms:	3
baths:	2
garage:	2-car
foundation types:	
basement standard	
crawl space	
slab	

special features

- a large porch and entry door with sidelights lead into a generous living room
- well-planned U-shaped kitchen features a laundry closet, built-in pantry and open peninsula
- master bedroom has its own bath with 4' shower
- convenient to the kitchen is an oversized two-car garage with service door to rear

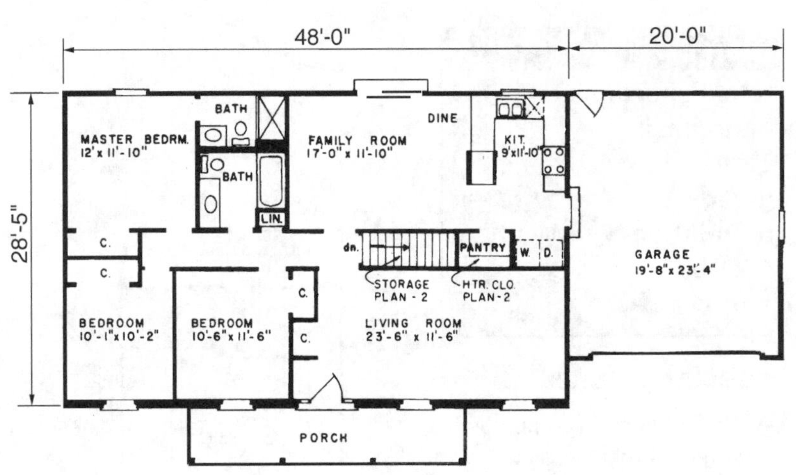

plan #584-018D-0006

price code B

plan information	
total living area:	1,742
bedrooms:	3
baths:	2
garage:	2-car
foundation types:	
slab standard	
crawl space	

special features

- efficient kitchen combines with the breakfast area and great room creating a spacious living area
- master bedroom includes a private bath with huge walk-in closet, shower and corner tub
- great room boasts a fireplace and access outdoors
- laundry room is conveniently located near the kitchen and garage

plan #584-016D-0037

price code B

plan information

total living area:	1,615
bedrooms:	3
baths:	2
garage:	2-car
foundation types:	
basement	
slab	
crawl space	
please specify when ordering	

special features

- master bedroom includes walk-in closet, spacious private bath with double vanity and a sloped ceiling with skylight
- family room has space for built-ins adjacent to the fireplace
- living and dining rooms are open to each other

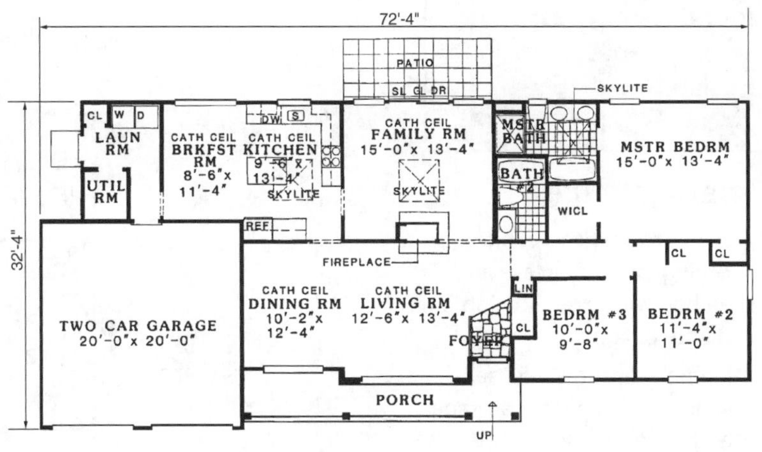

plan #584-006D-0001

price code B

plan information

total living area: 1,643
bedrooms: 3
baths: 2
garage: 2-car side entry
foundation types:
basement standard
slab
crawl space

special features

- family room has a vaulted ceiling, open staircase and arched windows allowing for plenty of light
- kitchen captures full use of space, with a pantry, storage, ample counterspace and work island
- roomy master bath has a skylight for natural lighting plus a separate tub and shower
- rear of house provides ideal location for future screened-in porch

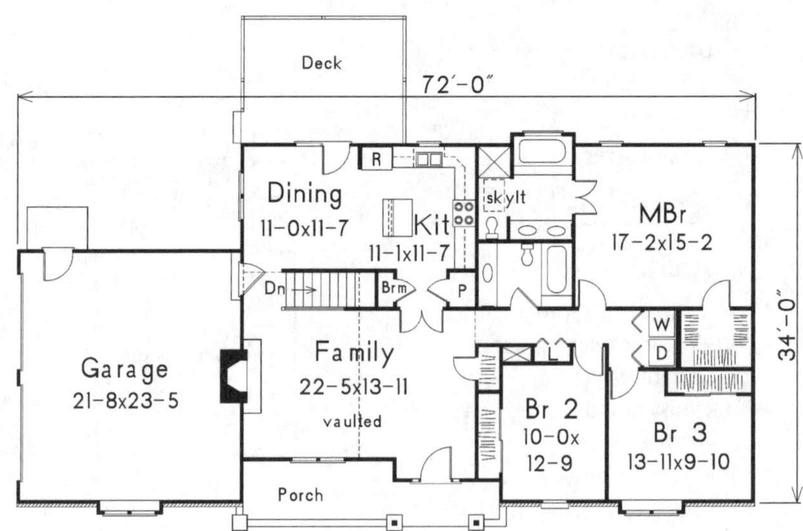

plan #584-020D-0002

price code A

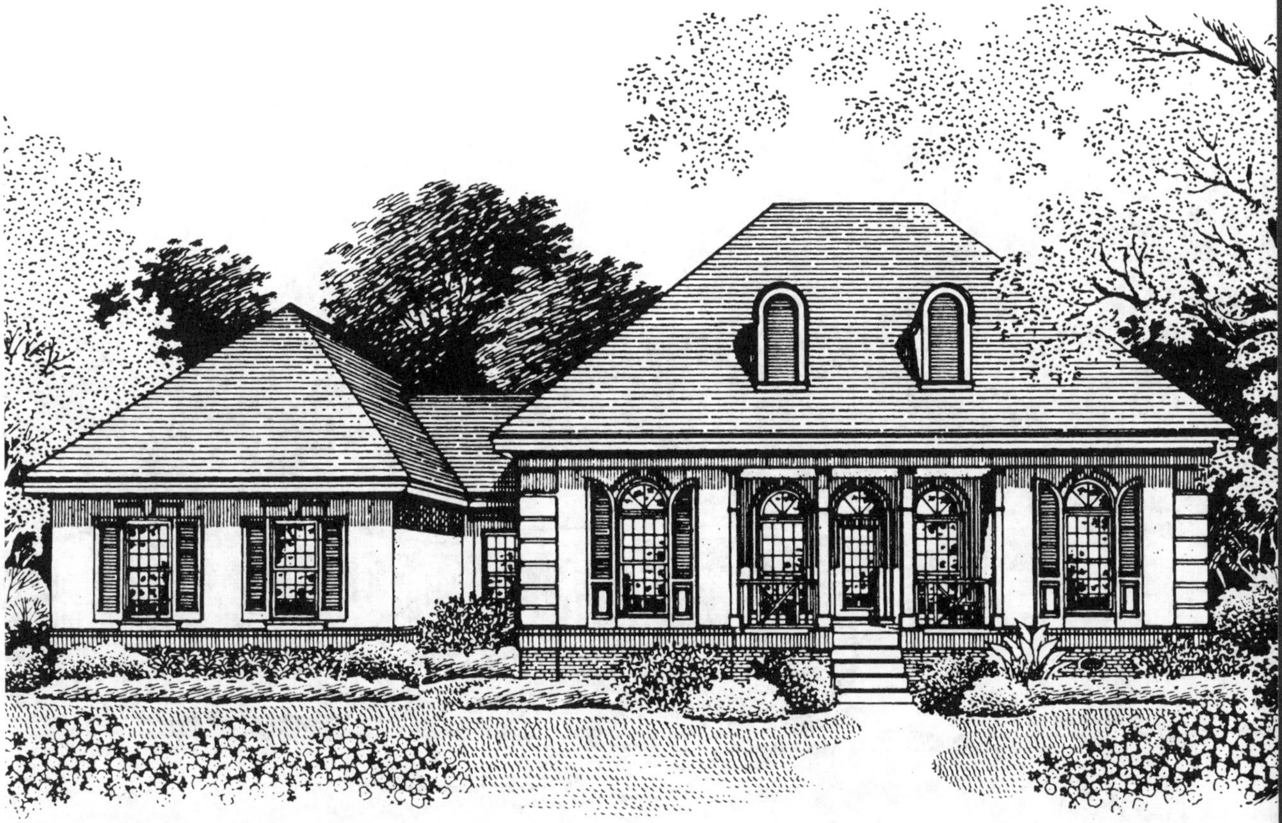

plan information

total living area:	1,434
bedrooms:	3
baths:	2
garage:	2-car side entry
foundation types:	
crawl space standard	
slab	

special features

- isolated master suite for privacy includes walk-in closet and bath
- elegant formal dining room
- efficient kitchen has an adjacent dining area which includes shelves and access to laundry facilities
- extra storage in garage

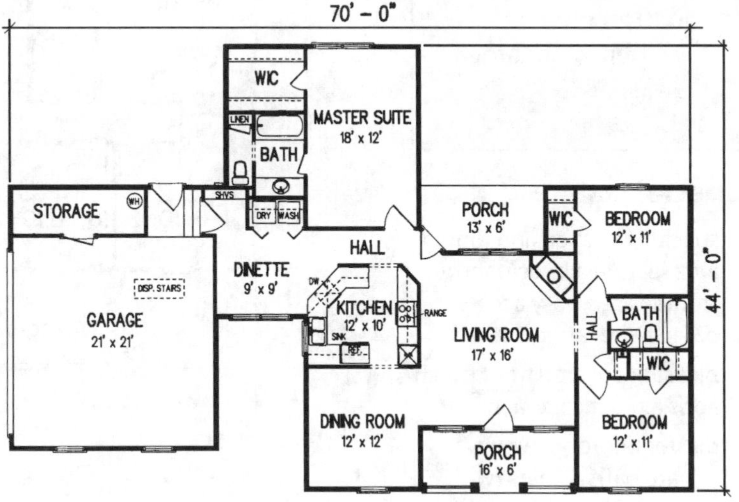

plan #584-001D-0029

price code A

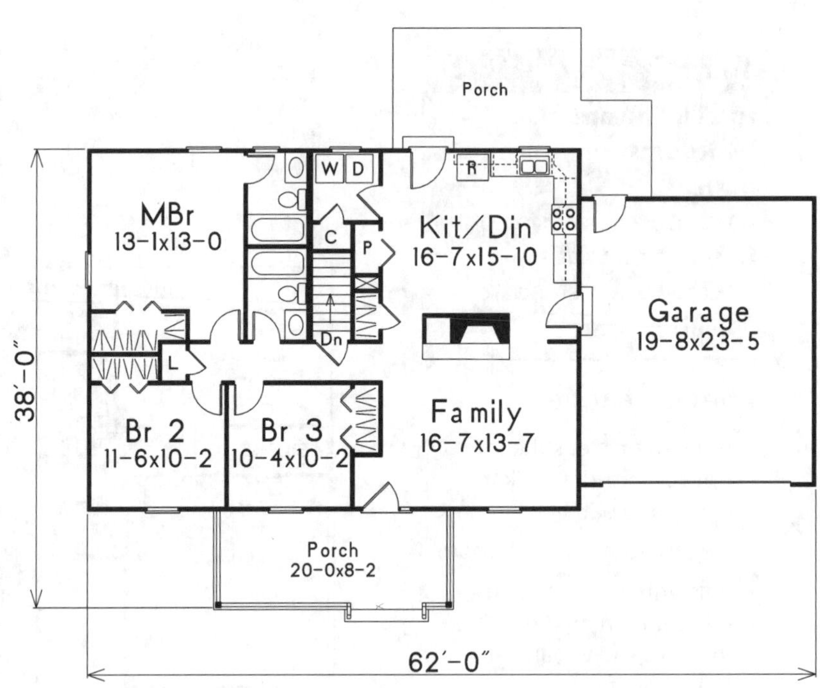

plan information

total living area:	1,260
bedrooms:	3
baths:	2
garage:	2-car
foundation types:	
basement standard	
crawl space	
slab	

special features

- spacious kitchen and dining area feature a large pantry, storage area, easy access to garage and laundry room
- pleasant covered front porch adds a practical touch
- master bedroom with a private bath adjoins two other bedrooms, all with plenty of closet space

plan #584-001D-0048

price code A

plan information

total living area:	1,400
bedrooms:	3
baths:	2
garage:	2-car
foundation types:	
crawl space standard	
basement	
slab	

special features

- front porch offers warmth and welcome
- large great room opens into dining room creating an open living atmosphere
- kitchen features convenient laundry area, pantry and breakfast bar

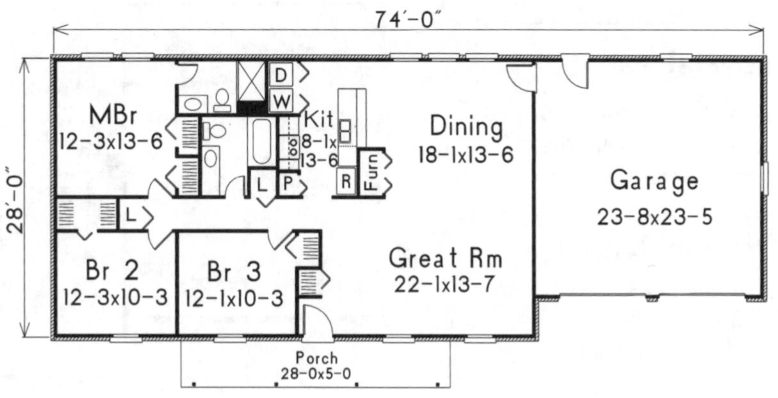

plan #584-058D-0021

price code A

plan information

total living area:	1,477
bedrooms:	3
baths:	2
garage:	2-car side entry
foundation type: basement	

special features

- oversized porch provides protection from the elements
- innovative kitchen employs step-saving design
- kitchen has snack bar which opens to the breakfast room with bay window
- extra storage in garage

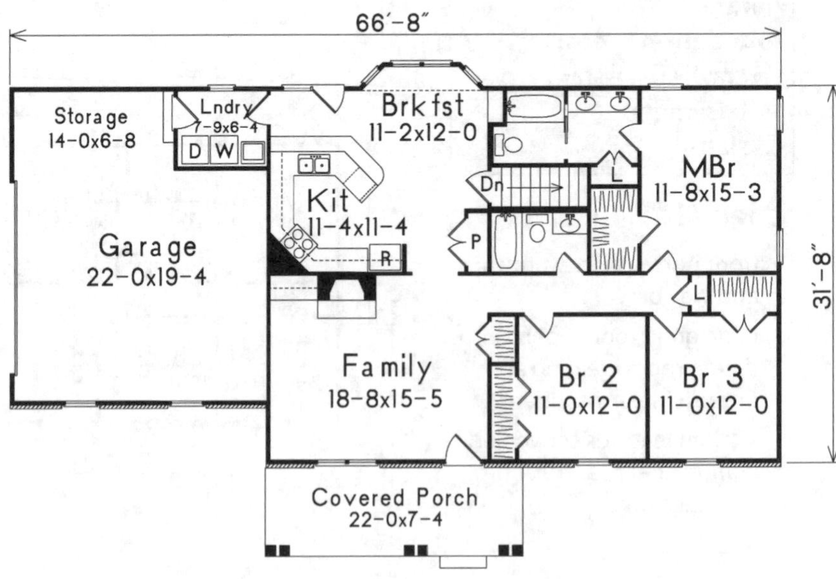

plan information

total living area:	1,756
bedrooms:	3
baths:	2
garage:	2-car
foundation type:	
basement	

special features

- kitchen features a wrap-around counter with eating bar that opens to dining room
- the family room boasts a 10' ceiling, fireplace and decorative columns leading to the dining room
- double-doors lead to the relaxing master bedroom which enjoys a large walk-in closet and private bath

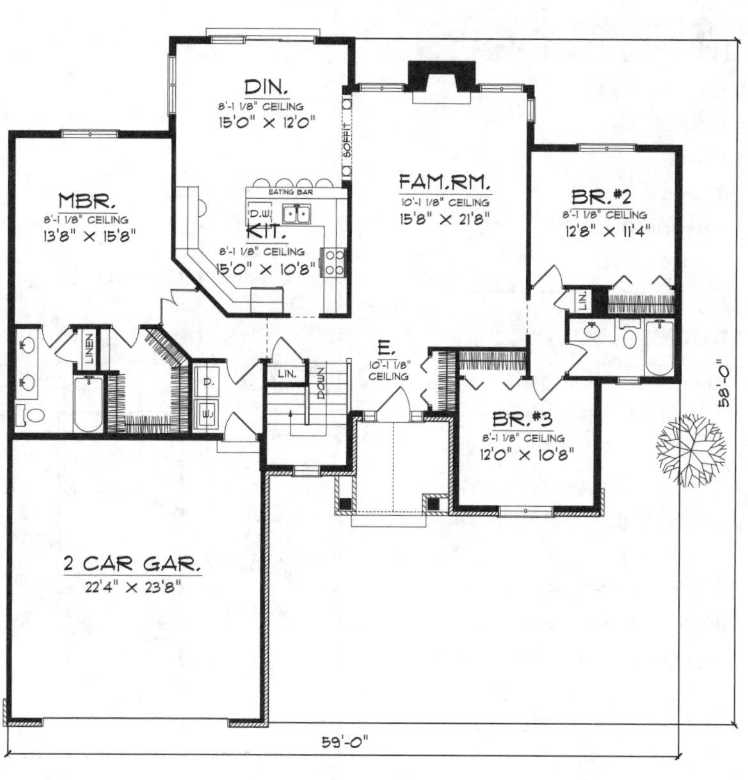

plan #584-045D-0009

price code B

plan information

total living area:	1,684
bedrooms:	3
baths:	2 1/2
garage:	2-car
foundation type:	
basement	

special features

- the bayed dining area boasts convenient double-door access onto the large deck
- the family room features several large windows for brightness
- bedrooms are separate from living areas for privacy
- master bedroom offers a bath with walk-in closet, double-bowl vanity and both a shower and a whirlpool tub

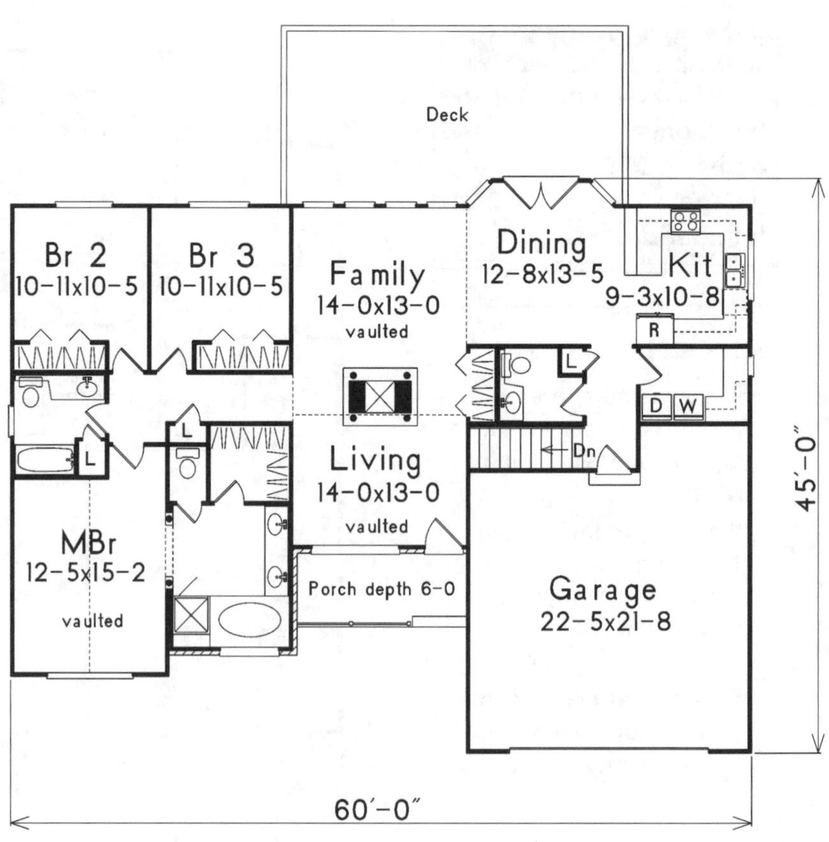

plan #584-016D-0049

price code B

plan information	
total living area:	1,793
bedrooms:	3
baths:	2
garage:	2-car side entry
foundation types:	
basement	
crawl space	
slab	
please specify when ordering	

special features

- beautiful foyer leads into the great room that has a fireplace flanked by two sets of beautifully transomed doors both leading to a large covered porch
- eat-in kitchen has lots of cabinets and workspace in an exciting angled shape
- delightful master bedroom has many amenities
- optional bonus room above the garage has an additional 779 square feet of living area

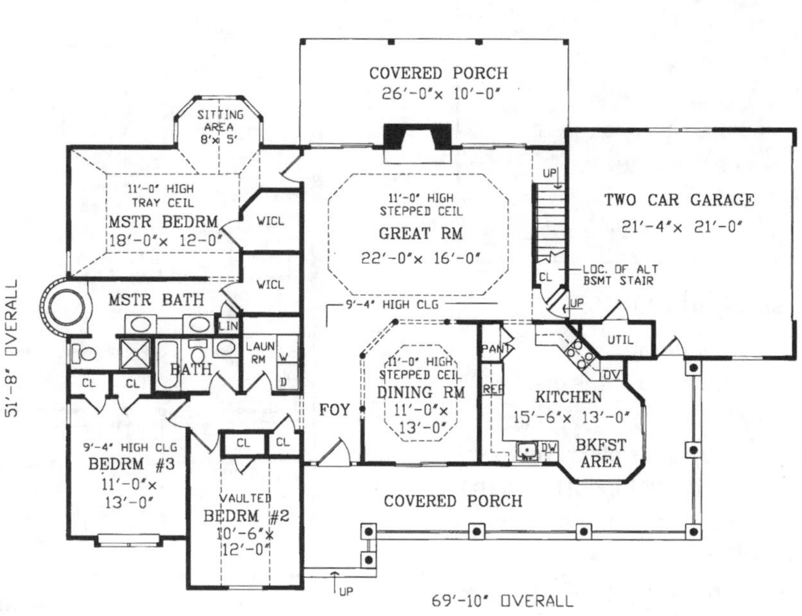

plan #584-055D-0017

price code B

plan information	
total living area:	1,525
bedrooms:	3
baths:	2
garage:	2-car
foundation types:	
basement	
walk-out basement	
crawl space	
slab	
please specify when ordering	

special features

- corner fireplace is highlighted in the great room
- unique glass block window over the whirlpool tub in the master bath brightens the interior
- open bar overlooks both the kitchen and great room
- breakfast room leads to an outdoor grilling and covered porch

plan #584-003D-0005

price code B

plan information

total living area:	1,708
bedrooms:	3
baths:	2
garage:	2-car
foundation types:	
basement standard	
crawl space	

special features

- massive family room is enhanced with several windows, a fireplace and access to the porch
- deluxe master bath is accented by a step-up corner tub flanked by double vanities
- closets throughout maintain organized living
- bedrooms are isolated from living areas

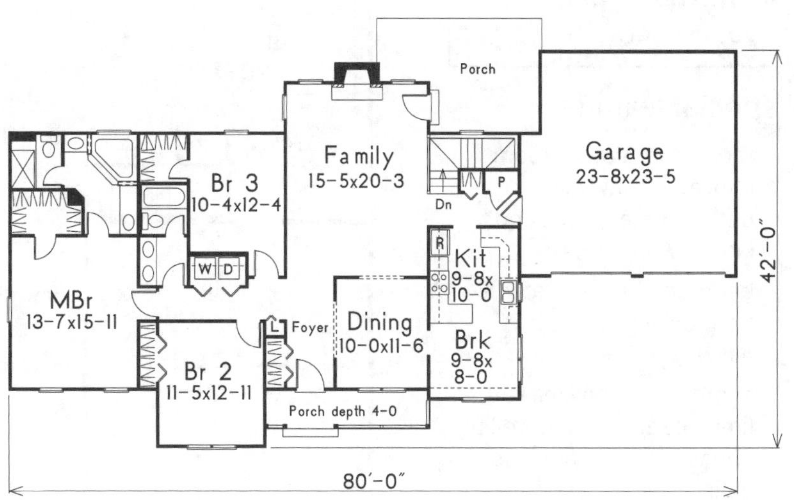

plan #584-058D-0016

price code B

plan information

total living area:	1,558
bedrooms:	3
baths:	2
garage:	2-car
foundation type: basement	

special features

- the spacious utility room is located conveniently between the garage and kitchen/dining area
- bedrooms are separated from the living area by hallway
- enormous living area with fireplace and vaulted ceiling opens to the kitchen and dining area
- master bedroom is enhanced with a large bay window, walk-in closet and private bath

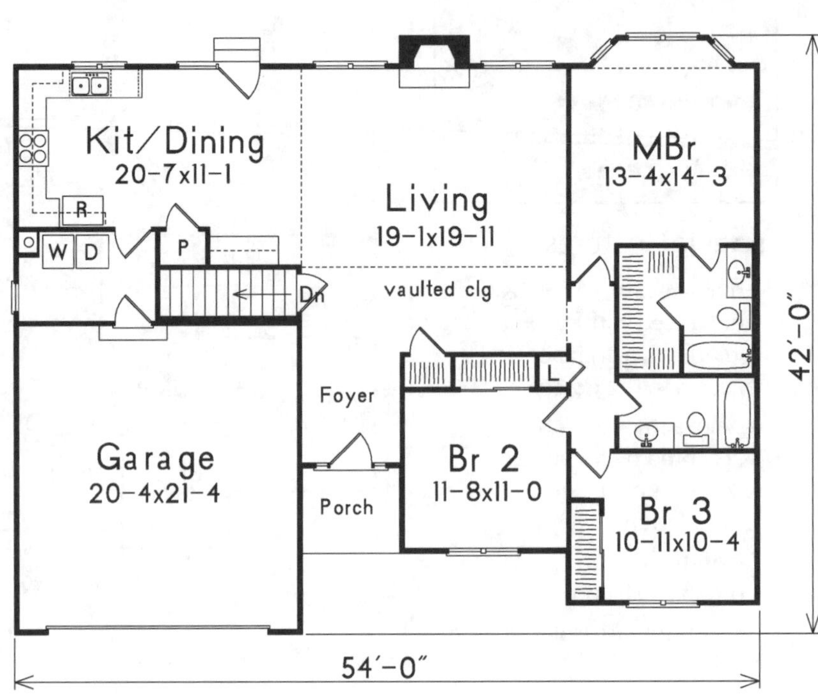

plan #584-022D-0019

price code A

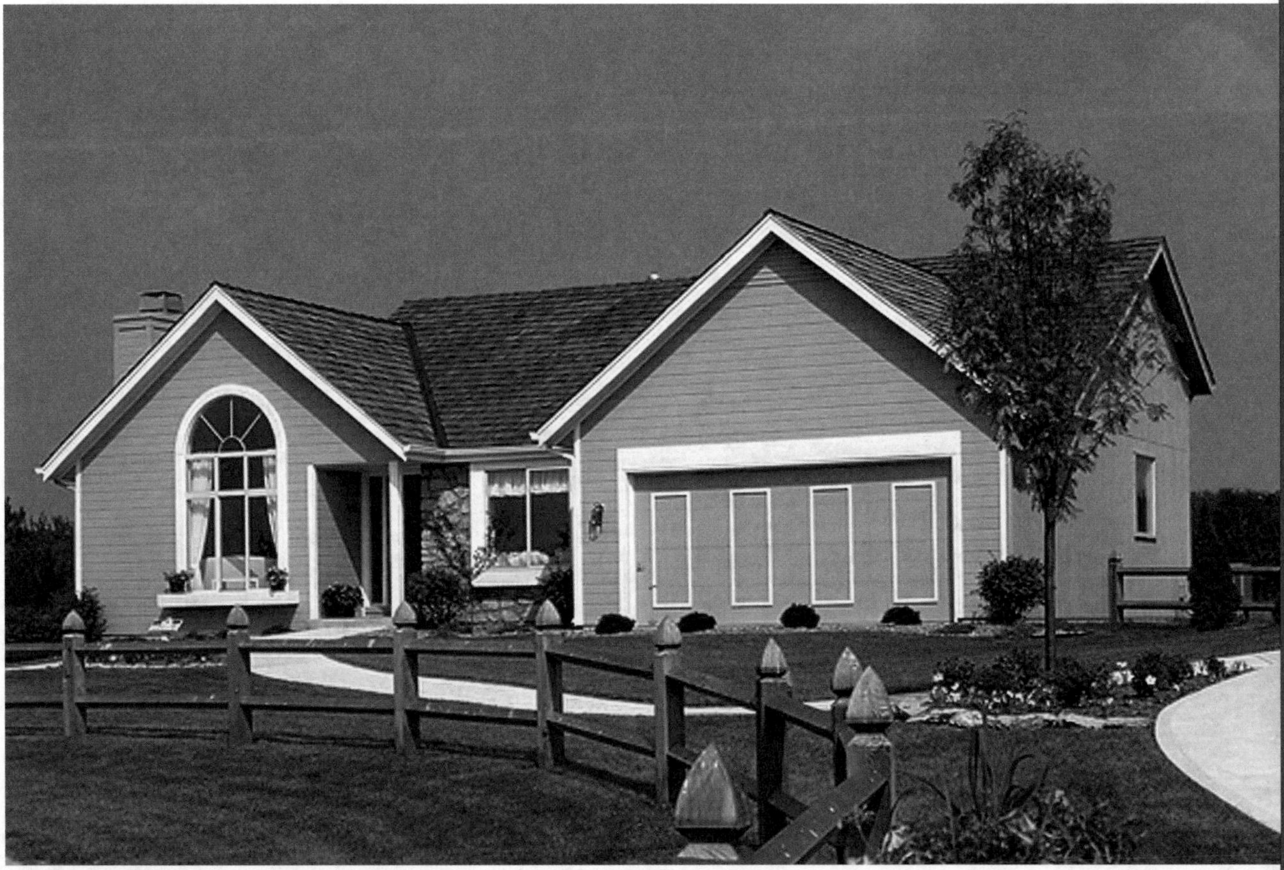

plan information	
total living area:	1,283
bedrooms:	3
baths:	2
garage:	2-car
foundation type: basement	

special features

- vaulted breakfast room has sliding doors that open onto deck
- kitchen features convenient corner sink and pass-through to dining room
- open living atmosphere in dining area and great room
- vaulted great room features a fireplace

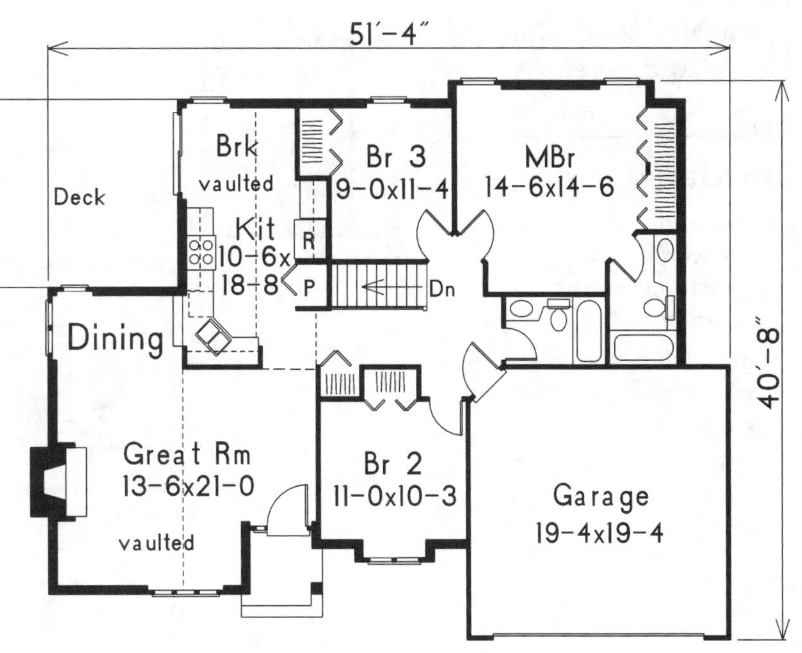

plan #584-025D-0010 price code B

plan information

total living area:	1,677
bedrooms:	3
baths:	2
garage:	2-car side entry
foundation type:	slab

special features

- master suite has a secluded feel with a private and remote location from other bedrooms
- great room is complete with fireplace and beautiful windows
- optional second floor has an additional 350 square feet of living area

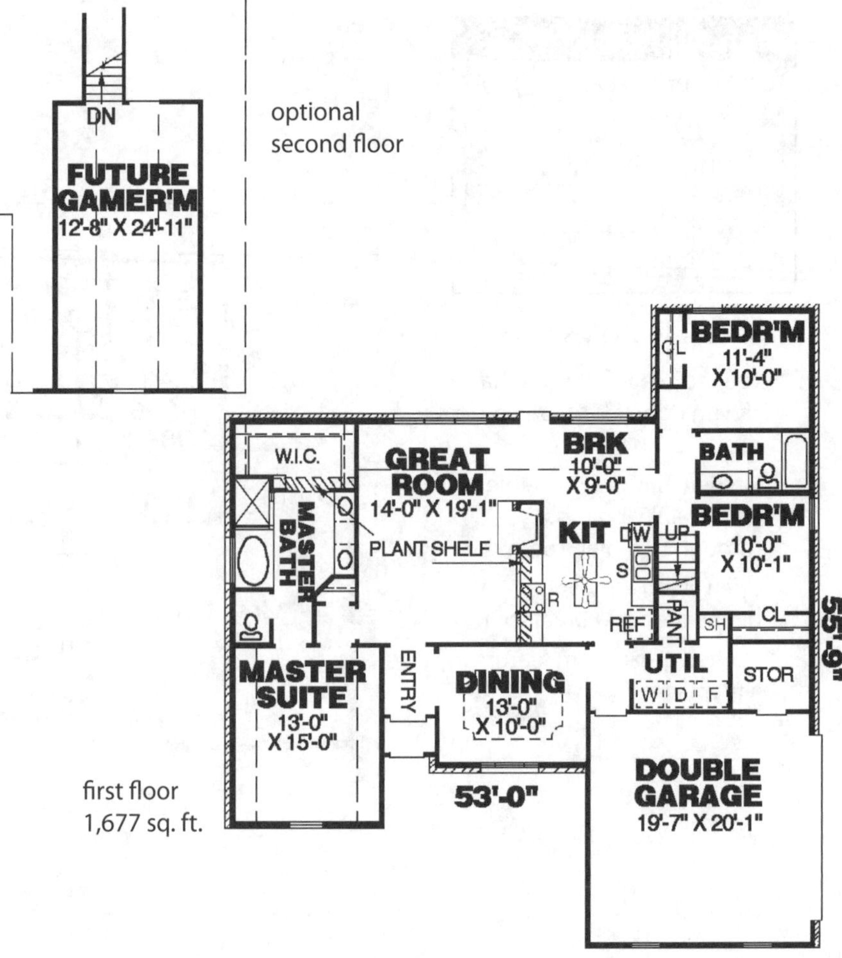

optional second floor

first floor 1,677 sq. ft.

plan #584-065D-0035

price code B

plan information

total living area:	1,798
bedrooms:	3
baths:	2
garage:	2-car
foundation type:	
basement	

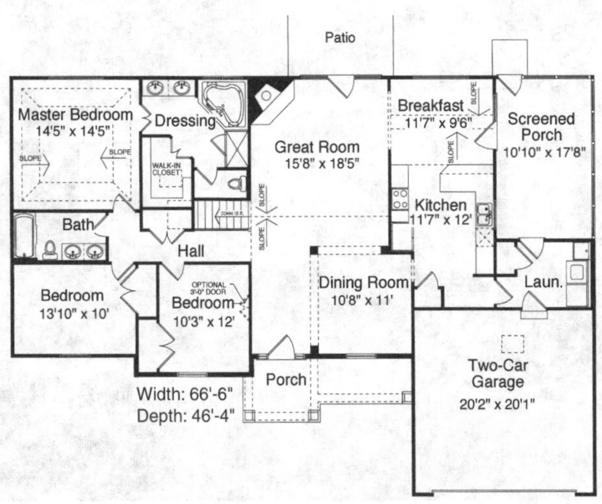

special features

- the expansive great room enjoys a fireplace and has access onto the rear patio
- the centrally located kitchen is easily accessible to the dining room and breakfast area
- the master bedroom boasts a sloped ceiling and deluxe bath with a corner whirlpool tub and large walk-in closet
- a screened porch offers relaxing outdoor living

---

plan #584-008D-0045

price code B

plan information

total living area:	1,540
bedrooms:	3
baths:	2
garage:	2-car
foundation types:	
basement standard	
crawl space	
slab	

special features

- porch entrance into foyer leads to an impressive dining area with full window and a half-circle window above
- kitchen/breakfast room features a center island and cathedral ceiling
- great room with cathedral ceiling and exposed beams is accessible from the foyer
- master bedroom includes a full bath and walk-in closet
- two additional bedrooms share a full bath

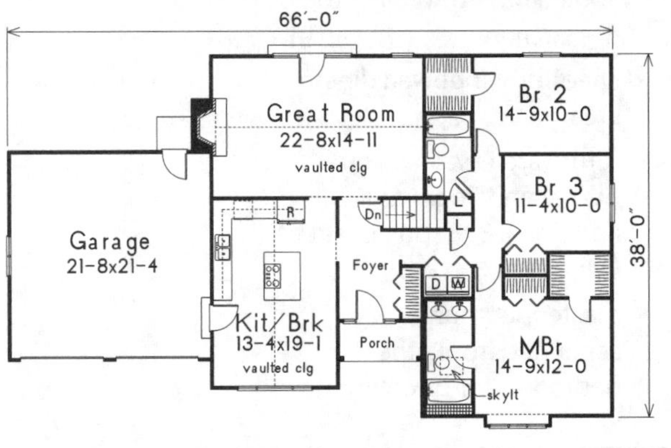

plan #584-017D-0007

price code C

plan information	
total living area:	1,567
bedrooms:	3
baths:	2
garage:	2-car side entry
foundation types:	
partial basement/crawl space - standard	
slab	

special features

- living room flows into the dining room shaped by an angled pass-through into the kitchen
- cheerful, windowed dining area
- future area available on the second floor has an additional 338 square feet of living area
- master bedroom is separated from other bedrooms for privacy

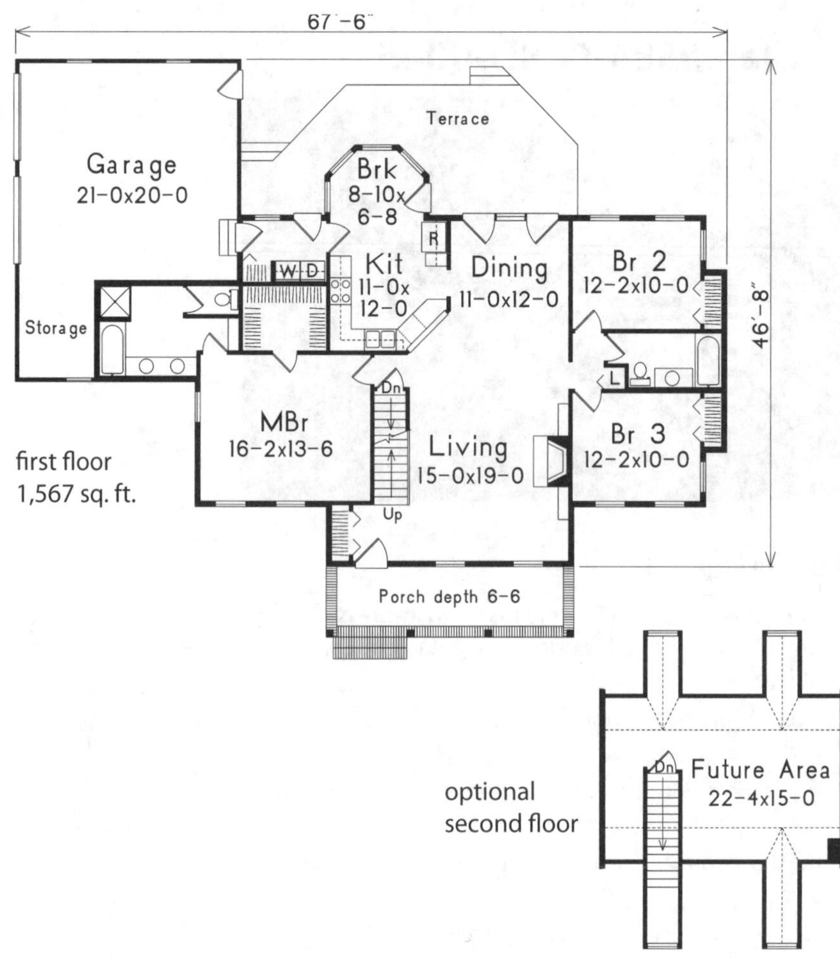

first floor
1,567 sq. ft.

optional
second floor

plan #584-001D-0067

price code B

plan information	
total living area:	1,285
bedrooms:	3
baths:	2
foundation types:	
crawl space standard	
basement	
slab	

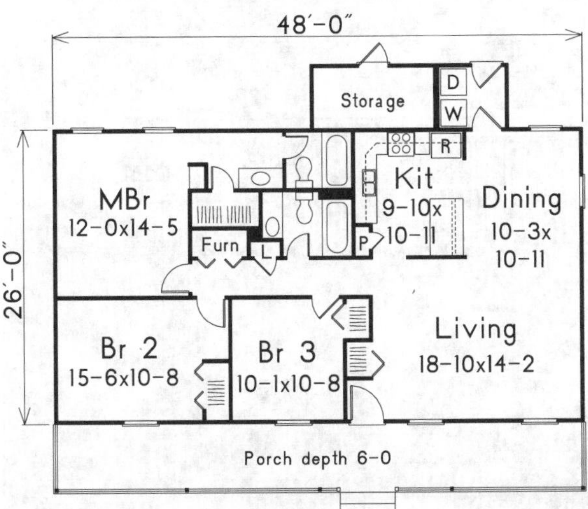

special features

- accommodating home with ranch-style porch
- large storage area on back of home
- master bedroom includes dressing area, private bath and built-in bookcase
- kitchen features pantry, breakfast bar and complete view to the dining room

---

plan #584-033D-0012

price code C

plan information	
total living area:	1,546
bedrooms:	3
baths:	2
garage:	2-car
foundation type:	
basement	

special features

- spacious, open rooms create a casual atmosphere
- master bedroom is secluded for privacy
- dining room features a large bay window
- kitchen and dinette combine for added space and include access to the outdoors
- large laundry room includes a convenient sink

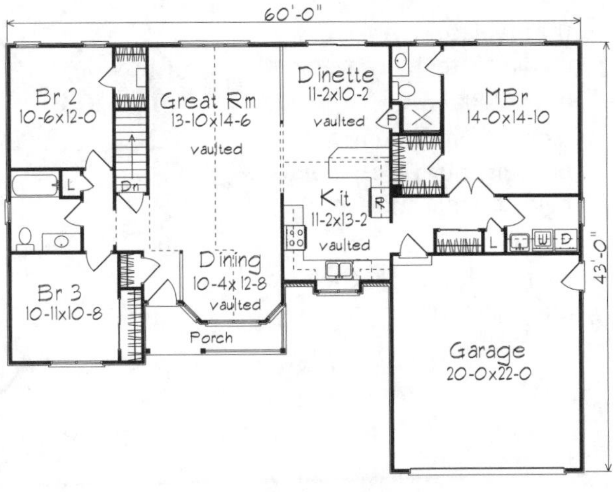

plan #584-016D-0057

price code C

plan information

total living area:	1,709
bedrooms:	3
baths:	2 1/2
garage:	2-car side entry
foundation types:	
basement	
crawl space	
slab	
please specify when ordering	

special features

- the fireplace is flanked by a media center for convenient relaxation
- dining room features a beautiful built-in cabinet to hold fine collectibles and china
- centrally located kitchen is a great gathering place

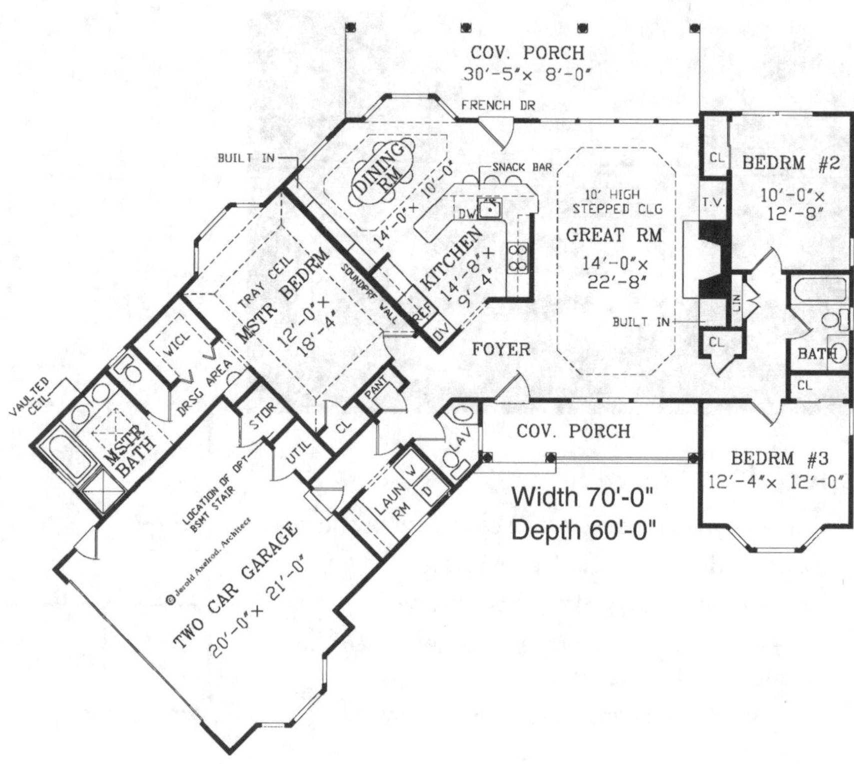

plan #584-007D-0049

price code C

plan information

total living area:	1,791
bedrooms:	4
baths:	2
garage:	2-car
foundation types:	
basement standard	
crawl space	
slab	

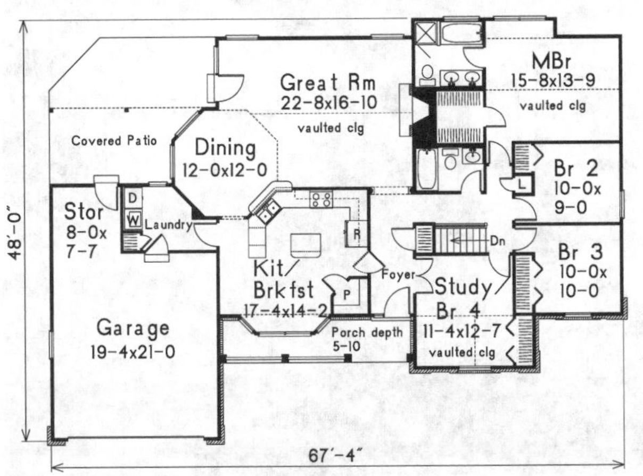

special features

- vaulted great room and octagon-shaped dining area enjoy the view of the covered patio
- kitchen features a pass-through to dining area, center island, large walk-in pantry and breakfast room with large bay window
- master bedroom is vaulted with sitting area
- extra storage in garage

plan #584-007D-0067

price code B

plan information

total living area:	1,761
bedrooms:	4
baths:	2
garage:	2-car side entry
foundation type:	
basement	

special features

- exterior window dressing, roof dormers and planter boxes provide visual warmth and charm
- great room boasts a vaulted ceiling, fireplace and opens to a pass-through kitchen
- the vaulted master bedroom includes a luxury bath and walk-in closet
- home features eight separate closets with an abundance of storage

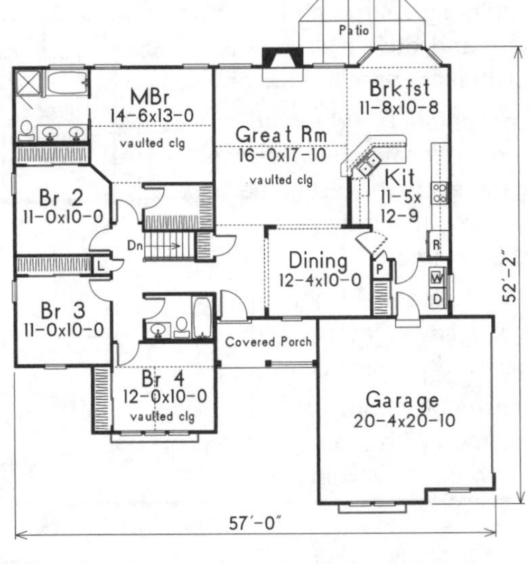

plan #584-006D-0003

price code B

plan information	
total living area:	1,674
bedrooms:	3
baths:	2
garage:	2-car
foundation types:	
basement standard	
crawl space	
slab	

special features

- vaulted great room, dining area and kitchen all enjoy a central fireplace and log bin
- convenient laundry/mud room is located between the garage and the rest of the home with handy stairs to the basement
- easily expandable screened porch and adjacent patio access the dining area
- master bedroom features a full bath with tub, separate shower and walk-in closet

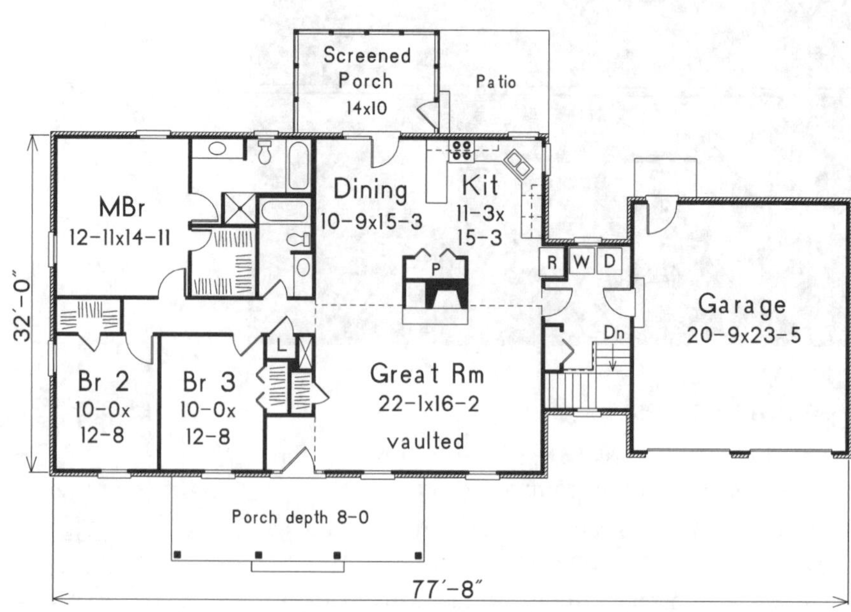

plan #584-048D-0011

price code B

plan information

total living area:	1,550
bedrooms:	3
baths:	2
garage:	2-car
foundation type:	
slab	

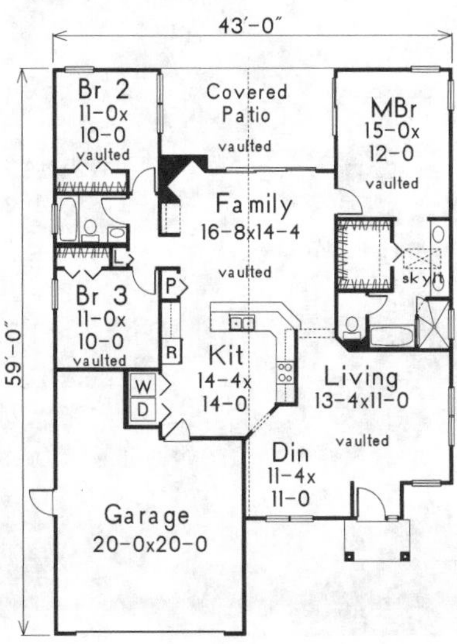

special features

- alcove in the family room can be used as a cozy corner fireplace or as a media center
- master bedroom features a large walk-in closet, skylight and separate tub and shower
- convenient laundry closet
- kitchen with pantry and breakfast bar connects to the family room
- family room and master bedroom access the covered patio

---

plan #584-001D-0024

price code A

plan information

total living area:	1,360
bedrooms:	3
baths:	2
garage:	2-car side entry
foundation types:	
basement standard	
crawl space	
slab	

68'-0"
30'-0"
Patio
Garage
22-4x23-5
Kit/Din
17-6x14-6
D
W
MBr
12-9x14-6
P
Dn
L
Family
17-6x14-7
Br 3
12-1x11-3
Br 2
12-2x11-3
workshop
10-8x6-0
Covered Porch
23-0x8-0

special features

- kitchen/dining room features island workspace and plenty of dining area
- master bedroom has a large walk-in closet and private bath
- laundry room is adjacent to the kitchen for easy access
- convenient workshop in garage
- large closets in secondary bedrooms

plan #584-005D-0001

price code B

plan information

total living area:	1,400
bedrooms:	3
baths:	2
garage:	2-car
foundation types:	
basement standard	
crawl space	

special features

- master bedroom is secluded for privacy
- large utility room has additional cabinet space
- covered porch provides an outdoor seating area
- roof dormers add great curb appeal
- living room and master bedroom feature vaulted ceilings
- oversized two-car garage has storage space

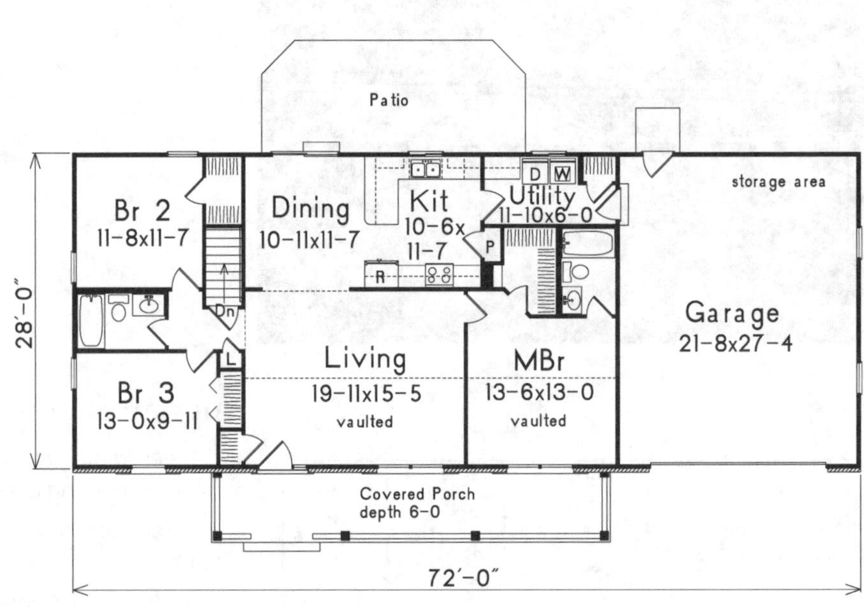

plan #584-053D-0029

price code A

plan information	
total living area:	1,220
bedrooms:	3
baths:	2
garage:	2-car drive under
foundation type: basement	

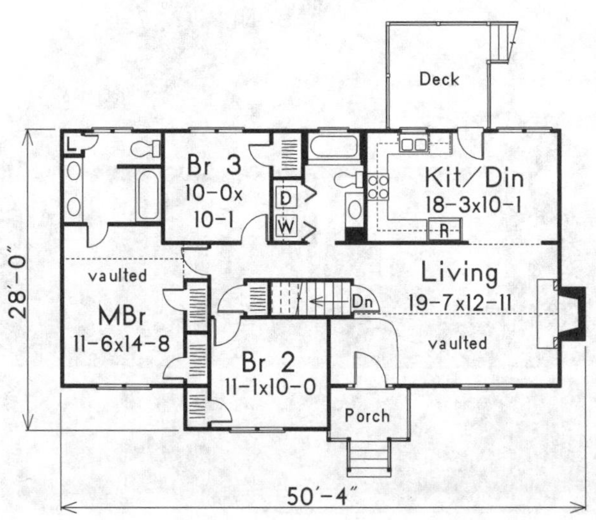

special features

- vaulted ceilings add luxury to the living room and master bedroom
- spacious living room is accented with a large fireplace and hearth
- gracious dining area is adjacent to the convenient wrap-around kitchen
- washer and dryer are handy to the bedrooms
- covered porch entry adds appeal
- rear deck adjoins dining area

---

plan #584-007D-0046

price code B

plan information	
total living area:	1,712
bedrooms:	3
baths:	2 1/2
garage:	2-car
foundation type: crawl space	

special features

- stylish stucco exterior enhances curb appeal
- sunken great room offers corner fireplace flanked by 9' wide patio doors
- well-designed kitchen features ideal view of the great room and fireplace through breakfast bar opening

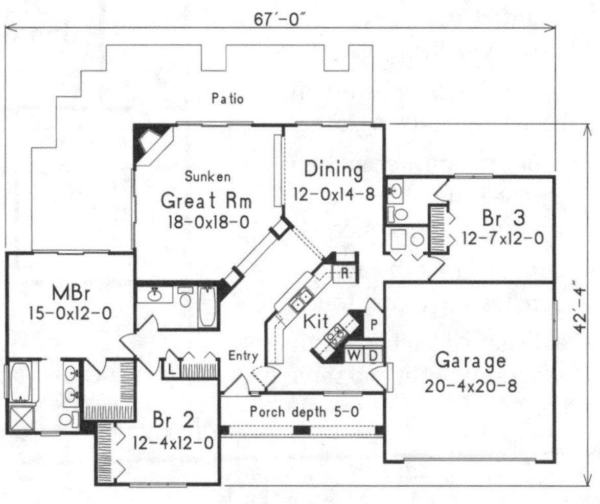

plan #584-021D-0010

price code A

plan information	
total living area:	1,444
bedrooms:	3
baths:	2
garage:	2-car side entry
foundation types:	
slab standard	
crawl space	

special features

- 11' ceilings in the living and dining rooms combine with a central fireplace to create a large open living area
- both secondary bedrooms have large walk-in closets
- large storage area in the garage is suitable for a workshop or play area
- front and rear covered porches add a cozy touch
- a U-shaped kitchen includes a laundry closet and serving bar

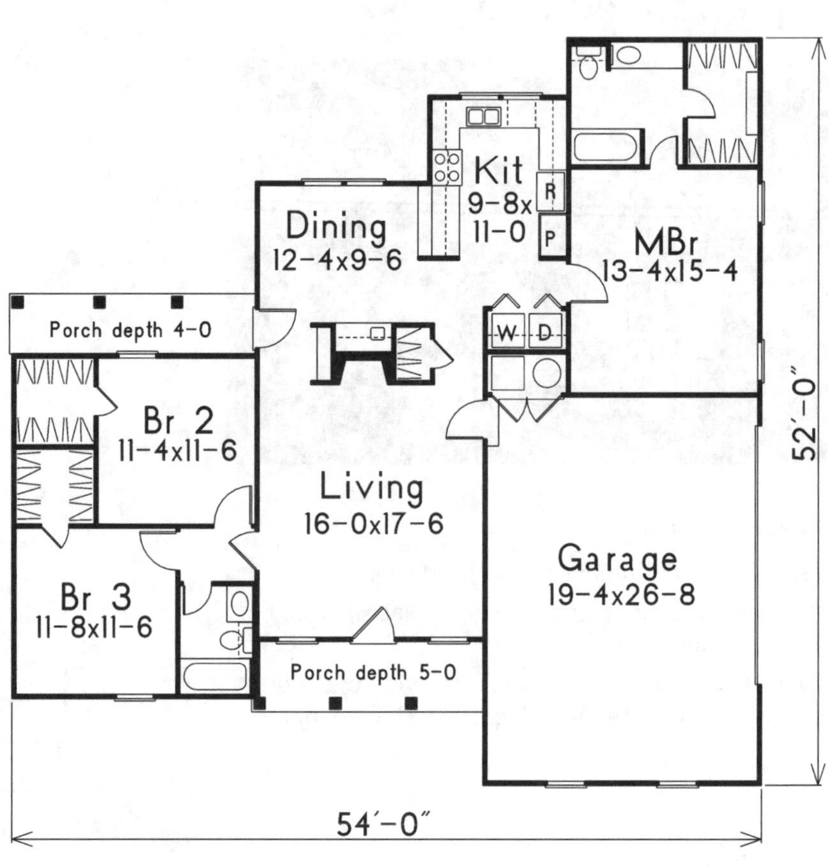

plan #584-037D-0012

price code B

plan information

total living area:	1,661
bedrooms:	3
baths:	2
garage:	2-car
foundation type:	
slab	

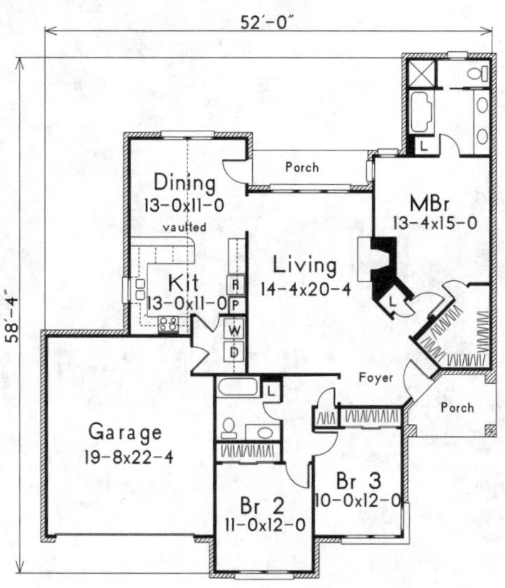

special features

- large open foyer with angled wall arrangement and high ceiling adds to spacious living room
- the kitchen and dining area have impressive cathedral ceilings and a French door allowing access to the patio
- utility room is conveniently located near the kitchen
- secluded master bedroom has a large walk-in closet, unique brick wall arrangement and 10' ceiling

---

plan #584-058D-0022

price code B

plan information

total living area:	1,578
bedrooms:	3
baths:	2
garage:	2-car
foundation type:	
basement	

special features

- plenty of closet, linen and storage space
- covered porches in the front and rear of home add charm to this design
- open floor plan has a unique angled layout

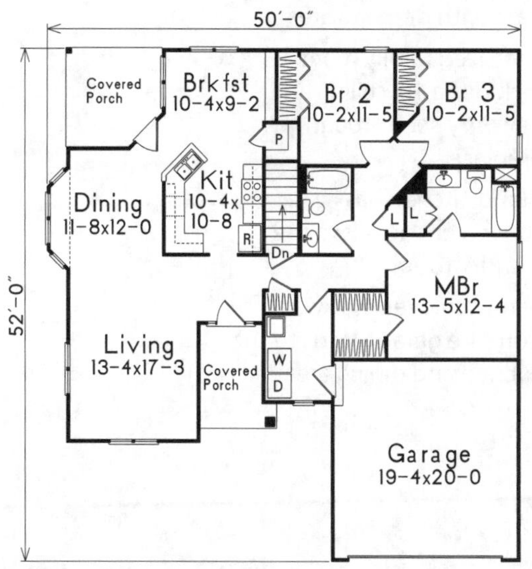

plan #584-040D-0015

price code B

plan information

total living area:	1,655
bedrooms:	3
baths:	2
garage:	2-car
foundation type:	
crawl space	

special features

- master bedroom features a 9' ceiling, walk-in closet and bath with dressing area
- oversized family room includes a 10' ceiling and masonry see-through fireplace
- island kitchen has convenient access to the laundry room
- handy covered walkway from the garage leads to the kitchen and dining area

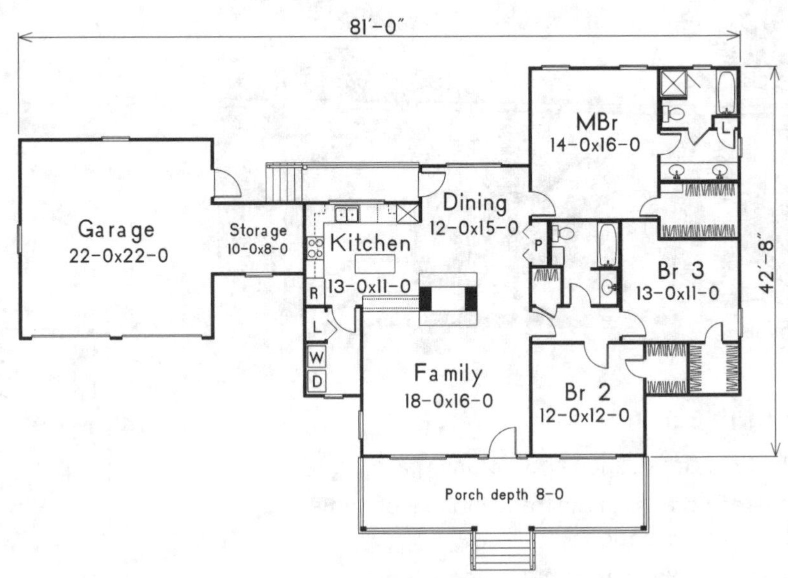

plan #584-001D-0018

price code AA

plan information

total living area:	988
bedrooms:	3
baths:	1
garage:	1-car
foundation types:	
basement standard	
crawl space	

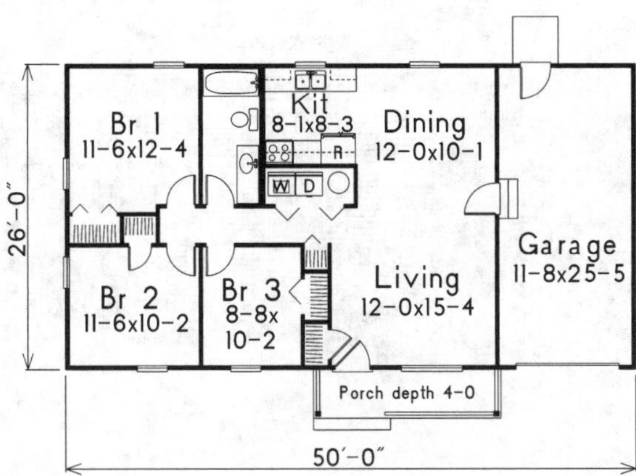

special features

- pleasant covered porch entry
- the kitchen, living and dining areas are combined to maximize space
- the entry has a convenient coat closet
- laundry closet is located adjacent to bedrooms

plan #584-053D-0004

price code B

plan information

total living area:	1,740
bedrooms:	3
baths:	2
garage:	2-car drive under
foundation type:	
basement	

special features

- the dining room boasts a coffered ceiling and specially treated ceilings grace the living room and master bedroom
- master bedroom features a large bath with walk-in closet, double-vanity, separate shower and tub
- both secondary bedrooms have ample closet space
- large breakfast area convenient to the laundry, pantry and rear deck

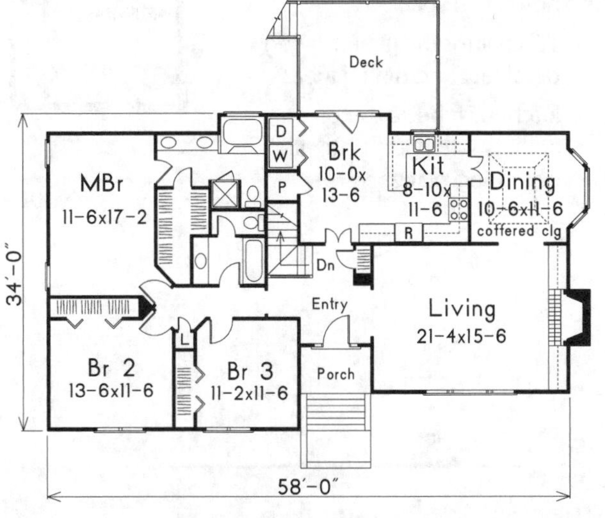

plan #584-020D-0006

price code B

plan information

total living area:	1,770
bedrooms:	3
baths:	2
garage:	2-car side entry
foundation types:	
slab standard	
crawl space	

special features

- open floor plan makes this home feel spacious
- 12' ceilings in kitchen, living, breakfast and dining areas
- kitchen is the center of activity with views into all gathering places

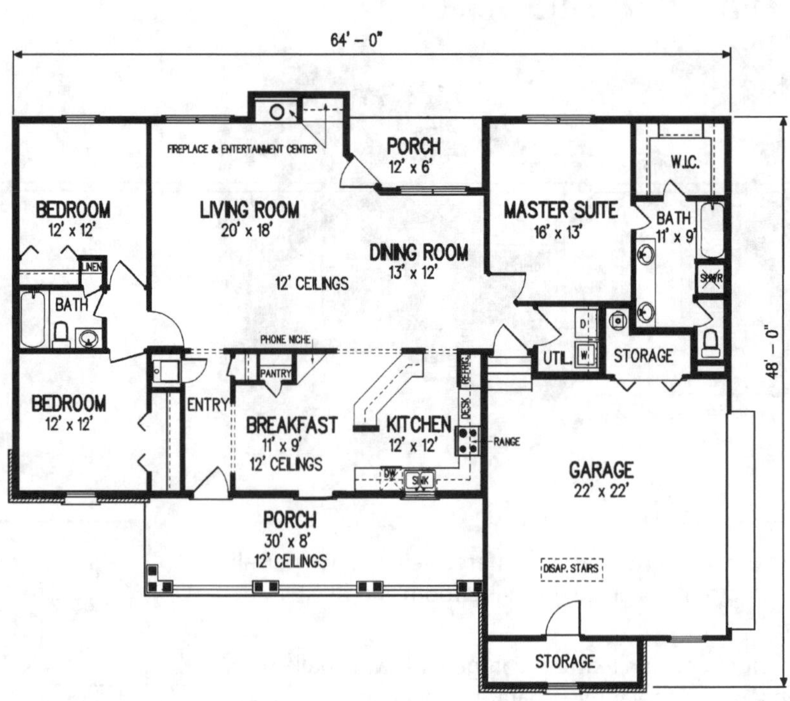

plan #584-001D-0043

price code AA

plan information

total living area: 1,104
bedrooms: 3
baths: 2
foundation types:
crawl space standard
basement
slab

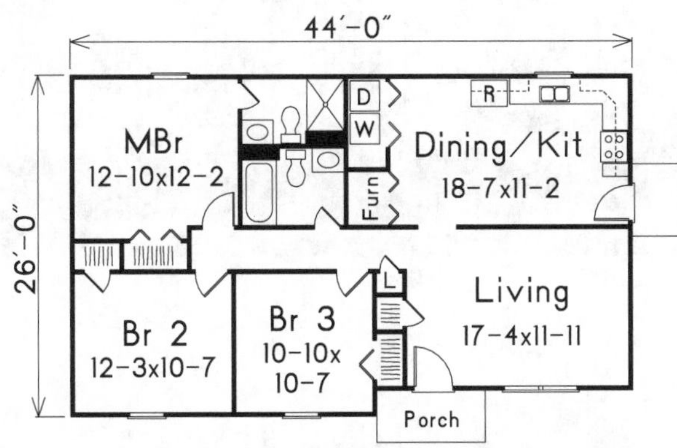

special features

- master bedroom includes a private bath
- convenient side entrance to the dining area/kitchen
- laundry area is located near the kitchen
- large living area creates a comfortable atmosphere

plan #584-053D-0032

price code A

plan information

total living area: 1,404
bedrooms: 3
baths: 2
garage: 2-car drive under
foundation types:
basement standard
partial crawl space

special features

- split-foyer entrance
- bayed living area features a unique vaulted ceiling and fireplace
- wrap-around kitchen has corner windows for added sunlight and a bar that overlooks dining area
- master bath features a garden tub with separate shower
- rear deck provides handy access to dining room and kitchen

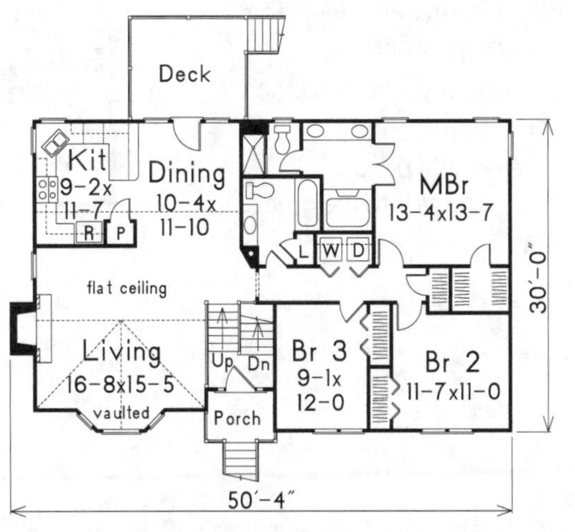

plan #584-025D-0013

price code B

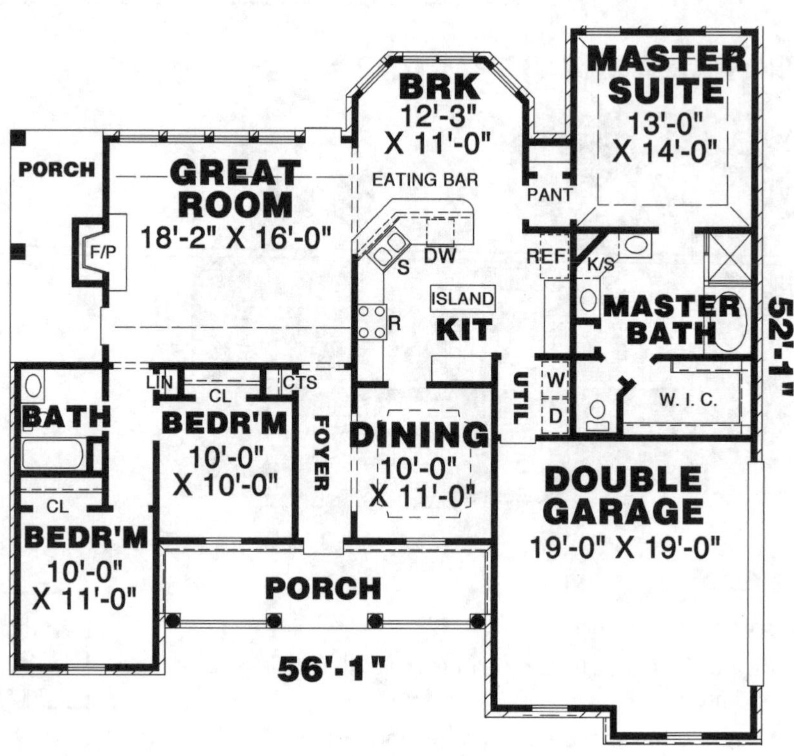

plan information

total living area:	1,686
bedrooms:	3
baths:	2
garage:	2-car side entry
foundation type:	slab

special features

- secondary bedrooms are separate from the master suite maintaining privacy
- island in kitchen is ideal for food preparation
- dramatic foyer leads to the great room
- covered side porch has direct access into the great room

plan #584-008D-0094

price code A

plan information

total living area:	1,364
bedrooms:	3
baths:	2
garage:	optional 2-car
foundation types:	
basement standard	
crawl space	

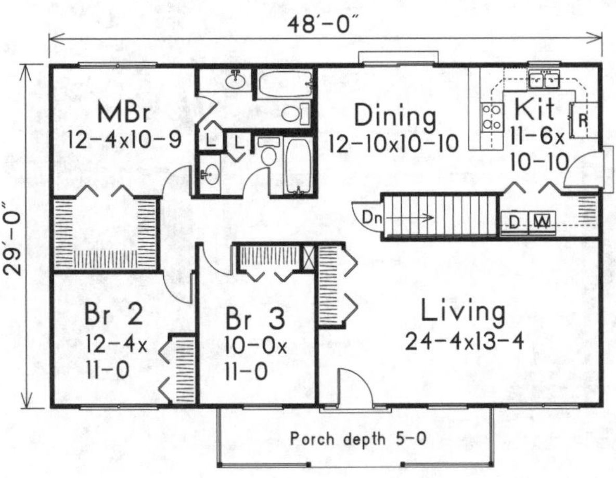

special features

- master bedroom features a spacious walk-in closet and private bath
- living room is highlighted with several windows
- kitchen with snack bar is adjacent to the dining area
- plenty of storage space throughout

---

plan #584-056D-0009

price code B

plan information

total living area:	1,606
bedrooms:	3
baths:	2
garage:	2-car
foundation type:	
slab	

special features

- kitchen has a snack bar which overlooks the dining area for convenience
- master bedroom has lots of windows with a private bath and large walk-in closet
- cathedral vault in the great room adds spaciousness

Width: 50'-0"
Depth: 42'-0"

plan #584-053D-0042

price code A

plan information

total living area:	1,458
bedrooms:	3
baths:	2
garage:	2-car
foundation types:	
crawl space standard	
slab	

special features

- convenient snack bar joins kitchen with breakfast room
- large living room has a fireplace, plenty of windows, vaulted ceiling and nearby plant shelf
- master bedroom offers a private bath, walk-in closet, plant shelf and coffered ceiling
- corner windows provide abundant light in breakfast room

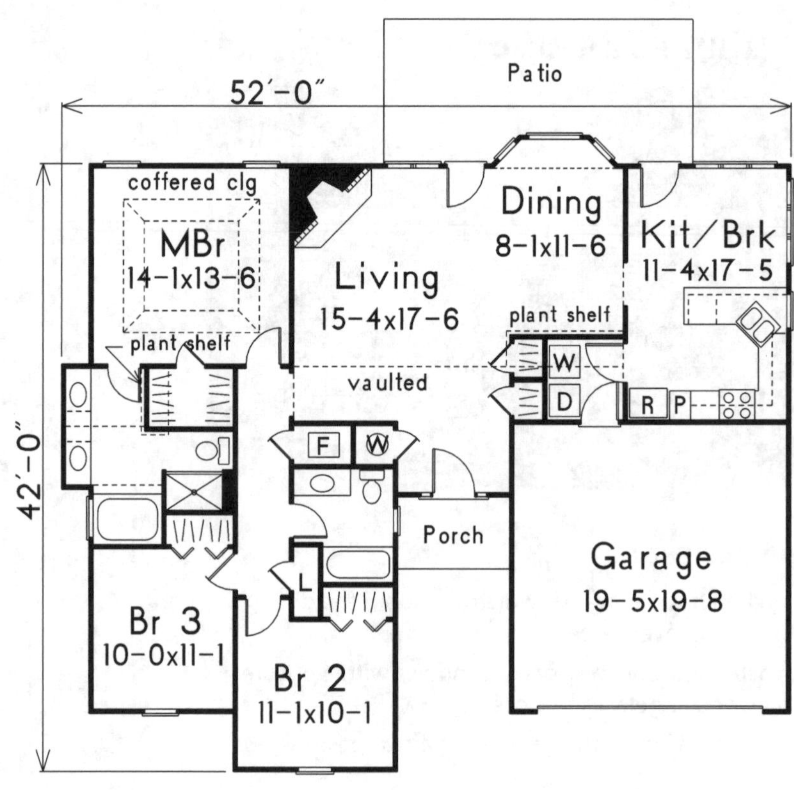

plan #584-026D-0165

price code A

plan information

total living area: 1,395
bedrooms: 3
baths: 2
garage: 2-car side entry
foundation type:
slab

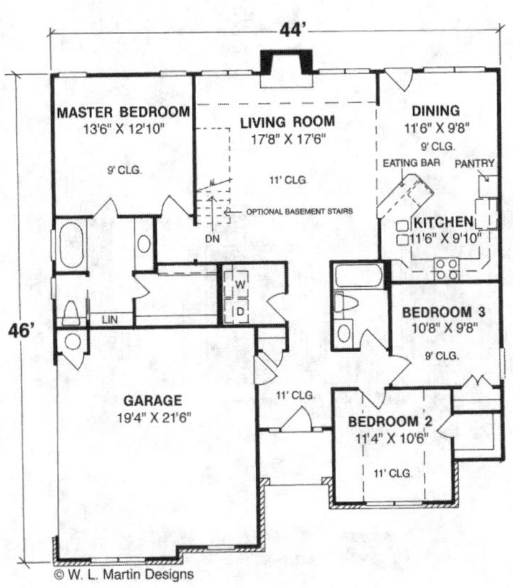

special features

- dining area and kitchen are separated by an angled eating bar
- 11' ceilings in entrance and living room create openness
- master bedroom and bedroom #2 feature walk-in closets

---

plan #584-037D-0022

price code B

plan information

total living area: 1,539
bedrooms: 3
baths: 2
garage: 2-car
foundation type:
slab

special features

- standard 9' ceilings
- master bedroom features 10' tray ceiling, access to porch, ample closet space and full bath
- serving counter separates kitchen and dining room
- foyer with handy coat closet opens to living area with fireplace
- handy utility room near kitchen

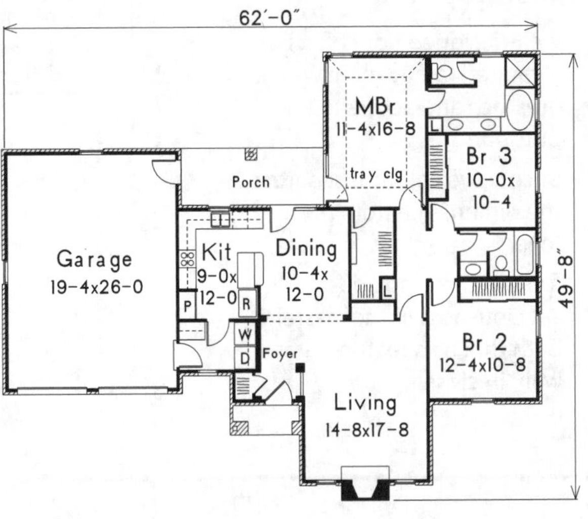

plan #584-035D-0028

price code B

plan information

total living area:	1,779
bedrooms:	3
baths:	2
garage:	2-car

foundation types:
walk-out basement
slab
crawl space
please specify when ordering

special features

- well-designed floor plan has a vaulted family room with fireplace and access to the outdoors
- decorative columns separate the dining area from the foyer
- a vaulted ceiling adds spaciousness in the master bath that also features a walk-in closet

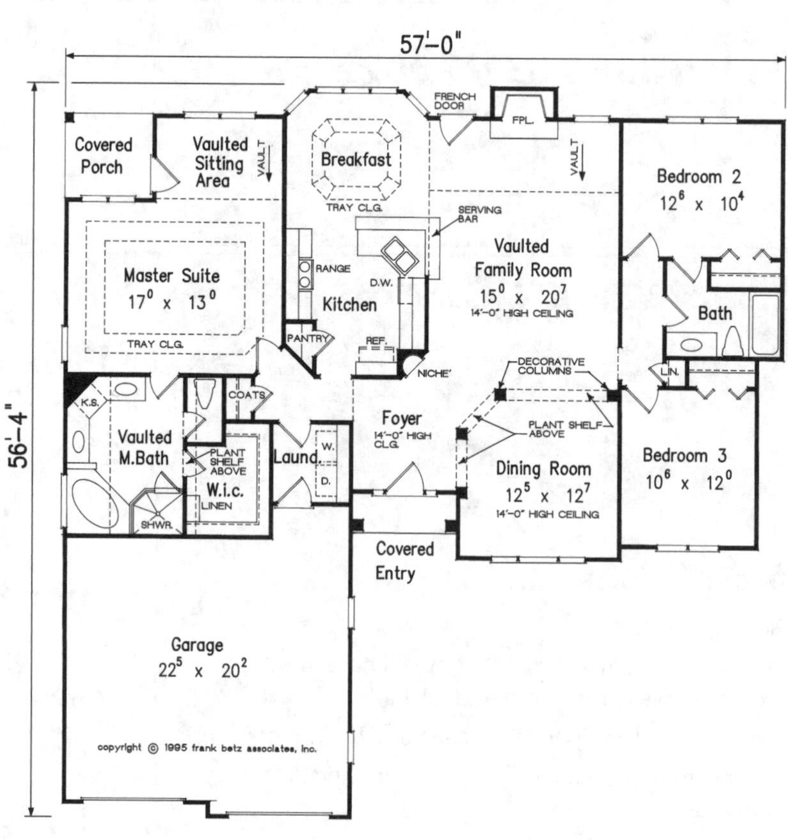

plan #584-040D-0008

price code B

plan information

total living area:	1,631
bedrooms:	3
baths:	2
garage:	2-car drive under
foundation type:	basement

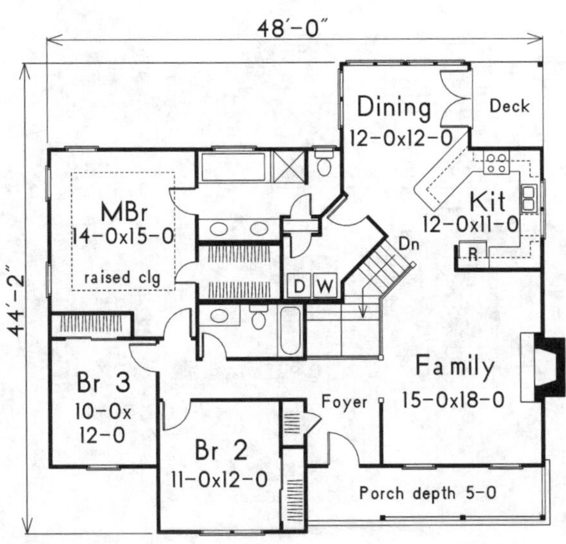

special features

- 9' ceilings throughout this home
- utility room is conveniently located near the kitchen
- roomy kitchen and dining area boast a breakfast bar and deck access
- raised ceiling accents master bedroom

---

plan #584-045D-0019

price code AA

plan information

total living area:	1,134
bedrooms:	2
baths:	1
garage:	2-car
foundation type:	basement

special features

- kitchen has plenty of counterspace, an island worktop, large pantry and access to the garage
- living room features a vaulted ceiling, fireplace and access to an expansive patio
- bedroom #1 has a large walk-in closet
- convenient linen closet in the hall

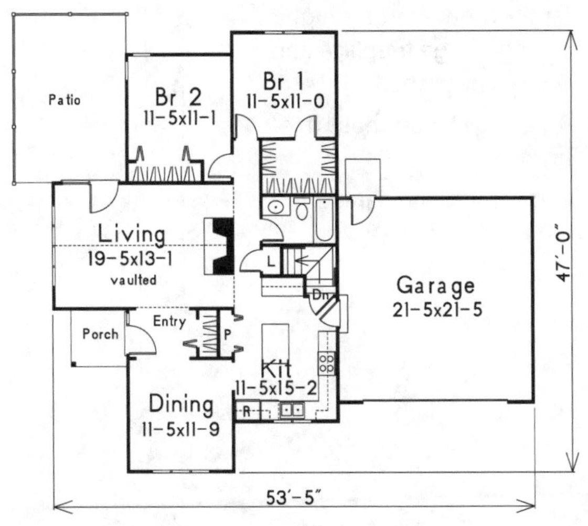

plan #584-039D-0009

price code B

plan information

total living area:	1,572
bedrooms:	3
baths:	2
garage:	2-car
foundation type:	
slab	

special features

- eating peninsula separates kitchen from traffic flow
- family room features high ceilings, large fireplace and built-in bookshelf
- 9' ceilings throughout this home
- extra storage in garage

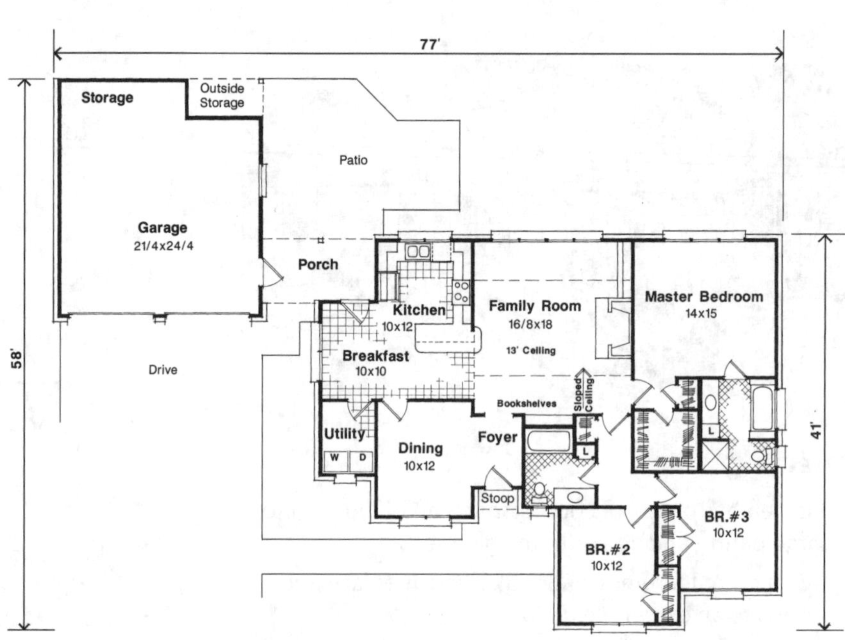

plan #584-065D-0026

price code D

plan information	
total living area:	2,269
bedrooms:	3
baths:	2
garage:	2-car
foundation type:	
basement	

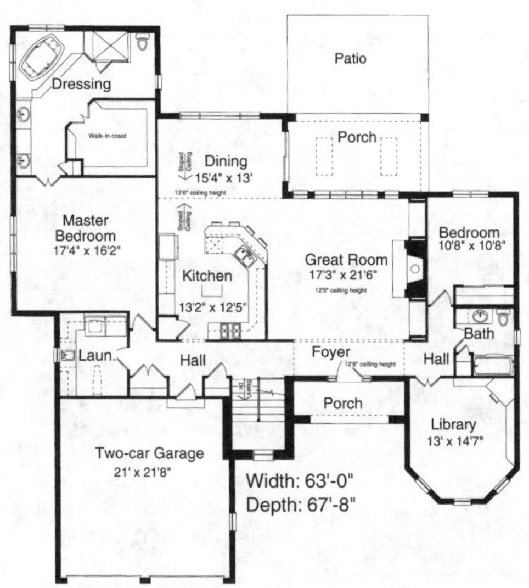

special features

- an open atmosphere encourages an easy flow of activities
- grand windows and a covered porch offer a cozy atmosphere
- the master bedroom boasts a double vanity, whirlpool tub and spacious walk-in closet

---

plan #584-022D-0026

price code D

plan information	
total living area:	1,993
bedrooms:	3
baths:	2
garage:	2-car
foundation type:	
basement	

special features

- spacious country kitchen boasts a fireplace and plenty of natural light from windows
- formal dining room features large bay window and steps down to the sunken living room
- master bedroom features corner windows, plant shelves and a deluxe private bath
- entry opens into the vaulted living room with windows flanking the fireplace

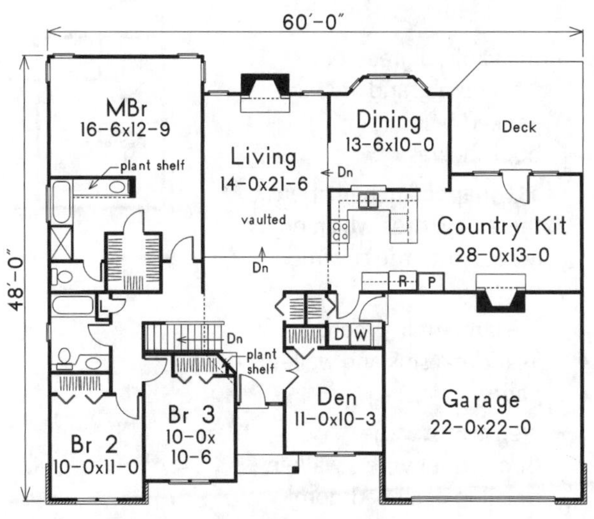

plan #584-077D-0003

price code D

plan information

total living area:	1,896
bedrooms:	3
baths:	2 1/2
garage:	2-car side entry

foundation types:
basement
crawl space
slab
please specify when ordering

special features

- the vaulted great room features a grand fireplace flanked by built-in bookshelves
- a U-shaped kitchen opens to the dining area which enjoys access onto the covered porch
- the large utility room includes a sink and walk-in pantry
- plenty of storage throughout with a walk-in closet in each bedroom

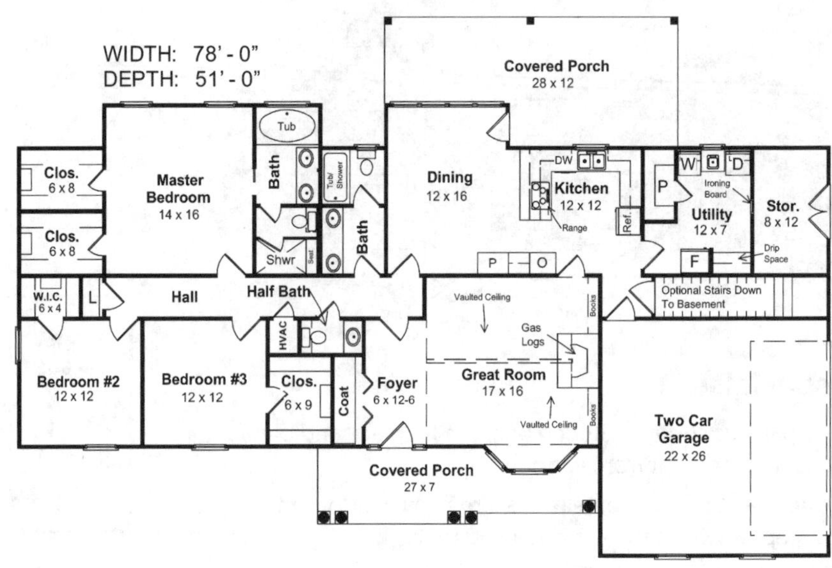

plan #584-055D-0114

price code C

plan information	
total living area:	2,050
bedrooms:	4
baths:	2
garage:	2-car
foundation types:	
crawl space	
slab	
please specify when ordering	

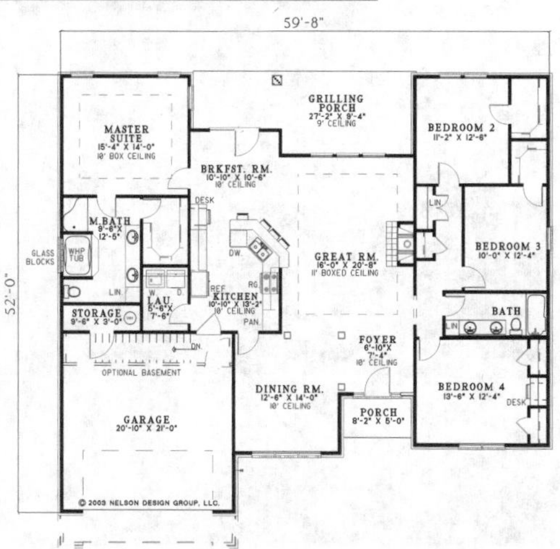

special features

- open living spaces allow for dining area, great room and breakfast room to flow together
- bedroom #4 has unique design with double closets and a built-in desk
- plenty of closet space throughout

---

plan #584-021D-0009

price code D

plan information	
total living area:	2,252
bedrooms:	4
baths:	2
garage:	2-car
foundation types:	
slab standard	
basement	
crawl space	

special features

- energy efficient home with 2" x 6" exterior walls
- central living area
- private master bedroom with large walk-in closet, dressing area and bath
- secondary bedrooms are in a suite arrangement with plenty of closet space
- sunny breakfast room looks out over the porch and patio
- large entry area is highlighted by circle-top transoms

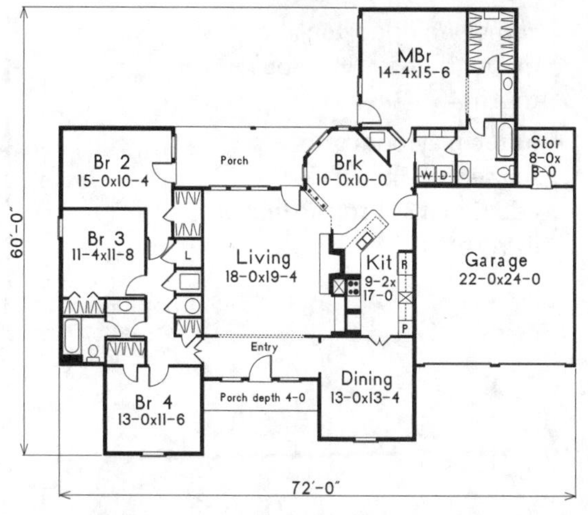

plan #584-025D-0048

price code D

plan information

total living area: 2,526
bedrooms: 4
baths: 3
garage: 2-car side entry
foundation types:
crawl space
slab
please specify when ordering

special features

- sunroom brightens dining area near kitchen
- corner whirlpool tub in master bath is a luxurious touch
- future playroom on the second floor has an additional 341 square feet of living area

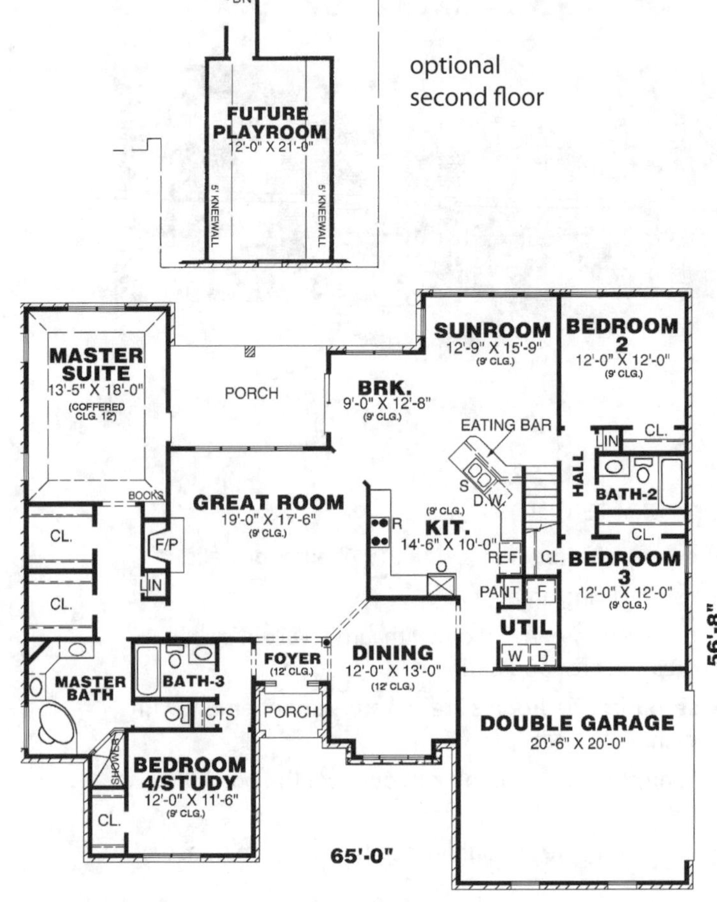

optional second floor

first floor
2,526 sq. ft.

plan #584-001D-0079

price code C

plan information	
total living area:	2,080
bedrooms:	4
baths:	2
garage:	2-car side entry
foundation types:	
crawl space standard	
basement	
slab	

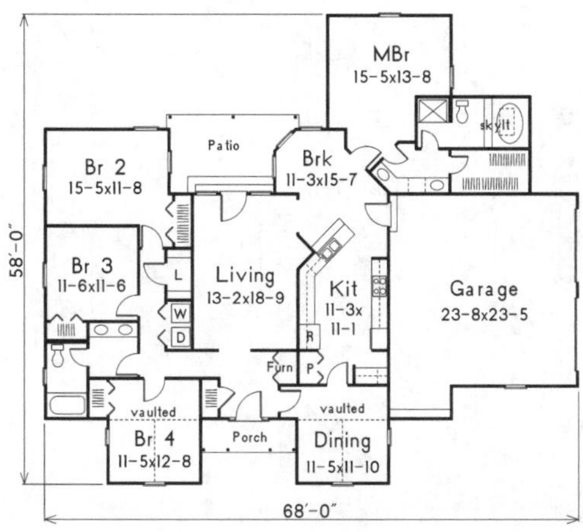

special features

- combined design elements create a unique facade
- foyer leads into a large living room with direct view to patio
- master bedroom includes spacious bath with garden tub, separate shower, walk-in closet and dressing area

---

plan #584-026D-0142

price code C

plan information	
total living area:	2,188
bedrooms:	3
baths:	2
garage:	3-car side entry
foundation type:	
basement	

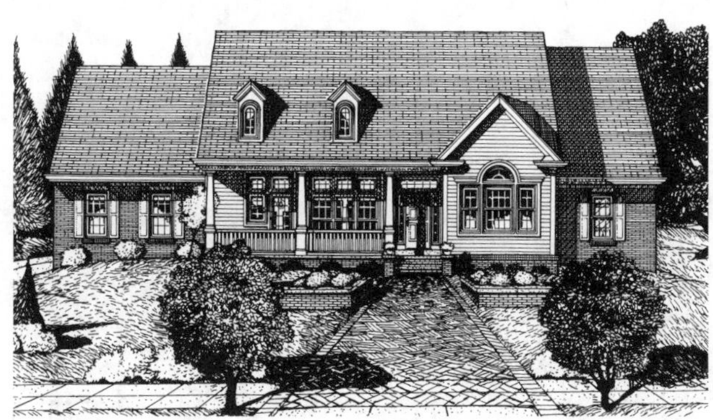

special features

- master bedroom includes a private covered porch, sitting area and two large walk-in closets
- spacious kitchen has center island, snack bar and laundry access
- great room has a 10' ceiling and a dramatic corner fireplace

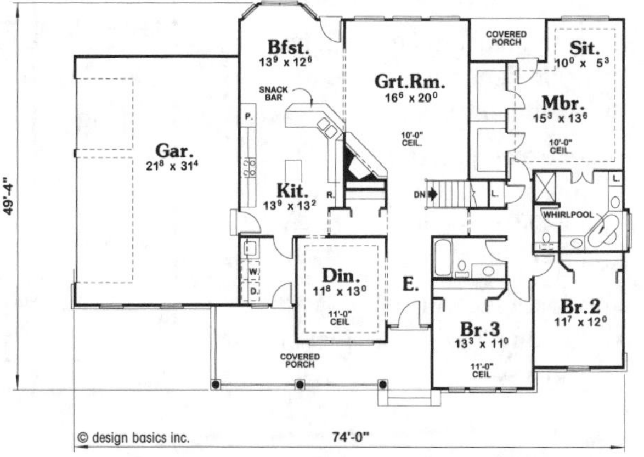

plan #584-077D-0002

price code D

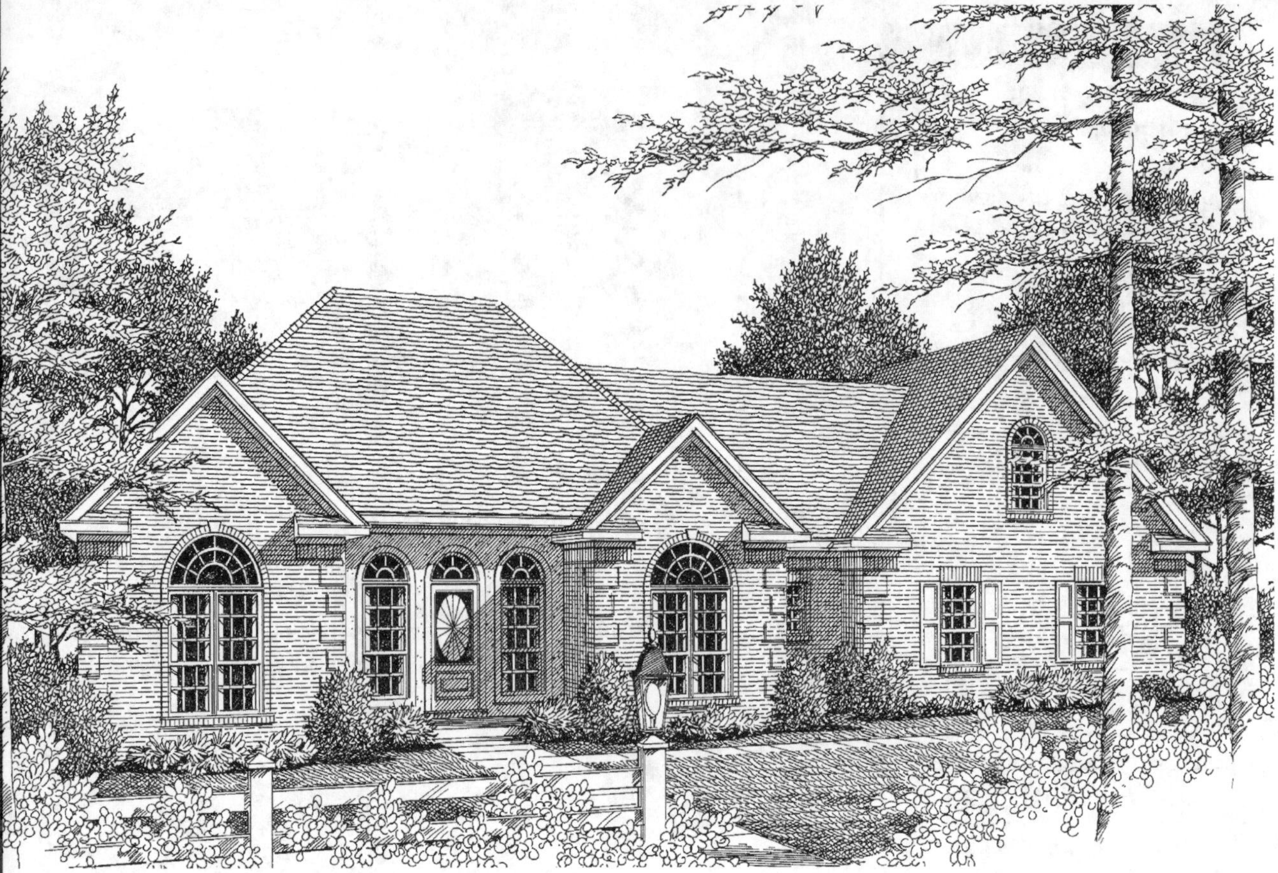

plan information

total living area:	1,855
bedrooms:	3
baths:	2 1/2
garage:	2-car side entry
foundation types:	
basement	
crawl space	
slab	
please specify when ordering	

special features

- the great room boasts a 12' ceiling and corner fireplace
- bayed breakfast area adjoins the kitchen that features a walk-in pantry
- the relaxing master bedroom includes a private bath with walk-in closet and garden tub
- optional second floor has an additional 352 square feet of living area

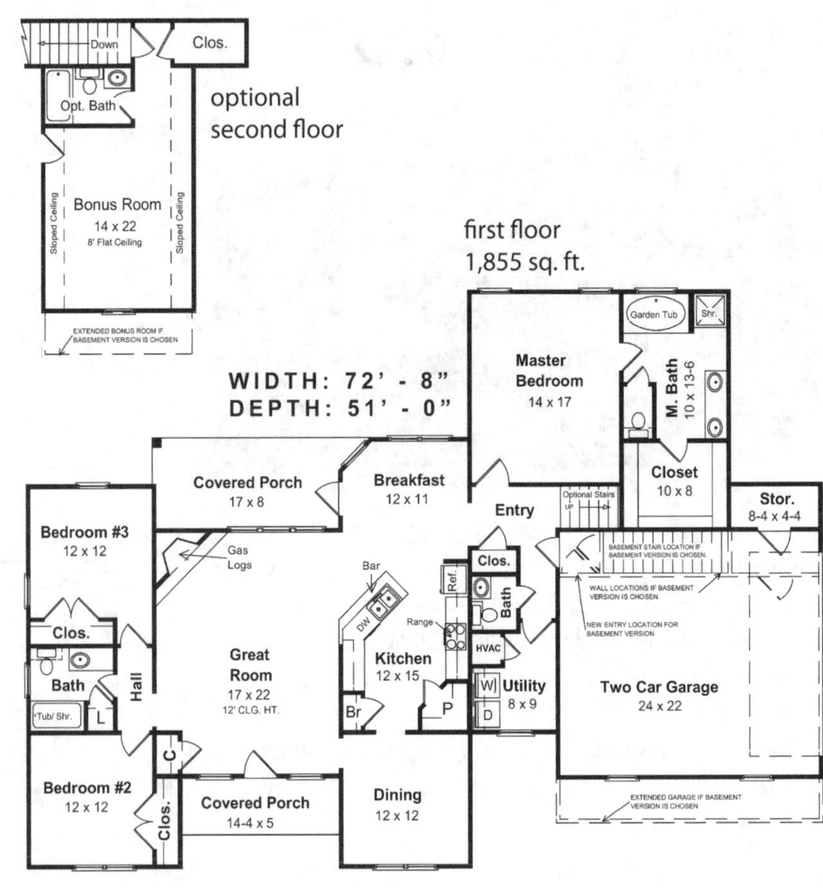

plan #584-014D-0015

price code C

plan information	
total living area:	1,941
bedrooms:	3
baths:	2 1/2
garage:	2-car
foundation type:	
crawl space	

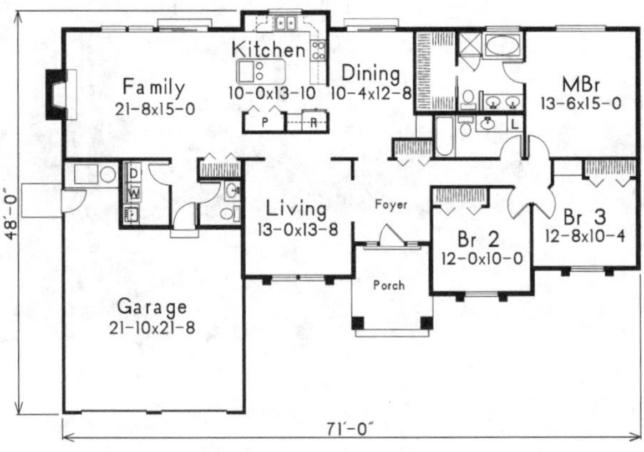

special features

- kitchen incorporates a cooktop island, a handy pantry and adjoins the dining and family rooms
- formal living room, to the left of the foyer, lends a touch of privacy
- raised ceilings enhance the foyer, kitchen, dining and living areas
- laundry room, half bath and closet are all located near the garage
- both the dining and family rooms have access outdoors through sliding doors

---

plan #584-041D-0001

price code D

plan information	
total living area:	2,003
bedrooms:	3
baths:	2
garage:	2-car
foundation type:	
basement	

special features

- octagon-shaped dining room boasts a tray ceiling and deck overlook
- the L-shaped island kitchen serves the living and dining rooms
- master bedroom boasts a luxury bath and walk-in closet
- living room features columns, elegant fireplace and a 10' ceiling

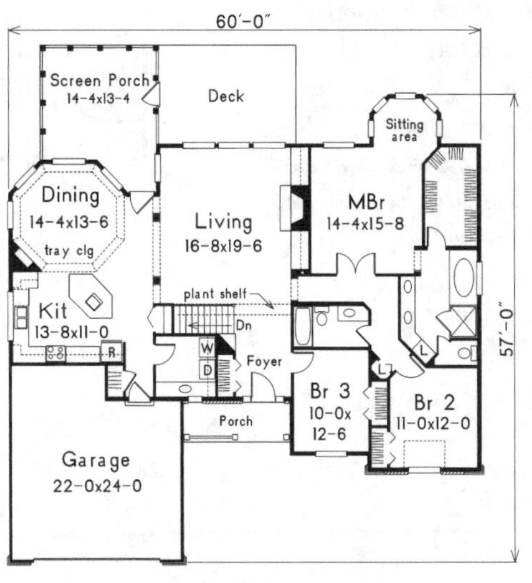

plan #584-047D-0037

price code D

plan information

total living area:	2,173
bedrooms:	3
baths:	2 1/2
garage:	3-car side entry
foundation type:	
slab	

special features

- enormous family room off kitchen has a fireplace surrounded by media shelves for state-of-the-art living
- the master bath has double walk-in closets as well as an oversized shower and whirlpool tub
- an arched entry graces the formal dining room

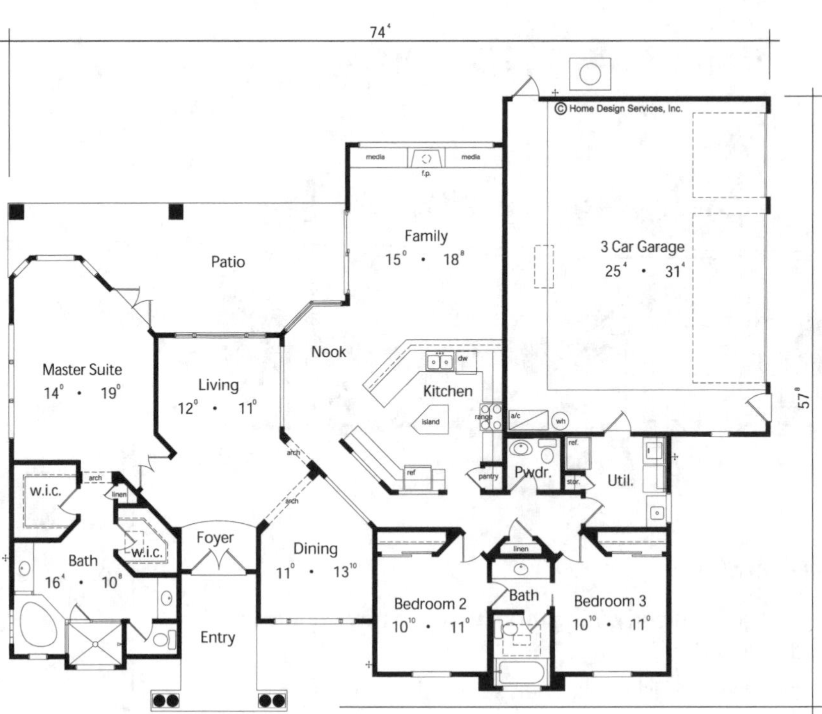

plan #584-051D-0103

price code D

plan information	
total living area:	1,821
bedrooms:	3
baths:	2
garage:	2-car
foundation type: basement	

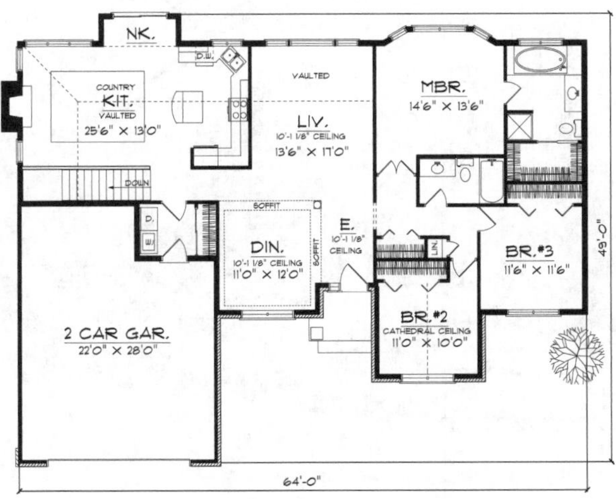

special features

- the foyer, living and dining rooms boast 10' ceilings creating a dramatic first impression
- the relaxing master bedroom features a double-door entry, large bay window and private bath with whirlpool tub and walk-in closet
- a cheerful nook and cozy fireplace grace the expansive kitchen

---

plan #584-053D-0005

price code C

plan information	
total living area:	1,833
bedrooms:	3
baths:	2
garage:	2-car drive under
foundation type: basement	

special features

- master bedroom suite comes with a garden tub, walk-in closet and bay window
- walk-through kitchen and the sunny breakfast room are easily accessble from many rooms of this home
- front bay windows offer a deluxe touch
- foyer with convenient coat closet opens into large vaulted living room with an attractive fireplace

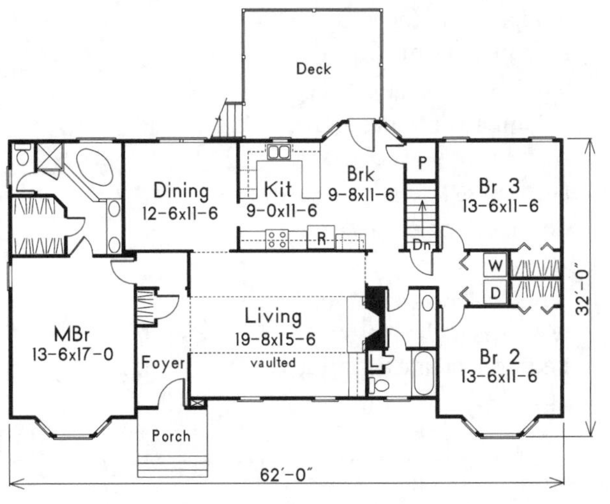

plan #584-068D-0001

price code D

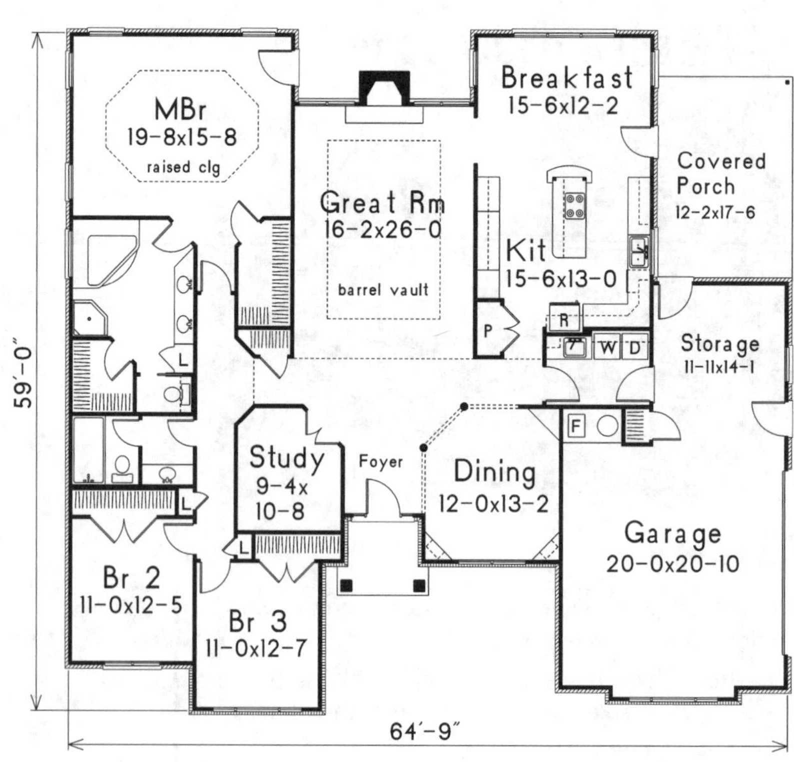

plan information

total living area:	2,437
bedrooms:	3
baths:	2
garage:	2-car side entry
foundation types:	
slab standard	
crawl space	

special features

- spacious breakfast area with access to the covered porch is adjacent to the kitchen and great room
- elegant dining area has a columned entrance and built-in corner cabinets
- cozy study has a handsome double-door entrance off a large foyer
- raised ceiling and lots of windows in the master bedroom create a spacious, open feel

plan #584-027D-0006

price code C

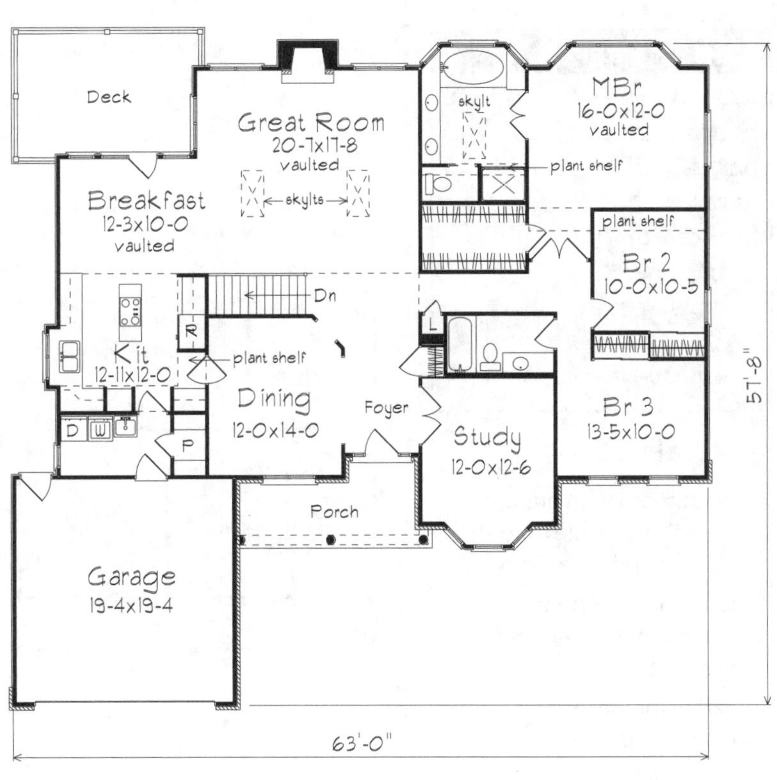

plan information	
total living area:	2,076
bedrooms:	3
baths:	2
garage:	2-car
foundation type: basement	

special features

- vaulted great room has a fireplace flanked by windows and skylights that welcome the sun
- kitchen leads to the vaulted breakfast room and rear deck
- study located off the foyer provides a great location for a home office
- large bay windows grace the master bedroom and bath

plan #584-016D-0024 price code D

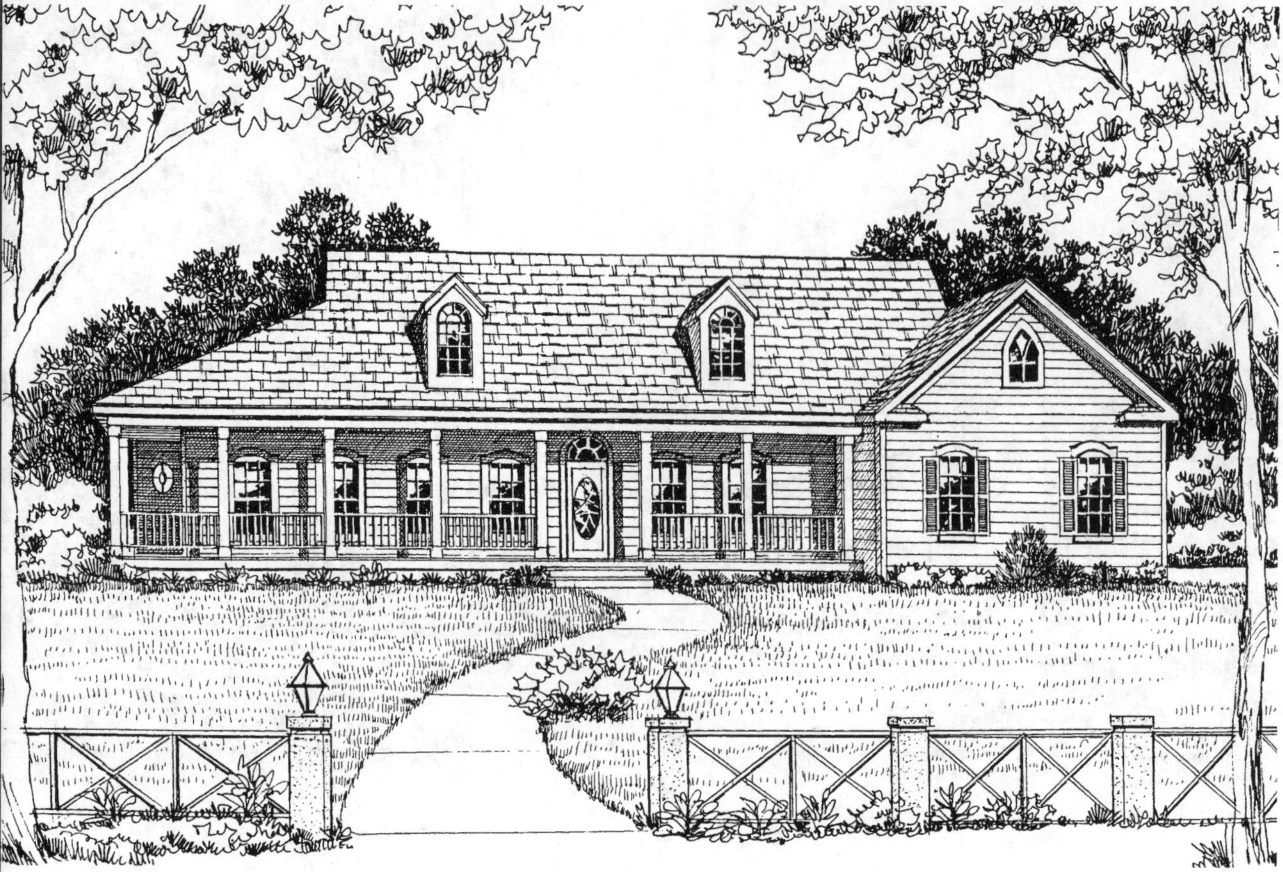

plan information

total living area:	1,902
bedrooms:	3
baths:	2
garage:	2-car side entry
foundation types:	
basement	
crawl space	
slab	
please specify when ordering	

special features

- great room with fireplace is easily viewable from the kitchen and breakfast area
- luxury master bedroom has a bay window and two walk-in closets
- extra storage in the garage makes organization easy

Width 75'-0"
Depth 45'-0"

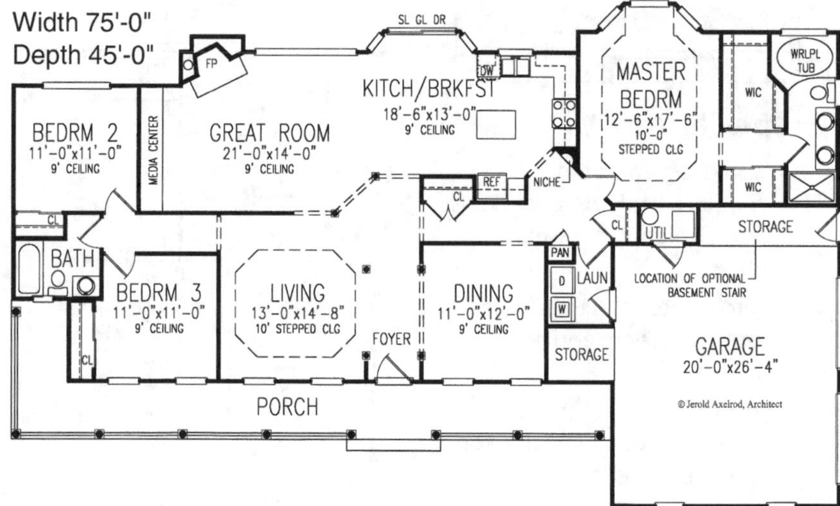

plan #584-077D-0006

price code D

plan information

total living area:	2,307
bedrooms:	3
baths:	2 1/2
garage:	2-car side entry
foundation types:	
basement	
crawl space	
slab	
please specify when ordering	

special features

- the bayed breakfast area warms the home with natural light
- the spacious master bedroom boasts two walk-in closets, private bath and a bonus area ideal for an office or nursery
- the vaulted great room includes a grand fireplace, built-in shelves and a double-door entry onto the covered porch

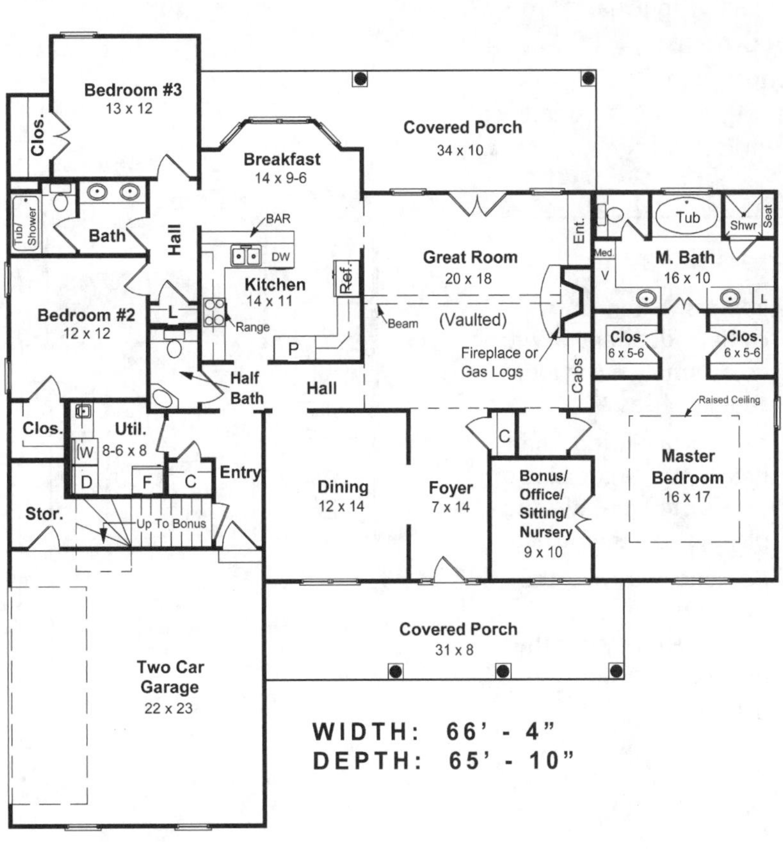

plan #584-026D-0163

price code F

plan information

total living area:	3,312
bedrooms:	3
baths:	2 1/2
garage:	3-car side entry
foundation type:	slab

special features

- impressive front entry commands attention with an enormous living room straight ahead
- a casual family room and breakfast area combine to create a terrific gathering place just off the kitchen
- a second entry near the master bedroom is a convenient way into the home directly from the garage

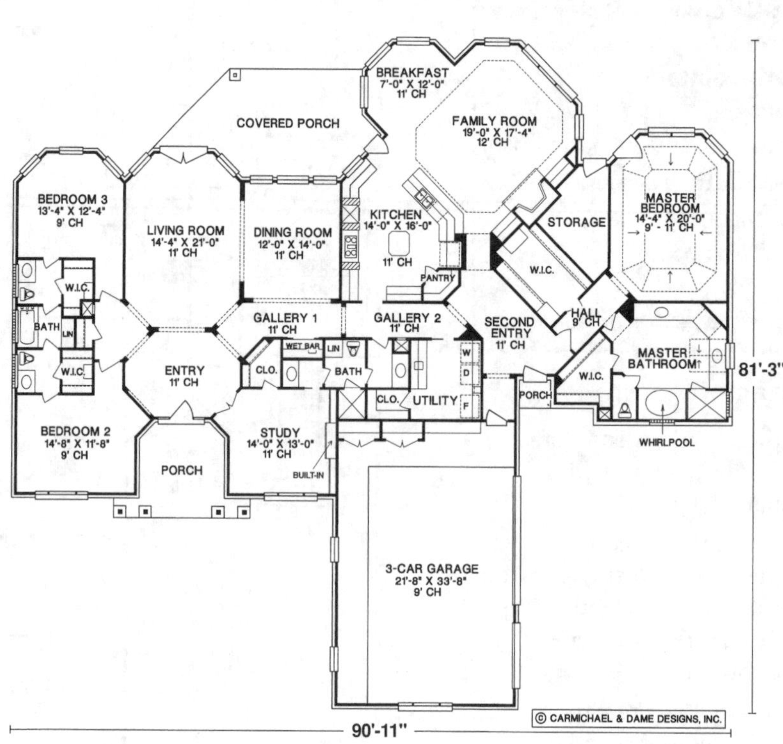

plan #584-035D-0021

price code C

plan information

total living area:	1,978
bedrooms:	3
baths:	2 1/2
garage:	2-car
foundation types:	
walk-out basement	
slab	
crawl space	
please specify when ordering	

special features

- elegant arched openings throughout interior
- vaulted living room off foyer
- master suite features a cheerful sitting room and a private bath

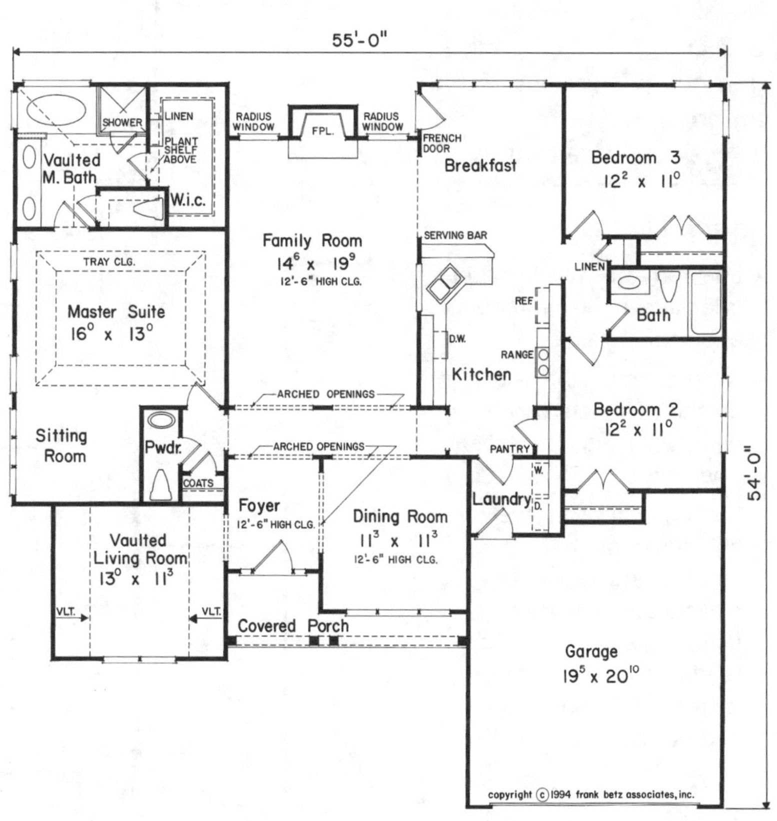

plan #584-065D-0041

price code E

plan information

total living area:	3,171
bedrooms:	3
baths:	2 1/2
garage:	3-car side entry
foundation type:	walk-out basement

special features

- an enormous walk-in closet is located in the master bath and dressing area
- the great room, breakfast area and kitchen combine with 12' ceilings to create an open feel
- the optional lower level has an additional 1,897 square feet of living area and is designed for entertaining featuring a wet bar with seating, a billiards room, large media room, two bedrooms and a full bath

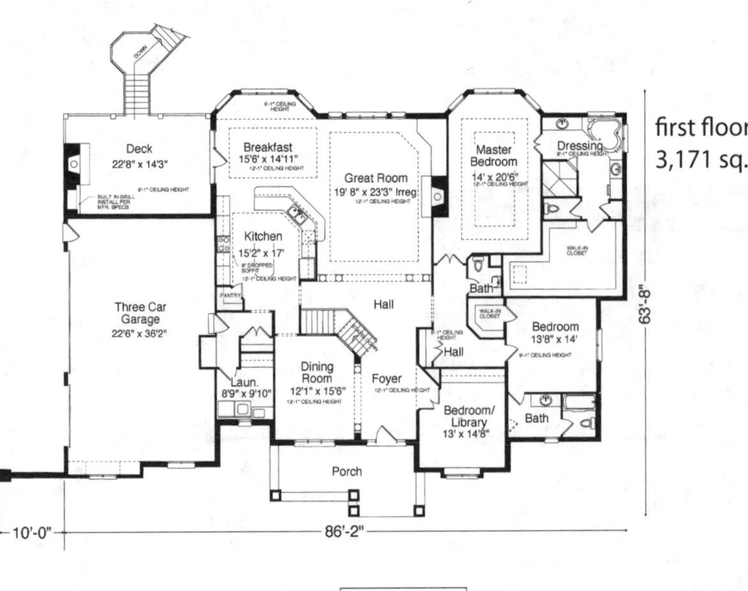

first floor
3,171 sq. ft.

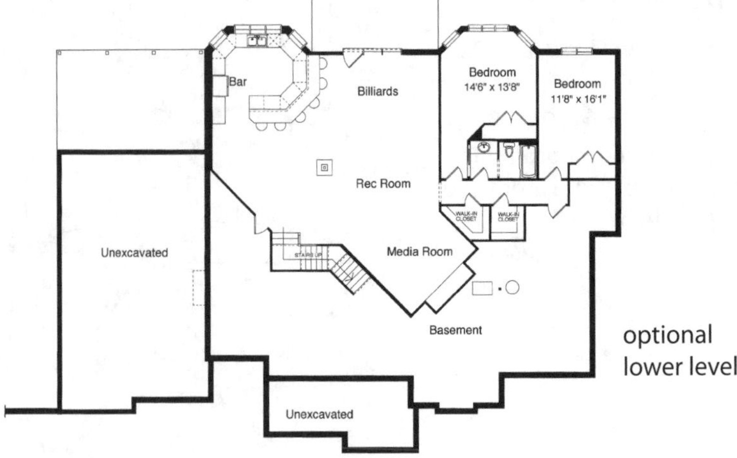

optional lower level

plan information

total living area:	2,671
bedrooms:	4
baths:	2 1/2
garage:	2-car side entry
foundation types:	
crawl space	
slab	
please specify when ordering	

special features

- spacious master suite has a luxurious bath with whirlpool tub, oversized shower and walk-in closet
- great room and breakfast room both access the grilling porch perfect for entertaining
- laundry room is conveniently located near all secondary bedrooms

plan #584-035D-0032

price code C

plan information

total living area:	1,856
bedrooms:	3
baths:	2
garage:	2-car side entry

foundation types:
- walk-out basement
- crawl space
- slab

please specify when ordering

special features

- beautiful covered porch creates a Southern accent
- kitchen has an organized feel with lots of cabinetry
- large foyer has a grand entrance and leads into the family room through columns and an arched opening

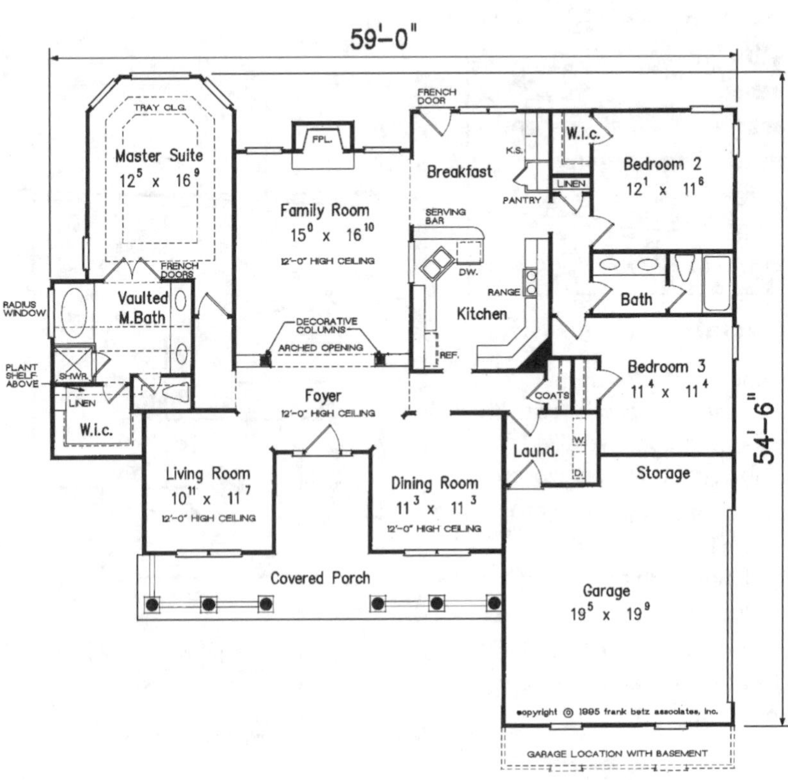

plan #584-013D-0022

price code C

plan information

total living area: 1,992
bedrooms: 4
baths: 3
garage: 2-car side entry
foundation types:
basement
crawl space
slab
please specify when ordering

special features

- interesting angled walls add drama to many of the living areas including the family room, master bedroom and breakfast area
- covered porch includes a spa and the outdoor kitchen with sink, refrigerator and cooktop
- enter the majestic master bath to find a dramatic corner oversized tub

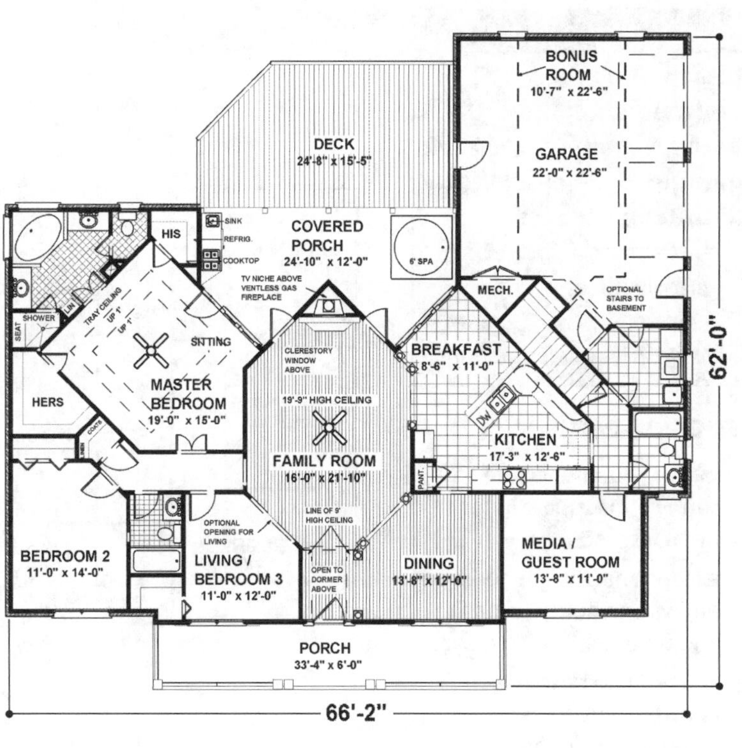

plan #584-013D-0026

price code C

plan information

total living area:	2,187
bedrooms:	4
baths:	2 1/2
garage:	2-car side entry
foundation types:	
basement	
crawl space	
slab	
please specify when ordering	

special features

- lots of windows create a sunny atmosphere in the breakfast room
- exceptional master bedroom enjoys an enormous bath and unique morning porch
- vaulted and raised ceilings adorn many rooms throughout this home
- the roomy deck may be accessed from the family room and master bedroom

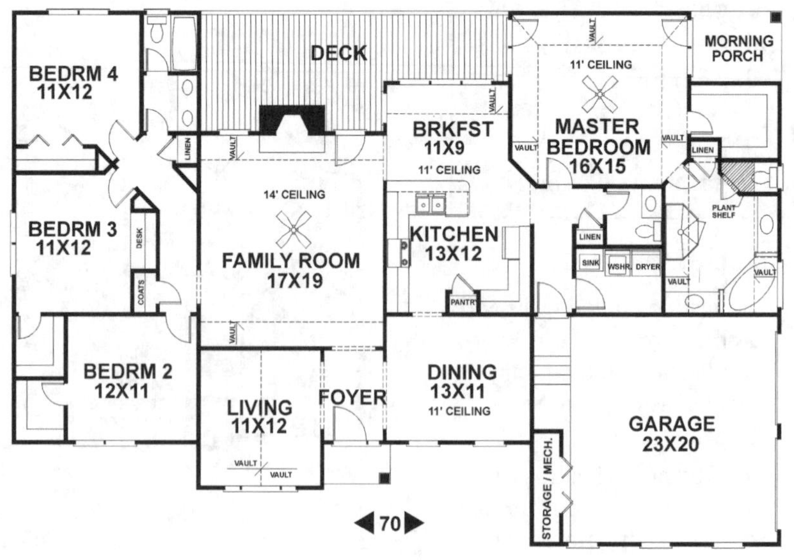

plan information

total living area: 1,945
bedrooms: 4
baths: 2
garage: 2-car side entry
foundation types:
walk-out basement
crawl space
slab
please specify when ordering

special features

- master suite is separate from other bedrooms for privacy
- vaulted breakfast room is directly off great room
- kitchen includes a built-in desk area
- elegant dining room has an arched window

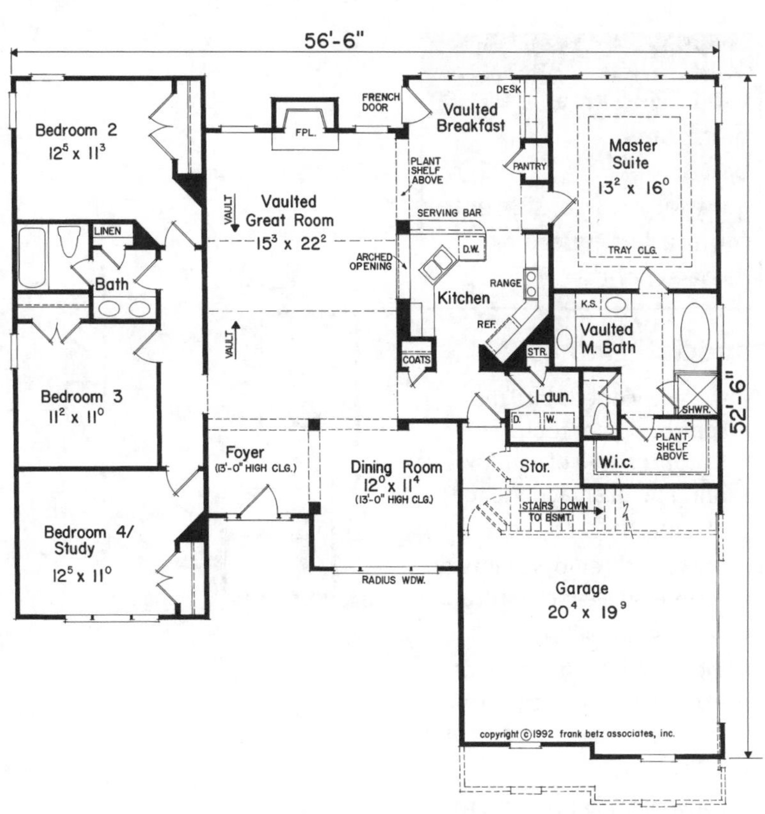

over 1,800 square feet plans

order 1-800-367-7667

plan #584-051D-0182

price code F

plan information	
total living area:	2,600
bedrooms:	3
baths:	2 1/2
garage:	3-car side entry
foundation type:	basement

special features

- the entry opens into the spacious great room which features a wall of windows bringing in an abundance of light
- the kitchen enjoys plenty of counterspace including an extra-large island
- the master bedroom boasts a double-door entry, sitting area, two walk-in closets and a private bath
- convenient laundry area includes a closet, sink and an alternate stairway to the basement

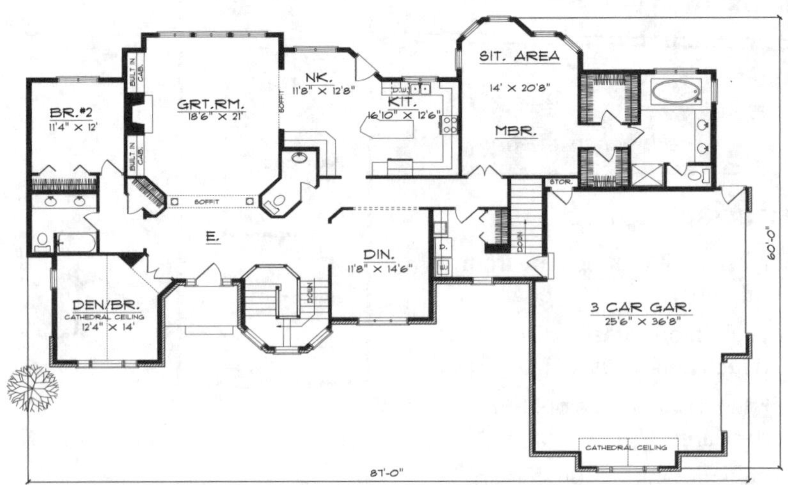

plan #584-011D-0013

price code D

plan information	
total living area:	2,001
bedrooms:	3
baths:	2
garage:	3-car
foundation type:	
crawl space	

special features

- large wrap-around counter in kitchen is accessible from the dining area
- a double-door entry keeps the den secluded from other living areas making it an ideal home office
- decorative columns adorn the entry leading into the great room

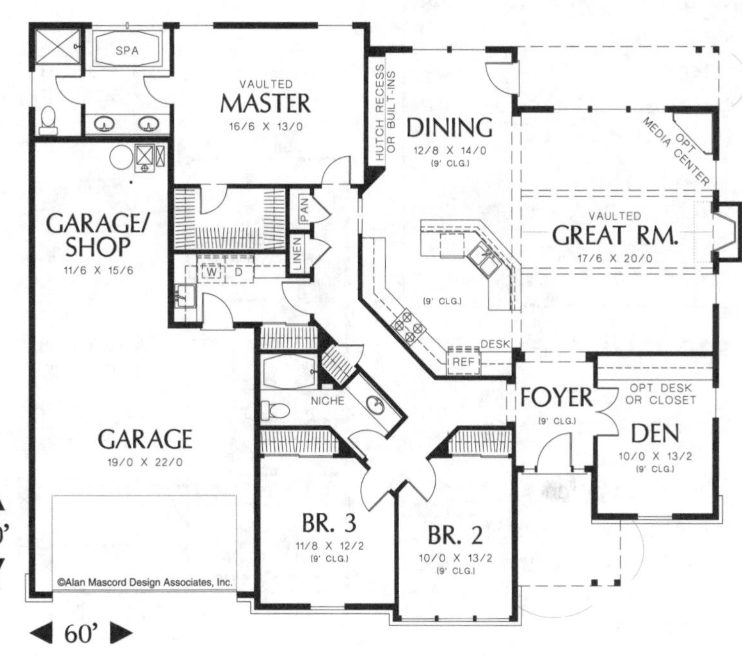

plan #584-013D-0019

price code C

plan information	
total living area:	1,992
bedrooms:	3
baths:	2 1/2
garage:	3-car side entry
foundation types:	
basement	
crawl space	
slab	
please specify when ordering	

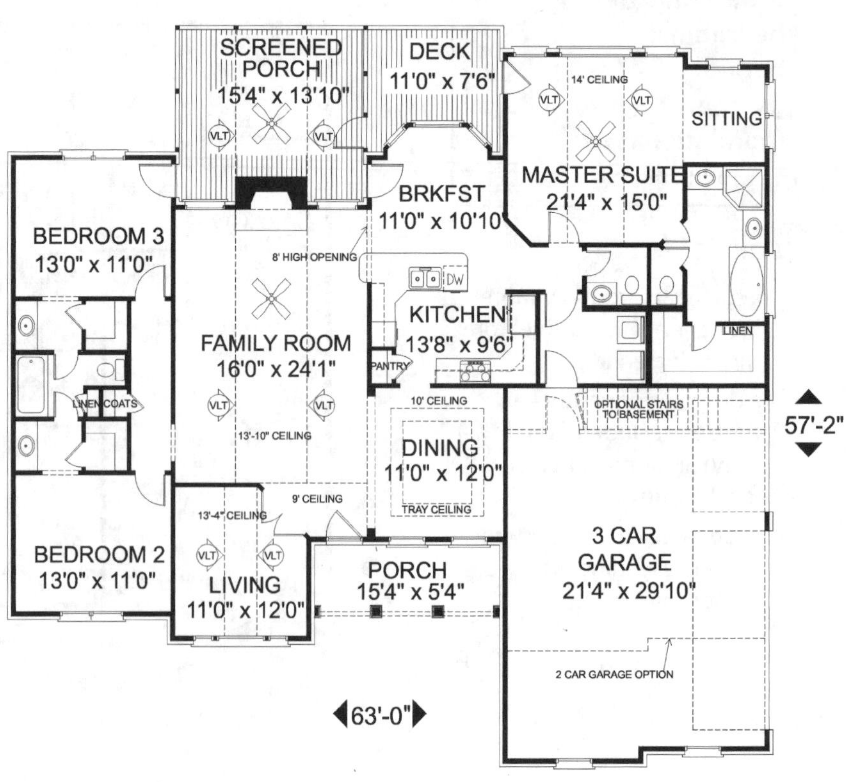

special features

- bayed breakfast room overlooks the outdoor deck and connects to the screened porch
- private formal living room in the front of the home could easily be converted to a home office or study
- compact, yet efficient kitchen is conveniently situated between the breakfast and dining rooms

plan #584-037D-0021

price code D

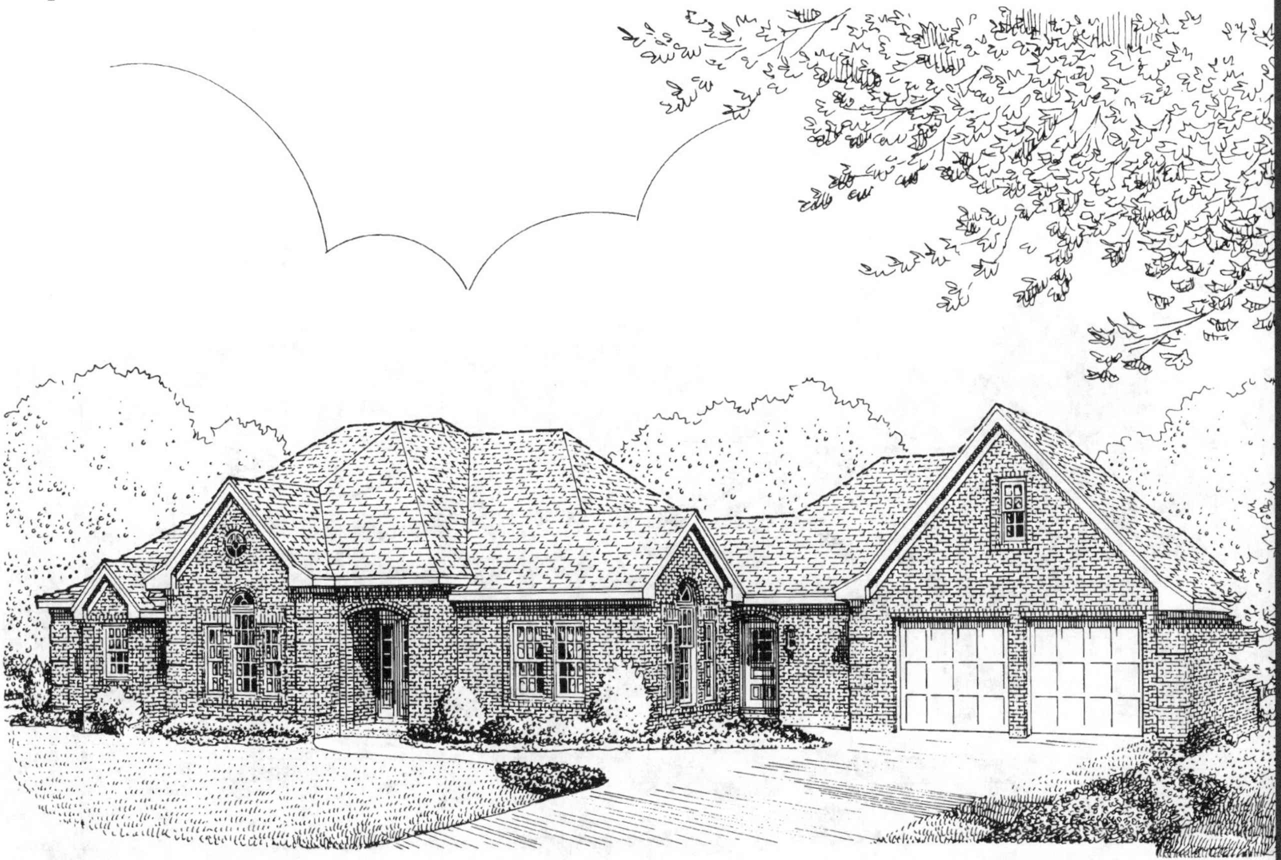

plan information

total living area:	2,260
bedrooms:	3
baths:	2
garage:	2-car
foundation type: slab	

special features

- luxurious master bedroom includes a raised ceiling, bath with oversized tub, separate shower and large walk-in closet
- convenient kitchen and breakfast area with ample pantry storage
- formal foyer leads into large living room with warming fireplace
- convenient secondary entrance for everyday traffic

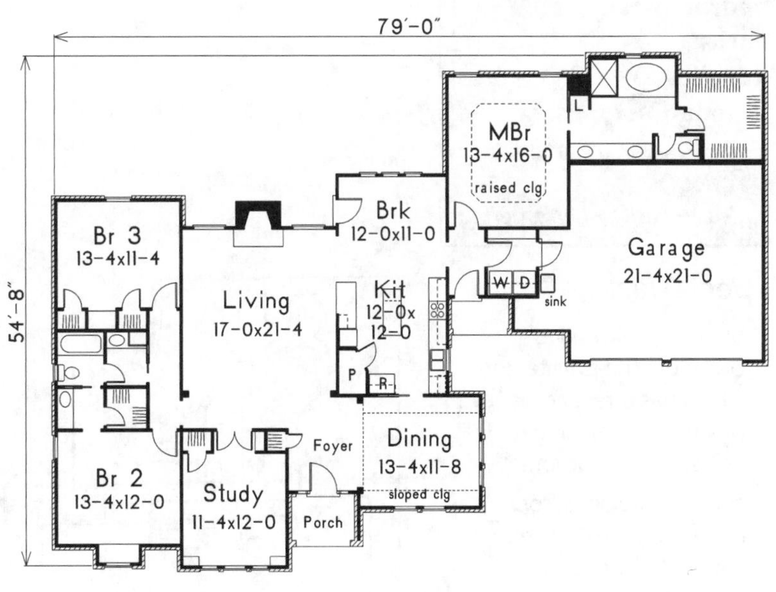

plan #584-026D-0124

price code D

plan information

total living area:	2,317
bedrooms:	1
baths:	2 1/2
garage:	3-car
foundation types:	
walk-out basement	
basement	
please specify when ordering	

special features

- built-in bookshelves complete the private den which has direct access to a private bath making it ideal as a second bedroom
- cheerful breakfast room is octagon-shaped and overlooks into the cozy hearth room
- optional lower level has an additional 1,475 square feet of living area

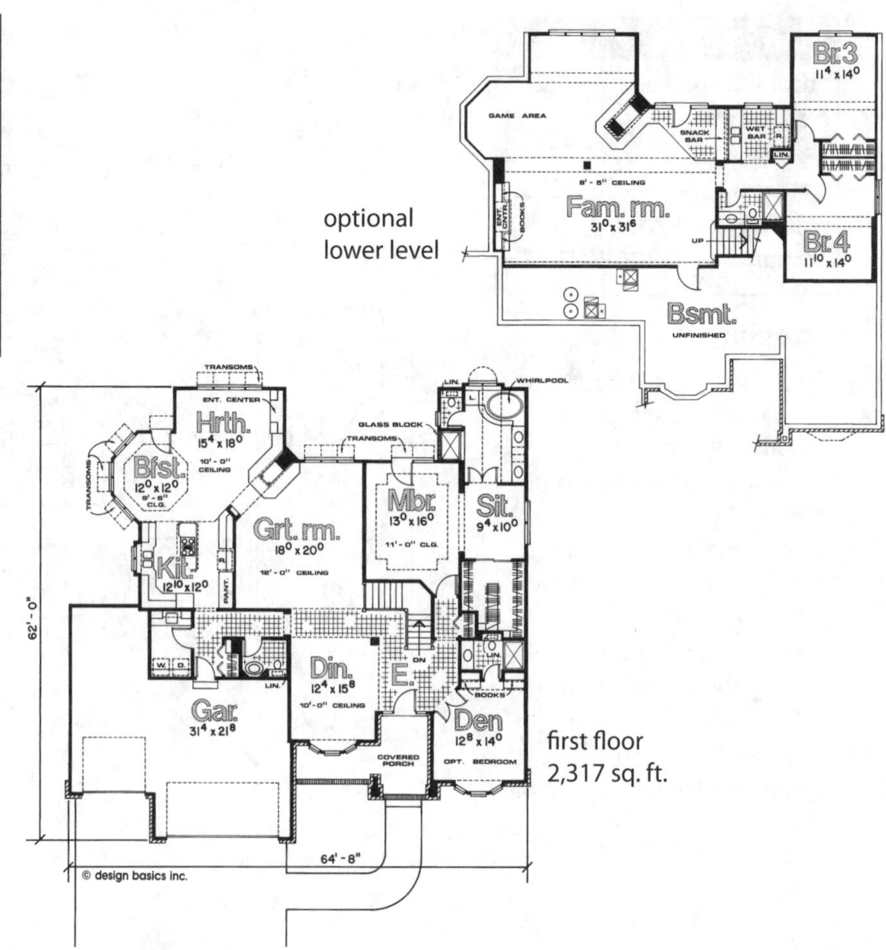

optional lower level

first floor
2,317 sq. ft.

plan #584-035D-0003

price code C

plan information

total living area: 2,115
bedrooms: 3
baths: 2
garage: 2-car side entry
foundation types:
walk-out basement
crawl space
slab
please specify when ordering

special features

- cozy living room/den has a double-door entry and makes an ideal office space
- kitchen has serving bar which overlooks vaulted breakfast area and family room
- master suite has all the amenities

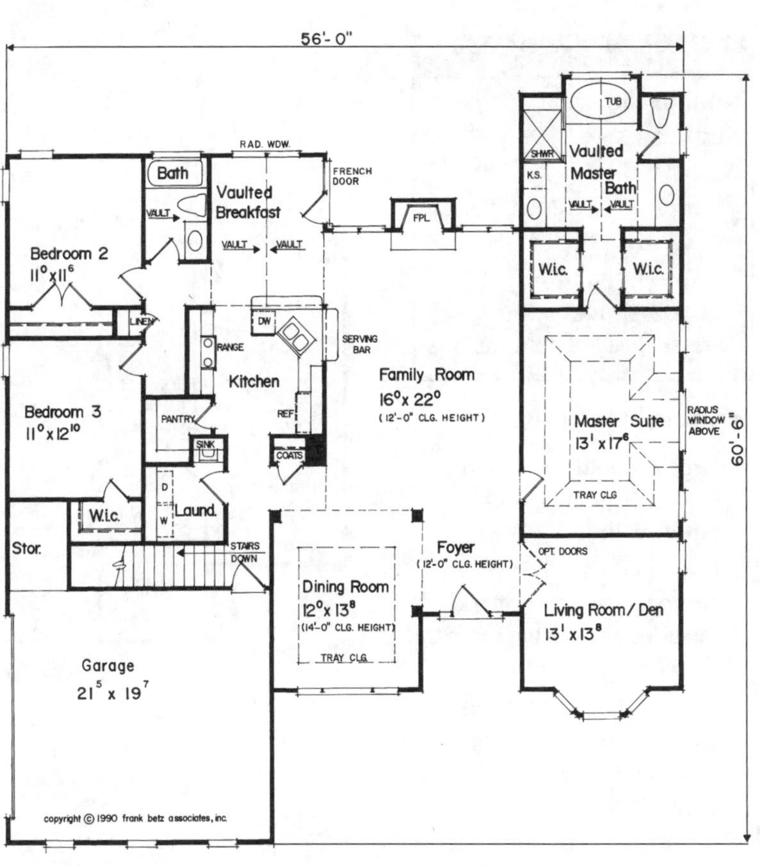

plan #584-069D-0017

price code C

plan information

total living area:	1,926
bedrooms:	3
baths:	2
garage:	2-car side entry
foundation types:	
slab	
crawl space	
please specify when ordering	

special features

- large covered rear porch is spacious enough for entertaining
- the L-shaped kitchen is compact yet efficient and includes a snack bar for extra dining space
- oversized utility room has counterspace, extra shelves and space for a second refrigerator
- secluded master suite has a private bath and a large walk-in closet

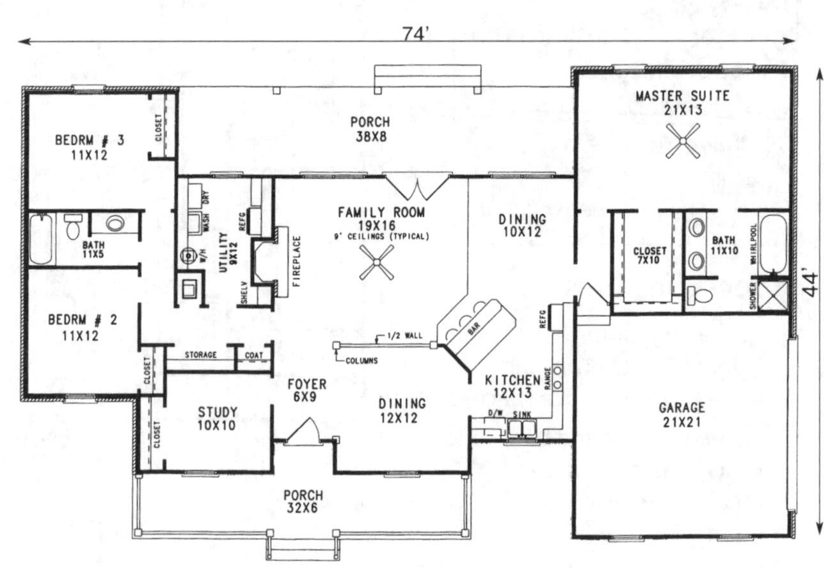

plan #584-048D-0006

price code C

plan information	
total living area:	2,153
bedrooms:	4
baths:	2
garage:	2-car
foundation type:	
slab	

special features

- foyer leads directly into the formal living room which accesses the porch
- master bedroom features a wall of windows and also accesses the porch
- family room boasts a 12' barrel vaulted ceiling and built-in bookshelves on each side of the dramatic fireplace
- varied ceiling heights throughout
- three bedrooms, a bath and the utility room are located off the family room

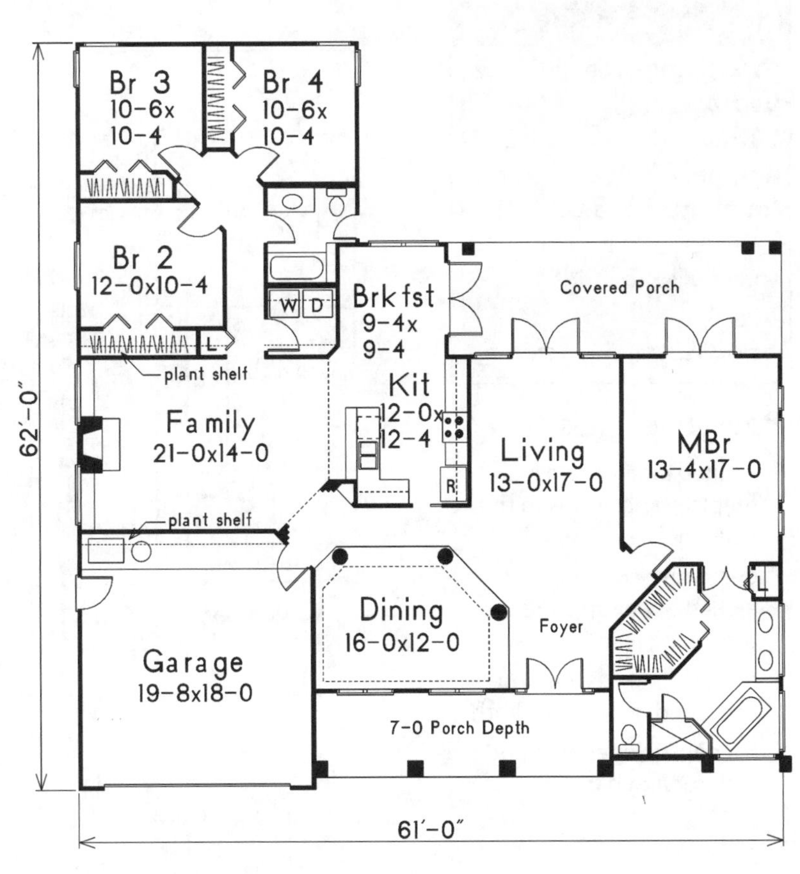

plan #584-035D-0035

price code D

plan information	
total living area:	2,322
bedrooms:	3
baths:	2 1/2
garage:	2-car side entry
foundation types:	
walk-out basement	
crawl space	
slab	
please specify when ordering	

special features

- vaulted family room has a fireplace and access to the kitchen
- decorative columns and arched openings surround the dining area
- master suite has a sitting room and grand-scale bath
- kitchen includes an island with serving bar

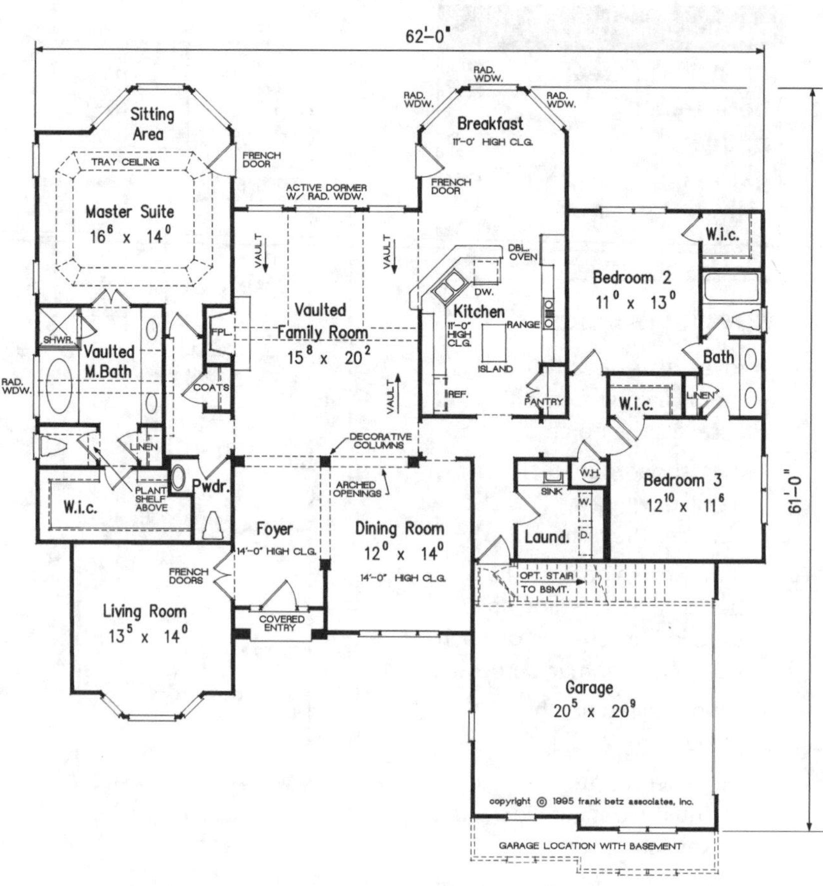

plan #584-051D-0057

price code D

plan information

total living area:	2,229
bedrooms:	3
baths:	2
garage:	2-car side entry
foundation type:	basement

special features

- welcoming and expansive front porch
- dining room has a tray ceiling
- sunny nook with arched soffit creates an inviting entry into this eating space

plan #584-013D-0025

price code C

plan information	
total living area:	2,097
bedrooms:	3
baths:	3
garage:	3-car side entry
foundation types:	
crawl space	
slab	
please specify when ordering	

special features

- angled kitchen, family room and eating area adds interest to this home
- family room includes a TV niche making this a cozy place to relax
- sumptuous master bedroom includes a sitting area, double walk-in closet and a full bath with double vanities

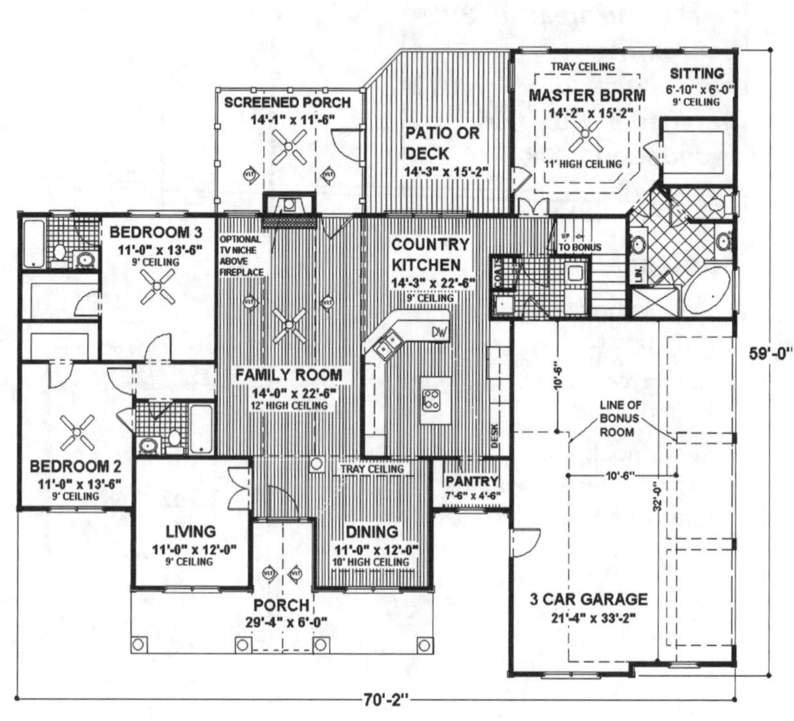

plan #584-035D-0048

price code C

plan information

total living area:	1,915
bedrooms:	4
baths:	3
garage:	2-car
foundation types:	
walk-out basement	
slab	
crawl space	
please specify when ordering	

special features

- large breakfast area overlooks the vaulted great room
- master suite has a cheerful sitting room and private bath
- plan features a unique in-law suite with private bath and walk-in closet

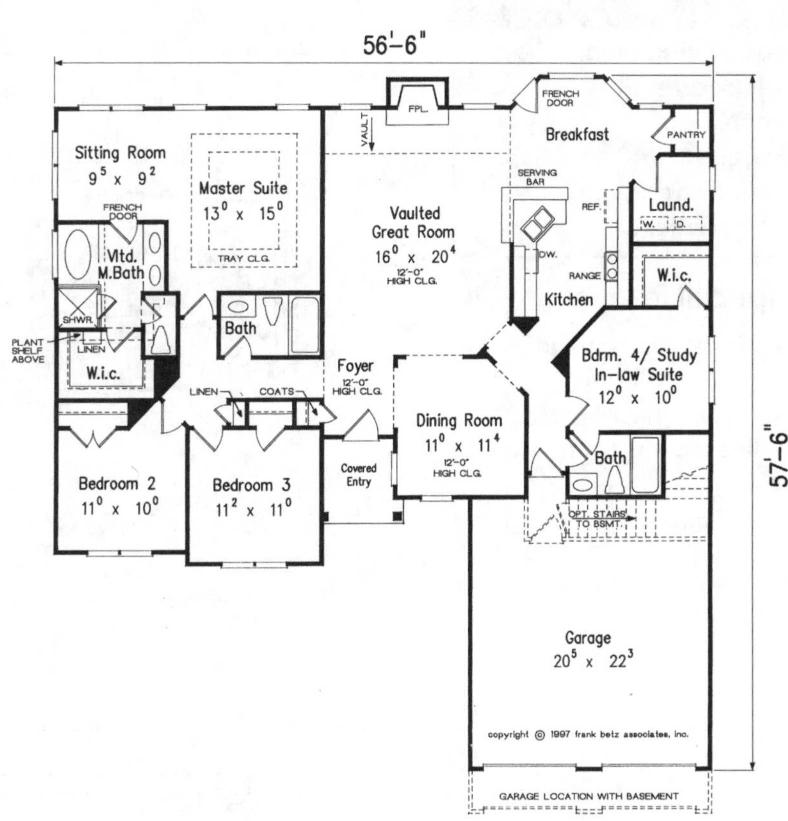

plan #584-026D-0125

price code D

plan information

total living area:	2,512
bedrooms:	3
baths:	2 1/2
garage:	3-car
foundation type: basement	

special features

- master bedroom and bath has all the luxuries
- dynamic breakfast room is flooded with light
- massive garage accommodates the largest of vehicles

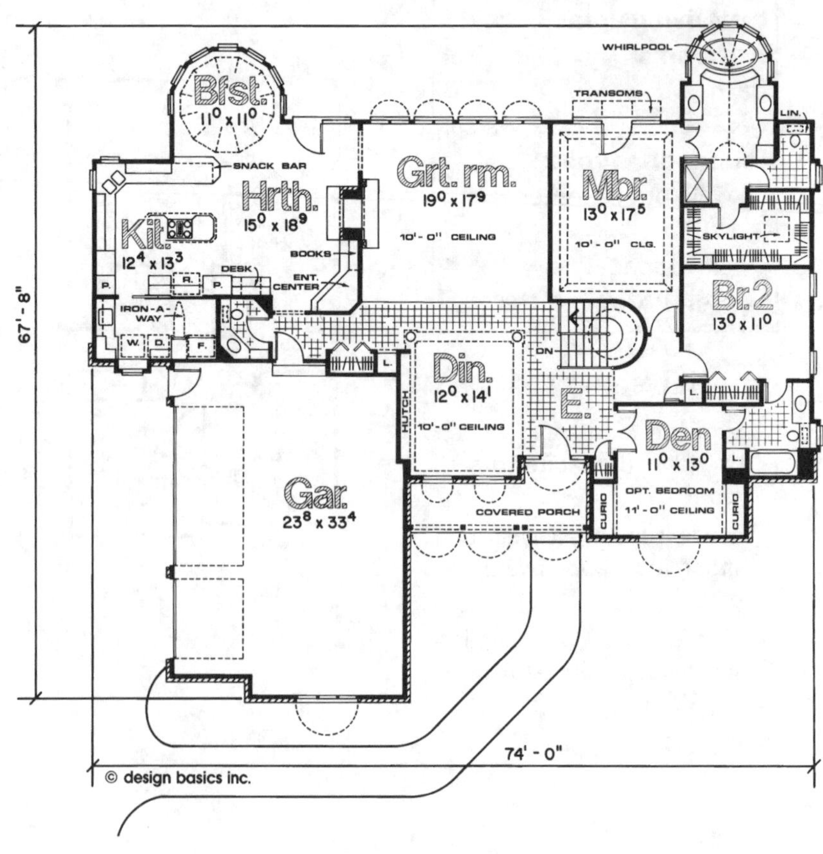

plan information

total living area:	2,033
bedrooms:	3
baths:	2 1/2
garage:	2-car
foundation type:	
walk-out basement	

special features

- vaulted living area is spacious and bright
- beautiful master bath with corner tub and large walk-in closet
- dining room with bay window

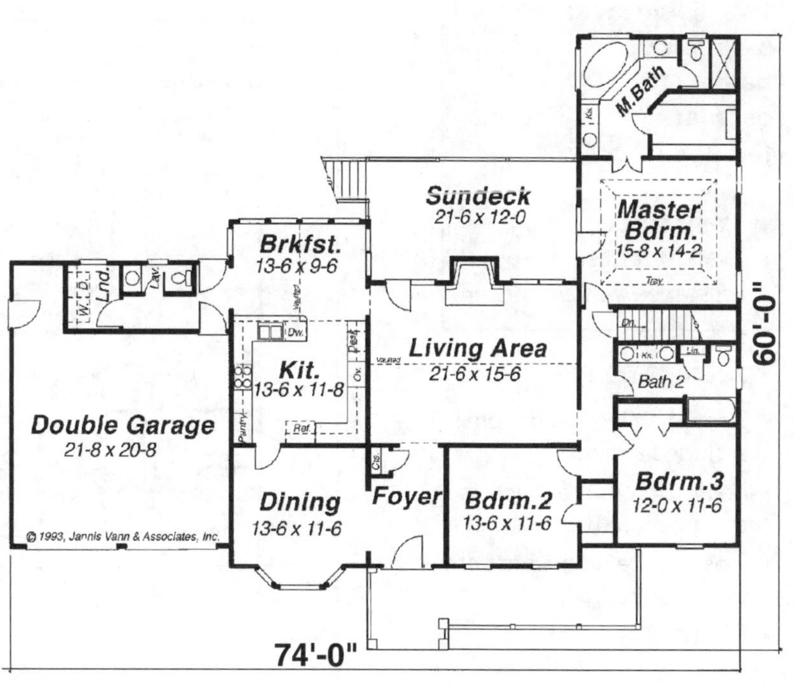

plan #584-035D-0037

price code D

plan information

total living area:	2,279
bedrooms:	4
baths:	3
garage:	2-car side entry

foundation types:

slab
crawl space
walk-out basement

please specify when ordering

special features

- formal vaulted living room is secluded and quiet
- breakfast room connects to the great room
- master suite is separate from the other bedrooms for privacy

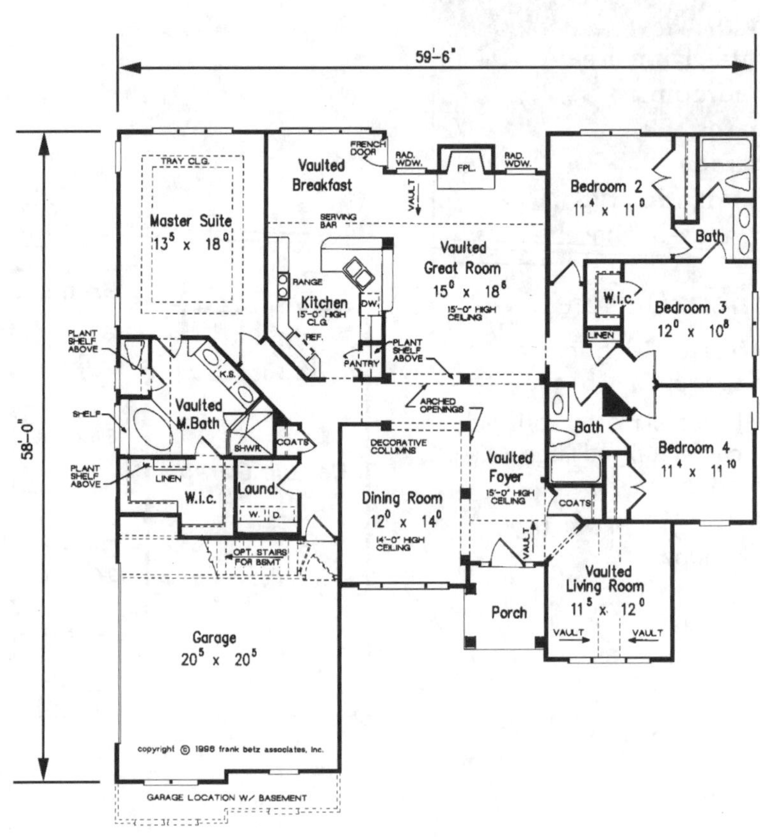

plan #584-052D-0080

price code D

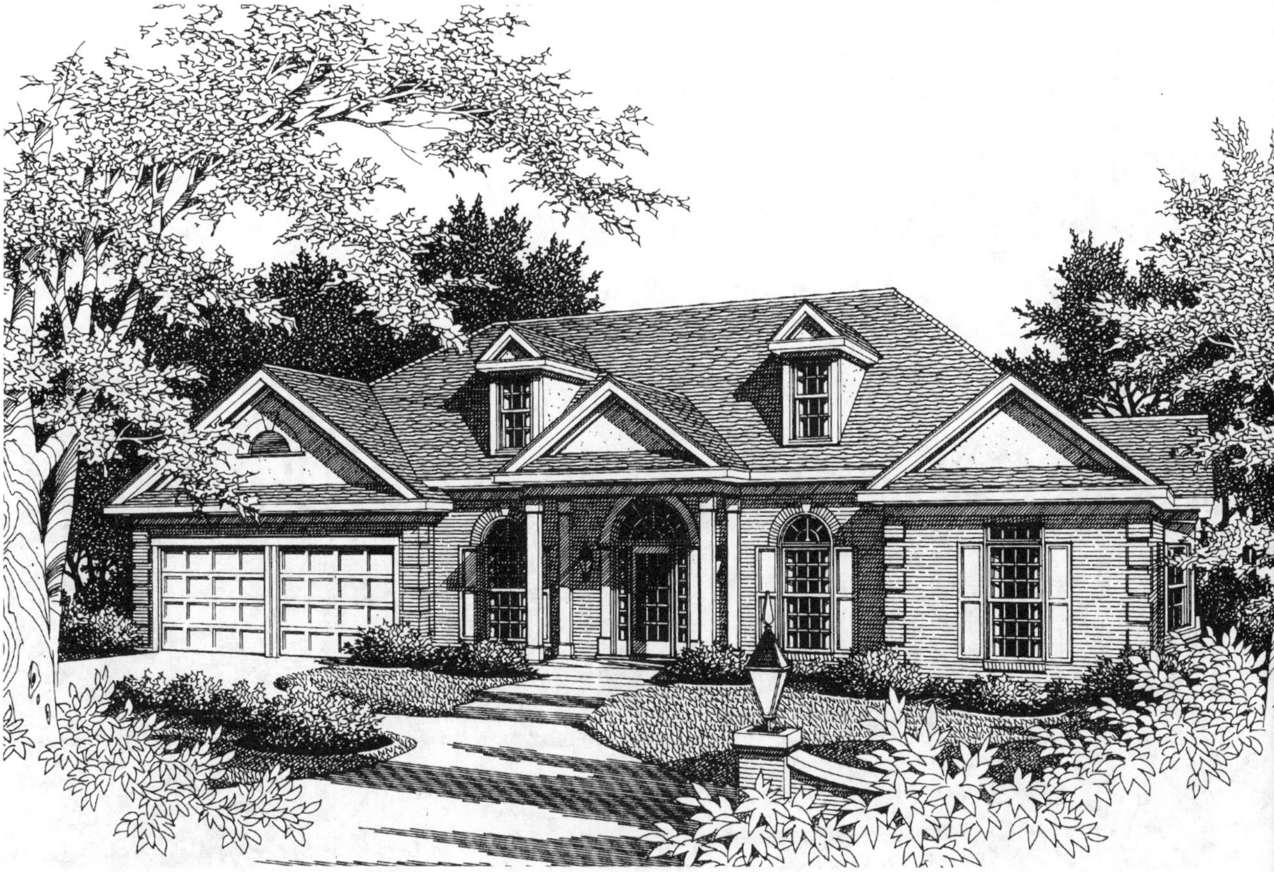

plan information

total living area:	2,542
bedrooms:	4
baths:	2 1/2
garage:	2-car
foundation types:	
walk-out basement	
crawl space	
slab	
please specify when ordering	

special features

- formal entry opens to living and dining rooms
- private master bedroom features double closets and access to the outdoors
- extra storage can be found throughout

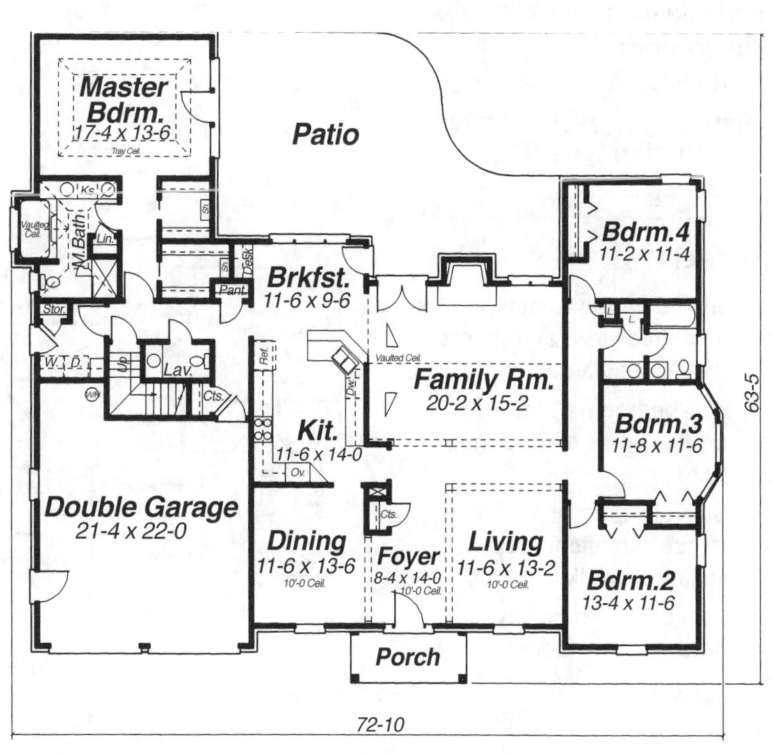

plan #584-047D-0046

price code D

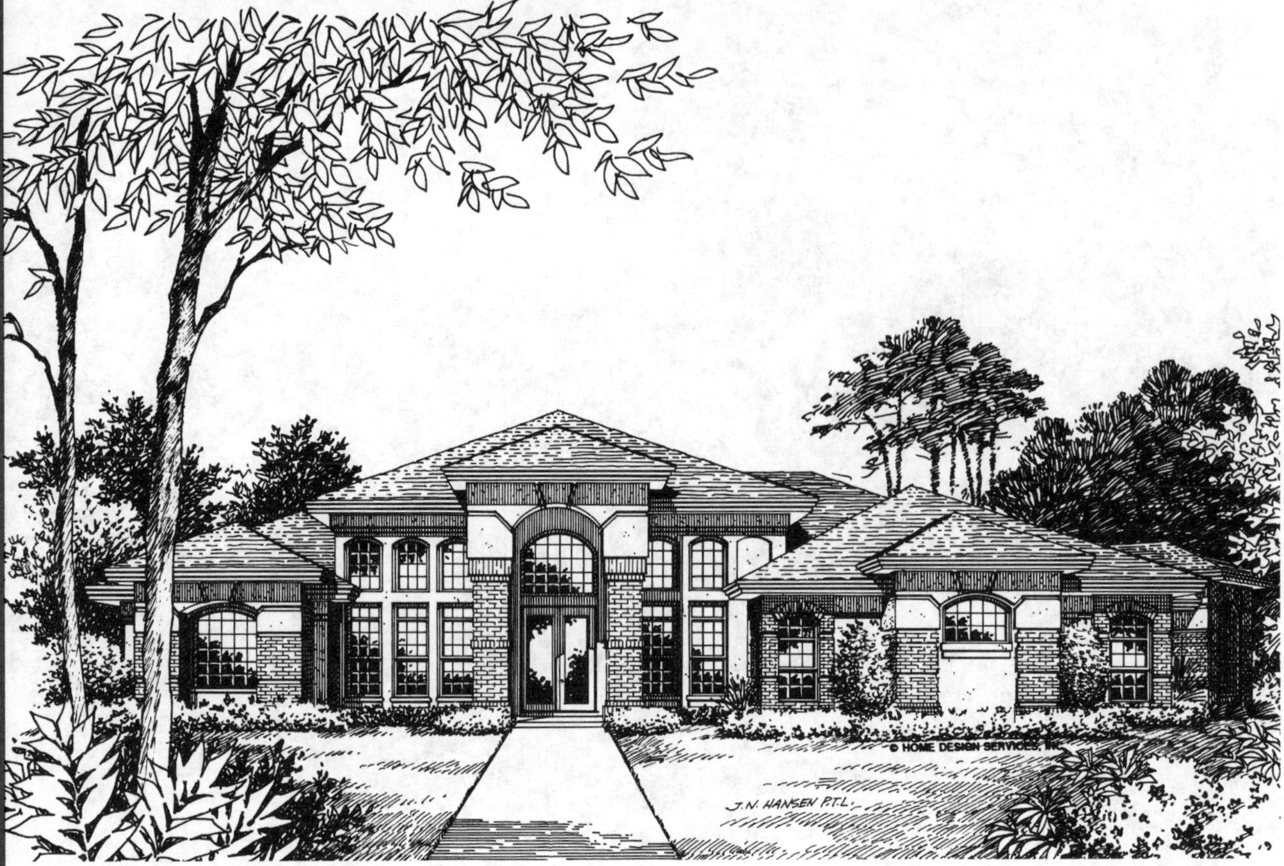

plan information

total living area:	2,597
bedrooms:	4
baths:	3
garage:	3-car rear entry
foundation type:	slab

special features

- angled design creates unlimited views and spaces that appear larger
- den/bedroom #4 makes a perfect home office or guest suite
- island kitchen with view to nook and family room includes a walk-in pantry
- pool bath is shared by outdoor and indoor areas

Width: 98'-6"
Depth: 50'-0"

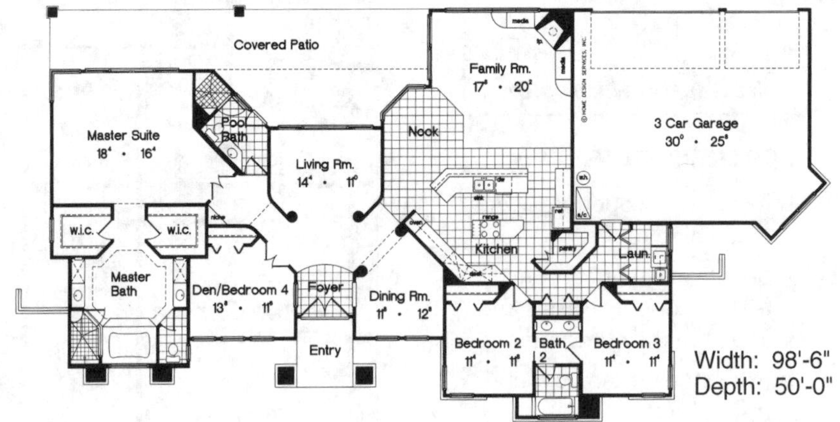

plan #584-055D-0085

price code C

plan information

total living area:	1,989
bedrooms:	4
baths:	3
garage:	2-car side entry
foundation types:	
crawl space	
siab	

please specify when ordering

special features

- dining room has 8" decorative columns
- master suite has optional door to rear covered porch
- laundry area is convenient to kitchen and garage

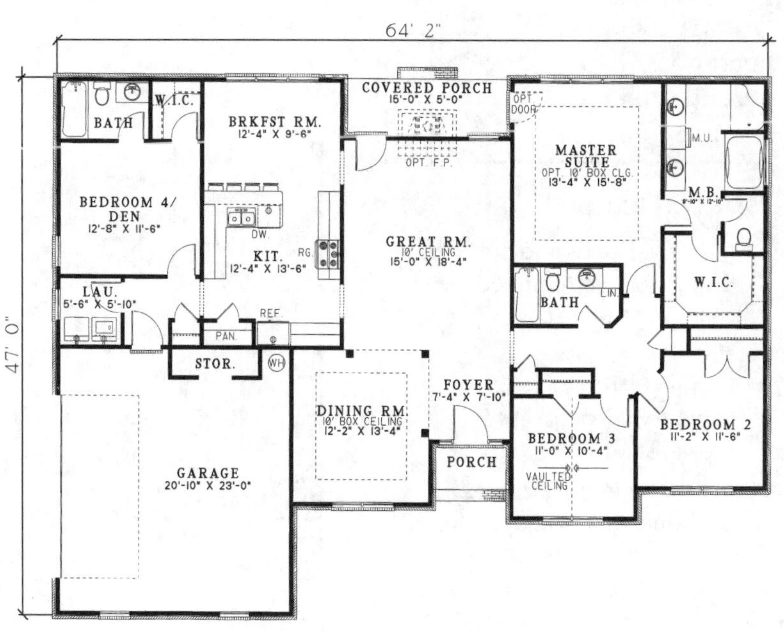

plan #584-048D-0002

price code D

plan information	
total living area:	2,467
bedrooms:	3
baths:	3
garage:	2-car
foundation type: slab	

special features

- tiled foyer leads into the living room with vaulted ceiling and large bay window
- kitchen features a walk-in pantry and adjacent breakfast nook
- master bedroom includes a bay window and bath with large walk-in closet

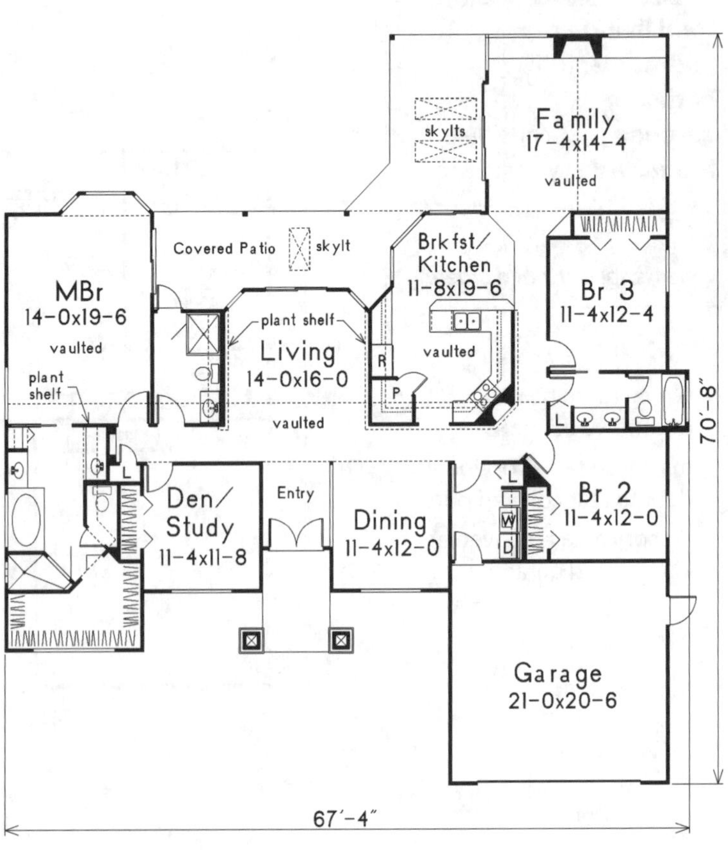

plan #584-055D-0095

price code C

© Michael E. Nelson
NELSON DESIGN GROUP, LLC

plan information

total living area:	2,189
bedrooms:	4
baths:	2
garage:	2-car side entry
foundation types:	
slab	
crawl space	
please specify when ordering	

special features

- bedroom #2 has double closets and accesses a full bath
- master bath has a whirlpool tub, separate shower, double vanities and a large walk-in closet
- front porch opens to the foyer with 13' ceiling

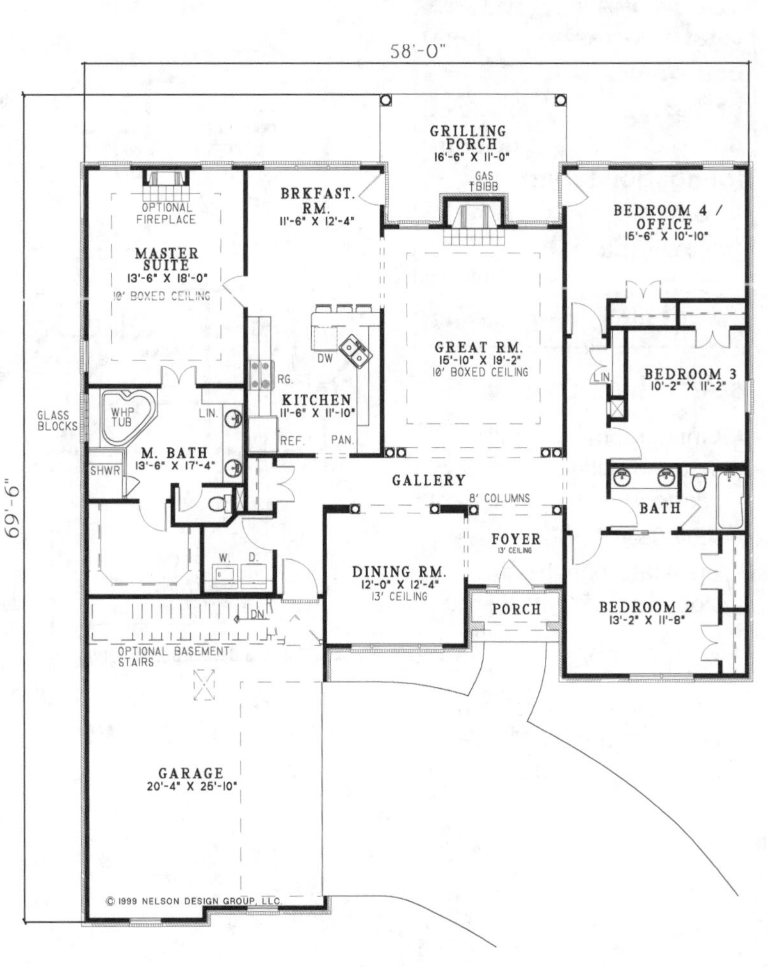

plan #584-016D-0047

price code D

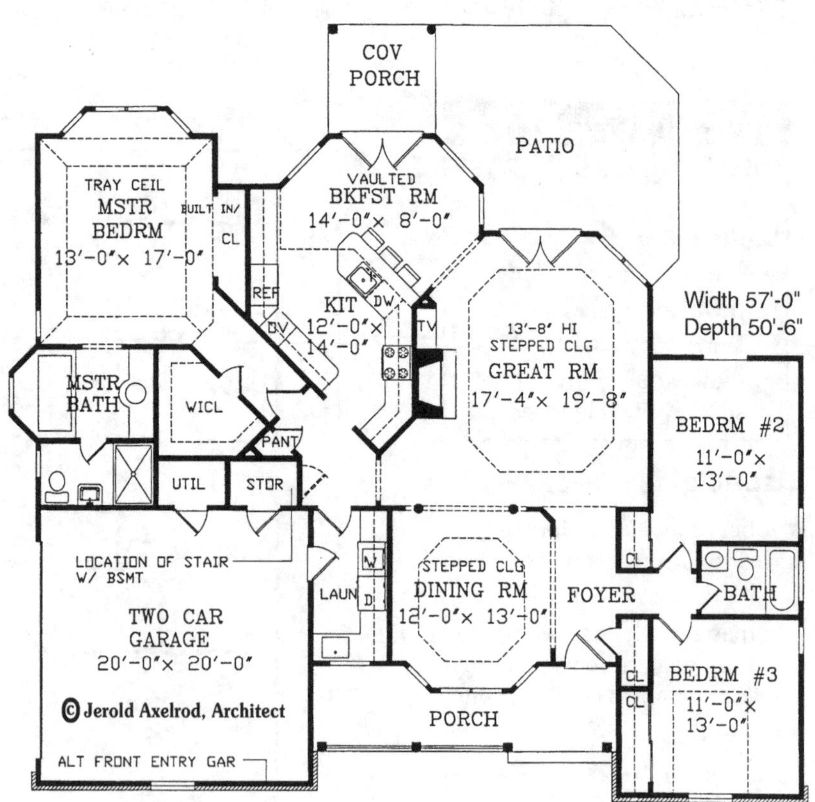

plan information

total living area:	1,860
bedrooms:	3
baths:	2
garage:	2-car side entry
foundation types:	
basement	
crawl space	
slab	
please specify when ordering	

special features

- dining room has an 11' stepped ceiling with a bay window creating a pleasant dining experience
- breakfast room has a 12' sloped ceiling with French doors leading to a covered porch
- great room has a columned arched entrance, a built-in media center and a fireplace

plan #584-053D-0031

price code C

plan information

total living area:	1,908
bedrooms:	3
baths:	2
garage:	2-car
foundation types:	
crawl space standard	
slab	

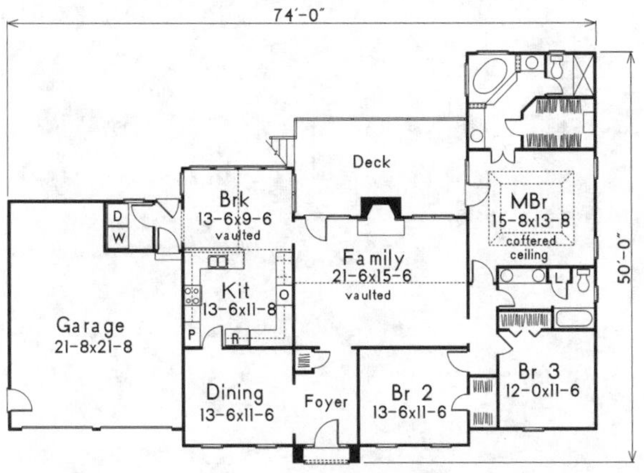

special features

- distinguished front entry features circle-top window and prominent center gable
- deck is nestled between living areas for easy access
- oversized two-car garage has large work/storage area and convenient laundry room
- vaulted ceiling and floor-to-ceiling windows in family and breakfast rooms create an open, unrestricted space
- master bedroom with deluxe bath, large walk-in closet and recessed ceiling

---

plan #584-068D-0004

price code C

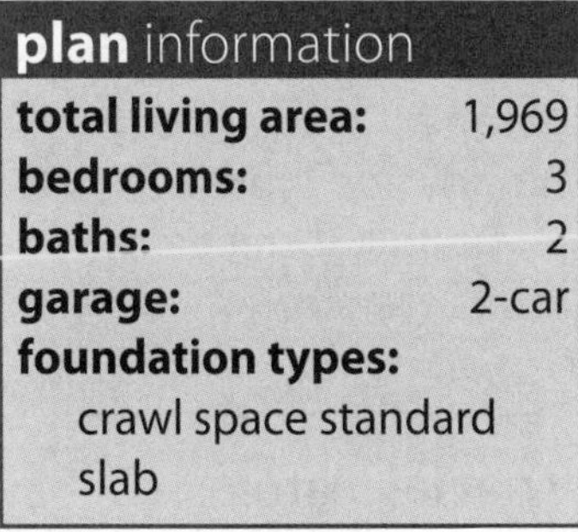

plan information

total living area:	1,969
bedrooms:	3
baths:	2
garage:	2-car
foundation types:	
crawl space standard	
slab	

special features

- master bedroom boasts a luxurious bath with double sinks, two walk-in closets and an oversized tub
- corner fireplace warms a conveniently located family area
- formal living and dining areas in the front of the home lend a touch of privacy when entertaining
- spacious utility room has counterspace and a sink

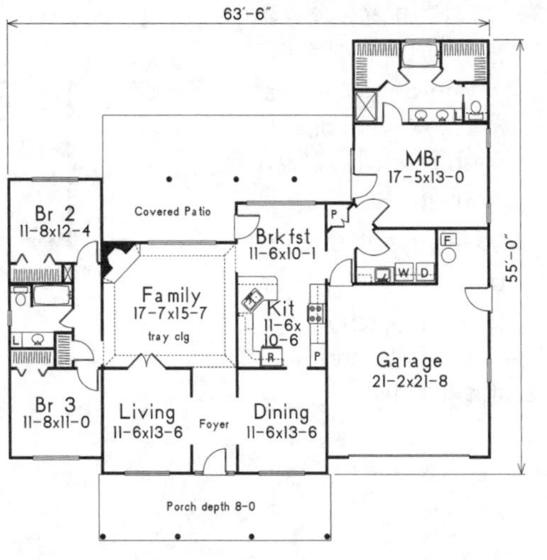

plan #584-001D-0032

price code D

plan information

total living area:	2,520
bedrooms:	4
baths:	2 1/2
garage:	2-car side entry
foundation types:	
basement standard	
crawl space	
slab	

special features

- open hearth fireplace warms family and breakfast rooms
- master bedroom features a private bath with deluxe tub, double-bowl vanity and large walk-in closet
- vaulted living and dining rooms flank foyer
- corner sink in kitchen overlooks family and breakfast rooms

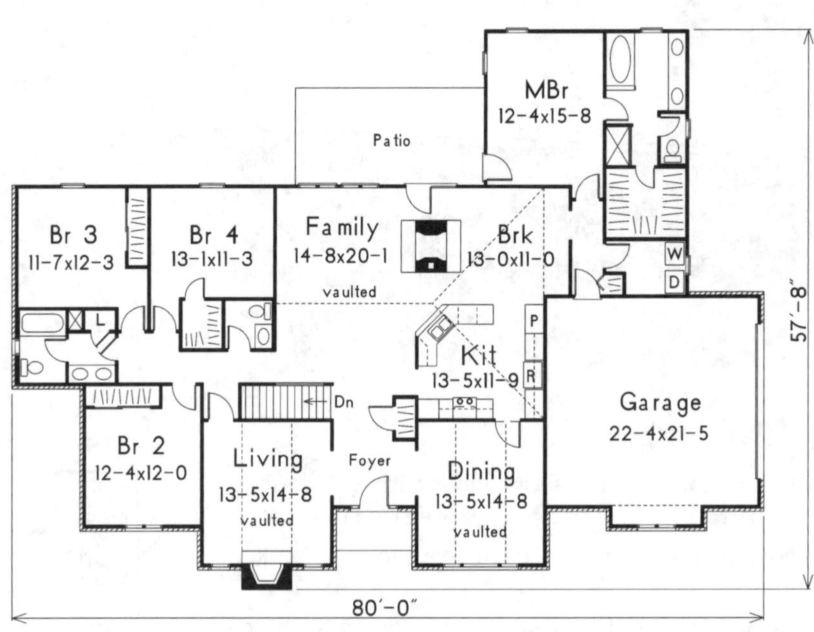

plan #584-053D-0055

price code C

plan information

total living area:	1,803
bedrooms:	3
baths:	2
garage:	3-car drive under
foundation type: basement	

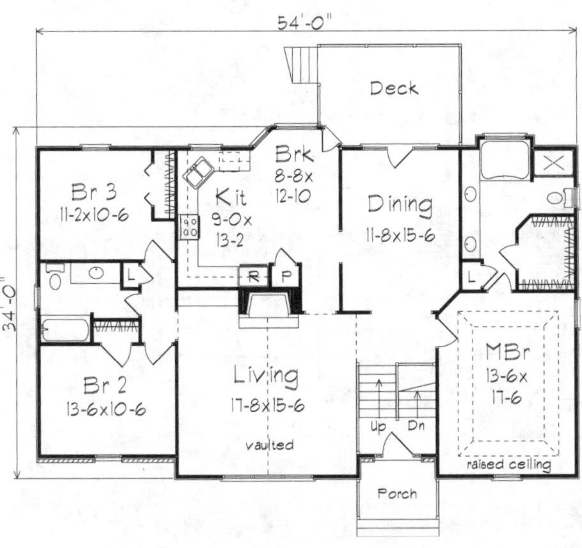

special features

- master bedroom features a raised ceiling and private bath with a walk-in closet, large double-bowl vanity and separate tub and shower
- a U-shaped kitchen includes a corner sink and convenient pantry
- vaulted living room is complete with a fireplace and built-in cabinet

plan #584-061D-0003

price code D

plan information

total living area:	2,255
bedrooms:	4
baths:	2 1/2
garage:	3-car
foundation type: slab	

special features

- walk-in closets in all bedrooms
- plant shelf graces hallway
- large functional kitchen adjoins the family room which features a fireplace and access outdoors
- master bath comes complete with a double vanity, enclosed toilet, separate tub and shower and cozy fireplace
- living/dining room combine for a large formal gathering room

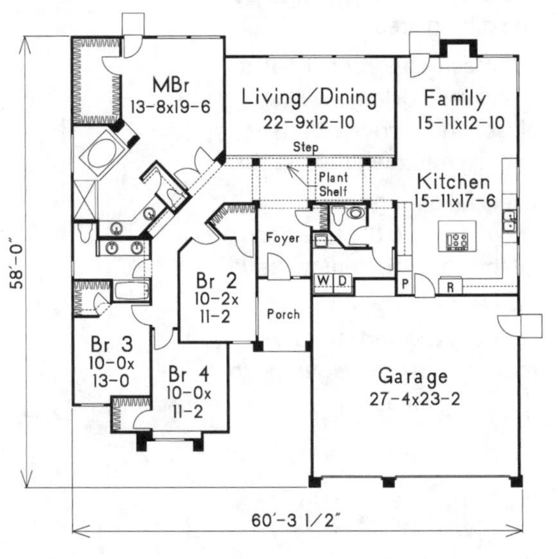

plan #584-004D-0002

price code C

plan information

total living area:	1,823
bedrooms:	3
baths:	2
garage:	2-car
foundation type:	basement

special features

- vaulted living room is spacious and easily accesses the dining area
- the master bedroom boasts a tray ceiling, large walk-in closet and a private bath with a corner whirlpool tub
- cheerful dining area is convenient to the U-shaped kitchen and also enjoys patio access
- centrally located laundry room connects the garage to the living areas

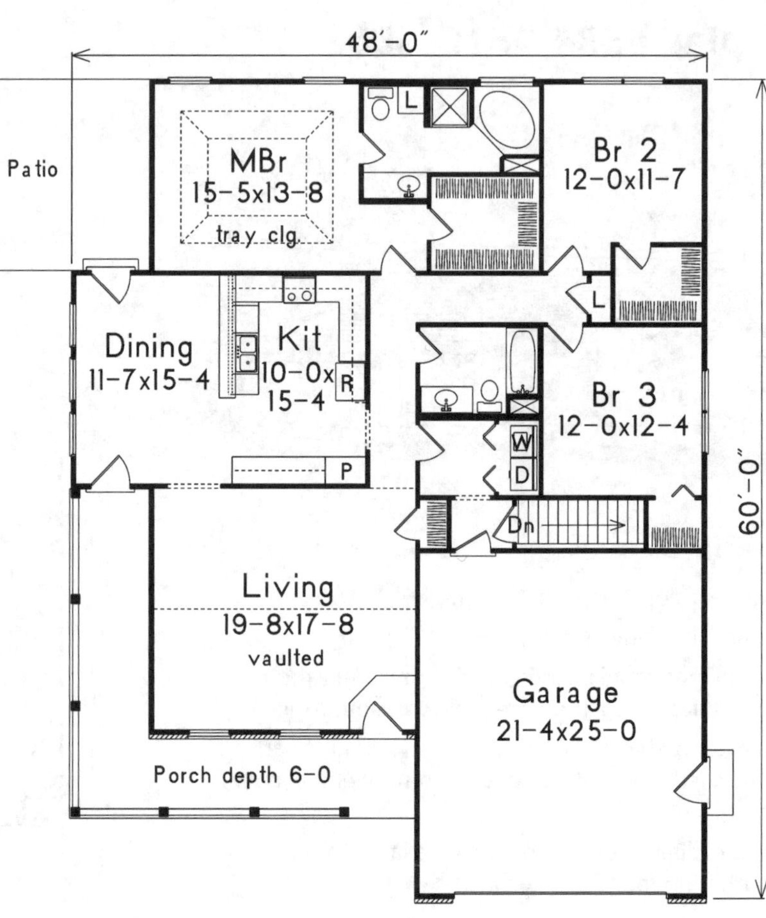

plan #584-058D-0023

price code C

plan information	
total living area:	1,883
bedrooms:	3
baths:	2 1/2
garage:	2-car side entry
foundation type:	
basement	

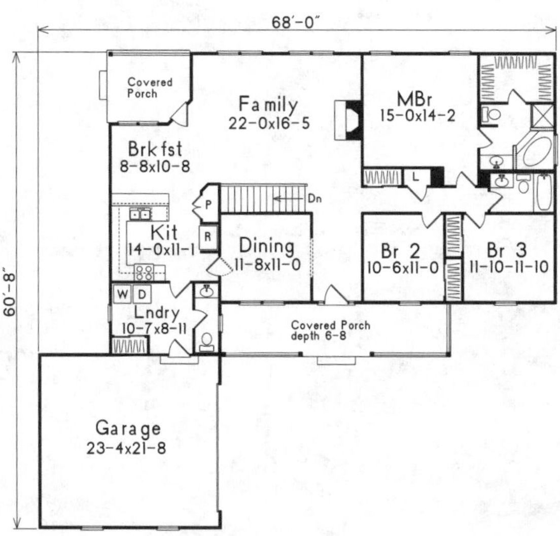

special features

- large laundry room located off the garage has a coat closet and half bath
- large family room with fireplace and access to the covered porch is a great central gathering room
- the U-shaped kitchen has a breakfast bar, large pantry and swing door to dining room for convenient serving

---

plan #584-061D-0002

price code C

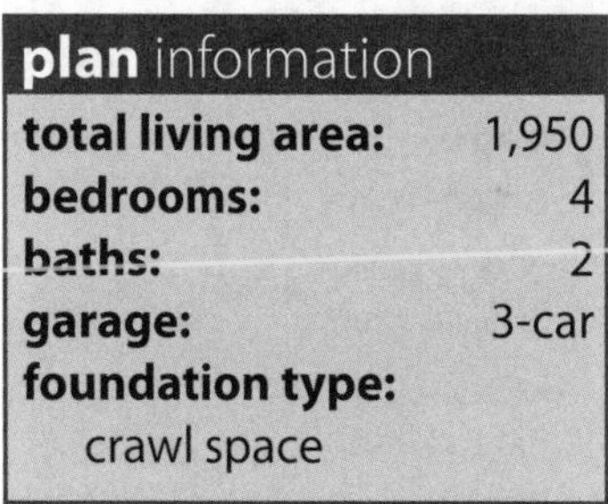

plan information	
total living area:	1,950
bedrooms:	4
baths:	2
garage:	3-car
foundation type:	
crawl space	

special features

- large corner kitchen with island cooktop opens to the family room
- master bedroom features a double-door entry, raised ceiling, double-bowl vanity and walk-in closet
- plant shelf accents hall

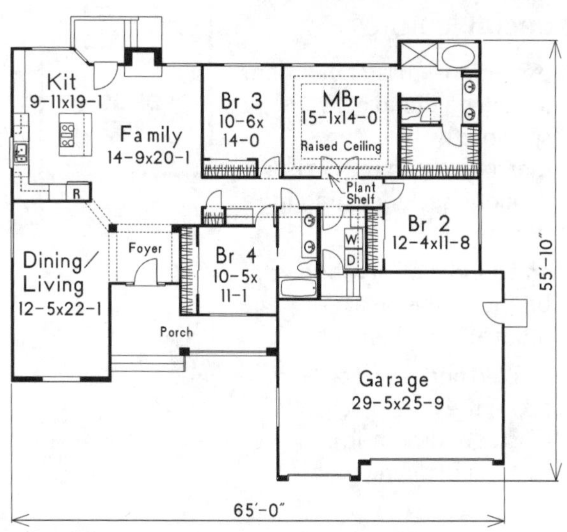

plan #584-013D-0024

price code C

plan information

total living area: 2,088
bedrooms: 3
baths: 2 1/2
garage: 2-car
foundation types:
- basement
- crawl space
- slab

please specify when ordering

special features

- exceptional master bedroom includes a grand bath, spacious walk-in closet, direct access to the deck and a unique secluded morning porch
- an abundance of windows brightens the breakfast room and kitchen
- vaulted and raised ceilings adorn the foyer, kitchen, master bedroom, living, family and dining rooms

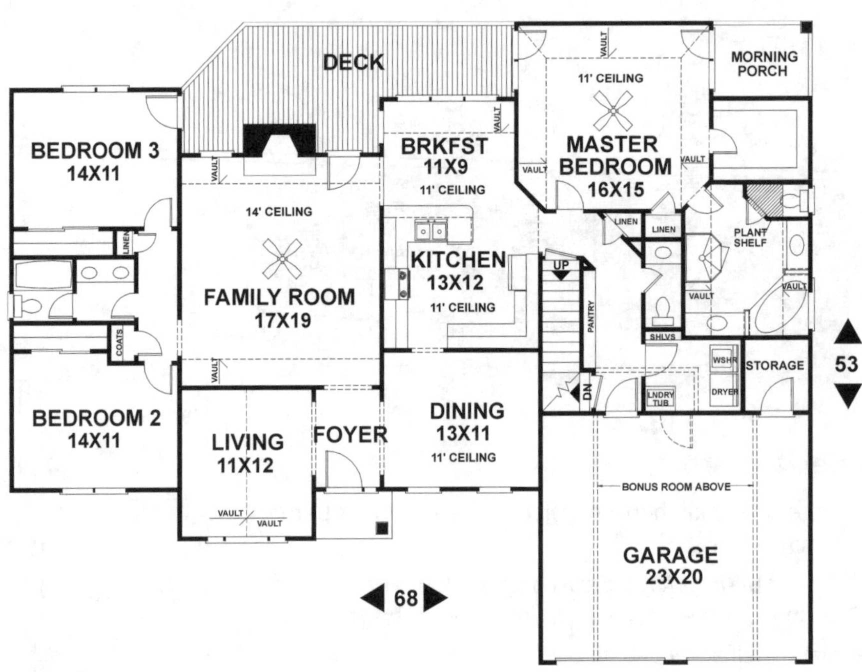

plan #584-058D-0026

price code C

plan information

total living area:	1,819
bedrooms:	3
baths:	2
garage:	2-car side entry
foundation type:	
basement	

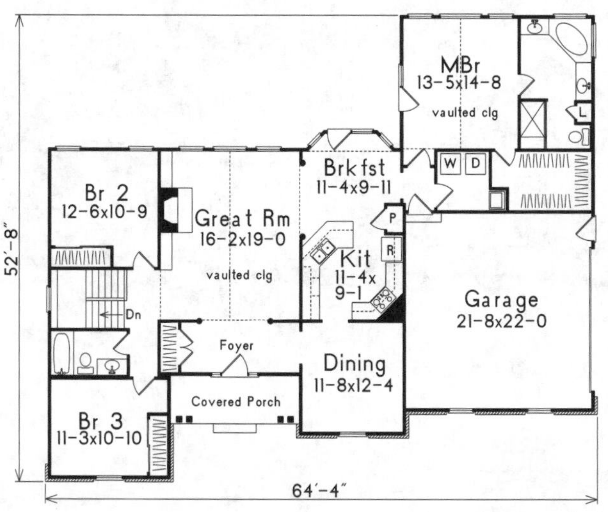

special features

- master bedroom features access to the outdoors, large walk-in closet and private bath
- 9' ceilings throughout
- formal foyer with coat closet opens into the vaulted great room with fireplace and formal dining room
- kitchen and breakfast room create a cozy and casual area

---

plan #584-058D-0027

price code D

plan information

total living area:	2,516
bedrooms:	3
baths:	2 1/2
garage:	3-car
foundation type:	
basement	

special features

- 12' ceilings in the living areas
- plenty of closet space in this open ranch plan
- large kitchen/breakfast area joins great room via see-through fireplace creating two large entering spaces flanking each side
- large three-car garage has extra storage area
- the master bedroom has an eye-catching bay window

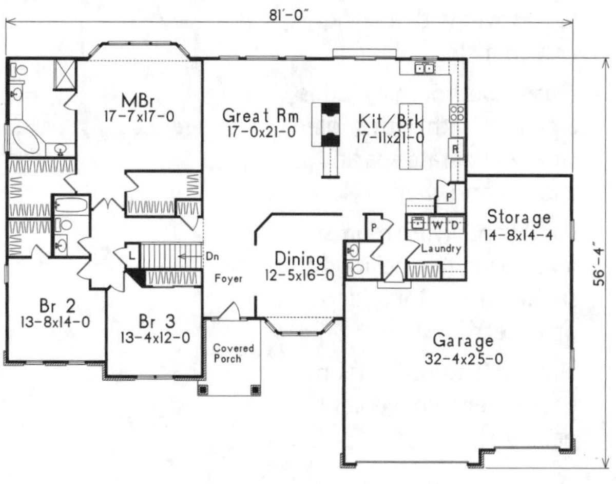

plan #584-014D-0001

price code C

plan information

total living area:	2,159
bedrooms:	3
baths:	2
garage:	2-car
foundation types:	
basement standard	
crawl space	
slab	

special features

- energy efficient home with 2" x 6" exterior walls
- covered entry opens into the large foyer with a skylight and coat closet
- master bedroom includes a private bath with angled vanity, separate spa and shower and walk-in closet
- family and living rooms feature vaulted ceilings and sunken floors for added openness
- kitchen features an island counter and convenient pantry

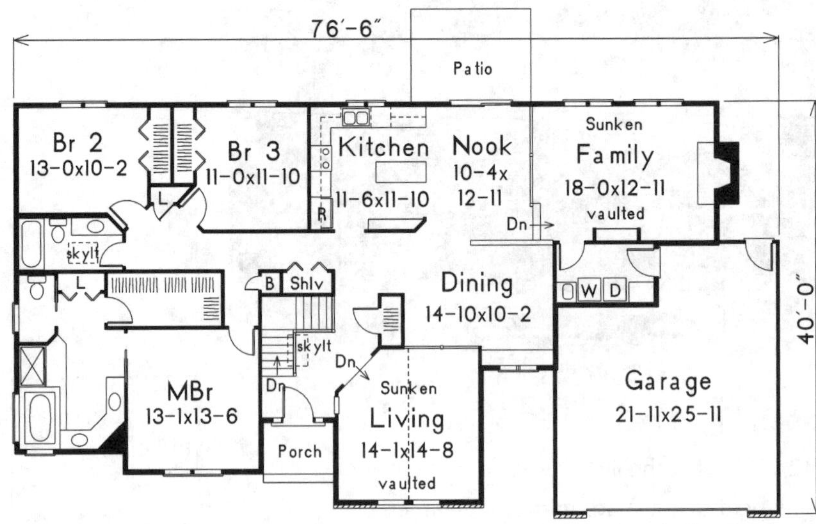

plan #584-045D-0003

price code C

plan information

total living area:	1,958
bedrooms:	3
baths:	2
garage:	2-car
foundation type:	
basement	

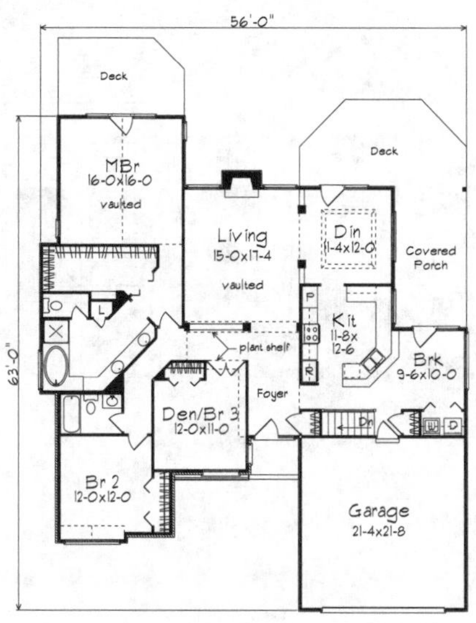

special features

- large wrap-around kitchen opens to a bright and cheerful breakfast area with access to large covered deck and open stairway to basement
- kitchen is nestled between the dining and breakfast rooms
- master bedroom includes large walk-in closet, double-bowl vanity, garden tub and separate shower
- foyer features an attractive plant shelf and opens into the living room that includes a lovely central fireplace

---

plan #584-053D-0046

price code C

plan information

total living area:	1,862
bedrooms:	3
baths:	2
garage:	2-car
foundation types:	
slab standard	
crawl space	

special features

- master bedroom includes a tray ceiling, bay window, access to the patio and a private bath with oversized tub and generous closet space
- corner sink and breakfast bar faces into the breakfast area and great room
- spacious great room features a vaulted ceiling, fireplace and access to the rear patio

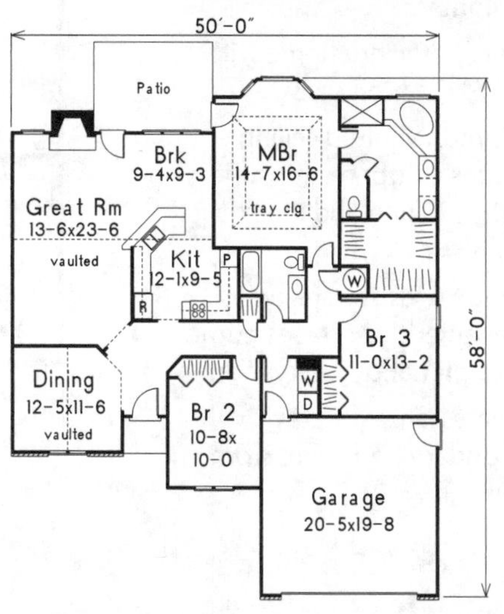

plan #584-021D-0014

price code C

plan information

total living area:	1,856
bedrooms:	3
baths:	2
garage:	2-car side entry
foundation types:	
slab standard	
crawl space	

special features

- living room features include fireplace, 12' ceiling and skylights
- energy efficient home with 2" x 6" exterior walls
- common vaulted ceiling creates an open atmosphere in the kitchen and breakfast room
- garage with storage areas conveniently accesses home through handy utility room
- private hall separates secondary bedrooms from living areas

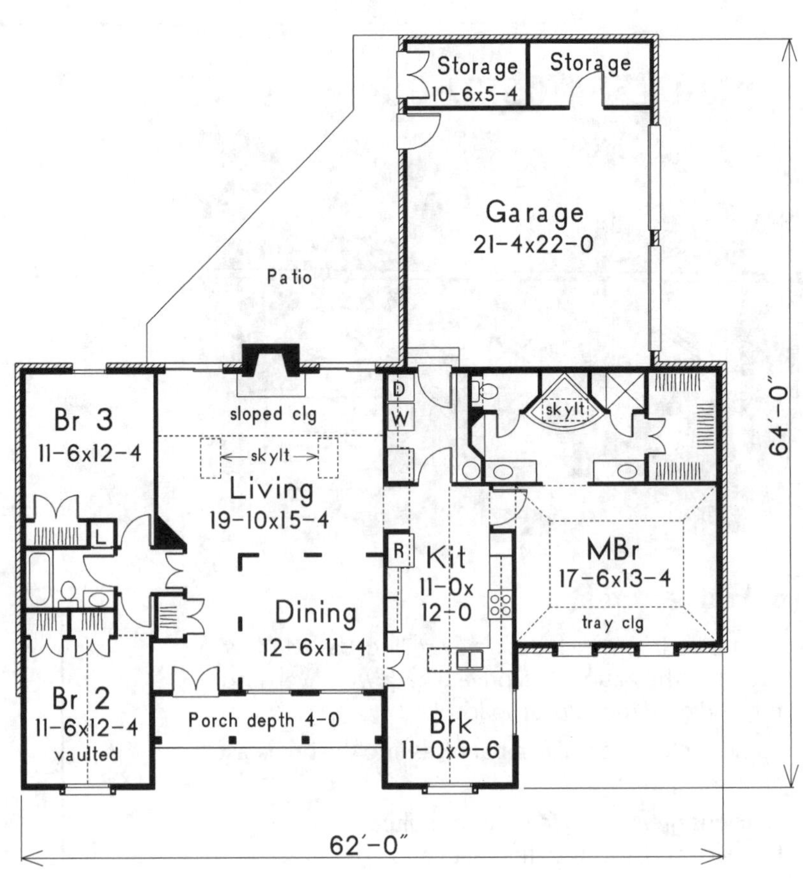

plan #584-047D-0035

price code C

plan information	
total living area:	2,077
bedrooms:	3
baths:	2
garage:	2-car side entry
foundation type:	
slab	

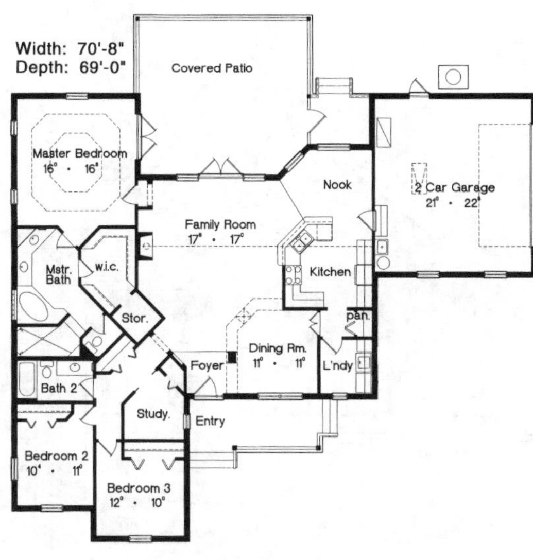

special features

- lots of storage space throughout
- enormous covered patio adds a lot of space when entertaining
- angled walls add appeal throughout this home

plan #584-051D-0055

price code C

plan information	
total living area:	1,907
bedrooms:	3
baths:	2 1/2
garage:	3-car
foundation type:	
basement	

special features

- vaulted entry and great room
- large three stall garage includes ample storage space for hobby materials
- covered porch directly off eating nook provides easy access to the outdoors

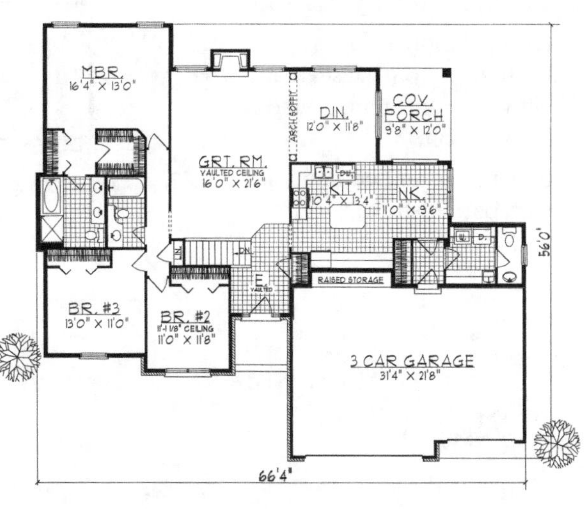

plan #584-026D-0112

price code C

plan information

total living area:	1,911
bedrooms:	3
baths:	2
garage:	2-car
foundation type:	basement

special features

- large entry opens into a beautiful great room with an angled see-through fireplace
- terrific design includes kitchen and breakfast area with adjacent sunny bayed hearth room
- private master bedroom with bath features skylight and walk-in closet

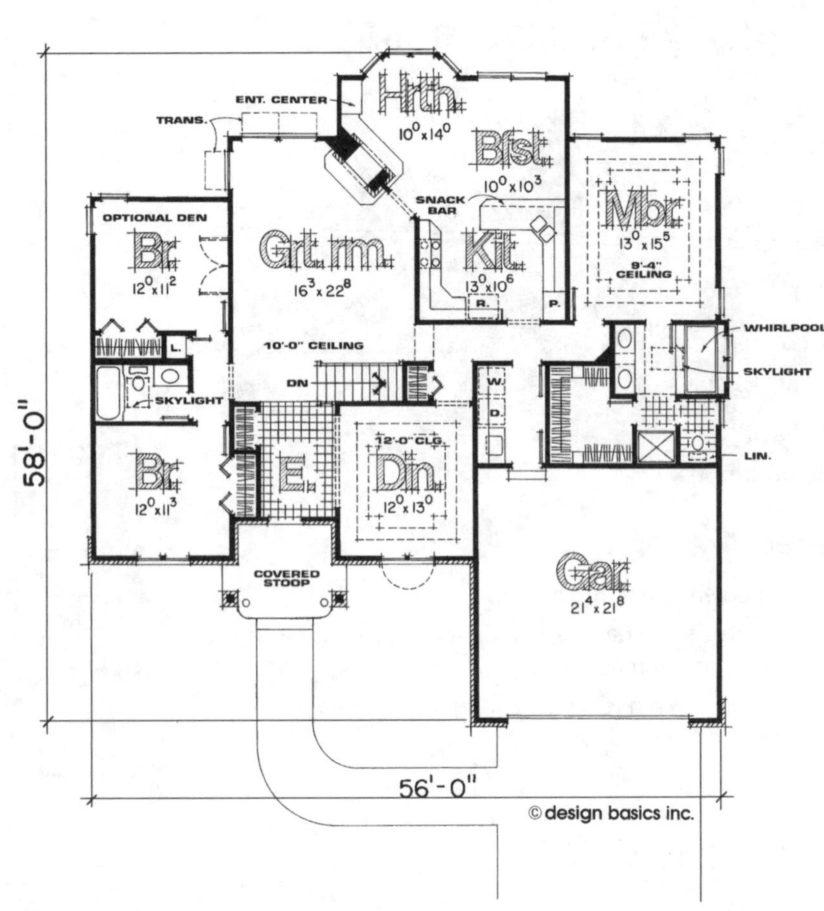

plan #584-048D-0009

price code C

plan information

total living area:	2,041
bedrooms:	4
baths:	2
garage:	2-car
foundation types:	
slab standard	
crawl space	

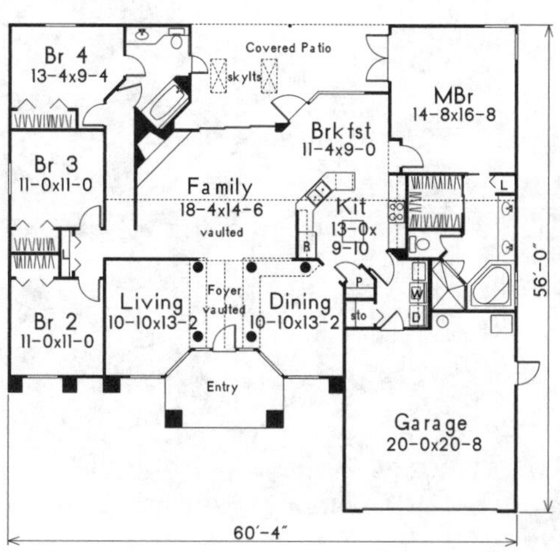

special features

- columned foyer projects past the living and dining rooms into the family room
- kitchen conveniently accesses the dining room and breakfast area
- master bedroom features double-door access to the patio and a pocket door to the private bath with walk-in closet, double-bowl vanity and tub

plan #584-023D-0012

price code D

plan information

total living area:	2,365
bedrooms:	4
baths:	2
garage:	2-car carport
foundation type:	
slab	

special features

- 9' ceilings throughout the home
- expansive central living room is complemented by a corner fireplace
- breakfast bay overlooks the rear porch
- master bedroom features a bath with two walk-in closets and vanities, separate tub and shower and handy linen closet
- peninsula keeps kitchen private

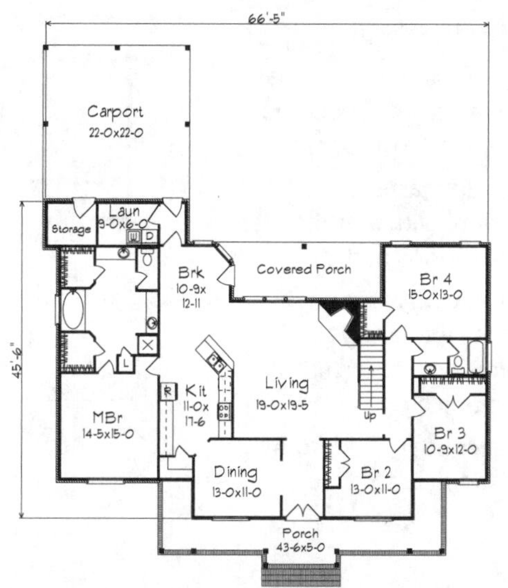

plan #584-013D-0027

price code C

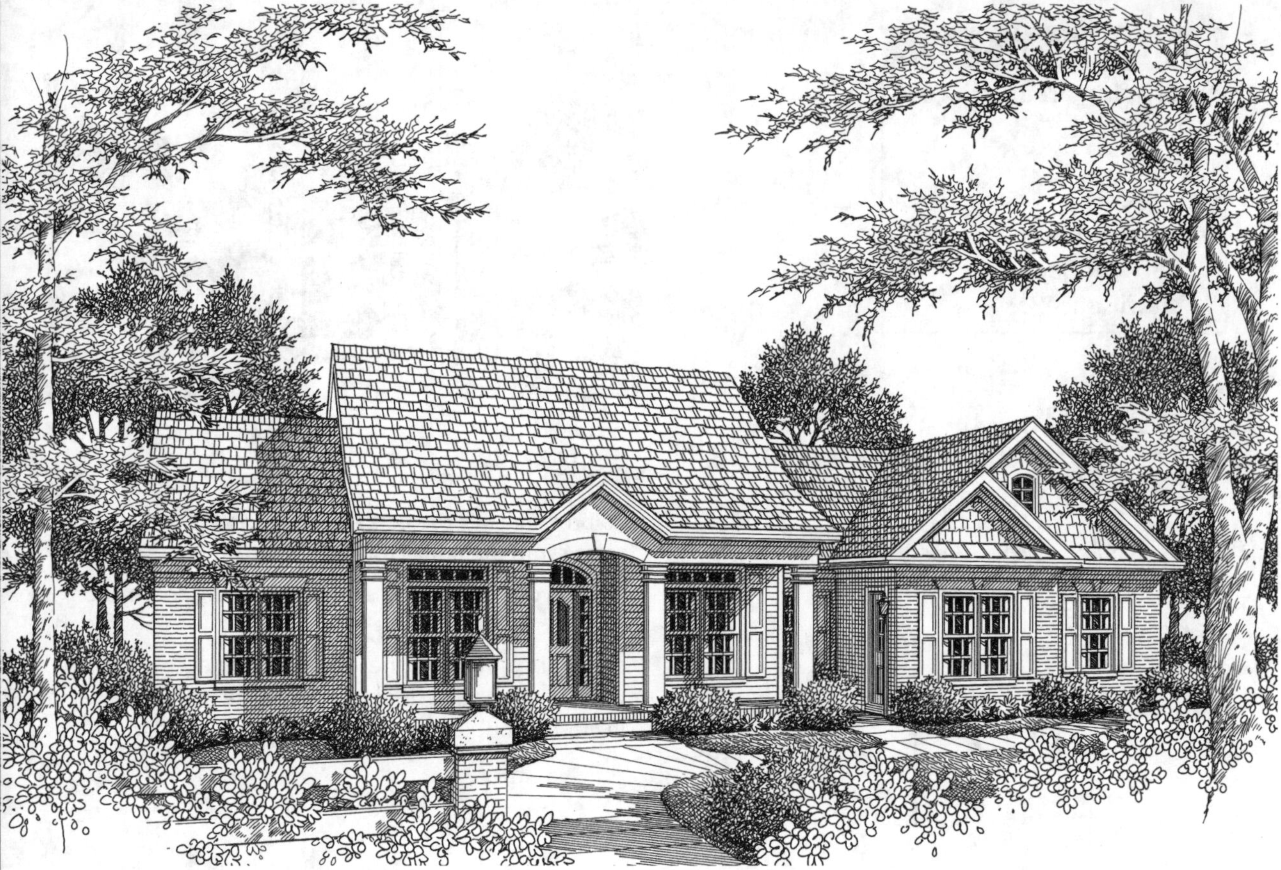

plan information

total living area:	2,184
bedrooms:	3
baths:	3
garage:	2-car side entry
foundation types:	
basement	
crawl space	
slab	
please specify when ordering	

special features

- delightful family room has access to the screened porch for enjoyable outdoor living
- secluded master suite is complete with a sitting area and luxurious bath
- formal living room has a double-door entry easily converting it to a study or home office
- two secondary bedrooms share a full bath

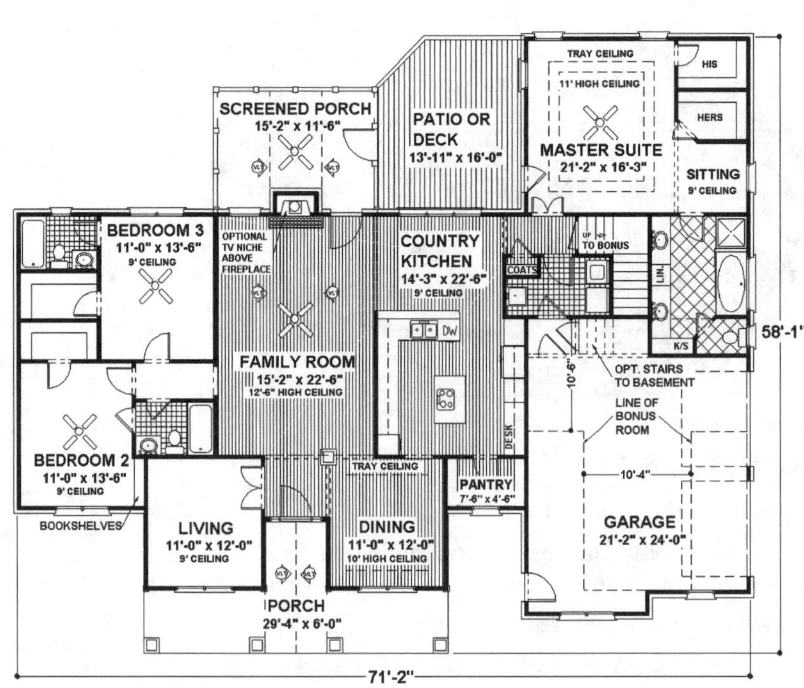

plan #584-037D-0003

price code D

plan information

total living area:	1,996
bedrooms:	3
baths:	2
garage:	2-car side entry

foundation types:
slab standard
crawl space

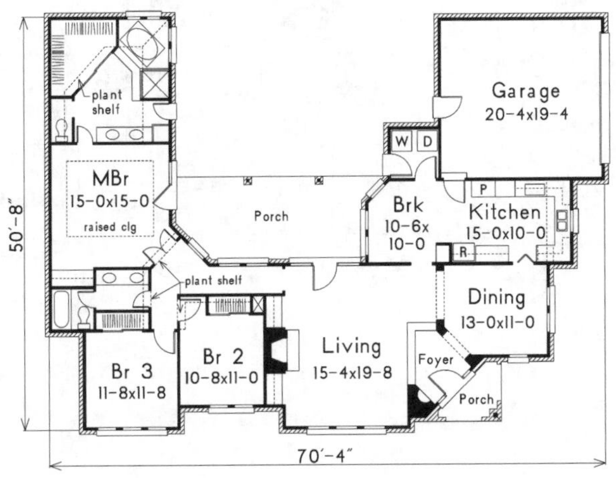

special features

- garden courtyard comes with large porch and direct access to master bedroom suite, breakfast room and garage
- sculptured entrance has artful plant shelves and special niche in foyer
- master bedroom boasts French doors, garden tub, desk with bookshelves and generous storage
- plant shelves and a high ceiling grace the hallway

---

plan #584-020D-0011

price code E

plan information

total living area:	2,259
bedrooms:	3
baths:	2 1/2
garage:	2-car

foundation types:
slab standard
crawl space

special features

- courtyard accesses home through the master bedroom, dining and living rooms
- fireplace in master bedroom warms surroundings
- extra storage area is provided off the garage

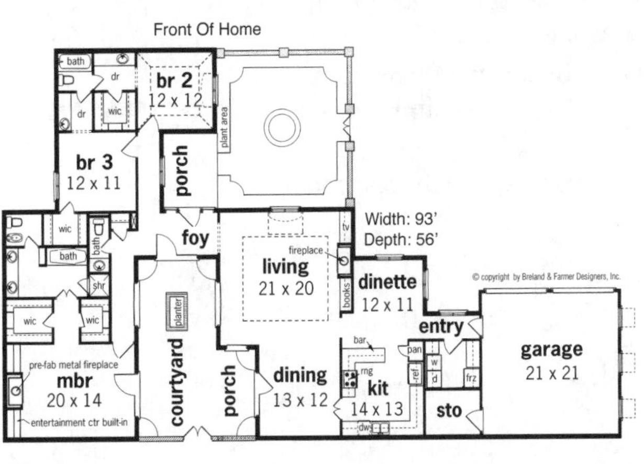

plan #584-026D-0166

price code C

plan information

total living area:	2,126
bedrooms:	3
baths:	2
garage:	2-car side entry
foundation type:	slab

special features

- elegant bay windows in the master bedroom welcome the sun
- double vanities in the master bath are separated by a large whirlpool tub
- secondary bedrooms each include a walk-in closet
- nook has access to the outdoors onto the rear porch

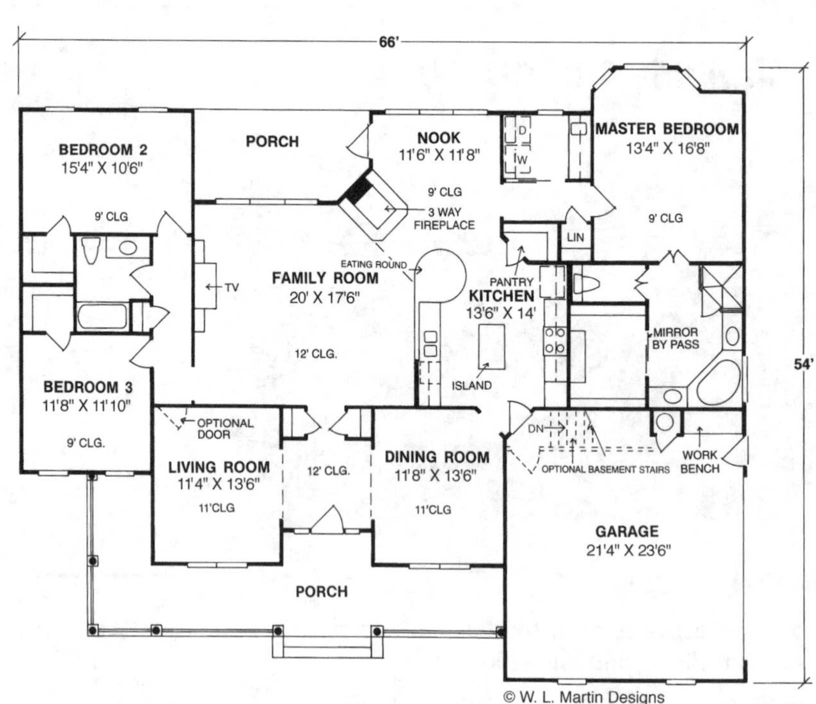

plan #584-052D-0054

price code C

plan information

total living area:	1,983
bedrooms:	3
baths:	2 1/2
garage:	2-car side entry

foundation types:

walk-out basement
slab
crawl space
please specify when ordering

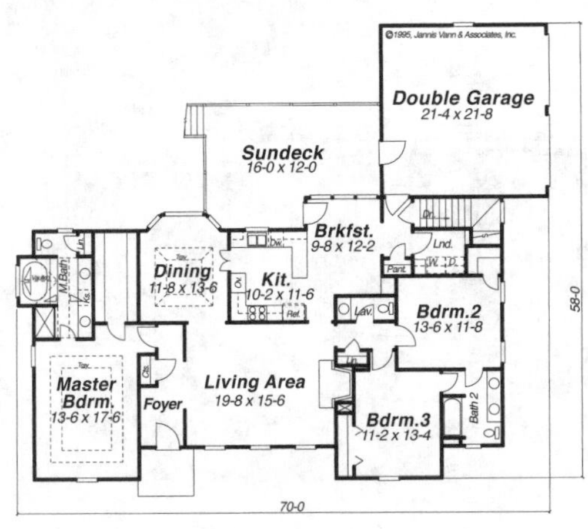

special features

- brightly lit breakfast area overlooks large sundeck in rear
- secondary bedrooms share bath
- interesting tray ceilings in dining area and master bedroom

---

plan #584-025D-0028

price code D

plan information

total living area:	2,350
bedrooms:	3
baths:	2 1/2
garage:	2-car side entry

foundation types:

walk-out basement
crawl space
slab
please specify when ordering

special features

- luxurious master suite enjoys a large bath and an enormous walk-in closet
- built-in hutch in breakfast room is eye-catching
- the terrific study is located in its own private hall and includes a half bath, two closets and a bookcase

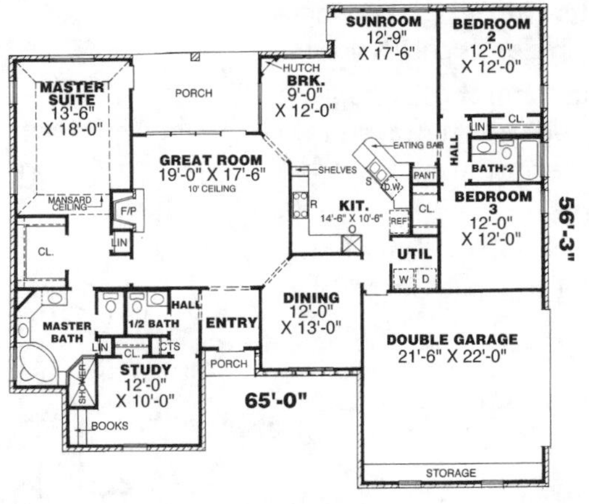

plan #584-040D-0009

price code D

plan information

total living area:	2,468
bedrooms:	3
baths:	2 1/2
garage:	2-car side entry
foundation type:	slab

special features

- open floor plan has a family room with columns, fireplace, triple French doors and a 12' ceiling
- master bath features double walk-in closets and vanities
- bonus room above garage has a private stairway and is included in the total square footage
- bedrooms are separate from main living space for privacy

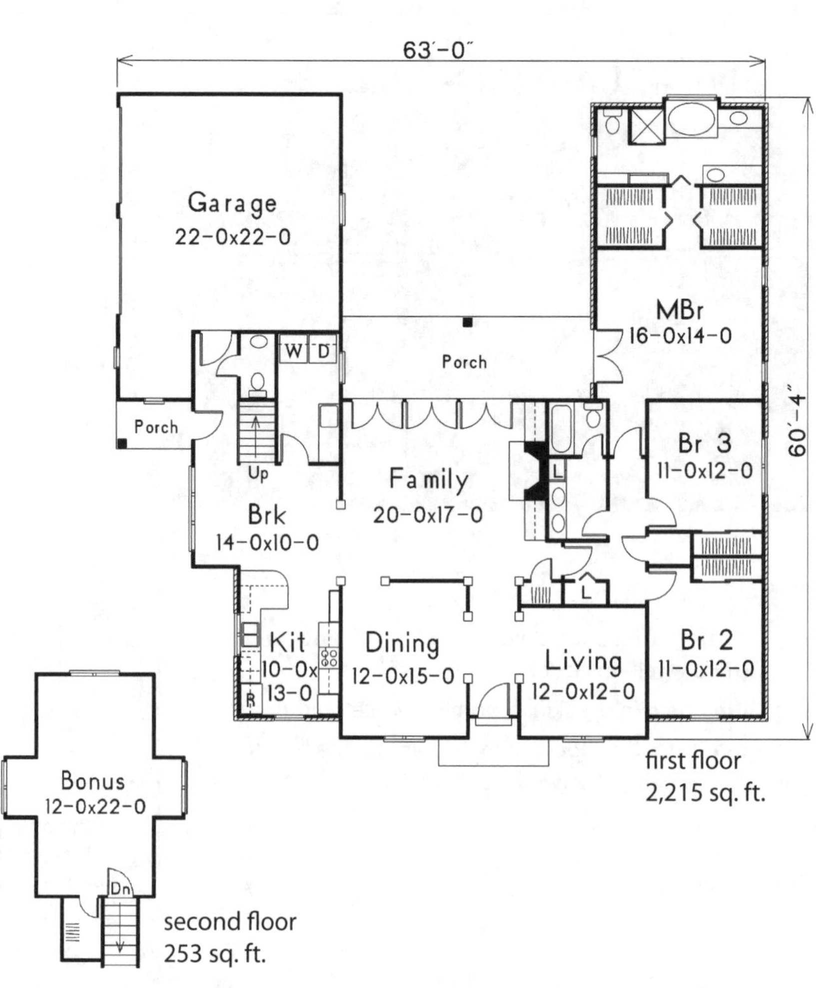

first floor
2,215 sq. ft.

second floor
253 sq. ft.

plan #584-055D-0081

price code C

plan information

total living area:	1,880
bedrooms:	4
baths:	2
garage:	2-car

foundation types:
slab
crawl space
basement
please specify when ordering

special features

- dining room conveniently accesses kitchen
- sunny breakfast room is brightened with a bay window
- master suite has a cozy fireplace and luxurious private bath

---

plan #584-065D-0049

price code C

plan information

total living area:	1,979
bedrooms:	3
baths:	2
garage:	2-car

foundation type:
walk-out basement

special features

- the formal dining room and great room form a large gathering space
- the breakfast area is surrounded by windows which provides a bright and cheery atmosphere
- the master bedroom enjoys a luxurious bath with a whirlpool tub, walk-in closet and double-bowl vanity

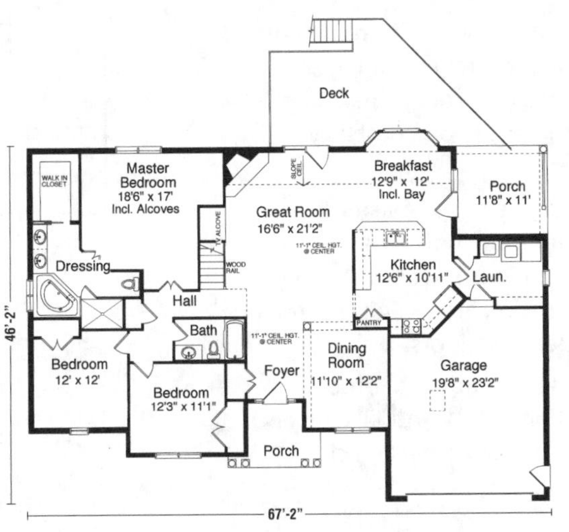

over 1,800 square feet plans

order 1-800-367-7667

plan #584-013D-0037

price code D

plan information

total living area:	2,564
bedrooms:	3
baths:	2 1/2
garage:	2-car side entry
foundation types:	
basement	
crawl space	
slab	
please specify when ordering	

special features

- hearth room is surrounded by the kitchen, dining and breakfast rooms making it the focal point of the living areas
- escape to the master bedroom which has a luxurious private bath and a sitting area leading to the deck outdoors
- the secondary bedrooms share a Jack and Jill bath and both have a walk-in closet

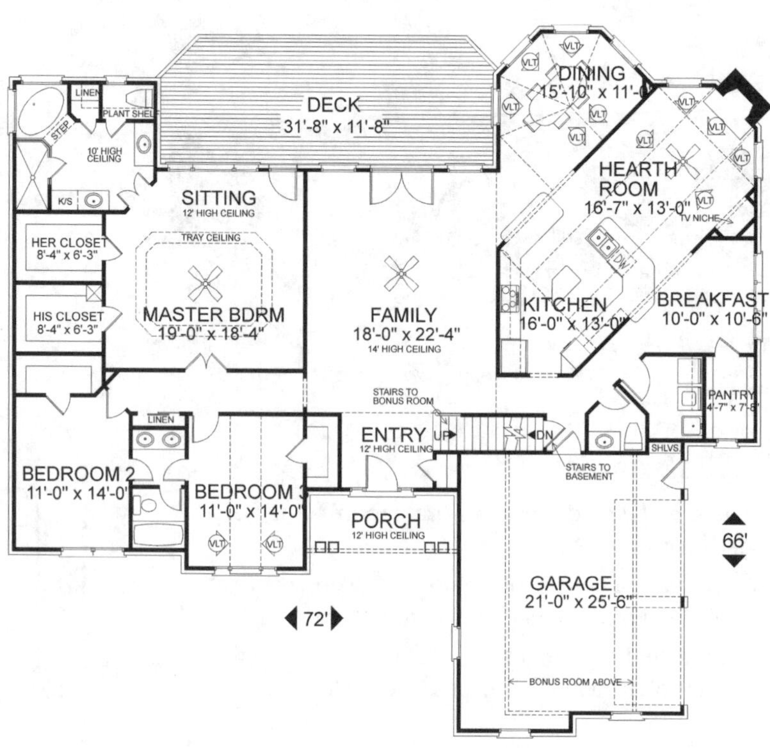

plan #584-047D-0051

price code E

plan information

total living area:	2,962
bedrooms:	4
baths:	3
garage:	3-car side entry
foundation type:	slab

special features

- vaulted breakfast nook is adjacent to the kitchen for convenience
- bedroom #4 is an ideal guest suite with private bath
- master bedroom includes see-through fireplace, bayed vanity and massive walk-in closet

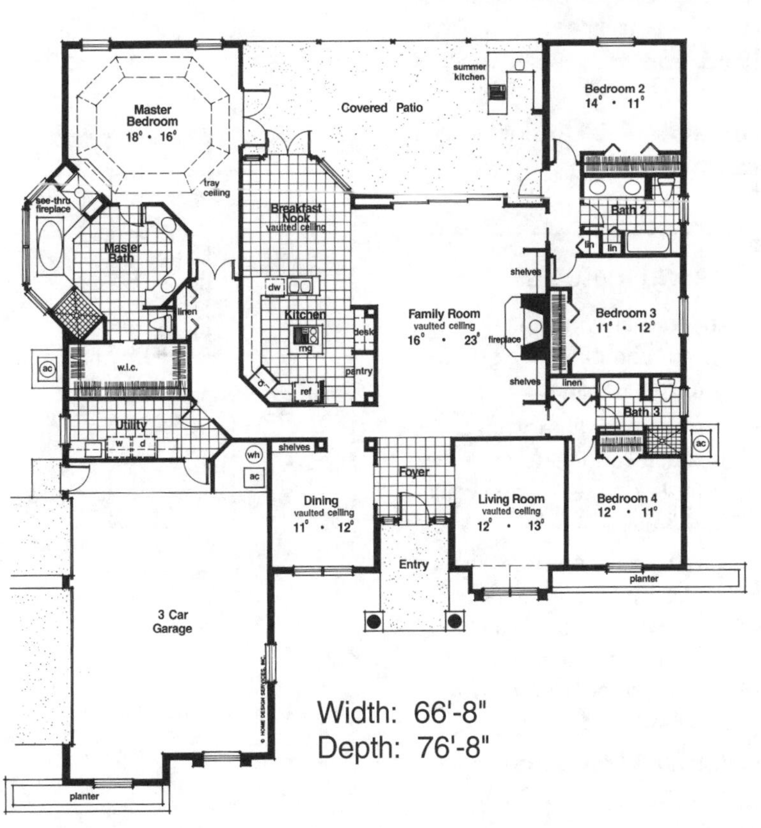

plan #584-051D-0105

price code F

plan information

total living area:	2,790
bedrooms:	3
baths:	2
garage:	2-car side entry
foundation type:	basement

special features

- the formal living and dining rooms combine for a grand entertaining space
- bedroom #3/library offers flexibility and features a double-door entry and walk-in closet
- the spacious master bedroom features a deluxe bath with a double vanity, extra-large walk-in closet and whirlpool tub set in a box-bay window
- the nook boasts a double-door entry onto the rear patio

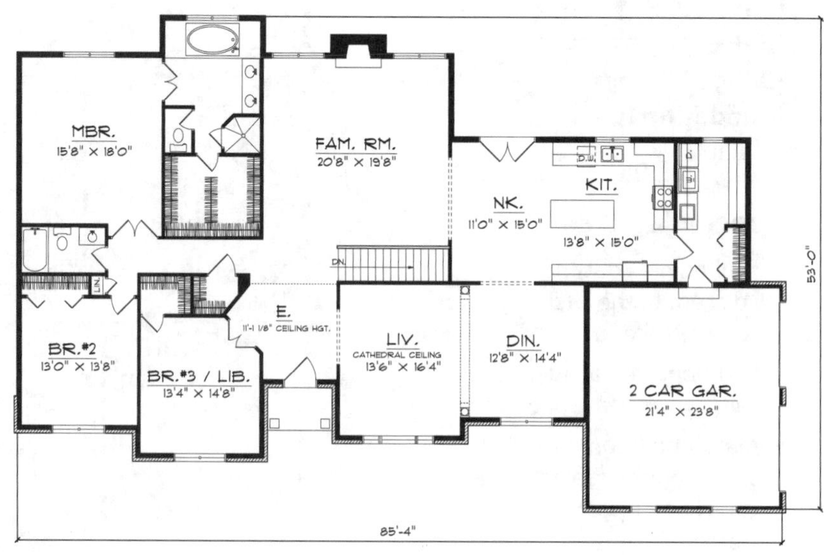

plan #584-069D-0019

price code C

plan information	
total living area:	2,162
bedrooms:	3
baths:	2
garage:	2-car
foundation types:	
crawl space	
slab	
please specify when ordering	

special features

- 10' ceilings in great room, dining room, master suite and foyer
- enormous great room overlooks kitchen with an oversized snack bar
- luxurious master bath boasts a triangular whirlpool tub drenched in light from large windows

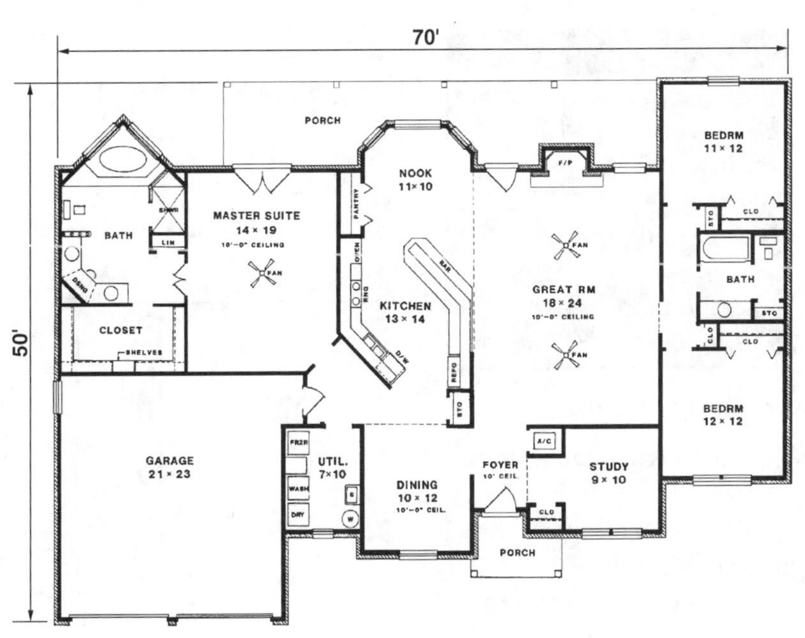

plan #584-069D-0018

price code C

plan information

total living area:	2,069
bedrooms:	3
baths:	2 1/2
garage:	2-car
foundation types:	
slab	
crawl space	
please specify when ordering	

special features

- 9' ceilings throughout this home
- kitchen has many amenities including a snack bar
- large front and rear porches

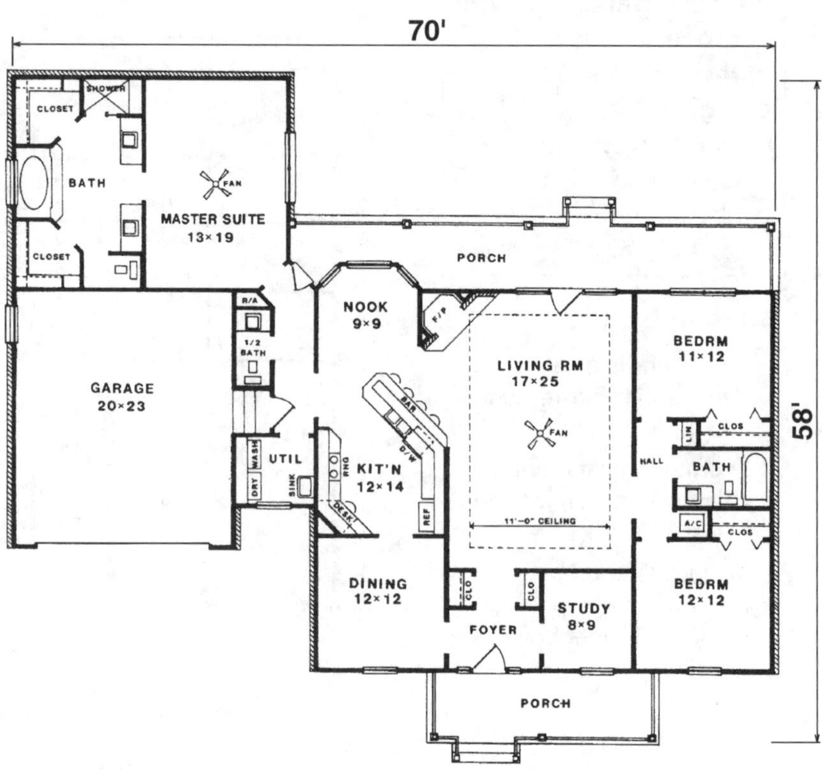

plan #584-055D-0031

price code C

plan information	
total living area:	2,133
bedrooms:	3
baths:	2
garage:	2-car side entry
foundation types:	
crawl space	
slab	
please specify when ordering	

special features

- master suite is separate from other bedrooms for privacy
- large hearth room shares a see-through fireplace with an open, airy great room
- efficiently designed kitchen

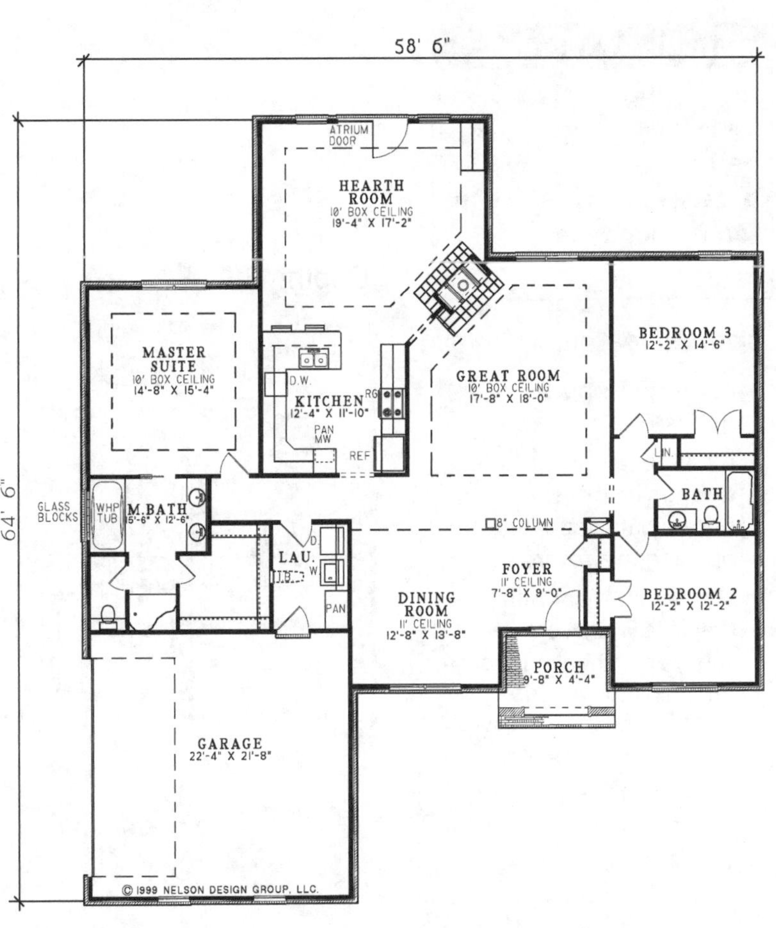

plan #584-047D-0059

price code F

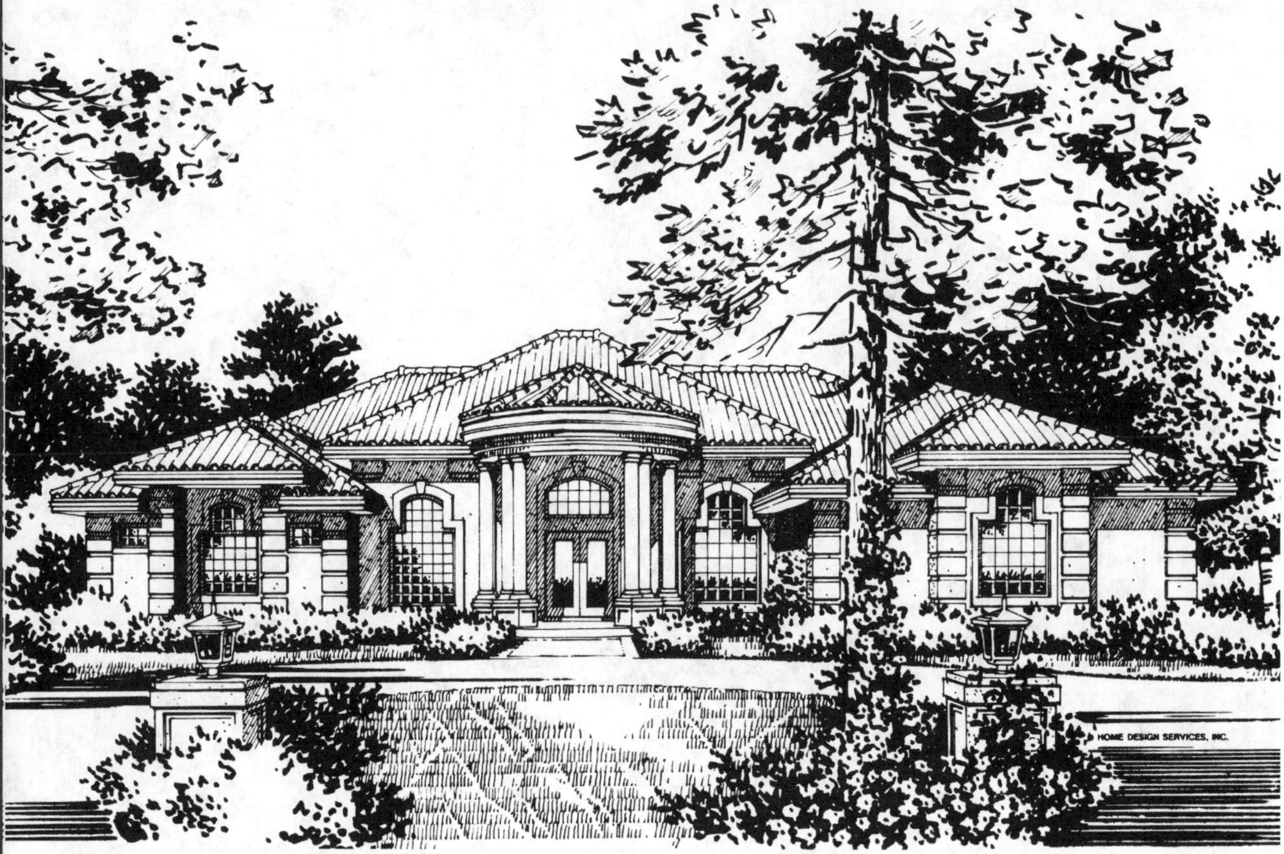

plan information	
total living area:	3,556
bedrooms:	4
baths:	3 1/2
garage:	3-car side entry
foundation type:	
slab	

special features

- curved portico welcomes guests
- master bedroom has a see-through fireplace, wet bar, private bath and sitting area opening to a covered patio
- cozy family room with fireplace is adjacent to a summer kitchen outdoors on the patio

Width: 85'-0"
Depth: 85'-0"

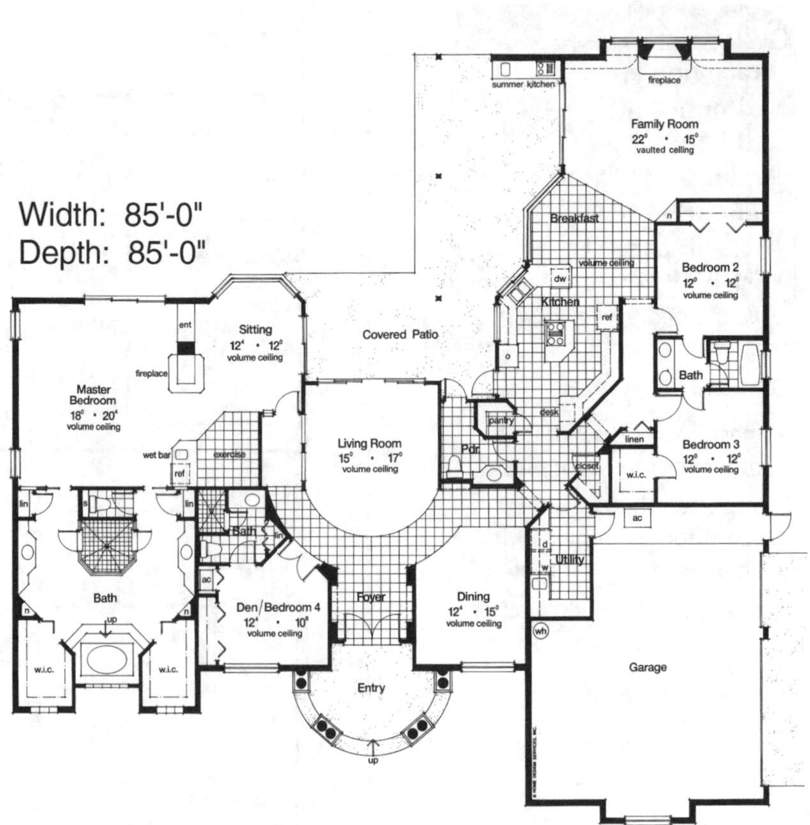

plan #584-065D-0044 price code D

plan information	
total living area:	2,203
bedrooms:	3
baths:	2 1/2
garage:	2-car
foundation type:	
basement	

special features

- the spacious great room with fireplace and entertainment alcove, dining area and kitchen combine to offer a large family gathering place
- three sets of French doors provide an abundance of warm natural light
- a spectacular covered porch with fireplace provides an exceptional entertaining area
- the private master bedroom enjoys a 10' ceiling and deluxe dressing room with a whirlpool

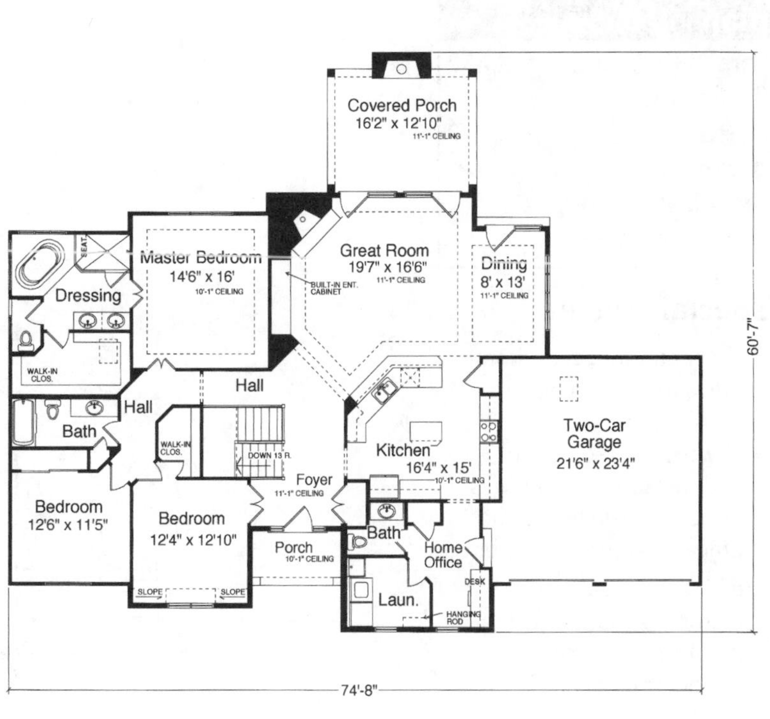

plan #584-007D-0008 price code D

plan information

total living area:	2,452
bedrooms:	3
baths:	2 1/2
garage:	3-car
foundation type:	
basement	

special features

- cheery and spacious home office room with private entrance and bath, two closets, vaulted ceiling and transomed window is perfect shown as a home office or a fourth bedroom
- delightful great room features a vaulted ceiling, fireplace, extra storage closets and patio doors to sundeck
- extra-large kitchen features walk-in pantry, cooktop island and bay window
- vaulted master bedroom includes transomed windows, walk-in closet and luxurious bath

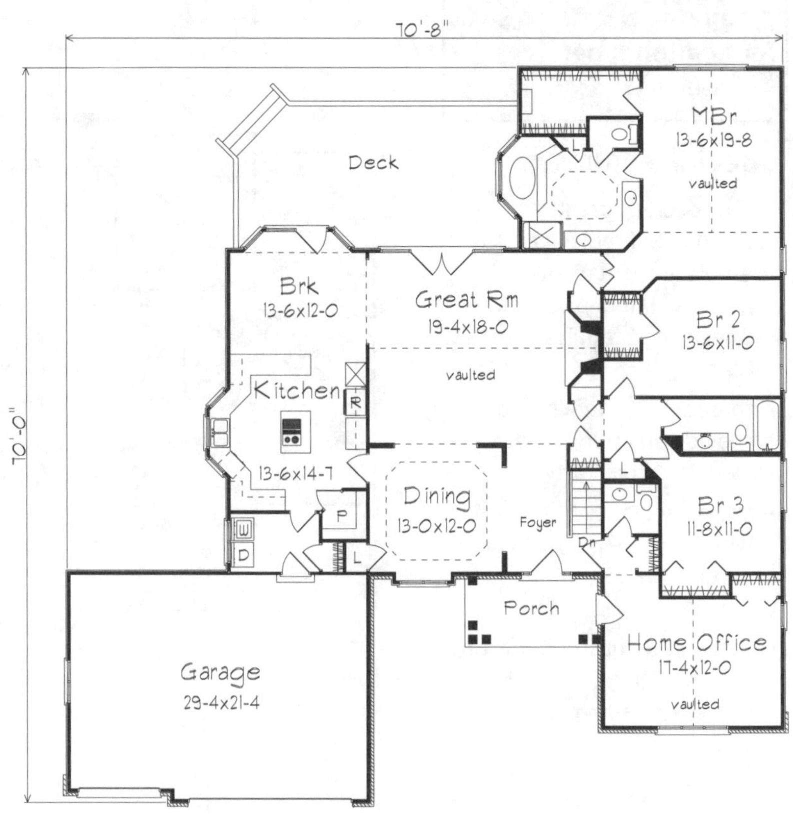

plan #584-055D-0109

price code C

plan information	
total living area:	2,217
bedrooms:	4
baths:	2
garage:	2-car
foundation types:	
crawl space	
slab	
please specify when ordering	

special features

- great room features a fireplace and is open to the foyer, breakfast and dining rooms
- laundry room and storage closet are located off the garage
- secluded master suite includes a bath with a corner whirlpool tub, split vanities, corner shower and a large walk-in closet

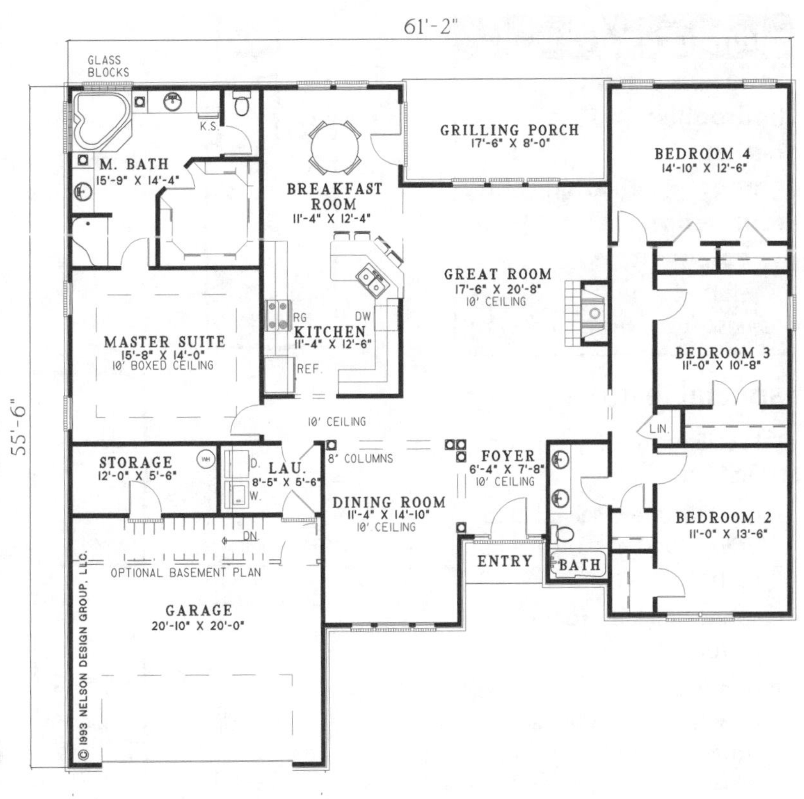

plan #584-056D-0008

price code E

plan information

total living area:	1,821
bedrooms:	3
baths:	2
garage:	2-car side entry
foundation types:	
basement	
slab	
please specify when ordering	

special features

- 9' ceilings throughout the first floor
- master suite is secluded for privacy and has a spacious bath
- sunny breakfast room features a bay window
- bonus room on the second floor has an additional 191 square feet of living area

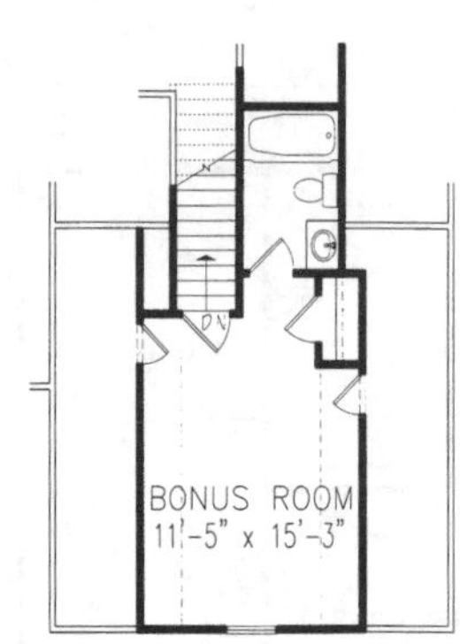

optional second floor

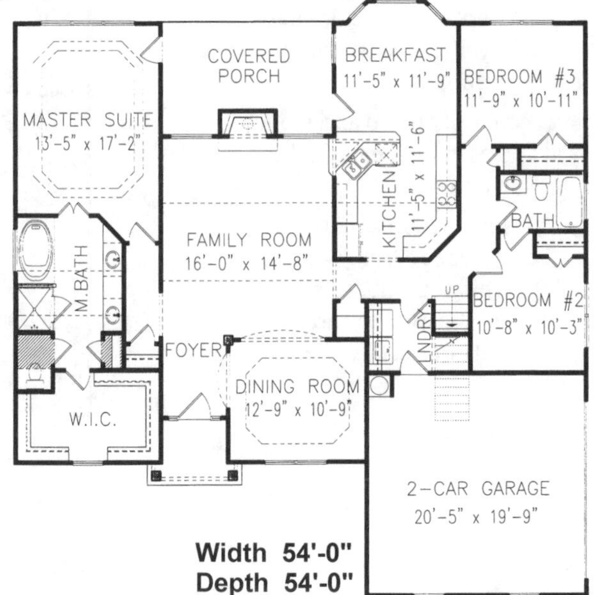

first floor
1,821 sq. ft.

Width 54'-0"
Depth 54'-0"

plan #584-047D-0052

price code F

plan information

total living area:	3,098
bedrooms:	4
baths:	4
garage:	3-car side entry
foundation type:	slab

special features

- master bedroom is ultra luxurious with a private bath, enormous walk-in closet and sitting area leading to the lanai
- vaulted family room has lots of windows and a corner fireplace
- secluded study has double closets and built-ins
- framing - only concrete block available
- optional second floor has an additional 849 square feet of living area

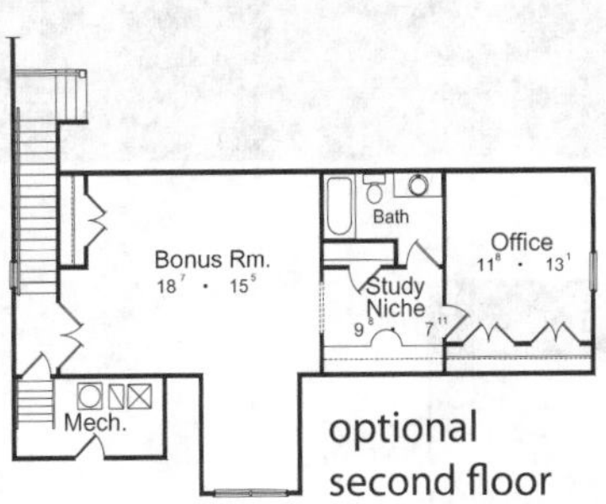

optional second floor

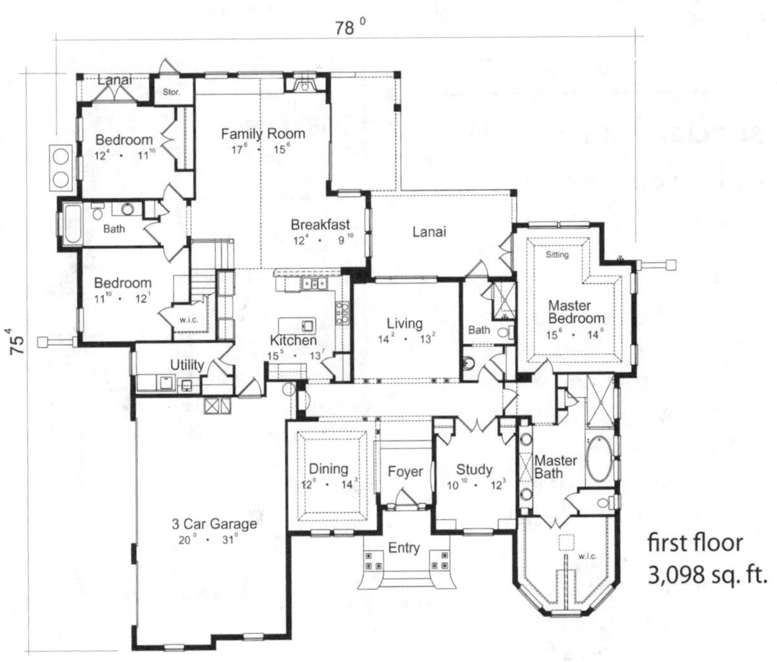

first floor
3,098 sq. ft.

plan #584-007D-0062 price code D

plan information	
total living area:	2,483
bedrooms:	4
baths:	2
garage:	2-car side entry
foundation type: basement	

special features

- a large entry porch with open brick arches and palladian door welcomes guests
- the vaulted great room features an entertainment center alcove and the ideal layout for furniture placement
- the dining room is extra large with a stylish tray ceiling
- bedroom #4/study is a versatile room that accommodates a families' needs

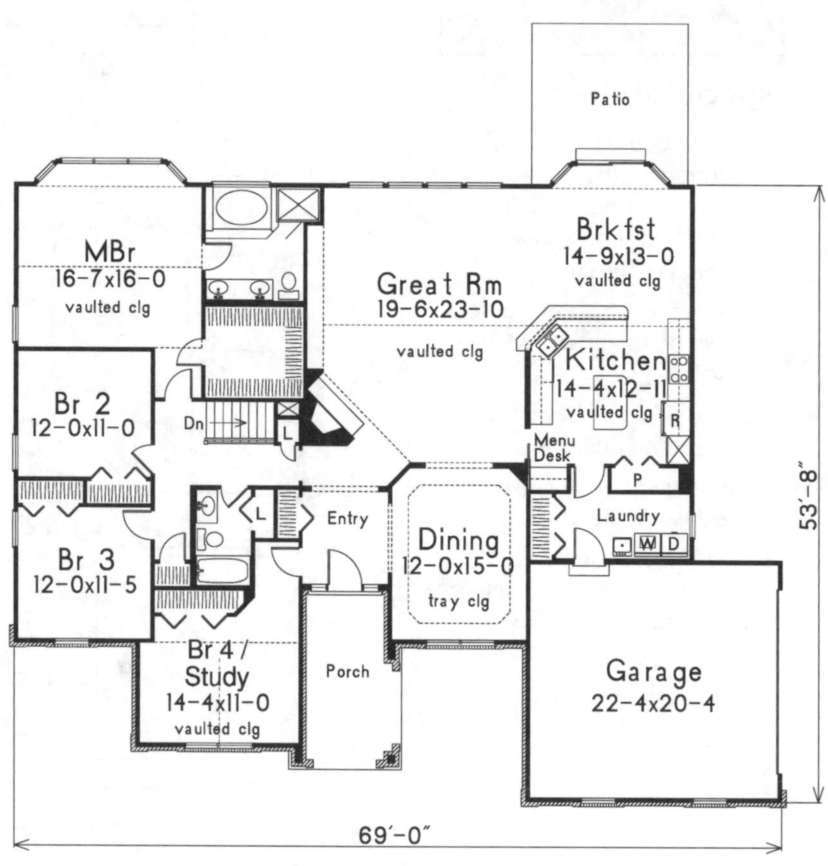

plan #584-027D-0003

price code D

plan information

total living area:	2,061
bedrooms:	3
baths:	2
garage:	2-car
foundation type:	
basement	

special features

- convenient entrance from garage into home through laundry room
- master bedroom features a walk-in closet and double-door entrance into master bath with an oversized tub
- formal dining room with tray ceiling
- kitchen features island cooktop and adjacent breakfast room

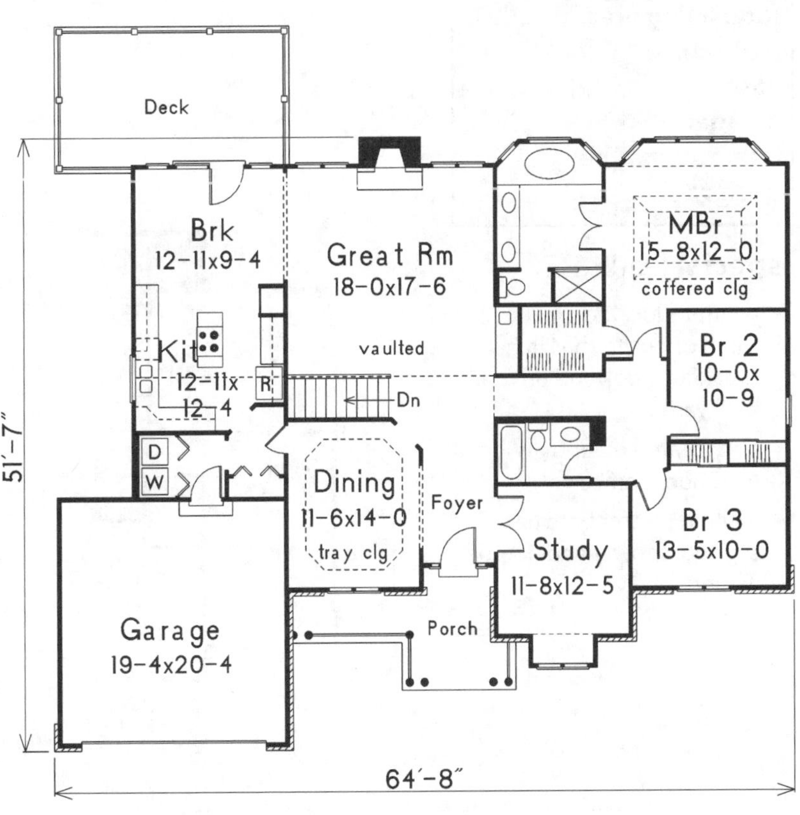

plan #584-011D-0010

price code C

plan information

total living area:	2,197
bedrooms:	3
baths:	2 1/2
garage:	3-car
foundation type:	
crawl space	

special features

- centrally located great room opens to the kitchen, breakfast nook and private backyard
- den located off entry is ideal for a home office
- vaulted master bath has a spa tub, shower and double vanity

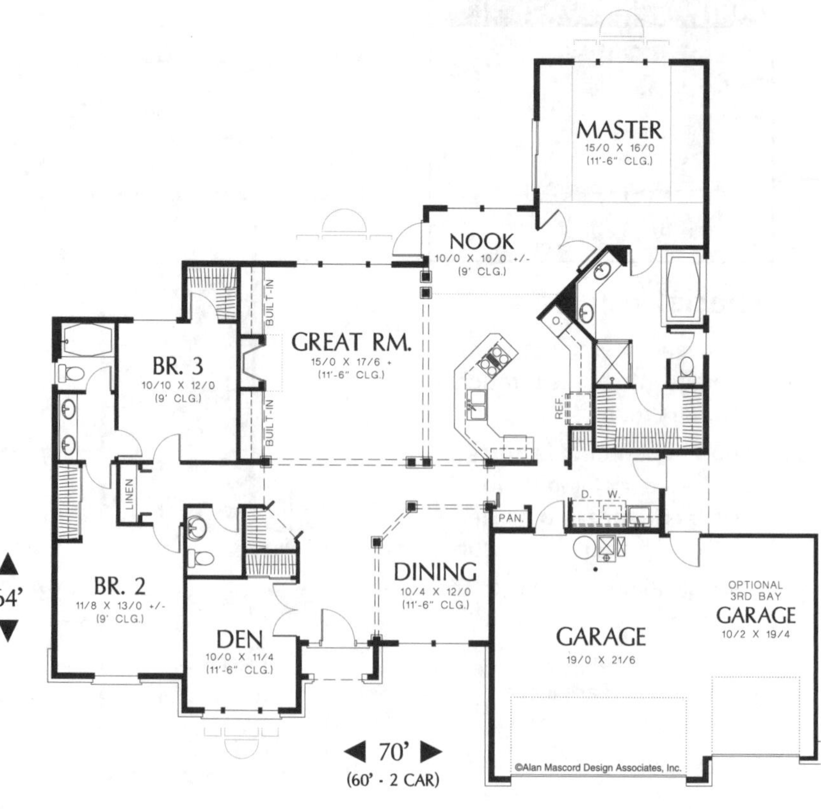

plan #584-007D-0055

price code D

plan information

total living area:	2,029
bedrooms:	4
baths:	2
garage:	2-car side entry
foundation types:	
basement standard	
crawl space	
slab	

special features

- stonework, gables, roof dormer and double porches create a country flavor
- kitchen has extravagant cabinetry and counterspace in a bay, island snack bar, built-in pantry and cheery dining area with tall windows
- angled stair descends from large entry with columns and is open to vaulted great room with fireplace
- master bedroom boasts two walk-in closets, a private bath and a secluded porch

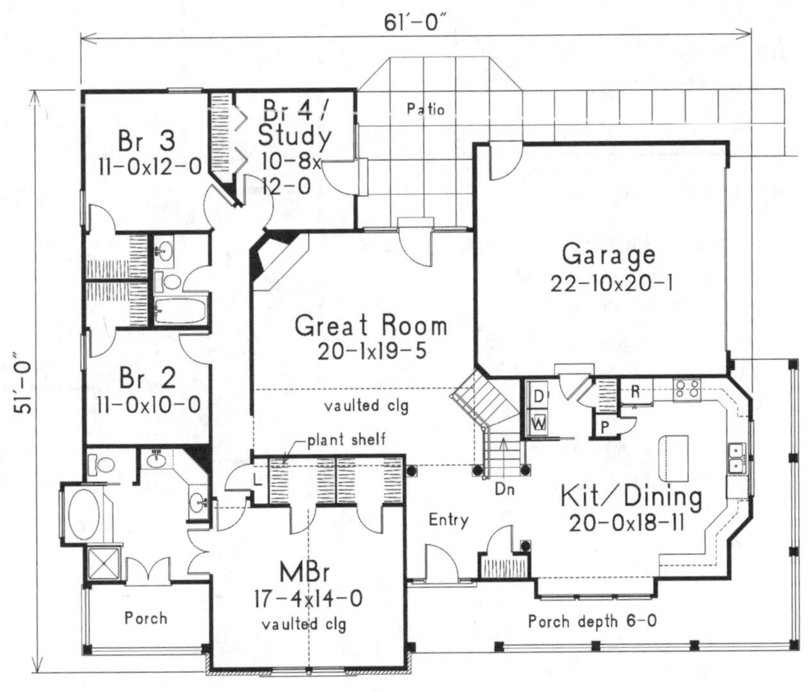

plan #584-048D-0005

price code E

plan information

total living area:	2,287
bedrooms:	4
baths:	2 1/2
garage:	2-car side entry
foundation type:	slab

special features

- a double-door entry leads into an impressive master bedroom which accesses the covered porch and features a deluxe bath with double closets and a step-up tub
- kitchen easily serves formal and informal areas of home
- the spacious foyer opens into formal dining and living rooms

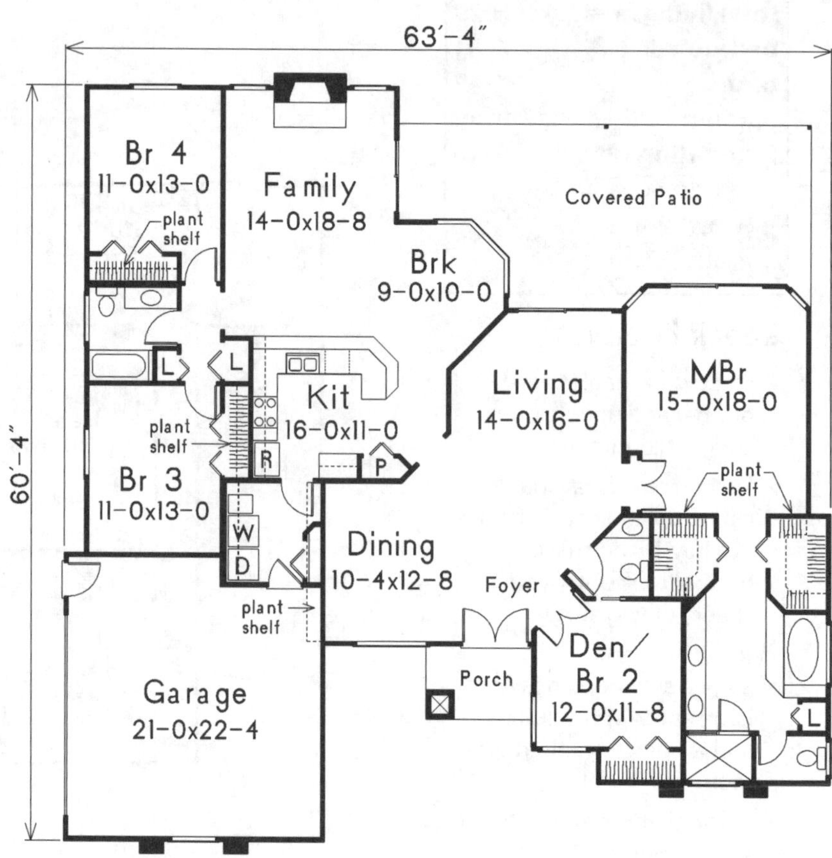

plan #584-065D-0013

price code C

plan information

total living area:	2,041
bedrooms:	3
baths:	2
garage:	2-car side entry
foundation type:	walk-out basement

special features

- great room accesses directly onto the covered rear deck with ceiling fan above
- private master bedroom has a beautiful octagon-shaped sitting area that opens and brightens the space
- two secondary bedrooms share a full bath

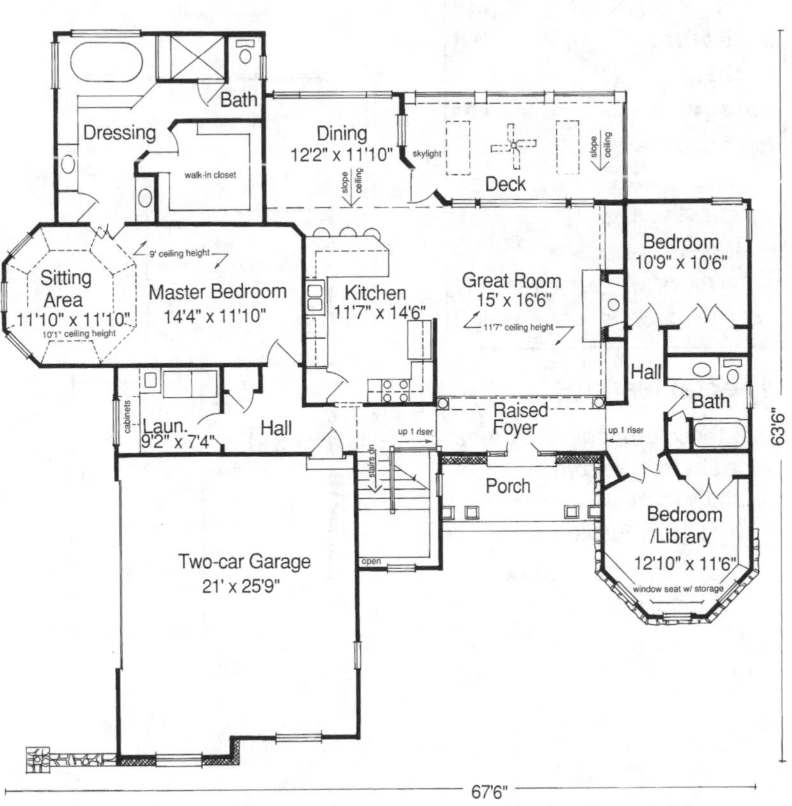

plan #584-055D-0032

price code D

plan information

total living area:	2,439
bedrooms:	4
baths:	3
garage:	2-car
foundation types:	
slab	
crawl space	
basement	
walk-out basement	
please specify when ordering	

special features

- enter columned gallery area just before reaching the family room with a see-through fireplace
- master bath has a corner whirlpool tub
- double-door entrance into the study

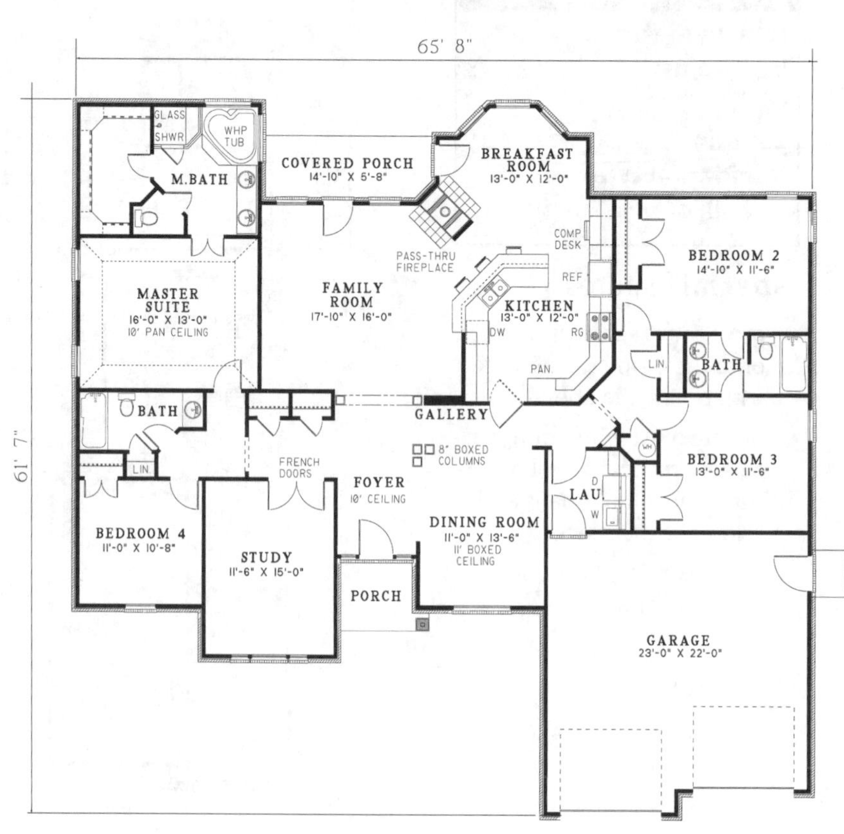

our blueprint packages offer...

Quality plans for building your future, with extras that provide unsurpassed value, ensure good construction and long-term enjoyment.

A quality home - one that looks good, functions well, and provides years of enjoyment - is a product of many things - design, materials, craftsmanship.

But it's also the result of outstanding blueprints - the actual plans and specifications that tell the builder exactly how to build your home.

And with our BLUEPRINT PACKAGES you get the absolute best. A complete set of blueprints is available for every design in this book. These "working drawings" are highly detailed, resulting in two key benefits:

- Better understanding by the contractor of how to build your home and...
- More accurate construction estimates.

Other helpful building aids are also available to help make your dream home a reality.

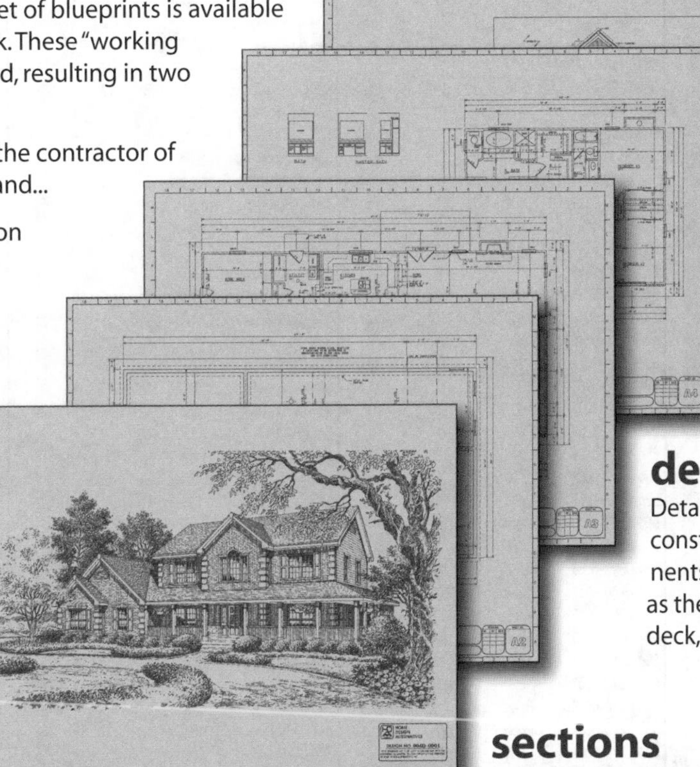

cover sheet

Included with many of our plans, the cover sheet is the artist's rendering of the exterior of the home. It will give you an idea of how your home will look when completed and landscaped.

interior elevations

Interior elevations provide views of special interior elements such as fireplaces, kitchen cabinets, built-in units and other features of the home.

foundation plan

The foundation plan shows the layout of the basement, crawl space, slab or pier foundation. All necessary notations and dimensions are included. See plan page for the foundation types included. If the home plan you choose does not have your desired foundation type, our Customer Service Representatives can advise you on how to customize your foundation to suit your specific needs or site conditions.

details

Details show how to construct certain components of your home, such as the roof system, stairs, deck, etc.

sections

Sections show detail views of the home or portions of the home as if it were sliced from the roof to the foundation. This sheet shows important areas such as load-bearing walls, stairs, joists, trusses and other structural elements, which are critical for proper construction.

floor plan

The floor plans show the placement of walls, doors, closets, plumbing fixtures, electrical outlets, columns, and beams for each level of the home.

exterior elevations

Exterior elevations illustrate the front, rear and both sides of the house, with all details of exterior materials and the required dimensions.

home plans index

what kind of plan package do you need?

Once you find the home plan you've been looking for, here are some suggestions on how to make your Dream Home a reality. To get started, order the type of plans that fit your particular situation.

Your Choices:

the 1-set package - We offer a 1-set plan package so you can study your home in detail. This one set is considered a study set and is marked "not for construction." It is a copyright violation to reproduce blueprints.

the minimum 5-set package - If you're ready to start the construction process, this 5-set package is the minimum number of blueprint sets you will need. It will require keeping close track of each set so they can be used by multiple subcontractors and tradespeople.

the standard 8-set package - For best results in terms of cost, schedule and quality of construction, we recommend you order eight (or more) sets of blueprints. Besides one set for yourself, additional sets of blueprints will be required by your mortgage lender, local building department, general contractor and all subcontractors working on foundation, electrical, plumbing, heating/air conditioning, carpentry work, etc.

reproducible masters - If you wish to make some minor design changes, you'll want to order reproducible masters. These drawings contain the same information as the blueprints but are printed on erasable and reproducible paper which clearly indicates your right to copy or reproduce. This will allow your builder or a local design professional to make the necessary drawing changes without the major expense of redrawing the plans. This package also allows you to print copies of the modified plans as needed. The right of building only one structure from these plans is licensed exclusively to the buyer. You may not use this design to build a second or multiple dwelling(s) without purchasing another blueprint. Each violation of the Copyright Law is punishable in a fine.

mirror reverse sets - Plans can be printed in mirror reverse. These plans are useful when the house would fit your site better if all the rooms were on the opposite side than shown. They are simply a mirror image of the original drawings causing the lettering and dimensions to read backwards. Therefore, when ordering mirror reverse drawings, you must purchase at least one set of right-reading plans. Some of our plans are offered mirror reverse right-reading. This means the plan, lettering and dimensions are flipped but read correctly. See the Home Plans Index on page 254 for availability.

other great products...

the legal kit - Avoid many legal pitfalls and build your home with confidence using the forms and contract featured in this kit. Included are request for proposal documents, various fixed price and cost plus contracts, instructions on how and when to use each form, warranty statements and more. Save time and money before you break ground on your new home or start a remodeling project. All forms are reproducible. The kit is ideal for homebuilders and contractors. **Cost: $35.00**

detail plan packages - framing, electrical and plumbing packages
Three separate packages offer homebuilders details for constructing various foundations; numerous floor, wall and roof framing techniques; simple to complex residential wiring; sump and water softener hookups; plumbing connection methods; installation of septic systems, and more. Each package includes three-dimensional illustrations and a glossary of terms. Purchase one or all three. Note: These drawings do not pertain to a specific home plan.
Cost: $20.00 each or all three for $40.00

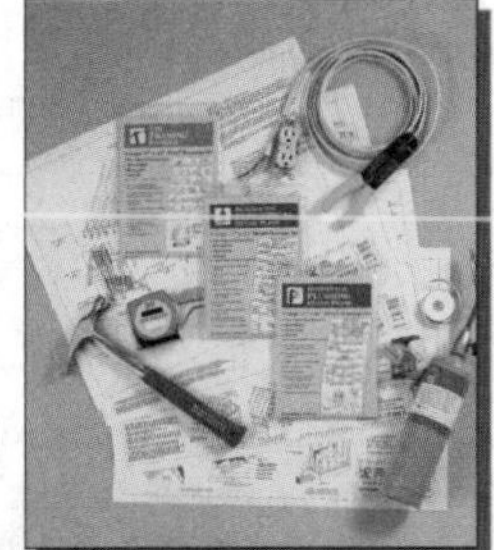

more helpful building aids...

Your Blueprint Package contains the necessary construction information to build your home. We also offer the following products and services to save you time and money in the building process.

express delivery - Most orders are processed within 24 hours of receipt. Please allow 7-10 business days for delivery. If you need to place a rush order, please call us by 11:00 a.m. Monday-Friday CST and ask for express service (allow 1-2 business days).

technical assistance - If you have questions, please call our technical support line at 1-314-770-2228 between 8:00 a.m. and 5:00 p.m. Monday-Friday CST. Whether it involves design modifications or field assistance, our designers are extremely familiar with all of our designs and will be happy to help you. We want your home to be everything you expect it to be.

material list - Material lists are available for many of the plans in this magazine. Each list gives you the quantity, dimensions and description of the building materials necessary to construct your home. You'll get faster and more accurate bids from your contractor while saving money by paying for only the materials you need. See the Home Plans Index on page 254 for availability. Note: Material lists are not refundable. **Cost: $125.00**

how to order

For fastest service, call toll-free

1-800-367-7667

24 HOURS A DAY

Three Easy Ways To Order

1. CALL toll-free 1-800-367-7667 for credit card orders. MasterCard, Visa, Discover and American Express are accepted.
2. FAX your order to 1-314-770-2226.
3. MAIL the Order Form to:

HDA, Inc.
944 Anglum Road
St. Louis, MO 63042

order form

Please send me -

PLAN NUMBER 584 - ____________

PRICE CODE ______ *(see page 254)*

Specify Foundation Type *(see plan page for availability)*

☐ Slab ☐ Crawl space ☐ Pier

☐ Basement ☐ Walk-out basement

☐ Reproducible Masters $ ______

☐ Eight-Set Plan Package $ ______

☐ Five-Set Plan Package $ ______

☐ One-Set Study Package *(no mirror reverse)* $ ______

☐ Additional Plan Sets*

______(Qty.) at $45.00 each $ ______

Mirror Reverse*

☐ Right-reading $150 one-time charge

(see index on page 254 for availability) $ ______

☐ Print in Mirror Reverse *(where right-reading is not available)*

______ (Qty.) at $15.00 each $ ______

☐ Material List* $125 *(see page 254)* $ ______

☐ Legal Kit *(see page 255)* $ ______

Detail Plan Packages: *(see page 255)*

☐ Framing ☐ Electrical ☐ Plumbing $ ______

SUBTOTAL $ ______

Sales Tax - MO residents add 6% $ ______

☐ Shipping/Handling *(see chart at right)* $ ______

TOTAL ENCLOSED *(US funds only)* $ ______

I hereby authorize HDA, Inc. to charge this purchase to my credit card account (check one):

☐ MasterCard ☐ VISA ☐ DISCOVER ☐ American Express Cards

Credit Card number ____________

Expiration date ____________

Signature ____________

Name ____________
(Please print or type)

Street Address ____________
(Please **do not** use PO Box)

City ____________

State ______ Zip ____________

Daytime phone number ( ) - ____________

I'm a ☐ Builder/Contractor ☐ Homeowner ☐ Renter

I ☐ have ☐ have not selected my general contractor

Thank you for your order!

important information to know before you order

■ **Exchange Policies** - Since blueprints are printed in response to your order, we cannot honor requests for refunds. However, if for some reason you find that the plan you have purchased does not meet your requirements, you may exchange that plan for another plan in our collection within 90 days of purchase. At the time of the exchange, you will be charged a processing fee of 25% of your original plan package price, plus the difference in price between the plan packages (if applicable) and the cost to ship the new plans to you.

Please note: Reproducible drawings can only be exchanged if the package is unopened.

■ **Building Codes & Requirements** - At the time the construction drawings were prepared, every effort was made to ensure that these plans and specifications meet nationally recognized codes. Our plans conform to most national building codes. Because building codes vary from area to area, some drawing modifications and/or the assistance of a professional designer or architect may be necessary to comply with your local codes or to accommodate specific building site conditions. We advise you to consult with your local building official for information regarding codes governing your area.

Questions? Call Our Customer Service Number
1-800-367-7667

blueprint price schedule

BEST VALUE

Price Code	1-Set*	SAVE $110 5-Sets	SAVE $200 8-Sets	Reproducible Masters
AAA	$225	$295	$340	$440
AA	$325	$395	$440	$540
A	$385	$455	$500	$600
B	$445	$515	$560	$660
C	$500	$570	$615	$715
D	$560	$630	$675	$775
E	$620	$690	$735	$835
F	$675	$745	$790	$890
G	$765	$835	$880	$980
H	$890	$960	$1005	$1105

Plan prices are subject to change without notice.
Please note that plans and material lists are not refundable.

■ **Additional Sets*** - Additional sets of the plan ordered are available for $45.00 each. Five-set, eight-set, and reproducible packages offer considerable savings.

■ **Mirror Reverse Plans*** - Available for an additional $15.00 per set, these plans are simply a mirror image of the original drawings causing the dimensions and lettering to read backwards. Therefore, when ordering mirror reverse plans, you must purchase at least one set of right-reading plans. Some of our plans are offered mirror reverse right-reading. This means the plan, lettering and dimensions are flipped but read correctly. To purchase a mirror reverse right-reading set, the cost is an additional $150.00. See the Home Plans Index on page 254 for availability.

■ **One-Set Study Package*** - We offer a one-set plan package so you can study your home in detail. This one set is considered a study set and is marked "not for construction." It is a copyright violation to reproduce blueprints.

Available only within 90 days after purchase of plan package or reproducible masters of same plan.

shipping & handling charges

U.S. SHIPPING - (AK and HI - express only)	1-4 Sets	5-7 Sets	8 Sets or Reproducibles
Regular (allow 7-10 business days)	$15.00	$17.50	$25.00
Priority (allow 3-5 business days)	$25.00	$30.00	$35.00
Express* (allow 1-2 business days)	$35.00	$40.00	$45.00

CANADA SHIPPING - (to/from) plans with suffix 062D	1-4 Sets	5-7 Sets	8 Sets or Reproducibles
Standard (allow 8-12 business days)	$25.00	$30.00	$35.00
Express* (allow 3-5 business days)	$40.00	$40.00	$45.00

Overseas Shipping/International - Call, fax, or e-mail (plans@hdainc.com) for shipping costs.

* For express delivery please call us by 11:00 a.m. Monday-Friday CST